Washington Irving

SELECTED PROSE

EDITED WITH AN INTRODUCTION BY
STANLEY T. WILLIAMS

HOLT, RINEHART AND WINSTON, INC.

NEW YORK • CHICAGO • SAN FRANCISCO • ATLANTA • DALLAS
MONTREAL • TORONTO • LONDON • SYDNEY

SBN: 03-009935-8

Introduction copyright, 1950, by Stanley T. Williams
Typography Design by Stefan Salter
Printed in the United States of America

01234   68   19181716151413121110

INTRODUCTION

THROUGHOUT HIS LITERARY CAREER of nearly sixty years (from the *Letters of Jonathan Oldstyle Gent.* to the *Life of George Washington*) Washington Irving recorded with sensitivity the manners and customs of six European nations. In the story of his life we need only notice for our purposes his successive indentures to the traditions of Holland, England, Germany, and Spain, glancing momentarily at his flirtations with Italy and France. When, at last, in 1832, he ended his second long stay in Europe, he had already lived abroad for nearly two-fifths of his fifty years; and in a decade he was to return for four years more, no longer an idler, but our distinguished Minister at the Court of Isabella the Second, in Madrid. In this intervening decade Irving mingled with the Osage Indians and endured good-naturedly the rigors of camp life. On his resultant narratives of the West may be based a redefinition of Irving as a frontier writer, an interpreter of pioneer, homespun America. Yet at its best this is a weak definition. Irving loved his country, particularly "Manna-hata" and the blue-shadowed hills of the Hudson, but on the prairie the Indian ponies reminded him of Andalusian steeds and the arching trees of Moorish mosques. He was, and he remained, perhaps more so than any writer of his generation, a thoroughly Europeanized American.

Presumably the chronology of these various European influences matters very little. In Irving's ductile mind England came first, in the stories he heard at his mother's knee. Yet these vicarious memories of Britain, these ships sailing from the pierheads to mysterious Spain, these gutturals of Holland audible on his way to school, were, in effect, simultaneous; all were early fused in his imagination with what he was to call in *The Sketch Book* Europe's "shadowy grandeurs of the past." On the traces of these antiquities he was always to fix a romantic yet an accurate eye. To the subtler meanings of these civilizations he never penetrated; instead he reported with respectful and often humorous precision on their picturesque ways of life. Thus in his youth, in his

v

native New York, he studied with relish the scrubbed Dutch kitchens and the rotund Dutch personalities. In 1805, during his first journey to Europe, he recognized with amusement in the immaculate inns, the broad-beamed maidens, and the pipe-smoking burgomasters the originals of his transplanted corner of the Netherlands in America; and he apparently vowed, even at the age of twenty-two, to do these justice in a book. Seventeen years later, when he had indeed done so in Diedrich Knickerbocker's *A History of New York* and in *The Sketch Book,* he was still fascinated during a second visit to Holland by scenes deserving, he declared, Paul Potter's pencil.

Skillful himself with pencil and brush, Irving loved the Flemish painters. Many of his set pieces in prose are better understood by remembering his familiarity with these artists and also his friendships with Charles Robert Leslie and Washington Allston, whom he persuaded to illustrate a third edition of his *History of New York.* Dutch painting, never adequately appraised in its influence on Irving's art, encouraged his portrayal of strong surfaces in scene or character at the same time that it ministered to his romantic passion for the past. For his curiosity about everything Dutch inspired him to prodigious labors in the history and legends of Old New York. He respected these heroic founders, but their idiosyncrasies offered him matchless material for broad satire. In these light-hearted years he inclined to believe his little English village of New York the hub of America; with impartial effrontery he ridiculed the Swedes in Delaware, the Yankees in New England, and the Dutch in "Manna-hata."

Thus the Dutch influence was partly responsible not merely for his burlesque history and his tales of the Catskills, but for either content or method in *Bracebridge Hall, Tales of a Traveller,* and even, with a touch of his old *insouciance,* for sections of *Wolfert's Roost,* published only four years before his death. Contemporary newspapers were quick to note the kinship of his work with that of the Dutch painters, and Maria Edgeworth remarked that such a tale as "The Stout Gentleman," in *Bracebridge Hall,* as well as "The Inn Yard" and "The Rookery," in the same book, were "all exquisite paintings in the high finish of the Flemish school." Perhaps so. The reader will recall more readily the vignettes of Derrick Van Bummel or Nicholas Vedder in "Rip Van Winkle" or the still-life picture of the Dutch country tea table belonging to Baltus Van Tassel in "The Legend of Sleepy Hollow."

This habit of mind of Irving's, this resolution of the Dutch past with what he saw with his own eyes and could record in his innumerable notebooks, was developed and refined by his prolonged immersion in the civilization of England. Of this fulfillment *The Sketch Book* and *Bracebridge Hall* are really one extended memorial; the Christmas pieces or the scenes from English rural life re-emphasize Irving's power to assimilate at least the surfaces of those materials for which the artist sought in vain in America. At last this English lode, too, was exhausted, but Irving himself, the antiquarian and observer—never! A year after the appearance of *Bracebridge Hall* he was mining the rich soil of Saxon legend, and in the following year he had turned to France, where if we trust his journals and the few ensuing *bagatelles*, his quest was least profitable.

As a matter of fact, his gleanings from Germany were hardly more so, for *Tales of a Traveller*, even when buttressed by memories of his early tour in Italy, was a spectacular failure, shaking his faith in himself for several years. Yet his absorption in German legend—he had talked with Scott about this—was ecstatic, and in Dresden he moved as in a happy dream amid feudalism's colorful legacy to the present. He knew German fairly well; it had been his anodyne in 1809 during his grief for the loss of Matilda Hoffman, and in 1817, six years before the winter in Germany, Otmar's tale of Peter Klaus's magic slumber had been on his table—perhaps too often—as he composed "Rip Van Winkle." So now, at the Court of King Frederick Augustus, he became more than ever convinced of the consanguinity of all legend and more than ever enamored of indigenous characters and time-defying customs. For the time being his integration with Germany was as complete as those with Holland and England. In his receptivity to folkways he seemed perpetually impressionable, a born chronicler of an undying past.

In Irving's sampling of the past and present of European civilizations, Spain was the climax. Here were legends related to those of Germany and of his own Catskills; his "Rip Van Winkle" had been readily adapted into Spanish, with oriental opiates instead of Dutch ale; instead of the rumbling ninepins one heard the clash of Moorish scimitars. Irving was happy. For three years he yielded his mind to the Spanish perspective, which reached back far beyond King Boabdil of Granada, beyond Roderick the Goth, beyond the Romans, into the lore of the continent of Africa. He read and spoke Spanish, and among his papers survive the dim souvenirs of his valiant assault on the Arabic. As he had devoured out-of-the-way Dutch histories, Elizabethan prose, and German mythology, so he now assailed, with an earnestness rivaling

Ticknor's or Prescott's, ancient Spanish folios and Columbian manuscripts just published by Martín Fernández de Navarrete. Yet he was more than *laudator temporis acti.* With intensity, so surprising to Longfellow when the poet visited him in Madrid in 1827, he also projected himself into the life of the Spanish present, living alone in the Alhambra with a coterie of Spanish peasants and discussing folklore with the Spanish novelist, Fernán Caballero. He liked her phrase for what he now knew to be his basic literary aim; he would "poetize reality."

Thus in the broadest sense the literary history of Washington Irving is that of his successive (and sometimes simultaneous) exposures to different European cultures. Indeed, it may be argued that after *The Life and Voyages of Christopher Columbus, The Conquest of Granada,* and *The Alhambra,* his literary life ended. His method of combining the antiquarian and the personal was to be less successful in its application to Western themes or to biographies of Goldsmith, Mahomet, and George Washington. In fact, after 1837, he was ill at ease, and we find him returning, whenever he was not engrossed by public life, to the old and now shopworn materials. "Irving," lamented Longfellow in 1839, "is writing away *like fury,* in the Knickerbocker;—*he had better not;* old remnants—odds and ends,—about Sleepy Hollow, and Granada. What a pity." It is dangerous to simplify; other elements qualify the easy labels that *A History of New York* was in origin Dutch; *The Sketch Book,* Dutch and English (a combination not always noted); *Tales of a Traveller,* German, Italian, and Dutch; or *The Alhambra,* Spanish. Yet these books, which together make up his most enduring writing, could not have come into being had his mind not responded in the fashion just summarized to variegated national patterns of legends and manners. Perhaps his conception of literature took form in that moment which he describes in the opening pages of *The Sketch Book:*

I . . . journeyed [he recalls] one long summer's day to the summit of the most distant hill, whence I stretched my eye over many a mile of *terra incognita,* and was astonished to find how vast a globe I inhabited.

For Irving, as later for Longfellow, Lowell, and Henry James, such a facing toward Europe, so typical of the temper of many civilized Americans, was not without advantages, however blind may seem to us, who are wise after the event, these fugitives from the latent literary treasures of America. Within the scope of the traditional, aims could be definite. In particular Irving, whose intellectual weight has been so often challenged, found reassurance in allying himself with such masters as Walter Scott in the tale of the supernatural, Miss Mitford in the essay of manners, or Fernán Caballero, in the *artículo de costumbres*. So he avoided easily, too easily, the problems of American themes, American mythology, or, so to speak, an American style. All these problems bolder writers, such as Hawthorne, Melville, or Mark Twain, were to attack and in some measure to solve. By temperament Irving's literary objectives were not profound, but they were enhanced by one of his most admirable traits, his consciousness of what he could and what he could not do. On these limitations I shall not dwell; each day they become more evident. Yet as we take him down again from the shelves, it is even plainer that in both his content and craft there were achievements, and with these we shall now be briefly concerned.

Irving's notebooks, which he continued with some interruptions until his sixtieth year, reveal the tireless craftsman. With interlineations and corrections recur his careful phrases, usually distinguished by definite cadences. Some of these he expanded into the passages in the essays, and others he incorporated without change, as in the last line of "Westminster Abbey": "his very monument becomes a ruin." In these faint pages, sometimes composed in inn or stagecoach, occur the favorite words or groups of words, such as "dimpling" or the "dilapidations of time," which in the later writings, such as *The Conquest of Granada*, harden into the unfortunate stereotypes and repetitions destined to alienate the modern reader, who is fond of stronger food. Here, with humorous drawings, are what he calls his "hints and memorandums," his "images" which delineate so sharply the color of a costume, the detail of a landscape, or the quality of an intense if transient mood. "A face," he wrote in 1817, "the title page to a volume of misery." Later he used these ten words in both *The Sketch Book* and *Bracebridge Hall*. In similar manner the rough draft of his unfinished novel "Rosalie" illustrates this vivid, pictorial method, a method ill-adapted to long narratives. Every jotting suggests his talent for the sketch or essay.

So in *The Sketch Book*, *Bracebridge Hall*, and *The Alhambra*, which form, rather than the histories, biographies, or other miscellaneous writing, the core of Irving's achievement, this craftsmanship attains realization. The unity of "Rip Van Winkle," with its beginning and ending in the afternoon or evening light of the Catskills, is characteristic. So is the slow, graceful exposition in his stories, with their ambiguities between the supernatural and the natural, always humorously weighted by Irving in favor of the latter. Certainly Brom Bones's ludicrous substitute for the head of the spectral horseman is not a well-kept secret. We recall Ichabod Crane's observation on his way to the Van Tassel party of the "yellow pumpkins . . . turning up their fair round bellies to the sun," and we understand Brom's uncontrollable laughter, after Katrina is safely his, at any mention of the shattered vegetable.

Unlike Hawthorne, Irving is not too equivocal concerning the supernatural, perhaps because of his own innate skepticism. One dark night in southern Spain he kept tryst with John Nalder Hall, a friend who had recently died, but, as he had expected, no whisper came to him from beyond the barrier of death. In his use of the supernatural his ambiguities are less serious than whimsical; and he is explicit to a degree perhaps unacceptable today when the reader demands, as in Henry James, a more balanced dubiety. He preferred, presumably, the neatly explanatory conclusions of the Gothic tale, as in "The Spectre Bridegroom." Yet without much belief in the occult, he often points a tale with more than one possible solution:

> The old Dutch inhabitants [so he concludes the story of Rip Van Winkle] . . . even to this day . . . never hear a thunder-storm of a summer afternoon about the Kaatskill, but they say Hendrick Hudson and his crew are at their game of ninepins.

In the essays and stories Irving uses for the most part moderately long, balanced sentences of no more than three, and often only two, clauses, reined up at intervals by a terse declarative sentence. The paragraphs, carefully planned, as the original manuscripts show, are often brief and sometimes reduced to two or three sentences; but they are tightly transitioned and always move forward, if ever so slowly, toward the master's gentle climax, such as Rip's return or our arrival at the actual resting place of Shakespeare. The vocabulary is Latinate but never pretentiously so; it is flecked with words unfamiliar today in Irving's particular sense, such as "rantipole," "hipped," or "slammerkin." The similes, especially the Homeric ones in *A History of New York*, are simple and usually humorous, and we are not bored by rhetoric or teased by the strain which is so characteristic of many modern essays.

Irving is old-fashioned also in his little, gossipy anecdotes, in his asides, in his confidences for the reader, and in his generosity of quotation, especially from English literature, in which he was deeply read. Has not the sentence on the "fair round bellies" of the "yellow pumpkins" an echo from *As You Like It* symbolic perhaps of what Ichabod is thinking? Within the narrative is a dialogue formal, but not without grace. All these devices conspire to establish the author's intimacy with us and to suggest rather deviously the kindliest and wisest of narrators. These discursive little pieces, part essay, part story, so different from the streamlined tales of our time, create an illusion of naïveté which is deceptive; this is a quality absent both in the life and in the writing of this sophisticated American. To dispel the illusion that this simplicity lacks art, imitate, if you can, the style of these essays; try to create, for instance, the same lucidity, the same easy movement of the opening paragraphs of "Rip Van Winkle"—and you will soon despair. All is calculated to attain that particular tone which is Irving himself, and which is as inseparable from this story or "The Legend of Sleepy Hollow" as was Irving's own pleasant, easy voice (which his friends always remembered) from his own personality.

No "preface," no theory of style, no study of writing for its own sake have come down to us to define the conscious techniques of this artist who so stimulated our aspiring young writers, among them Longfellow, Hawthorne, and Lowell. All that he says of writing, as in "The Literary Life" or "The Poor-Devil Author" (chapters in *Tales of a Traveller*) is outward rather than inward; he prefers to discuss Goldsmith's literary set rather than the secrets of his art. He is, in fact, never analytical concerning craftsmanship, and though a modern critic might christen the devices which are discernible in the notebooks, Irving himself never formulated a set of principles. Yet it is impossible to believe that such characteristics as have already been mentioned or more specific manipulations of language, to be discussed presently, were free from artifice. Passages in *A History of New York* which can be scanned as blank verse; the unified paragraphs with their suave transitions; balanced clauses, coordinate and dependent; an "elegant" but simple vocabulary; an over-all tone of leisure and friendly intimacy, with its inner variations, ranging from the sentimental in "The Pride of the Village" to the satirical in "The Spectre Bridegroom": all these he had mastered until he could play them as smoothly as the modulations on his beloved flute.

Irving's experimentation is most obvious, of course, in *Salmagundi* and *A History of New York* and most successful in *The Sketch Book* and in some sections of *Bracebridge Hall* and *The Alhambra*. In his later writings many of these ingenuities froze into formulas. But we can, as one example, observe his first exuberant delight in the device of the catalogue—which, like the epithet and the simile, he had encountered in Homer—in his comic history, in the boisterous roll call of warriors:

> Then came waddling on the sturdy chivalry of the Hudson. There were the Van Wycks, and the Van Dycks, and the Ten Eycks; the Van Nesses, the Van Tassels, the Van Grolls; the Van Hœsens, the Van Giesons, and the Van Blarcoms; the Van Warts, the Van Winkles, the Van Dams; the Van Pelts, the Van Rippers, and the Van Brunts. . . .

And so on for many lines more. Ten years later he adapted the trick to the whimsical catalogue of food upon the groaning board of Baltus Van Tassel:

> There was the doughty doughnut, the tenderer oly koek, and the crisp and crumbling cruller; sweet cakes and short cakes, ginger-cakes and honey-cakes, and the whole family of cakes. And then there were apple-pies and peach-pies and pumpkin-pies . . . preserved plums, and peaches, and pears. . . .

It is unwise to read the earlier passage to a Dutchman or the latter one to a hungry person, but the point is Irving's gradual refinement of all his mechanisms, culled from a reading which makes that of a formal education, which he lacked, seem a feeble substitute. Throughout his literary career he used with increasing sophistication if declining vigor: the mysterious manuscript; the hypothetical narrator, such as Diedrich Knickerbocker, Geoffrey Crayon, or Fray Antonio Agapida; the address to the reader; the quasi-autobiographical allusions; the humorous turn of a concluding sentence; or the Cervantean idiom of chivalry, which is so hilarious in *A History of New York* and so tedious in *The Conquest of Granada*.

Yet the homespun passage on the Van Tassel feast stimulates not only the literary memory of the reader, but also his ear. Surely those initial sounds in the catalogue are not accidental. Irving's toying with alliteration (or onomatopoeia, assonance, or metaphor) follows the development of his art, from enthusiastic curiosity in his youthful satires to strategic workmanship (based on trial and error in the note-books) in *The Sketch Book*. The following venture in alliteration, later to find finished expression in "St. Mark's Eve," typifies his study in the notebooks of the repetition of sounds:

> How the truth presses home upon us as we advance in life that every-

thing around us is transient & uncertain—It is one of those common truths that sleep in our ears—never hold it until we feel it withering at our hearts—until it is tolled in the funeral of our friends and written on the wrecks of our hopes & affections—

Even in these unpolished sentences we hear the melancholy cadence so characteristic of Irving's prose, of the *t*ruth of the *t*ransiency of life as it is *t*olled in the funeral bells of those we *h*old in our *h*earts, to echo only two of the sounds in this rough model of a later melodious paragraph.

Evidently in these crude notes he was learning what he could accomplish in expressing a favorite idea, by the interlinked repetition of "t," "h," "f," and "w." In a passage in *The Sketch Book* he tries out the dentals again, this time to make us feel the tarragon in Dame Van Winkle. She illustrated, says Irving, the truth that "a tart temper never mellows with age, and a sharp tongue is the only edged tool that grows keener with constant use." Then, in contrast to the exhausting din of his shrewish wife, we share the relative silence of Rip, in his "perpetual club of the sages, philosophers, and other idle personages of the village, sitting under the portrait of George the Third." This entire paragraph should be read carefully to appreciate Irving's artful antiphony of alliterative sounds, but we may perceive his communication of the mood of indolence (so strong a part of his own nature) through the liquids and sibilants, the slow movement of the sentences, the alternating long and short vowels, and the flat diminuendo of the last two words: "Here they used to sit in the shade through a long, lazy summer's day, talking listlessly over village gossip, or telling endless sleepy stories about nothing."

The antithesis between the high shrill voice of Dame Van Winkle and the quiet of Rip is partly humorous, but on a more poetic plane the equipoise between silence and sound elicits from Irving some of his most beautiful craftsmanship. In this particular story the stillness of the blue Catskills is always in our minds, and no doubt was in Irving's as, living in anxiety abroad, he wrote during a single intense night in Birmingham the entire story at one sitting. The family business had failed; to earn his living he was now writing *The Sketch Book*. The tale opens amid the peace of these "fairy mountains," and presently Rip, on the day of his fatal ramble, looks down from his green knoll upon the absolute quiet of hill and river. Against this background we hear at different times the echoes of Rip's gun, the strident calling of the crows (a human voice?), and the rumbling of the thunder-storm (ninepins?).

Likewise in Sleepy Hollow, "one of the quietest places in the whole world," we listen to the hoofbeats of Brom Bones's horse or the nasal chants of Ichabod Crane; in the silence of Westminster Abbey we are sensible of "casual footsteps" and of the "distant voice of the priest"; in these places or in the remote English village or in the hush surrounding Shakespeare's grave always echo these sounds from the busy world. Thus in Irving's imagination silence and sound are often opposed. The following passage illustrates the techniques already studied, and those to come. It suggests Irving's affinity, like Bryant's, with the Hudson River school of painters. Yet, most of all, for our immediate purpose, it indicates this counterpoint of sound and silence. As we share the tumult of Ichabod's thoughts during his ride toward the Van Tassels, so we likewise participate in this other world:

The wide bosom of the Tappan Zee lay motionless and glossy, excepting that here and there a gentle undulation waved and prolonged the blue shadow of the distant mountain. A few amber clouds floated in the sky, without a breath of air to move them. The horizon was of a fine golden tint, changing gradually into a pure apple-green, and from that into the deep blue of the mid-heaven. A slanting ray lingered on the woody crests of the precipices that overhung some parts of the river, giving greater depth to the dark-gray and purple of their rocky sides. A sloop was loitering in the distance, dropping slowly down with the tide, her sail hanging uselessly against the mast; and as the reflection of the sky gleamed along the still water, it seemed as if the vessel was suspended in the air.

The passage reveals still other variations in Irving's treatment of nature, among them, perhaps, his use of such descriptions to relieve his own inner craving for stillness, for peace; the words recur endlessly in his writing. More demonstrably, he displays a talent for describing landscape, a talent we have forgotten in our assumption of his interest in the city and the individual. It would be ridiculous to suggest that he rivaled Cooper in representations of prairie, lake, and mountain, ("sublime," said Balzac of the novelist), but it is unfair to think of these as mere backdrops. The panorama in the first pages of *The Sketch Book* of cataracts, rivers, and waters of "liquid silver" he parallels by others in the Spanish and Western books. Often, too, nature, instead of being contrapuntal to the world, is "sympathetic," reflecting the moods of his characters. The lassitude of Rip is mirrored in the slow-moving Hudson, and the peace of the dwellers in the Alhambra by the stillness of the vast *vega*. As Ichabod rides to possess (so he hopes) the abundance of the Van Tassels, he is aware of the "oppressive opulence" of the harvest season, but as, in the hush of midnight he bends his dejected course homeward, he is conscious of the enormous, sinister tulip tree and the "dusky and indistinct waste of waters" of the Tappan Zee.

Nature, then, is in a general sense a symbol. Yet to say that Irving, an adroit craftsman, used nature, legends, or characters in any planned system of symbolism is to state the matter inexactly. Plainly this lover of legends would speculate on their meanings, especially when he kept rediscovering identical ones in different civilizations. Why was the same story found in Dutch, German, and Spanish mountain villages unless it was a parable through which humanity clung tenaciously to some nub of wisdom? In devoting his art to these fables, he must have been aware of their latent meanings. It would seem so, but neither in notebook or journal, by explanation or hint, nor indeed in his attitude toward literature, does he encourage us toward analysis. No tale or sketch suffers readily a breakdown of component parts, a dismember-ment, a solemn exegesis. Surely, a tidy explanation of "Rip Van Winkle" would destroy these tangential, gossamer intimations about living which it so surely conveys to us. We must not break the spell. Let us, therefore, content ourselves with a suggestion of two or three meanings which reappear constantly throughout Irving's writings, and then, finally, ponder a little on the relation of these to his art in "Rip Van Winkle," this masterpiece of our first man of letters.

The two or three meanings are really attitudes or points of view. As a thinker no one, least of all he himself, has ever been able to take Irving seriously. These attitudes, such as his blending of past and pres-ent, already described during our study of his art, were emotional, instinctive, and, suffering little change during his development as an artist, were directly responsible for some of his best writing, namely that published between 1819 and 1832. The first attitude selected for more particular study concerns nature, which Irving perpetually bal-ances against the civilized activity of city, drawing room, or court— areas of life in which he was so completely at ease.

Nature, which in his own way he deeply loved, usually connotes for Irving tranquillity. This concept of nature appears in his earliest and latest Journals, in his tales of the Catskills (as we have seen), in the Spanish books, and in the Western narratives. In all of these he writes repeatedly of the quiet sunset, of the evening star, of the Angelus; indeed almost the last glimpse we have of him is at Sunnyside watching for hours the tranquil flow of the river. This Irving it is important to compare in our minds with Irving the courtier, the diplomat, the diner-out, the easygoing comrade of Walter Scott and Tom Moore. The concept is, of course, romantic; it is escapist; and it is entirely unintellectual, but it is causative in his writing. He was without philosophic interest in nature; he preferred Leigh Hunt to Wordsworth, and was puzzled by the New England Transcendentalists. He displayed no close observation of more than nature's outward grace; he never mentions Thoreau. He indulged in no speculations concerning nature's occult relations to man; he cared nothing for Emerson or Melville. Nevertheless, he turned to nature, and he believed in her power to calm.

A second attitude is a familiar one, that of his delight, especially in his prime, in the glitter, the pageantry of life. Even now, amid their somewhat dusty jests, we sense in the early writings his zest for living; and this is not wholly wanting in his last letters from Sunnyside. Despite Irving's ultimate union with the Church of England, despite his enervate moods, there is often in his essays a half-pagan satisfaction in the pleasures of this world, and little disposition, on the whole, to seek compensation in another. This mood, deep-seated, inclines to center in the pattern of young love as the best gift of life on this earth.

One is tempted to relate this conviction to his own tragic interlude with Matilda Hoffman, but the attitude, if explored in all his writing, reveals less a sentimental than an earthy and vigorous Irving. The lusty strength of Brom Bones and the buxom vitality of Katrina Van Tassel, not unrelated to passages in the notebooks which never found their way into print, intimate his sympathy with the mating of the young Dutch couple. Youthful love is a frequent theme in the essays and stories; and sometimes, as in *A History of New York*, it shows an unexpectedly robust range of experience. As Brom Bones and Katrina stand for the joys of youth, so the angular psalm-singing, materialistic Ichabod represents the enemies of these. After Irving's own boyhood passed he counted his advancing years almost like a woman; and he once referred to his old age as "the dregs of life." This mild hedonism is apparent in the three books of the central period; it is not a conclusion arrived at by reason, but an assumption, an instinctive way of looking at things. In the writings of the New Englanders, which he could not understand, life was a discipline, a preparation, or an emanation of the divine. Not for Irving. Life was life itself, and the best of it, after all, was young love.

So nature the tranquillizer and life in this world stimulated not his analytical faculties, which remained undeveloped, but his romantic imagination; and these two concepts he recorded in essay after essay— these and one other, which after his twenty-sixth year brought him as close to thought as he ever came. This concept was the fact of mutation. Again this was not really thought, but emotion, this deepening sense that the only unchanging principle in this life he loved was change. In one of the notebooks, evidently alarmed by the beginnings of melancholy, he exhorts himself to rise above his sensitivity to feelings and sentiments, "engendered by literature—which has produced a morbid sensibility and fostered all the melancholy tendencies." Other passages in the same notebook emphasize more and more the transiency of things, and in it occurs also his confession, meant for no eye but his own, of the "change" which obliterated his own youthful love; "the romance of life," so the manuscript ends, "is past." From now on this attitude colors everything he writes—*tempus edax rerum*.

Whatever the causes in Irving's own life, this intense consciousness of the mortality of man sets the tone of the books written within this period. This fact does not nullify previous suggestions about his attitudes toward nature and toward life in this world; in fact the sense of change increased his need for nature and intensified his belief, by reason of their brevity, in the experiences of youth. But the mood of change is ever in his mind. He ascribes it to Rip, after his return from the mountains; to King Boabdil as he casts his farewell glance on "bellissima Granada"; to Columbus, as misfortune overtakes him; and, not without absurdity, to Washington, in his declining years. Most of all, in the dozen or so superior essays this mood is dominant: in the moment when we stand before Shakespeare's grave or near the tombs of the rival queens in "Westminster Abbey" or in the court of Lindaraxa. In "The Mutability of Literature" Irving cannot forget the "dilapidations of time," and in "The Boar's Head Tavern, Eastcheap" he is distressed by the silence of the place where once rang out the laughter of Falstaff. Such meditation on our common doom is hardly unique; it was in debt, as he hinted, to his reading (to James Hervey and Sir Thomas Browne). Yet whether the attitude is palpably exploited in the sentimental fashion of the time, as in "The Pride of the Village," or whether, as in some parts of "Westminster Abbey," it flows from a natural melancholy, it became in the essays a basic mood, often served with all the techniques of which the stylist Irving was master.

No tale of Irving's portrays change so vividly as "Rip Van Winkle," and none is a better illustration, as we have seen, of the subtleties of his art. Thus it becomes the epitome of Irving the writer. There it still stands, outwardly just an old wives' fancy, a tale for the fireside, but actually sustaining Irving's fame through the years, if only as a reteller of ancient legends. As a story it has been popularized in play, opera, song, and parody. Yet it has survived all these corruptions, still casting over us, if we reread it now, its mysterious spell. This outward "Rip Van Winkle" has never been better described than by Hawthorne. When his character, Eustace Bright, is asked to tell the tale of Rip Van Winkle, Eustace replies that he cannot possibly do so because

> the story had been told once already, and better than it ever could be told again; and . . . nobody would have a right to alter a word of it, until it should have grown as old as "The Gorgon's Head," and "The Three Golden Apples," and the rest of those miraculous legends.

This is enough for most of us; "Rip Van Winkle" is the perfect version of a story which we seem always to have known. Yet from its immortality we might suspect that it is more; that the skill in craftsmanship was worthily bestowed, a situation not uniformly true of Irving's subjects. Here was the legend suited for his art; his was the art suited for the legend; in "Rip Van Winkle" occurs a fusion of craft and meaning.

At first this meaning, in the light of Irving's preoccupation with the law of change, seems only a projection of his own melancholy caused by this inexorable law. That is, without specifying symbols, we feel that his infatuation with this legend sprang from his reflections on change. Such is a familiar psychological reason for an author's interest in a parable, though the parable itself may by its very nature forbid a literal interpretation. We remember, for example, Matthew Arnold's use of a Danish legend for his poem, "The Forsaken Merman." If we attach meanings to the house on the windy hill or to the windless, sand-strewn caverns, the poem falls apart. Yet few nineteenth-century poets save Arnold would have been attracted by this legend's overtones of tumult and calm. So Irving, long after his boyhood days in the Catskills, still loved the old Dutch myth. Why? Again the notebooks help us. In passage after passage he reflects on wanderers returning home, on the consequences of absence, on altered ways of life. In this sense Rip's fate was his own. Like Rip, he too was to encounter the havoc wrought in his life by his charmed slumber (in Europe) for nearly—a curious coincidence—twenty years.

This personal meaning is interesting, but less important than others. Millions have read the story with complete ignorance of the loneliness of its creator. What moves some, if they regard "Rip Van Winkle" as more than a golden tale, is their own experience in the light of Rip's. *De te fabula narratur!* The machinery of the tale becomes inconsequential: the termagant, Dame Van Winkle; the loafer, Rip; the bowlers and their ninepins; the flagon; the villagers. The story is really an objectification of a tragic truth, a definition of what absence and the passage of time can do to us all. Of this law exist countless expressions, whether they are in the Bible or in the pages of Thomas Wolfe or Sherwood Anderson; where or how many does not matter. The law is always the same; remorseless, it applies to us who read the parable as to Irving, who wrote it and is now beyond its reach.

Because of its truth, it is tempting to pause over the details of the legend or over its antiquity. The German version is parallel, and so is the Spanish, even down to Rip's dog, though he is no longer Wolf, but an Andalusian hound named Tarfe! Probably there are hints in the indolence of Rip on that long, lazy summer's day of the eternal impulse to flee from life. In vain; no one escapes. In that curious dramatic pause in the tale, Rip hears distinctly, like a command, the sound of his own name, "Rip Van Winkle." It is a personal summons to experience the law of change. So at last Rip returns (like ourselves) to strange faces, new ways of life; another dog, a mocking counterpart of the devoted Wolf, growls at him. The twenty years' nap hints at every human being's shock at the swift passage of the years. Rip's destiny, though concentrated, is the destiny of us all.

To forget change, to escape time's winged chariot, which like most romantics, he heard constantly behind him, Irving had recourse to creating in art the tranquillity of nature and the joys of youth: Katrina, "the fair Julia," or Dolores. From this slightly different point of view his nature and his idealization of the life about him were really part of a world of dream and fantasy he had imagined, from his earliest youth until his dying day. Irving, we should not forget, is interested in Rip's experience in his dream world, a cosmos definitely superior, even if the product of a flagon of Dutch ale, to the world of the scolding shrew, Dame Van Winkle. Here Rip heard the reverberations of the ninepins but not, at any rate, his wife's voice. So in the versions of the old legends of Barbarossa, of Andrés Gazul, or of Rip, the dreams are all blissful ones. So were Irving's as he himself fled to an imaginary world of nature, of his own conception of youthful love, of his own half-melancholy, half-amorous dreams of change. Perhaps this fancy is the key to this writer, to whom the essential of life was the weaving of a dream. Listen to him, even in his sixtieth year:

How much of a life checquered by vicissitudes and clouded at times by sordid cares, has been lighted up and embellished by this unbought trickery of the mind. . . . Shadows have proved my substance; and from them I have derived many of my most exquisite enjoyments; while the substantial realities of life have turned to shadows in my grasp. . . . What revelry of the mind I have enjoyed; what fairy castles I have built—*and inhabited.*

·{ ❖❖❖ }·

BIOGRAPHICAL
AND BIBLIOGRAPHICAL NOTE

IRVING SPENT HIS EARLY YEARS in New York, where he was born in 1783, and from 1804 to 1806 he made his first journey abroad. After his return he abandoned his half-hearted study of the law and for almost a decade was variously engaged, in the family business, as staff officer in the War of 1812, as contributor to *The Analectic Magazine,* and as a writer of the first highly civilized satire in American literature. *Salmagundi* appeared in 1807 and Diedrich Knickerbocker's *A History of New York* in 1809. He was already deeply indebted to European thought; when he sailed again in 1815 for England he was to remain for seventeen years. His experiences included, after the publication of *The Sketch Book* (1819-1820) and *Bracebridge Hall* (1822), friendships with Walter Scott, Thomas Moore, Thomas Campbell, and others in the English literary set; a winter at the Saxon Court of Frederick Augustus; and three years in Spain, where for a time he lived with Spanish peasants in the Alhambra. *Tales of a Traveller* (1824) capitalized on his German experience, and his studies in Spain culminated in *A History of the Life and Voyages of Christopher Columbus* (1828); *A Chronicle of the Conquest of Granada* (1829); *Voyages and Discoveries of the Companions of Columbus* (1831); and what Prescott called his "Spanish Sketchbook," *The Alhambra* (1832). He now traveled in the West, took part in public life, and founded his famous home at Sunnyside. *The Crayon Miscellany* (1835), which included also his essays on Abbotsford and Newstead Abbey, recorded in "A Tour of the Prairies" his own experience, while *Astoria* (1836), and *The Rocky Mountains* (1837) were elaborate accounts of exploration based on journals and diaries of the far West. The climax of his public career was his service from 1842 to 1846 as United States Minister to Spain. After the western books, he wrote, besides various miscellanies, biographies of Goldsmith, Margaret Miller Davidson, Mahomet, and George Washington (1855-

1859). In the year of the publication of the fifth volume of this ambitious work he died, known with some reason in America and abroad as "our first man of letters."

In 1848-1850 G. P. Putnam brought out in fifteen volumes *The Works of Washington Irving* (Author's Revised edition). This work was issued under Irving's direct supervision, and though minor changes were made later by other hands, it appears to establish the text which had the final approval of its author. *The Works of Washington Irving* (Riverside Ed., New York, G. P. Putnam, 1851-1860, 21 vols.), which follows the Author's Revised Edition, has formed the basis of the present text. No changes have been made except a few silent corrections of typographical errors.

The four-volume family biography, still valuable for its source material, is Pierre M. Irving, *The Life and Letters of Washington Irving* (1862-1864). Later biographies include those by C. D. Warner (1890); H. W. Boynton (1901); G. S. Hellman (1925); and S. T. Williams (1935). A chapter on him appears in R. E. Spiller, *Literary History of the United States* (New York, 1948). Almost all the many journals and notebooks of Irving have been edited and published. Particularly useful to the student beginning the study of Irving are: P. M. Irving (cited above) and *Washington Irving Representative Selections with Introduction, Bibliography, and Notes,* Ed. Henry A. Pochmann (New York, 1934) and the chapter on Irving in Henry Seidel Canby's *Classic Americans* (New York, 1931).

CONTENTS

A HISTORY OF NEW YORK

BOOK IV

CONTAINING THE CHRONICLES OF THE REIGN
OF WILLIAM THE TESTY

CHAPTER I

Showing the Nature of History in General; Containing Farthermore the
Universal Acquirements of William the Testy, and How a Man May Learn
So Much as to Render Himself Good for Nothing

WHEN THE LOFTY THUCYDIDES is about to enter upon his description of the plague that desolated Athens, one of his modern commentators assures the reader, that the history is now going to be
exceeding solemn, serious, and pathetic, and hints, with that air
of chuckling gratulation with which a good dame draws forth
a choice morsel from a cupboard to regale a favorite, that this
plague will give his history a most agreeable variety.

In like manner did my heart leap within me, when I came to
the dolorous dilemma of Fort Goed Hoop, which I at once perceived to be the forerunner of a series of great events and entertaining disasters. Such are the true subjects for the historic
pen. For what is history, in fact, but a kind of Newgate calendar,
a register of the crimes and miseries that man has inflicted on his
fellow-man? It is a huge libel on human nature, to which we in-
dustriously add page after page, volume after volume, as if we
were building up a monument to the honor, rather than the infamy
of our species. If we turn over the pages of these chronicles that
man has written of himself, what are the characters dignified by
the appellation of great, and held up to the admiration of pos-

terity? Tyrants, robbers, conquerors, renowned only for the magnitude of their misdeeds, and the stupendous wrongs and miseries they have inflicted on mankind,—warriors, who have hired themselves to the trade of blood, not from motives of virtuous patriotism, or to protect the injured and defenceless, but merely to gain the vaunted glory of being adroit and successful in massacring their fellow-beings! What are the great events that constitute a glorious era?—The fall of empires; the desolation of happy countries; splendid cities smoking in their ruins; the proudest works of art tumbled in the dust; the shrieks and groans of whole nations ascending unto heaven!

It is thus the historian may be said to thrive on the miseries of mankind, like birds of prey which hover over the field of battle to fatten on the mighty dead. It was observed by a great projector of inland lock-navigation, that rivers, lakes, and oceans were only formed to feed canals. In like manner I am tempted to believe that plots, conspiracies, wars, victories, and massacres are ordained by Providence only as food for the historian.

It is a source of great delight to the philosopher, in studying the wonderful economy of nature, to trace the mutual dependencies of things, how they are created reciprocally for each other, and how the most noxious and apparently unnecessary animal has its uses. Thus those swarms of flies, which are so often execrated as useless vermin, are created for the sustenance of spiders; and spiders, on the other hand, are evidently made to devour flies. So those heroes, who have been such scourges to the world, were bounteously provided as themes for the poet and historian, while the poet and the historian were destined to record the achievements of heroes!

These, and many similar reflections, naturally arose in my mind as I took up my pen to commence the reign of William Kieft: for now the stream of our history, which hitherto has rolled in a tranquil current, is about to depart forever from its peaceful haunts, and brawl through many a turbulent and rugged scene.

As some sleek ox, sunk in the rich repose of a clover-field, dozing and chewing the cud, will bear repeated blows before it raises itself, so the province of Nieuw Nederlandts, having waxed fat under the drowsy reign of the Doubter, needed cuffs and kicks to rouse it into action. The reader will now witness the manner in which a peaceful community advances towards a state of war; which is apt to be like the approach of a horse to a drum, with much prancing and little progress, and too often with the wrong end foremost.

Wilhelmus Kieft, who in 1634 ascended the gubernatorial chair, (to borrow a favorite though clumsy appellation of modern phraseologists,) was of a lofty descent, his father being inspector of wind-mills in the ancient town of Saardam; and our hero, we are told, when a boy, made very curious investigations into the nature and operation of these machines, which was one reason why he afterwards came to be so ingenious a governor. His name, according to the most authentic etymologists, was a corruption of Kyver, that is to say, a *wrangler* or *scolder,* and expressed the characteristic of his family, which, for nearly two centuries, had kept the windy town of Saardam in hot water, and produced more tartars and brimstones than any ten families in the place; and so truly did he inherit this family peculiarity, that he had not been a year in the government of the province, before he was universally denominated William the Testy. His appearance answered to his name. He was a brisk, wiry, waspish little old gentleman; such a one as may now and then be seen stumping about our city in a broad-skirted coat with huge buttons, a cocked hat stuck on the back of his head, and a cane as high as his chin. His face was broad, but his features were sharp; his cheeks were scorched into a dusky red by two fiery little gray eyes; his nose turned up, and the corners of his mouth turned down, pretty much like the muzzle of an irritable pug-dog.

I have heard it observed by a profound adept in human physiology, that if a woman waxes fat with the progress of years, her tenure of life is somewhat precarious, but if haply she withers as she grows old, she lives forever. Such promised to be the case with William the Testy, who grew tough in proportion as he dried. He had withered, in fact, not through the process of years, but through the tropical fervor of his soul, which burnt like a vehement brush-light in his bosom, inciting him to incessant broils and bickerings. Ancient traditions speak much of his learning, and of the gallant inroads he had made into the dead languages, in which he had made captive a host of Greek nouns and Latin verbs and brought off rich booty in ancient saws and apothegms, which he was wont to parade in his public harangues, as a triumphant general of yore his *spolia opima*. Of metaphysics he knew enough to confound all hearers and himself into the bargain. In logic, he knew the whole family of syllogisms and dilemmas, and was so proud of his skill that he never suffered even a self-evident fact to pass unargued. It was observed, however, that he seldom got into an argument without getting into a perplexity, and then into a passion with his adversary for not being convinced gratis.

He had, moreover, skirmished smartly on the frontiers of several of the sciences, was fond of experimental philosophy, and prided himself upon inventions of all kinds. His abode, which he had fixed at a Bowerie or country-seat at a short distance from the city, just at what is now called Dutch Street, soon abounded with proofs of his ingenuity: patent smoke-jacks that required a horse to work them; Dutch ovens that roasted meat without fire; carts that went before the horses; weather-cocks that turned against the wind; and other wrong-headed contrivances that astonished and confounded all beholders. The house, too, was beset with paralytic cats and dogs, the subjects of his experimental philosophy; and the yelling and yelping of the latter unhappy victims of science, while aiding in the pursuit of knowledge, soon gained for the place the name of "Dog's Misery," by which it continues to be known even at the present day.

Thus in knowledge as in swimming: he who flounders and splashes on the surface makes more noise, and attracts more attention, than the pearl-diver who quietly dives in quest of treasures to the bottom. The vast acquirements of the new governor were the theme of marvel among the simple burghers of New Amsterdam; he figured about the place as learned a man as a Bonze at Pekin, who has mastered one half of the Chinese alphabet, and was unanimously pronounced a "universal genius!"

I have known in my time many a genius of this stamp; but, to speak my mind freely, I never knew one who, for the ordinary purposes of life, was worth his weight in straw. In this respect, a little sound judgment and plain common sense is worth all the sparkling genius that ever wrote poetry or invented theories. Let us see how the universal acquirements of William the Testy aided him in the affairs of government.

CHAPTER II

How William the Testy Undertook to Conquer by Proclamation—How He Was a Great Man Abroad, but a Little Man in His Own House

No SOONER HAD this bustling little potentate been blown by a whiff of fortune into the seat of government than he called his council together to make them a speech on the state of affairs.

Caius Gracchus, it is said, when he harangued the Roman populace, modulated his tone by an oratorical flute or pitch-pipe; Wilhelmus Kief, not having such an instrument at hand, availed himself of that musical organ or trump which nature has implanted in the midst of a man's face: in other words, he preluded his address by a sonorous blast of the nose,—a preliminary flourish much in vogue among public orators.

He then commenced by expressing his humble sense of his utter unworthiness of the high post to which he had been appointed; which made some of the simple burghers wonder why he undertook it, not knowing that it is a point of etiquette with a public orator never to enter upon office without declaring himself unworthy to cross the threshold. He then proceeded in a manner highly classic and erudite to speak of government generally, and of the governments of ancient Greece in particular, together with the wars of Rome and Carthage, and the rise and fall of sundry outlandish empires which the worthy burghers had never read nor heard of. Having thus, after the manner of your learned orator, treated of things in general, he came, by a natural, round-about transition, to the matter in hand, namely, the daring aggressions of the Yankees.

As my readers are well aware of the advantage a potentate has of handling his enemies as he pleases in his speeches and bulletins, where he has the talk all on his own side, they may rest assured that William the Testy did not let such an opportunity escape of giving the Yankees what is called "a taste of his quality." In speaking of their inroads into the territories of their High Mightinesses, he compared them with the Gauls who desolated Rome, the Goths and Vandals who overran the fairest plains of Europe; but when he came to speak of the unparalleled audacity with which they of Weathersfield had advanced their patches up to the very walls of Fort Goed Hoop, and threatened to smother the garrison in onions, tears of rage started into his eyes, as though he nosed the very offence in question.

Having thus wrought up his tale to a climax, he assumed a most belligerent look, and assured the council that he had devised an instrument, potent in its effects, and which he trusted would soon drive the Yankees from the land. So saying, he thrust his hand into one of the deep pockets of his broad-skirted coat and drew forth, not an infernal machine, but an instrument in writing, which he laid with great emphasis upon the table.

The burghers gazed at it for a time in silent awe, as a wary housewife does at a gun, fearful it may go off half-cocked. The document in question had a sinister look, it is true; it was crabbed in text, and from a broad red ribbon dangled the great seal of the province, about the size of a buckwheat pancake. Still, after all, it was but an instrument in writing. Herein, however, existed the wonder of the invention. The document in question was a PROCLAMATION, ordering the Yankees to depart instantly from the territories of their High Mightinesses, under pain of suffering all the forfeitures and punishment in such case made and provided. It was on the moral effect of this formidable instrument that Wilhelmus Kieft calculated, pledging his valor as a governor that, once fulminated against the Yankees, it would, in less than two months, drive every mother's son of them across the borders.

The council broke up in perfect wonder; and nothing was talked of for some time among the old men and women of New Amsterdam but the vast genius of the governor, and his new and cheap mode of fighting by proclamation.

As to Wilhelmus Kieft, having dispatched his proclamation to the frontiers, he put on his cocked hat and corduroy small-clothes, and mounting a tall raw-boned charger, trotted out to his rural retreat of Dog's Misery. Here, like the good Numa, he reposed from the toils of state, taking lessons in government, as from the nymph Egeria, but from the honored wife of his bosom; who was one of that class of females sent upon the earth a little after the flood, as a punishment for the sins of mankind, and commonly known by the appellation of *knowing women*. In fact, my duty as an historian obliges me to make known a circumstance which was a great secret at the time, and consequently was not a subject of scandal at more than half the tea-tables in New Amsterdam, but which, like many other great secrets, has leaked out in the lapse of years,—and this was, that Wilhelmus the Testy, though one of the most potent little men that ever breathed, yet submitted at home to a species of government, neither laid down in Aristotle nor Plato, in short, it partook of the nature of a pure, unmixed tyranny, and is familiarly denominated *petticoat government;*—an absolute sway, which, although exceedingly common in these modern days, was very rare among the ancients, if we may judge from the rout made about the domestic economy of honest Socrates; which is the only ancient case on record.

The great Kieft, however, warded off all the sneers and sarcasms of his particular friends, who are ever ready to joke with a man on sore points of the kind, by alleging that it was a government of his own election, to which he submitted through choice, adding at the same time a profound maxim which he had found in an ancient author, that "he who would aspire to *govern,* should first learn to *obey.*"

CHAPTER III

In Which Are Recorded the Sage Projects of a Ruler of Universal Genius—the Art of Fighting by Proclamation—and How that the Valiant Jacobus Van Curlet Came to Be Foully Dishonored at Fort Goed Hoop

NEVER WAS A MORE comprehensive, a more expeditious, or, what is still better, a more economical measure devised, than this of defeating the Yankees by proclamation,—an expedient, likewise, so gentle and humane, there were ten chances to one in favor of its succeeding; but then there was one chance to ten that it would not succeed,—as the ill-natured fates would have it, that single chance carried the day! The proclamation was perfect in all its parts, well constructed, well written, well sealed, and well published; all that was wanting to insure its effect was, that the Yankees should stand in awe of it; but, provoking to relate, they treated it with the most absolute contempt, applied it to an unseemly purpose; and thus did the first warlike proclamation come to a shameful end,—a fate which I am credibly informed has befallen but too many of its successors.

So far from abandoning the country, those varlets continued their encroachments, squatting along the green banks of the Varsche river, and founding Hartford, Stamford, New Haven, and other border-towns. I have already shown how the onion patches of Pyquag were an eye-sore to Jacobus Van Curlet and his garrisson; but now these moss-troopers increased in their atrocities, kidnapping hogs, impounding horses, and sometimes grievously rib-roasting their owners. Our worthy forefathers could scarcely stir abroad without danger of being out-jockeyed in horse-flesh, or taken in in bargaining; while, in their absence, some daring Yankee peddler would penetrate to their household, and nearly ruin the good housewives with tin ware and wooden bowls.*

* The following cases in point appear in Hazard's Collection of State Papers.
"In the meantime, they of Hartford have not onely usurped and taken in the lands of Connecticott, although unrighteously and against the lawes

I am well aware of the perils which environ me in this part of my history. While raking, with curious hand but pious heart, among the mouldering remains of former days, anxious to draw therefrom the honey of wisdom, I may fare somewhat like that valiant worthy, Samson, who, in meddling with the carcass of a dead lion, drew a swarm of bees about his ears. Thus, while narrating the many misdeeds of the Yanokie or Yankee race, it is ten chances to one but I offend the morbid sensibilities of certain of their unreasonable descendants, who may fly out and raise such a buzzing about this unlucky head of mine, that I shall need the tough hide of an Achilles, or an Orlando Furioso, to protect me from their stings.

Should such be the case, I should deeply and sincerely lament, —not my misfortune in giving offence, but the wrong-headed perverseness of an ill-natured generation, in taking offence at anything I say. That their ancestors did use my ancestors ill is true, and I am very sorry for it. I would, with all my heart, the fact were otherwise; but as I am recording the sacred events of history, I'd not bate one nail's breadth of the honest truth, though I were sure the whole edition of my work would be bought up and burnt by the common hangman of Connecticut. And in sooth, now that these testy gentlemen have drawn me out, I will make bold to go farther, and observe that this is one of the grand purposes for which we impartial historians are sent into the world, —to redress wrongs and render justice on the heads of the guilty. So that though a powerful nation may wrong its neighbors with

of nations but have hindered our nation in sowing theire own purchased broken up lands, but have also sowed them with corne in the night, which the Nederlanders had broken up and intended to sowe: and have beaten the servants of the high and mighty the honored companie, which were laboring upon theire master's lands, from theire lands, with sticks and plow staves in hostile manner laming, and among the rest, struck Ever Duckings [Evert Duyckink] a hole in his head, with a stick, so that the bloode ran downe very strongly downe upon his body."

"Those of Hartford sold a hogg, that belonged to the honored companie, under pretence that it had eaten of theire grounde grass, when they had not any foot of inheritance. They proffered the hogg for 5s. if the commissioners would have given 5s. for damage; which the commissioners denied, because noe man's own hogg (as men used to say) can trespass upon his owne master's grounde."

temporary impunity, yet sooner or later an historian springs up, who wreaks ample chastisement on it in return.

Thus these moss-troopers of the east little thought, I'll warrant it, while they were harassing the inoffensive province of Nieuw Nederlandts, and driving its unhappy governor to his wit's end, that an historian would ever arise, and give them their own, with interest. Since, then, I am but performing my bounden duty as an historian, in avenging the wrongs of our revered ancestors, I shall make no further apology; and, indeed, when it is considered that I have all these ancient borderers of the east in my power, and at the mercy of my pen, I trust that it will be admitted I conduct myself with great humanity and moderation.

It was long before William the Testy could be persuaded that his much-vaunted war-measure was ineffectual; on the contrary, he flew in a passion whenever it was doubted, swearing that, though slow in operating, yet when it once began to work, it would soon purge the land of these invaders. When convinced, at length, of the truth, like a shrewd physician he attributed the failure to the quantity, not the quality of the medicine, and resolved to double the dose. He fulminated, therefore, a second proclamation, more vehement than the first, forbidding all intercourse with these Yankee intruders, ordering the Dutch burghers on the frontiers to buy none of their pacing horses, measly pork, apple-sweet-meats, Weathersfield onions, or wooden bowls, and to furnish them with no supplies of gin, gingerbread, or sourkrout.

Another interval elapsed, during which the last production was as little regarded as the first; and the non-intercourse was especially set at naught by the young folks of both sexes, if we may judge by the active bundling which took place along the borders.

At length, one day the inhabitants of New Amsterdam were aroused by a furious barking of dogs, great and small, and beheld, to their surprise, the whole garrison of Fort Goed Hoop straggling into town all tattered and wayworn, with Jacobus Van Curlet at their head, bringing the melancholy intelligence of the capture of Fort Goed Hoop by the Yankees.

The fate of this important fortress is an impressive warning to all military commanders. It was neither carried by storm nor famine; nor was it undermined; nor bombarded; nor set on fire by red-hot shot; but was taken by a stratagem no less singular than effectual, and which can never fail of success, whenever an opportunity occurs of putting it in practice.

It seems that the Yankees had received intelligence that the garrison of Jacobus Van Curlet had been reduced nearly one eighth by the death of two of his most corpulent soldiers, who had overeaten themselves on fat salmon caught in the Varsche river. A secret expedition was immediately set on foot to surprise the fortress. The crafty enemy, knowing the habits of the garrison to sleep soundly after they had eaten their dinners and smoked their pipes, stole upon them at the noontide of a sultry summer's day, and surprised them in the midst of their slumbers.

In an instant the flag of their High Mightinesses was lowered, and the Yankee standard elevated in its stead, being a dried codfish, by way of a spread eagle. A strong garrison was appointed, of long-sided, hard-fisted Yankees, with Weathersfield onions for cockades and feathers. As to Jacobus Van Curlet and his men, they were seized by the nape of the neck, conducted to the gate, and one by one dismissed with a kick in the crupper, as Charles XII. dismissed the heavy-bottomed Russians at the battle of Narva; Jacobus Van Curlet receiving two kicks in consideration of his official dignity.

CHAPTER IV

Containing the Fearful Wrath of William the Testy, and the Alarm of New Amsterdam—How the Governor Did Strongly Fortify the City—Of the Rise of Antony the Trumpeter, and the Windy Addition to the Armorial Bearings of New Amsterdam

LANGUAGE CANNOT EXPRESS the awful ire of William the Testy on hearing of the catastrophe at Fort Goed Hoop. For three good hours his rage was too great for words, or rather the words were too great for him, (being a very small man,) and he was nearly choked by the misshapen, nine-cornered Dutch oaths and epithets which crowded at once into his gullet. At length his words found vent, and for three days he kept up a constant discharge, anathematizing the Yankees, man, woman, and child, for a set of dieven, schobbejacken, deugenieten, twistzoekeren, blaes-kaken, loosenschalken, kakken-bedden, and a thousand other names, of which, unfortunately for posterity, history does not make mention. Finally, he swore that he would have nothing more to do with such a squatting, bundling, guessing, questioning, swapping, pumpkin-eating, molasses-daubing, shingle-splitting, cider-watering, horse-jockeying, notion-peddling crew; that they might stay at Fort Goed Hoop and rot, before he would dirty his hands by attempting to drive them away: in proof of which he ordered the new-raised troops to be marched forthwith into winter-quarters, although it was not as yet quite midsummer. Great despondency now fell upon the city of New Amsterdam. It was feared that the conquerors of Fort Goed Hoop, flushed with victory and apple-brandy, might march on to the capital, take it by storm, and annex the whole province to Connecticut. The name of Yankee became as terrible among the Nieuw Nederlanders as was that of Gaul among the ancient Romans; insomuch that the good wives of the Manhattoes used it as a bugbear wherewith to frighten their unruly children.

Everybody clamored around the governor, imploring him to put the city in a complete posture of defence; and he listened to their clamors. Nobody could accuse William the Testy of being idle in time of danger, or at any other time. He was never idle, but then he was often busy to very little purpose. When a youngling, he had been impressed with the words of Solomon, "Go to the ant, thou sluggard, observe her ways and be wise;" in conformity to which he had ever been of a restless, ant-like turn, hurrying hither and thither, nobody knew why or wherefore, busying himself about small matters with an air of great importance and anxiety, and toiling at a grain of mustard-seed in the full conviction that he was moving a mountain. In the present instance, he called in all his inventive powers to his aid, and was continually pondering over plans, making diagrams, and worrying about with a troop of workmen and projectors at his heels. At length, after a world of consultation and contrivance, his plans of defence ended in rearing a great flag-staff in the centre of the fort, and perching a wind-mill on each bastion.

These warlike preparations in some measure allayed the public alarm, especially after an additional means of securing the safety of the city had been suggested by the governor's lady. It has already been hinted in this most authentic history, that in the domestic establishment of William the Testy "the gray mare was the better horse"; in other words, that his wife "ruled the roast," and in governing the governor, governed the province, which might thus be said to be under petticoat government.

Now it came to pass, that about this time there lived in the Manhattoes a jolly, robustious trumpeter, named Antony Van Corlear, famous for his long wind; and who, as the story goes, could twang so potently upon his instrument, that the effect upon all within hearing was like that ascribed to the Scotch bagpipe when it sings right lustily i' the nose.

This sounder of brass was moreover a lusty bachelor, with a pleasant, burly visage, a long nose, and huge whiskers. He had his little *bowerie,* or retreat, in the country, where he led a roistering life, giving dances to the wives and daughters of the burghers of the Manhattoes, insomuch that he became a prodigious favorite with all the women, young and old. He is said to have been the first to collect that famous toll levied on the fair sex at Kissing Bridge, on the highway to Hellgate.*

To this sturdy bachelor the eyes of all the women were turned in this time of darkness and peril, as the very man to second and carry out the plans of defence of the governor. A kind of petticoat council was forthwith held at the government house, at which the governor's lady presided; and this lady, as has been hinted, being

* The bridge here mentioned by Mr. Knickerbocker still exists, but it is said that the toll is seldom collected nowadays, excepting on sleighing-parties, by the descendants of the patriarchs, who still preserve the traditions of the city.

all potent with the governor, the result of these councils was the elevation of Antony the Trumpeter to the post of commandant of wind-mills and champion of New Amsterdam.

The city being thus fortified and garrisoned, it would have done one's heart good to see the governor snapping his fingers and fidgeting with delight, as the trumpeter strutted up and down the ramparts, twanging defiance to the whole Yankee race, as does a modern editor to all the principalities and powers on the other side of the Atlantic. In the hands of Antony Van Corlear this windy instrument appeared to him as potent as the horn of the paladin Astolpho, or even the more classic horn of Alecto; nay, he had almost the temerity to compare it with the rams' horns celebrated in holy writ, at the very sound of which the walls of Jericho fell down.

Be all this as it may, the apprehensions of hostilities from the east gradually died away. The Yankees made no further invasion; nay, they declared they had only taken possession of Fort Goed Hoop as being erected within their territories. So far from manifesting hostility, they continued to throng to New Amsterdam with the most innocent countenances imaginable, filling the market with their notions, being as ready to trade with the Nederlanders as ever, and not a whit more prone to get to the windward of them in a bargain.

The old wives of the Manhattoes, who took tea with the governor's lady, attributed all this affected moderation to the awe inspired by the military preparations of the governor, and the windy prowess of Antony the Trumpeter.

There were not wanting illiberal minds, however, who sneered at the governor for thinking to defend his city as he governed it, by mere wind; but William Kieft was not to be jeered out of his wind-mills: he had seen them perched upon the ramparts of his native city of Saardam, and was persuaded they were connected with the great science of defence; nay, so much piqued was he by having them made a matter of ridicule, that he introduced them into the arms of the city, where they remain to this day, quartered with the ancient beaver of the Manhattoes, an emblem and memento of his policy.

I must not omit to mention that certain wise old burghers of the Manhattoes, skilful in expounding signs and mysteries, after events have come to pass, consider this early intrusion of the wind-mill into the escutcheon of our city, which before had been wholly occupied by the beaver, as portentous of its after fortune, when the quiet Dutchman would be elbowed aside by the enterprising Yankee, and patient industry overtopped by windy speculation.

CHAPTER V

Of the Jurisprudence of William the Testy, and His Admirable Expedients for the Suppression of Poverty

AMONG THE WRECKS and fragments of exalted wisdom, which have floated down the stream of time from venerable antiquity, and been picked up by those humble but industrious wights who ply along the shores of literature, we find a shrewd ordinance of Charondas the Locrian legislator. Anxious to preserve the judicial code of the State from the additions and amendments of country members and seekers of popularity, he ordained that, whoever proposed a new law should do it with a halter about his neck; whereby, in case his proposition were rejected, they just hung him up—and there the matter ended.

The effect was, that for more than two hundred years there was but one trifling alteration in the judicial code; and legal matters were so clear and simple that the whole race of lawyers starved to death for want of employment. The Locrians, too, being freed from all incitement to litigation, lived very lovingly together, and were so happy a people that they make scarce any figure in history; it being only your litigious, quarrelsome, rantipole nations who make much noise in the world.

I have been reminded of these historical facts in coming to treat of the internal policy of William the Testy. Well would it have been for him had he in the course of his universal acquirements stumbled upon the precaution of the good Charondas, or had he looked nearer home at the protectorate of Oloffe the Dreamer, when the community was governed without laws. Such legislation, however, was not suited to the busy, meddling mind of William the Testy. On the contrary, he conceived that the true wisdom of legislation consisted in the multiplicity of laws. He accordingly had great punishments for great crimes, and little punishments for little offences. By degrees the whole surface of society was cut up by ditches and fences, and quickset hedges of the law, and even the sequestered paths of private life so beset by petty rules and ordinances, too numerous to be remembered, that one could scarce walk at large without the risk of letting off a spring-gun or falling into a man-trap.

In a little while the blessings of innumerable laws became apparent; a class of men arose to expound and confound them. Petty courts were instituted to take cognizance of petty offences, pettifoggers began to abound; and the community was soon set together by the ears.

Let me not be thought as intending anything derogatory to the profession of the law, or to the distinguished members of that illustrious order. Well am I aware that we have in this ancient city innumerable worthy gentlemen, the knights-errant of modern days, who go about redressing wrongs and defending the defenceless, not for the love of filthy lucre, nor the selfish cravings of renown, but merely for the pleasure of doing good. Sooner would I throw this trusty pen into the flames, and cork up my ink-bottle forever, than infringe even for a nail's breadth upon the dignity of these truly benevolent champions of the distressed. On the contrary, I allude merely to those caitiff scouts who, in these latter days of evil, infest the skirts of the profession, as did the recreant Cornish knights of yore the honorable order of chivalry,—who, under its auspices, commit flagrant wrongs,—who thrive by quibbles, by quirks and chicanery, and like vermin increase the corruption in which they are engendered.

Nothing so soon awakens the malevolent passions as the facility of gratification. The courts of law would never be so crowded with petty, vexatious, and disgraceful suits, were it not for the herds of pettifoggers. These tamper with the passions of the poorer and more ignorant classes, who, as if poverty were not a sufficient misery in itself, are ever ready to imbitter it by litigation. These, like quacks in medicine, excite the malady to profit by the cure, and retard the cure to augment the fees. As the quack exhausts the constitution, the pettifogger exhausts the purse; and as he who has once been under the hands of a quack is forever after prone to dabble in drugs, and poison himself with infallible prescriptions, so the client of the pettifogger is ever after prone to embroil himself with his neighbors, and impoverish himself with successful lawsuits. My readers will excuse this digression into which I have been unwarily betrayed; but I could not avoid giving a cool and unprejudiced account of an abomination too prevalent in this excellent city, and with the effects of which I am ruefully acquainted: having been nearly ruined by a lawsuit which was decided against me; and my ruin having been completed by another, which was decided in my favor.

To return to our theme. There was nothing in the whole range of moral offences against which the jurisprudence of William the Testy was more strenuously directed than the crying sin of poverty. He pronounced it the root of all evil, and determined to cut it up, root and branch, and extirpate it from the land. He had been struck, in the course of his travels in the old countries of Europe, with the wisdom of those notices posted up in country towns, that "any vagrant found begging there would be put in the stocks," and he had observed that no beggars were to be seen in these neighborhoods; having doubtless thrown off their rag and their poverty, and become rich under the terror of the law. He determined to improve upon this hint. In a little while a new machine, of his own invention, was erected hard by Dog's Misery. This was nothing more nor less than a gibbet, of a very strange, uncouth, and unmatchable construction, far more efficacious, as he boasted, than the stocks, for the punishment of poverty. It was for altitude not a whit inferior to that of Haman so renowned in Bible history; but the marvel of the contrivance was, that the culprit, instead of being suspended by the neck, according to venerable custom, was hoisted by the waistband, and kept dangling and sprawling between heaven and earth for an hour or two at a time—to the infinite entertainment and edification of the respectable citizens who usually attend exhibitions of the kind.

It is incredible how the little governor chuckled at beholding caitiff vagrants and sturdy beggars thus swinging by the crupper, and cutting antic gambols in the air. He had a thousand pleasantries and mirthful conceits to utter upon these occasions. He called them his dandle-lions—his wild-fowl—his high-fliers—his spread-eagles—his goshawks—his scare-crows—and finally, his *gallows-birds;* which ingenious appellation, though originally confined to worthies who had taken the air in this strange manner, has since grown to be a cant name given to all candidates for legal elevation. This punishment, moreover, if we may credit the assertions of certain grave etymologists, gave the first hint for a kind of harnessing, or strapping, by which our forefathers braced up their multifarious breeches, and which has of late years been revived, and continues to be worn at the present day.

Such was the punishment of all petty delinquents, vagrants and beggars and others detected in being guilty of poverty in a small way; as to those who had offended on a great scale, who had been guilty of flagrant misfortunes and enormous backslidings of the purse, and who stood convicted of large debts, which they were unable to pay, William Kieft had them straightway inclosed within the stone walls of a prison, there to remain until they should reform and grow rich. This notable expedient, however, does not appear to have been more efficacious under William the Testy than in more modern days: it being found that the longer a poor devil was kept in prison the poorer he grew.

CHAPTER VI

Projects of William the Testy for Increasing the Currency—He Is Out-witted by the Yankees—The Great Oyster War

NEXT TO HIS PROJECTS for the suppression of poverty may be classed those of William the Testy, for increasing the wealth of New Amsterdam. Solomon, of whose character for wisdom the little governor was somewhat emulous, had made gold and silver as plenty as the stones in the streets of Jerusalem. William Kieft could not pretend to vie with him as to the precious metals, but he determined, as an equivalent, to flood the streets of New Amsterdam with Indian money. This was nothing more nor less than strings of beads wrought of clams, periwinkles, and other shell-fish, and called seawant or wampum. These had formed a native currency among the simple savages, who were content to take them of the Dutchmen in exchange for peltries. In an un-lucky moment, William the Testy, seeing this money of easy pro-duction, conceived the project of making it the current coin of the province. It is true it had an intrinsic value among the Indians, who used it to ornament their robes and moccasons, but among the honest burghers it had no more intrinsic value than those rags which form the paper currency of modern days. This consider-ation, however, had no weight with William Kieft. He began by paying all the servants of the company, and all the debts of gov-ernment, in strings of wampum. He sent emissaries to sweep the shores of Long Island, which was the Ophir of this modern Solo-mon, and abounded in shell-fish. These were transported in loads to New Amsterdam, coined into Indian money, and launched into circulation.

And now, for a time, affairs went on swimmingly; money be-came as plentiful as in the modern days of paper currency, and, to use the popular phrase, "a wonderful impulse was given to pub-lic prosperity." Yankee traders poured into the province, buying everything they could lay their hands on, and paying the worthy

Dutchmen their own price—in Indian money. If the latter, however, attempted to pay the Yankees in the same coin for their tin ware and wooden bowls, the case was altered; nothing would do but Dutch guilders and such like "metallic currency." What was worse, the Yankees introduced an inferior kind of wampum made of oyster-shells, with which they deluged the province, carrying off in exchange all the silver and gold, the Dutch herrings, and Dutch cheeses: thus early did the knowing men of the east manifest their skill in bargaining the New Amsterdammers out of the oyster, and leaving them the shell.*

It was a long time before William the Testy was made sensible how completely his grand project of finance was turned against him by his eastern neighbors; nor would he probably have ever found it out, had not tidings been brought him that the Yankees had made a descent upon Long Island, and had established a kind of mint at Oyster Bay, where they were coming up all the oyster-banks.

Now this was making a vital attack upon the province in a double sense, financial and gastronomical. Ever since the council-dinner of Oloffe the Dreamer at the founding of New Amsterdam, at which banquet the oyster figured so conspicuously, this divine shell-fish has been held in a kind of superstitious reverence at the Manhattoes; as witness the temples erected to its cult in every street and lane and alley. In fact, it is the standard luxury of the place, as is the terrapin at Philadelphia, the soft crab at Baltimore, or the canvas-back at Washington.

* In a manuscript record of the province, dated 1659, Library of the New York Historical Society, is the following mention of Indian money:

"*Seawant* alias wampum. Beads manufactured from the *Quahang* or *wilk:* a shell-fish formerly abounding on our coasts, but lately of more rare occurrence, of two colors, black and white; the former twice the value of the latter. Six beads of the white and three of the black for an English penny. The seawant depreciates from time to time. The New-England people make use of it as a means of barter, not only to carry away the best cargoes which we send thither, but to accumulate a large quantity of beavers and other furs; by which the company is defrauded of her revenues, and the merchants disappointed in making returns with that speed with which they might wish to meet their engagements; while their commissioners and the inhabitants remain overstocked with seawant,—a sort of currency of no value except with the New Netherland savages, &c."

The seizure of Oyster Bay, therefore, was an outrage not merely on the pockets, but the larders of the New Amsterdammers; the whole community was aroused, and an oyster crusade was immediately set on foot against the Yankees. Every stout trencherman hastened to the standard; nay, some of the most corpulent Burgomasters and Schepens joined the expedition as a *corps de reserve*, only to be called into action when the sacking commenced.

The conduct of the expedition was intrusted to a valiant Dutchman, who for size and weight might have matched with Colbrand the Danish champion, slain by Guy of Warwick. He was famous throughout the province for strength of arm and skill at quarterstaff, and hence was named Stoffel Brinkerhoff, or rather, Brinkerhoofd, that is to say, Stoffel the head-breaker.

This sturdy commander, who was a man of few words but vigorous deeds, led his troops resolutely on through Nineveh, and Babylon, and Jericho, and Patch-hog, and other Long Island towns, without encountering any difficulty of note; though it is said that some of the burgomasters gave out at Hardscramble Hill and Hungry Hollow, and that others lost heart and turned back at Puss-panick. With the rest he made good his march until he arrived in the neighborhood of Oyster Bay.

Here he was encountered by a host of Yankee warriors, headed by Preserved Fish, and Habakkuk Nutter, and Return Strong, and Zerubbabel Fisk, and Determined Cock! at the sound of whose names Stoffel Brinkerhoff verily believed the whole parliament of Praise-God Barebones had been let loose upon him. He soon found, however, that they were merely the "selectmen" of the settlement, armed with no weapon but the tongue, and disposed only to meet him on the field of argument. Stoffel had but one mode of arguing, that was, with the cudgel; but he used it with such effect that he routed his antagonists, broke up the settlement, and would have driven the inhabitants into the sea if they had not managed to escape across the Sound to the mainland by the Devil's stepping-stones, which remain to this day monuments of this great Dutch victory over the Yankees.

Stoffel Brinkerhoff made great spoil of oysters and clams, coined and uncoined, and then set out on his return to the Manhattoes.

A grand triumph, after the manner of the ancients, was prepared for him by William the Testy. He entered New Amsterdam as a conqueror, mounted on a Narraganset pacer. Five dried codfish on poles, standards taken from the enemy, were borne before him, and an immense store of oysters and clams, Weathersfield onions, and Yankee "notions" formed the *spolia opima;* while several coiners of oyster-shells were led captive to grace the hero's triumph.

The procession was accompanied by a full band of boys and negroes, performing on the popular instruments of rattle-bones and clam-shells, while Antony Van Corlear sounded his trumpet from the ramparts.

A great banquet was served up in the stadthouse from the clams and oysters taken from the enemy; while the governor sent the shells privately to the mint, and had them coined into Indian money, with which he paid his troops.

It is moreover said that the governor, calling to mind the practice among the ancients to honor their victorious general with public statues, passed a magnanimous decree, by which every tavern-keeper was permitted to paint the head of Stoffel Brinkerhoff upon his sign!

CHAPTER VII

Growing Discontents of New Amsterdam under the Government of William the Testy

IT HAS BEEN REMARKED by the observant writer of the Stuyvesant manuscript, that under the administration of William Kieft the disposition of the inhabitants of New Amsterdam experienced an essential change, so that they became very meddlesome and factious. The unfortunate propensity of the little governor to experiment and innovation, and the frequent exacerbations of his temper, kept his council in a continual worry; and the council being to

the people at large what yeast or leaven is to a batch, they threw
the whole community in a ferment; and the people at large being
to the city what the mind is to the body, the unhappy commotions
they underwent operated most disastrously upon New Amsterdam,
—insomuch that, in certain of their paroxysms of consternation
and perplexity, they begat several of the most crooked, distorted,
and abominable streets, lanes, and alleys, with which this metropolis is disfigured.

The fact was, that about this time the community, like Balaam's
ass, began to grow more enlightened than its rider, and to show a
disposition for what is called "self-government." This restive propensity was first evinced in certain popular meetings, in which the
burghers of New Amsterdam met to talk and smoke over the com-
plicated affairs of the province, gradually obfuscating themselves
with politics and tobacco-smoke. Hither resorted those idlers and
squires of low degree who hang loose on society and are blown
about by every wind of doctrine. Cobblers abandoned their stalls
to give lessons on political economy; blacksmiths suffered their
fires to go out while they stirred up the fires of faction; and even
tailors, though said to be the ninth parts of humanity, neglected
their own measures to criticize the measures of government.

Strange! that the science of government, which seems to be so
generally understood, should invariably be denied to the only one
called upon to exercise it. Not one of the politicians in question,
but, take his word for it, could have administered affairs ten times
better than William the Testy.

Under the instructions of these political oracles the good people
of New Amsterdam soon became exceedingly enlightened, and,
as a matter of course, exceedingly discontented. They gradually
found out the fearful error in which they had indulged, of thinking
themselves the happiest people in creation, and were convinced
that, all circumstances to the contrary notwithstanding, they were
a very unhappy, deluded, and consequently ruined people!

We are naturally prone to discontent, and avaricious after imaginary causes of lamentation. Like lubberly monks we belabor our
own shoulders, and take a vast satisfaction in the music of our
own groans. Nor is this said by way of paradox; daily experience

shows the truth of these observations. It is almost impossible to elevate the spirits of a man groaning under ideal calamities; but nothing is easier than to render him wretched, though on the pinnacle of felicity; as it would be an Herculean task to hoist a man to the top of a steeple, though the merest child could topple him off thence.

I must not omit to mention that these popular meetings were generally held at some noted tavern, these public edifices possessing what in modern times are thought the true fountains of political inspiration. The ancient Greeks deliberated upon a matter when drunk, and reconsidered it when sober. Mob-politicians in modern times dislike to have two minds upon a subject, so they both deliberate and act when drunk; by this means a world of delay is spared; and as it is universally allowed that a man when drunk sees double, it follows conclusively that he sees twice as well as his sober neighbors.

CHAPTER VIII

Of the Edict of William the Testy against Tobacco—Of the Pipe-Plot, and the Rise of Feuds and Parties

WILHELMUS KIEFT, as has already been observed, was a great legislator on a small scale, and had a microscopic eye in public affairs. He had been greatly annoyed by the factious meeting of the good people of New Amsterdam, but, observing that on these occasions the pipe was ever in their mouth, he began to think that the pipe was at the bottom of the affair, and that there was some mysterious affinity between politics and tobacco-smoke. Determined to strike at the root of the evil, he began forthwith to rail at tobacco, as a noxious, nauseous weed, filthy in all its uses; and as to smoking, he denounced it as a heavy tax upon the public pocket,—a vast consumer of time, a great encourager of idleness, and a deadly bane to the prosperity and morals of the people. Finally he issued an edict, prohibiting the smoking of tobacco throughout the New Netherlands. Ill-fated Kieft! Had he lived in the present age and attempted to check the unbounded license of the press, he could not have struck more sorely upon the sensibilities of the million. The pipe, in fact, was the great organ of reflection and deliberation of the New Netherlander. It was his constant companion and solace: was he gay, he smoked; was he sad, he smoked; his pipe was never out of his mouth; it was a part of his physiognomy; without it his best friends would not know him. Take away his pipe? You might as well take away his nose!

The immediate effect of the edict of William the Testy was a popular commotion. A vast multitude, armed with pipes and tobacco-boxes, and an immense supply of ammunition, sat themselves down before the governor's house, and fell to smoking with tremendous violence. The testy William issued forth like a wrathful spider, demanding the reason of this lawless fumigation. The sturdy rioters replied by lolling back in their seats, and puffing away with redoubled fury, raising such a murky cloud that the governor was fain to take refuge in the interior of his castle.

A long negotiation ensued through the medium of Antony the Trumpeter. The governor was at first wrathful and unyielding, but was gradually smoked into terms. He concluded by permitting the smoking of tobacco, but he abolished the fair long pipes used in the days of Wouter Van Twiller, denoting ease, tranquillity, and sobriety of deportment; these he condemned as incompatible with the despatch of business, in place whereof he substituted little captious short pipes, two inches in length, which, he observed, could be stuck in one corner of the mouth, or twisted in the hatband, and would never be in the way. Thus ended this alarming insurrection, which was long known by the name of The Pipe-Plot, and which, it has been somewhat quaintly observed, did end, like most plots and seditions, in mere smoke.

But mark, oh, reader! the deplorable evils which did afterwards result. The smoke of these villainous little pipes, continually ascending in a cloud about the nose, penetrated into and befogged the cerebellum, dried up all the kindly moisture of the brain, and rendered the people who use them as vaporish and testy as the governor himself. Nay, what is worse, from being goodly, burly, sleek-conditioned men, they became, like our Dutch yeomanry who smoke short pipes, a lantern-jawed, smoked-dried, leathern-hided race.

Nor was this all. From this fatal schism in tobacco-pipes we may date the rise of parties in the Nieuw Nederlands. The rich and self-important burghers who had made their fortunes, and could afford to be lazy, adhered to the ancient fashion, and formed a kind of aristocracy known as the *Long Pipes;* while the lower order, adopting the reform of William Kieft as more convenient in their handicraft employments, were branded with the plebeian name of *Short Pipes.*

A third party sprang up, headed by the descendants of Robert Chewit, the companion of the great Hudson. These discarded pipes altogether and took to chewing tobacco; hence they were called *Quids,*—an appellation since given to those political mongrels, which sometimes spring up between two great parties, as a mule is produced between a horse and an ass.

And here I would note the great benefit of party distinctions in saving the people at large the trouble of thinking. Hesiod divides mankind into three classes,—those who think for themselves, those who think as others think, and those who do not think at all. The second class comprises the great mass of society; for most people require a set creed and a file-leader. Hence the origin of party: which means a large body of people, some few of whom think, and all the rest talk. The former take the lead and discipline the latter; prescribing what they must say, what they must approve, what they must hoot at, whom they must support, but, above all, whom they must hate; for no one can be a right good partisan, who is not a thorough-going hater.

The enlightened inhabitants of the Manhattoes, therefore, being divided into parties, were enabled to hate each other with great accuracy. And now the great business of politics went bravely on, the long pipes and short pipes assembling in separate beer-houses, and smoking at each other with implacable vehemence, to the great support of the State and profit of the tavern-keepers. Some, indeed, went so far as to bespatter their adversaries with those odoriferous little words which smell so strong in the Dutch language, believing, like true politicians, that they served their party, and glorified themselves in proportion as they bewrayed their neighbors. But, however they might differ among themselves, all parties agreed in abusing the governor, seeing that he was not a governor of their choice, but appointed by others to rule over them.

Unhappy William Kieft! exclaims the sage writer of the Stuyvesant manuscript, doomed to contend with enemies too knowing to be entrapped, and to reign over a people too wise to be governed. All his foreign expeditions were baffled and set at naught by the all-pervading Yankees; all his home measures were canvassed and condemned by "numerous and respectable meetings" of pothouse politicians.

In the multitude of counsellors, we are told, there is safety; but the multitude of counsellors was a continual source of perplexity to William Kieft. With a temperament as hot as an old radish, and a mind subject to perpetual whirlwinds and tornadoes, he never failed to get into a passion with every one who undertook to advise him. I have observed, however, that your passionate little men, like small boats with large sails, are easily upset or blown out of their course; so was it with William the Testy, who was prone to be carried away by the last piece of advice blown into his ear. The consequence was, that, though a projector of the first class, yet by continually changing his projects he gave none a fair trial; and by endeavoring to do everything, he in sober truth did nothing.

In the mean time, the sovereign people got into the saddle, showed themselves, as usual, unmerciful riders; spurring on the little governor with harangues and petitions, and thwarting him with memorials and reproaches, in much the same way as holiday apprentices manage an unlucky devil of a hack-horse,—so that Wilhelmus Kieft was kept at a worry or a gallop throughout the whole of his administration.

CHAPTER IX

Of the Folly of Being Happy in Time of Prosperity—Of Troubles to the South Brought On by Annexation—Of the Secret Expedition of Jan Jansen Alpendam, and His Magnificent Reward

IF WE COULD BUT GET a peep at the tally of dame Fortune, where like a vigilant landlady she chalks up the debtor and creditor accounts of thoughtless mortals, we should find that every good is checked off by an evil, and that, however we may apparently revel scot-free for a season, the time will come when we must ruefully pay off the reckoning. Fortune in fact is a pestilent shrew, and withal an inexorable creditor; and though for a time she may be all smiles and courtesies, and indulge us in long credits, yet sooner or later she brings up her arrears with a vengeance, and washes out her scores with our tears. "Since," says good old Boetius, "no man can retain her at his pleasure; what are her favors but sure prognostications of approaching trouble and calamity?"

This is the fundamental maxim of that sage school of philosophers, the croakers, who esteem it true wisdom to doubt and despond when other men rejoice, well knowing that happiness is at best but transient,—that, the higher one is elevated on the seesaw balance of fortune, the lower must be his subsequent depression,—that he who is on the uppermost round of a ladder has most to suffer from a fall, while he who is at the bottom runs very little risk of breaking his neck by tumbling to the top.

Philosophical readers of this stamp must have doubtless indulged in dismal forebodings all through the tranquil reign of Walter the Doubter, and considered it what Dutch seamen call a weather-breeder. They will not be surprised, therefore, that the foul weather which gathered during his days should now be rattling from all quarters on the head of William the Testy.

The origin of some of these troubles may be traced quite back to the discoveries and annexations of Hans Reinier Oothout, the explorer, and Wynant Ten Breeches, the land-measurer, made in the twilight days of Oloffe the Dreamer; by which the territories of the Nieuw Nederlands were carried far to the south, to Delaware river and parts beyond. The consequence was, many disputes and brawls with the Indians, which now and then reached the drowsy ears of Walter the Doubter and his council, like the muttering of distant thunder from behind the mountains, without, however, disturbing their repose. It was not till the time of William the Testy that the thunderbolt reached the Manhattoes. While the little governor was diligently protecting his eastern boundaries from the Yankees, word was brought him of the irruption of a vagrant colony of Swedes in the south, who had landed on the banks of the Delaware and displayed the banner of that redoubtable virago Queen Christina, and taken possession of the country in her name. These had been guided in their expedition by one Peter Minuits, or Minnewits, a renegade Dutchman, formerly in the service of their High Mightinesses, but who now declared himself governor of all the surrounding country, to which was given the name of the province of NEW SWEDEN.

It is an old saying that "a little pot is soon hot," which was the case with William the Testy. Being a little man, he was soon in a passion, and once in a passion, he soon boiled over. Summoning his council on the receipt of this news, he belabored the Swedes in the longest speech that had been heard in the colony since the wordy warfare of Ten Breeches and Tough Breeches. Having thus taken off the fire-edge of his valor, he resorted to his favorite measure of proclamation, and despatched a document of the kind, ordering the renegade Minnewits and his gang of Swedish vagabonds to leave the country immediately, under pain of the vengeance of their High Mightinesses the Lords States General, and of the potentates of the Manhattoes.

This strong measure was not a whit more effectual than its predecessors, which had been thundered against the Yankees; and William Kieft was preparing to follow it up with something still more formidable, when he received intelligence of other invaders on his southern frontier, who had taken possession of the banks of the Schuylkill, and built a fort there. They were represented as a gigantic, gunpowder race of men, exceedingly expert at boxing, biting, gouging, and other branches of the rough-and-tumble mode of warfare, which they had learned from their prototypes and cousins-german, the Virginians, to whom they have ever borne considerable resemblance. Like them, too, they were great roisters, much given to revel on hoe-cake and bacon, mint-julep and apple-toddy; whence their newly formed colony had already acquired the name of Merryland, which, with a slight modification, it retains to the present day.

In fact, the Merrylanders and their cousins, the Virginians, were represented to William Kieft as offsets from the same original stock as his bitter enemies the Yanokie, or Yankee tribes of the east, having both come over to this country for the liberty of conscience, or, in other words, to live as they pleased: the Yankees taking to praying and money-making, and converting quakers; and the Southerners to horse-racing and cock-fighting, and breeding negroes.

Against these new invaders Wilhelmus Kieft immediately despatched a naval armament of two sloops and thirty men, under Jan Jansen Alpendam, who was armed to the very teeth with one of the little governor's most powerful speeches, written in vigorous Low Dutch.

Admiral Alpendam arrived without accident in the Schuylkill, and came upon the enemy just as they were engaged in a great "barbecue," a kind of festivity or carouse much practised in Merryland. Opening upon them with the speech of William the Testy, he denounced them as a pack of lazy, canting, julep-tippling, cock-fighting, horse-racing, slave-trading, tavern-hunting, Sabbath-breaking, mulatto-breeding upstarts, and concluded by ordering them to evacuate the country immediately: to which they laconically replied in plain English, "they'd see him d--d first!"

Now, this was a reply on which neither Jan Jansen Alpendam nor Wilhelmus Kieft had made any calculation. Finding himself, therefore, totally unprepared to answer so terrible a rebuff with suitable hostility, the admiral concluded his wisest course would be to return home and report progress. He accordingly steered his course back to New Amsterdam, where he arrived safe, having accomplished this hazardous enterprise at small expense of treasure and no loss of life. His saving policy gained him the universal appellation of the Saviour of his Country; and his services were suitably rewarded by a shingle monument, erected by subscription on the top of Flattenbarrack Hill, where it immortalized his name for three whole years, when it fell to pieces and was burnt for firewood.

CHAPTER X

Troublous Times on the Hudson—How Killian Van Rensellaer Erected a Feudal Castle, and How He Introduced Club-Law into the Province

ABOUT THIS TIME the testy little governor of the New Netherlands appears to have had his hands full, and with one annoyance and the other to have been kept continually on the bounce. He was on the very point of following up the expedition of Jan Jansen Alpendam by some belligerent measures against the marauders of Merryland, when his attention was suddenly called away by belligerent troubles springing up in another quarter, the seeds of which had been sown in the tranquil days of Walter the Doubter.

The reader will recollect the deep doubt into which that most pacific governor was thrown on Killian Van Rensellaer's taking possession of Bearn Island by *wapen recht*. While the governor doubted and did nothing, the lordly Killian went on to complete his sturdy little castellum of Rensellaerstein, and to garrison it with a number of his tenants from the Helderberg, a mountain region famous for the hardest heads and hardest fists in the province. Nicholas Koorn, a faithful squire of the patroon, accustomed to strut at his heels, wear his cast-off clothes, and imitate his lofty bearing, was established in this post as wacht-meester. His duty it was to keep an eye on the river, and oblige every vessel that passed, unless on the service of their High Mightinesses, to strike its flag, lower its peak, and pay toll to the lord of Rensellaer-stein.

This assumption of sovereign authority within the territories of the Lords States General, however it might have been tolerated by Walter the Doubter, had been sharply contested by William the Testy on coming into office; and many written remonstrances had been addressed by him to Killian Van Rensellaer, to which the latter never deigned a reply. Thus, by degrees, a sore place, or, in Hibernian parlance, a *raw*, had been established in the irritable soul of the little governor, insomuch that he winced at the very name of Rensellaerstein.

Now it came to pass, that, on a fine sunny day, the Company's yacht, the Half-Moon, having been on one of its stated visits to Fort Aurania, was quietly tiding it down the Hudson. The commander, Govert Lockerman, a veteran Dutch skipper of few words but great bottom, was seated on the high poop, quietly smoking his pipe under the shadow of the proud flag of Orange, when, on arriving abreast of Bearn Island, he was saluted by a stentorian voice from the shore, "Lower thy flag, and be d—d to thee!"

Govert Lockerman, without taking his pipe out of his mouth, turned up his eye from under his broad-brimmed hat to see who hailed him thus discourteously. There, on the ramparts of the fort, stood Nicholas Koorn, armed to the teeth, flourishing a brass-hilted sword, while a steeple-crowned hat and cock's tail-feather, formerly worn by Killian Van Rensellaer himself, gave an inexpressible loftiness to his demeanor.

Govert Lockerman eyed the warrior from top to toe, but was not to be dismayed. Taking the pipe slowly out of his mouth, "To whom should I lower my flag?" demanded he. "To the high and mighty Killian Van Rensellaer, the lord of Rensellaerstein!" was the reply.

"I lower it to none but the Prince of Orange and my masters the Lords States General." So saying, he resumed his pipe and smoked with an air of dogged determination.

Bang! went a gun from the fortress; the ball cut both sail and rigging. Govert Lockerman said nothing, but smoked the more doggedly.

Bang! went another gun; the shot whistled close astern.

"Fire, and be d—d," cried Govert Lockerman, cramming a new charge of tobacco into his pipe, and smoking with still increasing vehemence.

Bang! went a third gun. The shot passed over his head, tearing a hole in the "princely flag of Orange."

This was the hardest trial of all for the pride and patience of Govert Lockerman. He maintained a stubborn, though swelling silence; but his smothered rage might be perceived by the short vehement puffs of smoke emitted from his pipe, by which he might be tracked for miles, as he slowly floated out of shot and out of sight of Bearn Island. In fact he never gave vent to his passion until he got fairly among the highlands of the Hudson; when he let fly whole volleys of Dutch oaths, which are said to linger to this very day among the echoes of the Dunderberg, and to give particular effect to the thunder-storms in that neighborhood.

It was the sudden apparition of Govert Lockerman at Dog's Misery, bearing in his hand the tattered flag of Orange, that arrested the attention of William the Testy, just as he was devising a new expedition against the marauders of Merryland. I will not pretend to describe the passion of the little man when he heard of the outrage of Rensellaerstein. Suffice it to say, in the first transports of his fury, he turned Dog's Misery topsy-turvy; kicked every cur out of doors, and threw the cats out of the window; after which, his spleen being in some measure relieved, he went into a council of war with Govert Lockerman, the skipper, assisted by Antony Van Corlear, the Trumpeter.

CHAPTER XI

Of the Diplomatic Mission of Antony the Trumpeter to the Fortress of
Rensellaerstein—And How He Was Puzzled by a Cabalistic Reply

THE EYES OF ALL New Amsterdam were now turned to see what
would be the end of this direful feud between William the Testy
and the patroon of Rensellaerwick; and some, observing the consultations of the governor with the skipper and the trumpeter,
predicted warlike measures by sea and land. The wrath of William
Kieft, however, though quick to rise, was quick to evaporate. He
was a perfect brush-heap in a blaze, snapping and crackling for
a time, and then ending in smoke. Like many other valiant potentates, his first thoughts were all for war, his sober second thoughts
for diplomacy.

Accordingly, Govert Lockerman was once more despatched up
the river in the Company's yacht, the Goed Hoop, bearing Antony
the Trumpeter as ambassador, to treat with the belligerent powers
of Rensellaerstein. In the fulness of time the yacht arrived before
Bearn Island, and Antony the Trumpeter, mounting the poop,
sounded a parley to the fortress. In a little while the steeple-
crowned hat of Nicholas Koorn, the wacht-meester, rose above the
battlements, followed by his iron visage, and ultimately his whole
person, armed, as before, to the very teeth; while, one by one, a
whole row of Helderbergers reared their round burly heads above
the wall, and beside each pumpkin-head peered the end of a rusty
musket. Nothing daunted by this formidable array, Antony Van
Corlear drew forth and read with audible voice a missive from
William the Testy, protesting against the usurpation of Bearn
Island, and ordering the garrison to quit the premises, bag and
baggage, on pain of the vengeance of the potentate of the Manhattoes.

In reply, the wacht-meester applied the thumb of his right hand
to the end of his nose, and the thumb of his left hand to the little
finger of the right, and spreading each hand like a fan, made an

aërial flourish with his fingers. Antony Van Corlear was sorely perplexed to understand this sign, which seemed to him something mysterious and masonic. Not liking to betray his ignorance, he again read with a loud voice the missive of William the Testy, and again Nicholas Koorn applied the thumb of his right hand to the end of his nose, and the thumb of his left hand to the little finger of the right, and repeated this kind of nasal weather-cock. Antony Van Corlear now persuaded himself that this was some short-hand sign or symbol, current in diplomacy, which, though unintelligible to a new diplomat, like himself, would speak volumes to the experienced intellect of William the Testy; considering his embassy therefore at an end, he sounded his trumpet with great complacency, and set sail on his return down the river, every now and then practising this mysterious sign of the wacht-meester, to keep it accurately in mind.

Arrived at New Amsterdam, he made a faithful report of his embassy to the governor, accompanied by a manual exhibition of the response of Nicholas Koorn. The governor was equally perplexed with his embassy. He was deeply versed in the mysteries of freemasonry; but they threw no light on the matter. He knew every variety of wind-mill and weather-cock, but was not a whit the wiser as to the aërial sign in question. He had even dabbled in Egyptian hieroglyphics and the mystic symbols of the obelisks, but none furnished a key to the reply of Nicholas Koorn. He called a meeting of his council. Antony Van Corlear stood forth in the midst, and putting the thumb of his right hand to his nose, and the thumb of his left hand to the finger of the right, he gave a faithful facsimile of the portentous sign. Having a nose of unusual dimensions, it was as if the reply had been put in capitals; but all in vain: the worthy burgomasters were equally perplexed with the governor. Each one put his thumb to the end of his nose, spread his fingers like a fan, imitated the motion of Antony Van Corlear, and then smoked in dubious silence. Several times was Antony obliged to stand forth like a fugleman and repeat the sign, and each time a circle of nasal weather-cocks might be seen in the council-chamber.

Perplexed in the extreme, William the Testy sent for all the soothsayers, and fortune-tellers, and wise men of the Manhattoes, but none could interpret the mysterious reply of Nicholas Koorn. The council broke up in sore perplexity. The matter got abroad, and Antony Van Corlear was stopped at every corner to repeat the signal to a knot of anxious newsmongers, each of whom departed with his thumb to his nose and his fingers in the air, to carry the story home to his family. For several days, all business was neglected in New Amsterdam; nothing was talked of but the diplomatic mission of Antony the Trumpeter,—nothing was to be seen but knots of politicians with their thumbs to their noses. In the meantime the fierce feud between William the Testy and Killiam Van Rensellaer, which at first had menaced deadly warfare, gradually cooled off, like many other war-questions, in the prolonged delays of diplomacy.

Still to this early affair of Rensellaerstein may be traced the remote origin of those windy wars in modern days which rage in the bowels of the Helderberg, and have wellnigh shaken the great patroonship of the Van Rensellaers to its foundation; for we are told that the bully boys of the Helderberg, who served under Nicholas Koorn the wacht-meester, carried back to their mountains the hieroglyphic sign which had so sorely puzzled Antony Van Corlear and the sages of the Manhattoes; so that to the present day the thumb to the nose and the fingers in the air is apt to be the reply of the Helderbergers whenever called upon for any long arrears of rent.

CHAPTER XII

Containing the Rise of the Great Amphictyonic Council of the Pilgrims, with the Decline and Final Extinction of William the Testy

IT WAS ASSERTED by the wise men of ancient times, who had a nearer opportunity of ascertaining the fact, that at the gate of Jupiter's palace lay two huge tuns, one filled with blessings, the other with misfortunes; and it would verily seem as if the latter had been completely overturned and left to deluge the unlucky province of Nieuw Nederlands: for about this time, while harassed and annoyed from the south and the north, incessant forays were made by the border-chivalry of Connecticut upon the pig-sties and hen-roosts of the Nederlanders. Every day or two some broad-bottomed express-rider, covered with mud and mire, would come floundering into the gate of New Amsterdam, freighted with some new tale of aggression from the frontier; whereupon Antony Van Corlear, seizing his trumpet, the only substitute for a newspaper in those primitive days, would sound the tidings from the ramparts with such doleful notes and disastrous cadence as to throw half the old women in the city into hysterics; all which tended greatly to increase his popularity; there being nothing for which the public are more grateful than being frequently treated to a panic,—a secret well known to the modern editors.

But, oh ye powers! into what a paroxysm of passion did each new outrage of the Yankees throw the choleric little governor! Letter after letter, protest after protest, bad Latin, worse English, and hideous Low Dutch, were incessantly fulminated upon them, and the four-and-twenty letters of the alphabet, which formed his standing army, were worn out by constant campaigning. All, however, was ineffectual; even the recent victory at Oyster Bay, which had shed such a gleam of sunshine between the clouds of his foul-weather reign, was soon followed by a more fearful gathering up of those clouds, and indications of more portentous tempest; for the Yankee tribe on the banks of the Connecticut, finding on this memorable occasion their incompetency to cope, in fair fight, with the sturdy chivalry of the Manhattoes, had called to their aid all the ten tribes of their brethren who inhabit the east country, which from them has derived the name of Yankee-land. This call was promptly responded to. The consequence was a great confederacy of the tribes of Massachusetts, Connecticut, New Plymouth, and New Haven, under the title of the "United Colonies of New England"; the pretended object of which was mutual defence against the savages, but the real object the subjugation of the Nieuw Nederlands.

For, to let the reader into one of the great secrets of history, the Nieuw Nederlands had long been regarded by the whole Yankee race as the modern land of promise, and themselves as the chosen and peculiar people destined, one day or other, by hook or by crook, to get possession of it. In truth, they are a wonderful and all-prevalent people, of that class who only require an inch to gain an ell, or a halter to gain a horse. From the time they first gained a foothold on Plymouth Rock, they began to migrate, progressing and progressing from place to place, and land to land, making a little here and a little there, and controverting the old proverb, that a rolling stone gathers no moss. Hence they have facetiously received the nickname of THE PILGRIMS: that is to say, a people who are always seeking a better country than their own.

The tidings of this great Yankee league struck William Kieft with dismay, and for once in his life he forgot to bounce on receiving a disagreeable piece of intelligence. In fact, on turning over in his mind all that he had read at the Hague about leagues and combinations, he found that this was a counterpart of the Amphictyonic league, by which the states of Greece attained such power and supremacy; and the very idea made his heart quake for the safety of his empire at the Manhattoes.

The affairs of the confederacy were managed by an annual council of delegates held at Boston, which Kieft denominated the Delphos of this truly classic league. The very first meeting gave evidence of hostility to the Nieuw Nederlanders, who were charged, in their dealings with the Indians, with carrying on a traffic in "guns, powther and shott,—a trade damnable and injurious to the colonists." It is true the Connecticut traders were fain to dabble a little in this damnable traffic; but then they always dealt in what were termed Yankee guns, ingeniously calculated to burst in the pagan hands which used them.

The rise of this potent confederacy was a death-blow to the glory of William the Testy, for from that day forward he never held up his head, but appeared quite crestfallen. It is true, as the grand council augmented in power, and the league, rolling onward, gathered about the red hills of New Haven, threatening to overwhelm the Nieuw Nederlands, he continued occasionally to fulminate proclamations and protests, as a shrewd sea-captain fires his guns into a waterspout; but alas! they had no more effect than so many blank cartridges.

Thus end the authenticated chronicles of the reign of William the Testy; for henceforth, in the troubles, perplexities, and confusion of the times, he seems to have been totally overlooked, and to have slipped forever through the fingers of scruplous history. It is a matter of deep concern that such obscurity should hang over his latter days; for he was in truth a mighty and great-little man, and worthy of being utterly renowned, seeing that he was the first potentate that introduced into this land the art of fighting by proclamation, and defending a country by trumpeters and windmills.

It is true, that certain of the early provincial poets, of whom there were great numbers in the Nieuw Nederlands, taking advantage of his mysterious exit, have fabled, that, like Romulus, he was translated to the skies, and forms a very fiery little star, somewhere on the left of the Crab; while others, equally fanciful, declare that he had experienced a fate similar to that of the good king Arthur, who, we are assured by ancient bards, was carried away to the delicious abodes of fairy-land, where he still exists in pristine worth and vigor, and will one day or another return to restore the gallantry, the honor, and the immaculate probity, which prevailed in the glorious days of the Round Table.*

All these, however, are but pleasing fantasies, the cobweb visions of those dreaming varlets, the poets, to which I would not have my judicious readers attach any credibility. Neither am I disposed to credit an ancient and rather apocryphal historian, who asserts that the ingenious Wilhelmus was annihilated by the blowing

---

* The old Welsh bards believed that king Arthur was not dead, but carried awaie by the fairies into some pleasant place, where he sholde remaine for a time, and then returne againe and reigne in as great authority as ever.— HOLLINSHED.

The Britons suppose that he shall come yet and conquere all Britaigne, for certes, this is the prophicye of Merlyn—He say'd that his deth shall be doubteous; and said soth, for men thereof yet have doubte and shullen for ever more—for men wyt not whether that he lyveth or is dede.—DR. LEEW. CHRON.

down of one of his wind-mills; nor a writer of latter times, who affirms that he fell a victim to an experiment in natural history, having the misfortune to break his neck from a garret-window of the stadthouse in attempting to catch swallows by sprinkling salt upon their tails. Still less do I put my faith in the tradition that he perished at sea in conveying home to Holland a treasure of golden ore, discovered somewhere among the haunted regions of the Catskill mountains.*

The most probable account declares, that, what with the constant troubles on his frontiers, the incessant schemings and projects going on in his own pericranium, the memorials, petitions, remonstrances, and sage pieces of advice of respectable meetings of the sovereign people, and the refractory disposition of his councillors, who were sure to differ from him on every point, and uniformly to be in the wrong, his mind was kept in a furnace-heat, until he became as completely burnt out as a Dutch family-pipe which has passed through three generations of hard smokers. In this manner

* Diedrich Knickerbocker, in his scrupulous search after truth, is sometimes too fastidious in regard to facts which border a little on the marvellous. The story of the golden ore rests on something better than mere tradition. The venerable Adrian Van der Donck, Doctor of Laws, in his description of the New Netherlands, asserts it from his own observation as an eye-witness. He was present, he says, in 1645, at a treaty between Governor Kieft and the Mohawk Indians, in which one of the latter, in painting himself for the ceremony, used a pigment, the weight and shining appearance of which excited the curiosity of the governor and Mynheer Van der Donck. They obtained a lump, and gave it to be proved by a skilful doctor of medicine, Johannes de la Montagne, one of the councillors of the New Netherlands. It was put into a crucible, and yielded two pieces of gold, worth about three guilders. All this, continues Adrian Van der Donck, was kept secret. As soon as peace was made with the Mohawks, an officer and a few men were sent to the mountain, (in the region of the Kaatskill,) under the guidance of an Indian, to search for the precious mineral. They brought back a bucket full of ore; which, being submitted to the crucible, proved as productive as the first. William Kieft now thought the discovery certain. He sent a confidential person, Arent Corsen, with a bag full of the mineral, to New Haven, to take passage in an English ship for England, thence to proceed to Holland. The vessel sailed at Christmas, but never reached her port. All on board perished.

In the year 1647, Wilhelmus Kieft himself embarked on board the Princess, taking with him specimens of the supposed mineral. The ship was never heard of more!

Some have supposed that the mineral in question was not gold, but did he undergo a kind of animal combustion, consuming away like a farthing rushlight: so that when grim death finally snuffed him out, there was scarce left enough of him to bury!

It would appear, however, that these golden treasures of the Kaatskill always brought ill luck: as is evidenced in the fate of Arent Corsen and Wilhelmus Kieft, and the wreck of the ships in which they attempted to convey the treasure across the ocean. The golden mines have never since been explored, but remain among the mysteries of the Kaatskill mountains, and under the protection of the goblins which haunt them.

BOOK V

CONTAINING THE FIRST PART OF THE REIGN OF PETER STUY-
VESANT, AND HIS TROUBLES WITH THE AMPHICTYONIC COUNCIL

CHAPTER I

In Which the Death of a Great Man Is Shown to Be No Very Inconsolable Matter of Sorrow—And How Peter Stuyvesant Acquired a Great Name from the Uncommon Strength of His Head

To A PROFOUND PHILOSOPHER like myself, who am apt to see clear through a subject, where the penetration of ordinary people extends but half-way, there is no fact more simple and manifest than that the death of a great man is a matter of very little im-

---

pyrites; but we have the assertion of Adrian Van der Donck, an eye-witness, and the experiment of Johannes de la Montagne, a learned doctor of medicine, on the golden side of the question. Cornelius Van Tienhooven, also, at that time secretary of the New Netherlands, declared in Holland that he had tested several specimens of the mineral, which proved satisfactory. (See Van der Donck's "Description of the New Netherlands." Collect. New York Hist. Society, Vol. I, p. 161.)

portance. Much as we may think of ourselves, and much as we may excite the empty plaudits of the million, it is certain that the greatest among us do actually fill but an exceeding small space in the world; and it is equally certain, that even that small space is quickly supplied when we leave it vacant. "Of what consequence is it," said Pliny, "that individuals appear, or make their exit? the world is a theatre whose scenes and actors are continually changing." Never did philosopher speak more correctly; and I only wonder that so wise a remark could have existed so many ages, and mankind not have laid it more to heart. Sage follows on in the footsteps of sage; one hero just steps out of his triumphal car, to make way for the hero who comes after him; and of the proudest monarch it is merely said, that "he slept with his fathers, and his successor reigned in his stead."

The world, to tell the private truth, cares but little for their loss, and if left to itself would soon forget to grieve; and though a nation has often been figuratively drowned in tears on the death of a great man, yet it is ten to one if an individual tear has been shed on the occasion, excepting from the forlorn pen of some hungry author. It is the historian, the biographer, and the poet, who have the whole burden of grief to sustain,—who—kind souls! —like undertakers in England, act the part of chief mourners,— who inflate a nation with sighs it never heaved, and deluge it with tears it never dreamt of shedding. Thus, while the patriotic author is weeping and howling, in prose, in blank verse, and in rhyme, and collecting the drops of public sorrow into his volume, as into a lachrymal vase, it is more than probable his fellow-citizens are eating and drinking, fiddling and dancing, as utterly ignorant of the bitter lamentations made in their name as are those men of straw, John Doe and Richard Roe, of the plaintiffs for whom they are generously pleased to become sureties.

The most glorious hero that ever desolated nations might have mouldered into oblivion among the rubbish of his own monument, did not some historian take him into favor, and benevolently transmit his name to posterity; and much as the valiant William Kieft worried, and bustled, and turmoiled, while he had the destinies of a whole colony in his hand, I question seriously whether he will not be obliged to this authentic history for all his future celebrity.

His exit occasioned no convulsion in the city of New Amsterdam nor its vicinity: the earth trembled not, neither did any stars shoot from their spheres; the heavens were not shrouded in black, as poets would fain persuade us they have been, on the death of a hero; the rocks (hardhearted varlets!) melted not into tears, nor did the trees hang their heads in silent sorrow; and as to the sun, he lay abed the next night just as long, and showed as jolly a face when he rose as he ever did on the same day of the month in any year, either before or since. The good people of New Amsterdam, one and all, declared that he had been a very busy, active, bustling little governor; that he was "the father of his country"; that he was "the noblest work of God"; that "he was a man, take him for all in all, they ne'er should look upon his like again"; together with sundry other civil and affectionate speeches regularly said on the death of all great men; after which they smoked their pipes, thought no more about him, and Peter Stuyvesant succeeded to his station.

Peter Stuyvesant was the last, and, like the renowned Wouter Van Twiller, the best of our ancient Dutch governors. Wouter having surpassed all who preceded him, and Peter, or Piet, as he was sociably called by the old Dutch burghers, who were ever prone to familiarize names, having never been equalled by any successor. He was in fact the very man fitted by nature to retrieve the desperate fortunes of her beloved province, had not the fates, those most potent and unrelenting of all ancient spinsters, destined them to inextricable confusion.

To say merely that he was a hero, would be doing him great injustice: he was in truth a combination of heroes; for he was of a sturdy, raw-boned make, like Ajax Telamon, with a pair of round shoulders that Hercules would have given his hide for (meaning his lion's hide) when he undertook to ease old Atlas of his load. He was, moreover, as Plutarch describes Coriolanus, not only terrible for the force of his arm, but likewise of his voice, which sounded as though it came out of a barrel; and, like the self-same warrior, he possessed a sovereign contempt for the sovereign people, and an iron aspect, which was enough of itself to make the very bowels of his adversaries quake with terror and dismay. All this martial excellency of appearance was inexpressibly heightened by an accidental advantage, with which I am surprised that neither Homer nor Virgil have graced any of their heroes. This was nothing less than a wooden leg, which was the only prize he had gained in bravely fighting the battles of his country, but of which he was so proud, that he was often heard to declare he valued it more than all his other limbs put together; indeed so highly did he esteem it, that he had it gallantly enchased and relieved with silver devices, which caused it to be related in divers histories and legends that he wore a silver leg.*

Like that choleric warrior Achilles, he was somewhat subject to extempore bursts of passion, which were rather unpleasant to his favorites and attendants, whose perceptions he was apt to quicken, after the manner of his illustrious imitator, Peter the Great, by anointing their shoulders with his walking-staff.

Though I cannot find that he had read Plato, or Aristotle, or Hobbes, or Bacon, or Algernon Sydney, or Tom Paine, yet did he sometimes manifest a shrewdness and sagacity in his measures, that one would hardly expect from a man who did not know Greek, and had never studied the ancients. True it is, and I confess it with sorrow, that he had an unreasonable aversion to experiments, and was fond of governing his province after the simplest manner; but then he contrived to keep it in better order than did the erudite Kieft, though he had all the philosophers, ancient and modern, to assist and perplex him. I must likewise own that he made but very few laws; but then, again, he took care that those few were rigidly and impartially enforced; and I do not know but justice, on the whole, was as well administered as if there had been volumes of sage acts and statutes yearly made, and daily neglected and forgotten.

He was, in fact, the very reverse of his predecessors, being neither tranquil and inert, like Walter the Doubter, nor restless and fidgeting, like William the Testy,—but a man, or rather a governor, of such uncommon activity and decision of mind, that

* See the histories of Masters Josselyn and Blome.

he never sought nor accepted the advice of others,—depending bravely upon his single head, as would a hero of yore upon his single arm, to carry him through all difficulties and dangers. To tell the simple truth, he wanted nothing more to complete him as a statesman than to think always right; for no one cay say but that he always acted as he thought. He was never a man to flinch when he found himself in a scrape, but to dash forward through thick and thin, trusting, by hook or by crook, to make all things straight in the end. In a word, he possessed, in an eminent degree, that great quality in a statesman, called perseverance by the polite, but nicknamed obstinacy by the vulgar,—a wonderful slave for official blunders, since he who perseveres in error without flinching gets the credit of boldness and consistency, while he who wavers in seeking to do what is right gets stigmatized as a trimmer. This much is certain; and it is a maxim well worthy the attention of all legislators, great and small, who stand shaking in the wind, irresolute which way to steer, that a ruler who follows his own will pleases himself, while he who seeks to satisfy the wishes and whims of others runs great risk of pleasing nobody. There is nothing, too, like putting down one's foot resolutely when in doubt, and letting things take their course. The clock that stands still points right twice in the four-and-twenty hours, while others may keep going continually and be continually going wrong.

Nor did this magnanimous quality escape the discernment of the good people of Nieuw Nederlands; on the contrary, so much were they struck with the independent will and vigorous resolution displayed on all occasions by their new governor, that they universally called him Hard-Koppig Piet, or Peter the Headstrong, —a great compliment to the strength of his understanding.

If, from all that I have said, thou dost not gather, worthy reader, that Peter Stuyvesant was a tough, sturdy, valiant, weather-beaten, mettlesome, obstinate, leathern-sided, lion-hearted, generous-spirited old governor, either I have written to but little purpose, or thou art very dull at drawing conclusions.

This most excellent governor commenced his administration on the 29th of May, 1647,—a remarkably stormy day, distinguished in all the almanacs of the time which have come down to us by the name of *Windy Friday*. As he was very jealous of his personal and official dignity, he was inaugurated into office with great ceremony,—the goodly oaken chair of the renowned Wouter Van Twiller being carefully preserved for such occasions, in like manner as the chair and stone were reverentially preserved at Schone, in Scotland, for the coronation of the Caledonian monarchs.

I must not omit to mention that the tempestuous state of the elements, together with its being that unlucky day of the week termed "hanging-day," did not fail to excite much grave speculation and divers very reasonable apprehensions among the more ancient and enlightened inhabitants; and several of the sager sex, who were reputed to be not a little skilled in the mystery of astrology and fortune-telling, did declare outright that they were omens of a disastrous administration;—an event that came to be lamentably verified, and which proves beyond dispute the wisdom of attending to those preternatural intimations furnished by dreams and visions, the flying of birds, falling of stones, and cackling of geese, on which the sages and rulers of ancient times placed such reliance; or to those shooting of stars, eclipses of the moon, howlings of dogs, and flarings of candles, carefully noted and interpreted by the oracular sibyls of our day,—who, in my humble opinion, are the legitimate inheritors and preservers of the ancient science of divination. This much is certain, that Governor Stuyvesant succeeded to the chair of state at a turbulent period: when foes thronged and threatened from without; when anarchy and stiff-necked opposition reigned rampant within; when the authority of their High Mightinesses the Lords States General, though supported by economy and defended by speeches, protests, and proclamations, yet tottered to its very centre; and when the great city of New Amsterdam, though fortified by flag-staffs, trumpeters, and wind-mills, seemed, like some fair lady of easy virtue, to lie open to attack, and ready to yield to the first invader.

CHAPTER II

Showing How Peter the Headstrong Bestirred Himself among the Rats and Cobwebs on Entering into Office—His Interview with Antony the Trumpeter, and His Perilous Meddling with the Currency

THE VERY FIRST MOVEMENTS of the great Peter, on taking the reins of government, displayed his magnanimity, though they occasioned not a little marvel and uneasiness among the people of the Manhattoes. Finding himself constantly interrupted by the opposition, and annoyed by the advice of his privy council, the members of which had acquired the unreasonable habit of thinking and speaking for themselves during the preceding reign, he determined at once to put a stop to such grievous abominations. Scarcely, therefore, had he entered upon his authority, than he turned out of office all the meddlesome spirits of the factious cabinet of William the Testy; in place of whom he chose unto himself counsellors from those fat, somniferous, respectable burghers who had flourished and slumbered under the easy reign of Walter the Doubter. All these he caused to be furnished with abundance of fair long pipes, and to be regaled with frequent corporation dinners, admonishing them to smoke, and eat, and sleep for the good of the nation, while he took the burden of government upon his own shoulders,—an arrangement to which they all gave hearty acquiescence.

Nor did he stop here, but made a hideous rout among the inventions and expedients of his learned predecessor,—rooting up his patent gallows, where caitiff vagabonds were suspended by the waistband,—demolishing his flag-staffs and wind-mills, which, like mighty giants, guarded the ramparts of New Amsterdam,— pitching to the duyvel whole batteries of quaker guns,—and, in a word, turning topsy-turvy the whole philosophic, economic, and wind-mill system of the immortal sage of Saardam.

The honest folk of New Amsterdam began to quake now for

the fate of their matchless champion, Antony the Trumpeter, who had acquired prodigious favor in the eyes of the women, by means of his whiskers and his trumpet. Him did Peter the Headstrong cause to be brought into his presence, and eying him for a moment from head to foot, with a countenance that would have appalled anything else than a sounder of brass,—"Pr'ythee, who and what art thou?" said he. "Sire," replied the other, in no wise dismayed, "for my name, it is Antony Van Corlear; for my parentage, I am the son of my mother; for my profession, I am champion and garrison of this great city of New Amsterdam." "I doubt me much," said Peter Stuyvesant, "that thou art some scurvy costard-monger knave. How didst thou acquire this paramount honor and dignity?" "Marry, sir," replied the other, "like many a great man before me, simply *by sounding my own trumpet.*" "Ay, is it so?" quoth the governor; "why, then let us have a relish of thy art." Whereupon the good Antony put his instrument to his lips, and sounded a charge with such a tremendous outset, such a delectable quaver, and such a triumphant cadence, that it was enough to make one's heart leap out of one's mouth only to be within a mile of it. Like as a war-worn charger, grazing in peaceful plains, starts at a strain of martial music, pricks up his ears, and snorts, and paws, and kindles at the noise, so did the heroic Peter joy to hear the clangor of the trumpet; for of him might truly be said, what was recorded of the renowned St. George of England, "there was nothing in all the world that more rejoiced his heart than to hear the pleasant sound of war, and see the soldiers brandish forth their steeled weapons." Casting his eye more kindly, therefore, upon the sturdy Van Corlear, and finding him to be a jovial varlet, shrewd in his discourse, yet of great discretion and immeasurable wind, he straightway conceived a vast kindness for him, and discharging him from the troublesome duty of garrisoning, defending, and alarming the city, ever after retained him about his person, as his chief favorite, confidential envoy, and trusty squire. Instead of disturbing the city with disastrous notes, he was instructed to play so as to delight the governor while at his repasts, as did the minstrels of yore in the days of glorious chivalry,—and on all public occasions to rejoice the ears of the people with warlike melody,—thereby keeping alive a noble and martial spirit.

But the measure of the valiant Peter which produced the greatest agitation in the community, was his laying his hand upon the currency. He had old-fashioned notions in favor of gold and silver, which he considered the true standards of wealth and mediums of commerce; and one of his first edicts was, that all duties to government should be paid in those precious metals, and that seawant, or wampum, should no longer be a legal tender.

Here was a blow at public prosperity! All those who speculated on the rise and fall of this fluctuating currency, found their calling at an end; those, too, who had hoarded Indian money by barrels full, found their capital shrunk in amount; but, above all, the Yankee traders, who were accustomed to flood the market with newly coined oyster-shells, and to abstract Dutch merchandise in exchange, were loud-mouthed in decrying this "tampering with the currency." It was clipping the wings of commerce; it was checking the development of public prosperity; trade would be at an end; goods would moulder on the shelves; grain would rot in the granaries; grass would grow in the market-place. In a word, no one who has not heard the outcries and howlings of a modern Tarshish, at any check upon "paper-money," can have any idea of the clamor against Peter the Headstrong, for checking the circulation of oyster-shells.

In fact, trade did shrink into narrower channels; but then the stream was deep as it was broad; the honest Dutchmen sold less goods; but then they got the worth of them, either in silver and gold, or in codfish, tin ware, apple-brandy, Weathersfield onions, wooden bowls, and other articles of Yankee barter. The ingenious people of the east, however, indemnified themselves another way for having to abandon the coinage of oyster-shells; for about this time we are told that wooden nutmegs made their first appearance in New Amsterdam, to the great annoyance of the Dutch housewives.

NOTE

From a manuscript record of the province; Lib. N. Y. Hist. Society.—We have been unable to render your inhabitants wiser and prevent their being further imposed upon than to declare absolutely and peremptorily that henceforward seawant shall be bullion,—not longer admissible in trade, without any value, as it is indeed. So that every one may be upon his guard to barter no longer away his wares and merchandises for these bubbles,—at least not to accept them at a higher rate, or in a larger quantity, than as they may want them in their trade with the savages.

In this way your English [Yankee] neighbors shall no longer be enabled to draw the best wares and merchandises from our country for nothing,— the beavers and furs not excepted. This has indeed long since been insufferable, although it ought chiefly to be imputed to the imprudent penuriousness of our own merchants and inhabitants, who, it is to be hoped, shall through the abolition of this seawant become wiser and more prudent.

2*7th January,* 1662.

Seawant falls into disrepute; duties to be paid in silver coin.

CHAPTER III

How the Yankee League Waxed More and More Potent; and How It Outwitted the Good Peter in Treaty-Making

NOW IT CAME TO PASS, that, while Peter Stuyvesant was busy regulating the internal affairs of his domain, the great Yankee league, which had caused such tribulation to William the Testy, continued to increase in extent and power. The grand Amphictyonic council of the league was held at Boston, where it spun a web, which threatened to link within it all the mighty principalities and powers of the east. The object proposed by this formidable combination was, mutual protection and defence against their savage neighbors; but all the world knows the real aim was to form a grand crusade against the Nieuw Nederlands, and to get possession of the city of the Manhattoes,—as devout an object of enterprise and ambition to the Yankees as was ever the capture of Jerusalem to ancient crusaders.

In the very year following the inauguration of Governor Stuyvesant, a grand deputation departed from the city of Providence (famous for its dusty streets and beauteous women) in behalf of the plantation of Rhode Island, praying to be admitted into the league.

The following minute of this deputation appears in the ancient records of the council.*

"Mr. Will. Cottington and Captain Partridg of Rhoode Island presented this insewing request to the commissioners in wrighting—

"Our request and motion is in behalfe of Rhoode Iland, that wee the Ilanders of Roode-Iland may be rescauied into combination with all the united colonyes of New England in a firme and perpetual league of friendship and amity of ofence and defence, mutuall advice and succor upon all just occasions for our mutuall safety and wellfaire, etc.   WILL COTTINGTON,

"ALICXSANDER PARTRIDG."

There was certainly something in the very physiognomy of this document that might well inspire apprehension. The name of Alexander, however misspelt, has been warlike in every age; and though its fierceness is in some measure softened by being coupled with the gentle cognomen of Partridge, still, like the color of scarlet, it bears an exceeding great resemblance to the sound of a trumpet. From the style of the letter, moreover, and the soldier-like ignorance of orthography displayed by the noble Captain Alicxsander Partridg in spelling his own name, we may picture to ourselves this mighty man of Rhodes, strong in arms, potent in the field, and as great a scholar as though he had been educated among that learned people of Thrace, who, Aristotle assures us, could not count beyond the number four.

The result of this great Yankee league was agumented audacity on the part of the moss-troopers of Connecticut,—pushing their encroachments farther and farther into the territories of their High Mightinesses, so that even the inhabitants of New Amsterdam began to draw short breath and to find themselves exceedingly cramped for elbow-room.

Peter Stuyvesant was not a man to submit quietly to such in-

* Haz. Col. Stat. Pap.

trusions; his first impulse was to march at once to the frontier
and kick these squatting Yankees out of the country; but, be-
thinking himself in time that he was now a governor and legislator,
the policy of the statesman for once cooled the fire of the old
soldier, and he determined to try his hand at negotiation. A cor-
respondence accordingly ensued between him and the grand council
of the league; and it was agreed that commissioners from either
side should meet at Hartford, to settle boundaries, just grievances,
and establish a "perpetual and happy peace."

The commissioners on the part of the Manhattoes were chosen,
according to immemorial usage of that venerable metropolis, from
among the "wisest and weightiest" men of the community, that is
to say, men with the oldest heads and heaviest pockets. Among
these sages the veteran navigator, Hans Reinier Oothout, who
had made such extensive discoveries during the time of Oloffe the
Dreamer, was looked up to as an oracle in all matters of the kind;
and he was ready to produce the very spy-glass with which he
first spied the mouth of the Connecticut river from his mast-head;
and all the world knows the discovery of the mouth of a river gives
prior right to all the lands drained by its waters.

It was with feelings of pride and exultation that the good
people of the Manhattoes saw two of the richest and most ponderous burghers departing on this embassy,—men whose word on
'change was oracular, and in whose presence no poor man ventured
to appear without taking off his hat: when it was seen, too, that
the veteran Reinier Oothout accompanied them with his spy-glass
under his arm, all the old men and old women predicted that men
of such weight, with such evidence, would leave the Yankees no
alternative but to pack up their tin kettles and wooden wares,
put wife and children in a cart, and abandon all the lands of their
High Mightinesses, on which they had squatted.

In truth, the commissioners sent to Hartford by the league
seemed in no wise calculated to compete with men of such capacity.
They were two lean Yankee lawyers, litigious-looking varlets, and
evidently men of no substance, since they had no rotundity in
the belt, and there was no jingling of money in their pockets;
it is true, they had longer heads than the Dutchmen; but if the

heads of the latter were flat at top, they were broad at bottom, and what was wanting in height of forehead was made up by a double chin.

The negotiation turned as usual upon the good old corner-stone of original discovery,—according to the principle that he who first sees a new country has an unquestionable right to it. This being admitted, the veteran Oothout, at a concerted signal, stepped forth in the assembly with the identical trapauling spy-glass in his hand, with which he had discovered the mouth of the Connecticut, while the worthy Dutch commissioners lolled back in their chairs, secretly chuckling at the idea of having for once got the weather-gage of the Yankees; but what was their dismay when the latter produced a Nantucket whaler with a spy-glass twice as long, with which he discovered the whole coast, quite down to the Manhattoes, and so crooked, that he had spied with it up the whole course of the Connecticut river. This principle pushed home, therefore, the Yankees had a right to the whole country bordering on the Sound; nay, the city of New Amsterdam was a mere Dutch squatting-place on their territories.

I forbear to dwell upon the confusion of the worthy Dutch commissioners at finding their main pillar of proof thus knocked from under them; neither will I pretend to describe the consternation of the wise men at the Manhattoes when they learned how their commissioner had been out-trumped by the Yankees, and how the latter pretended to claim to the very gates of New Amsterdam.

Long was the negotiation protracted, and long was the public mind kept in a state of anxiety. There are two modes of settling boundary questions when the claims of the opposite are irreconcilable. One is by an appeal to arms, in which case the weakest party is apt to lose its right, and get a broken head into the bargain; the other mode is by compromise, or mutual concession,—that is to say, one party cedes half of its claims, and the other party half of its rights; he who grasps most gets most, and the whole is pronounced an equitable division, "perfectly honorable to both parties."

The latter mode was adopted in the present instance. The

Yankees gave up claims to vast tracts of the Nieuw Nederlands which they had never seen, and all right to the land of Manna-hata and the city of New Amsterdam, to which they had no right at all; while the Dutch, in return, agreed that the Yankees should retain possession of the frontier places where they had squatted, and of both sides of the Connecticut river.

When the news of this treaty arrived at New Amsterdam, the whole city was in an uproar of exultation. The old women rejoiced that there was to be no war, the old men that their cabbage-gardens were safe from invasion; while the political sages pro-nounced the treaty a great triumph over the Yankees, considering how much they had claimed, and how little they had been "fobbed off with."

And now my worthy reader is, doubtless, like the great and good Peter, congratulating himself with the idea that his feelings will no longer be harassed by afflicting details of stolen horses, broken heads, impounded hogs, and all the other catalogue of heart-rending cruelties that disgraced these border wars. But if he should indulge in such expectations, it is a proof that he is but little versed in the paradoxical ways of cabinets; to convince him of which, I solicit his serious attention to my next chapter, wherein I will show that Peter Stuyvesant has already committed a great error in politics, and, by effecting a peace, has materially hazarded the tranquillity of the province.

CHAPTER IV

Containing Divers Speculations on War and Negotiations—Showing that a Treaty of Peace Is a Great National Evil

IT WAS THE OPINION of that poetical philosopher, Lucretius, that war was the original state of man, whom he described as being primitively a savage beast of prey, engaged in a constant state of hostility with his own species, and that this ferocious spirit was tamed and ameliorated by society. The same opinion has been advocated by Hobbes,* nor have there been wanting many other philosophers to admit and defend.

For my part, though prodigiously fond of these valuable speculations, so complimentary to human nature, yet, in this instance, I am inclined to take the proposition by halves, believing with Horace,† that, though war may have been originally the favorite amusement and industrious employment of our progenitors, yet, like many other excellent habits, so far from being ameliorated, it has been cultivated and confirmed by refinement and civilization, and increases in exact proportion as we approach towards that state of perfection which is the *ne plus ultra* of modern philosophy.

The first conflict between man and man was the mere exertion of physical force, unaided by auxiliary weapons; his arm was his buckler, his fist was his mace, and a broken head the catastrophe of his encounters. The battle of unassisted strength was succeeded by the more rugged one of stones and clubs, and war assumed a sanguinary aspect. As man advanced in refinement, as his faculties expanded, and as his sensibilities became more exquisite, he grew rapidly more ingenious and experienced in the art of murdering his fellow-beings. He invented a thousand devices to defend and to assault: the helmet, the cuirass, and the buckler, the sword, the dart, and the javelin, prepared him to elude the wound as well as to launch the blow. Still urging on, in the career of philanthropic invention, he enlarges and heightens his powers of defence and injury:—The Aries, the Scorpio, the Balista, and the Catapulta, give a horror and sublimity to war, and magnify its glory, by increasing its desolation. Still insatiable, though armed with machinery that seemed to reach the limits of destructive invention, and to yield a power of injury commensurate even with the

---

* Hobbes's Leviathan. Part i. ch. 13.
† Quum prorepserunt primis animalia terris,
  Mutuum ac turpe pecus, glandem atque cubilia propter,
  Unguibus et pugnis, dein fustibus, atque ita porro
  Pugnabant armis, quæ post fabricaverat usus.
  Hor. Sat. L. i. S. 3.

desires of revenge,—still deeper researches must be made in the
diabolical arcana. With furious zeal he dives into the bowels of
the earth; he toils midst poisonous minerals and deadly salts,
—the sublime discovery of gunpowder blazes upon the world—
and finally the dreadful art of fighting by proclamation seems to
endow the demon of war with ubiquity and omnipotence!

This, indeed, is grand!—this, indeed, marks the powers of
mind, and bespeaks that divine endowment of reason, which dis-
tinguishes us from the animals, our inferiors. The unenlightened
brutes content themselves with the native force which Providence
has assigned them. The angry bull butts with his horns, as did his
progenitors before him; the lion, the leopard, and the tiger seek
only with their talons and their fangs to gratify their sanguinary
fury; and even the subtle serpent darts the same venom, and uses
the same wiles, as did his sire before the flood. Man alone, blessed
with the inventive mind, goes on from discovery to discovery,—
enlarges and multiplies his powers of destruction,—arrogates the
tremendous weapons of Deity itself, and tasks creation to assist
him in murdering his brother-worm!

In proportion as the art of war has increased in improvement
has the art of preserving peace advanced in equal ratio; and as
we have discovered, in this age of wonders and inventions, that
proclamation is the most formidable engine in war, so have we
discovered the no less ingenious mode of maintaining peace by
perpetual negotiations.

A treaty, or, to speak more correctly, a negotiation, therefore,
according to the acceptation of experienced statesmen, learned in
these matters, is no longer an attempt to accommodate differences,
to ascertain rights, and to establish an equitable exchange of kind
offices, but a contest of skill between two powers, which shall over-
reach and take in the other. It is a cunning endeavor to obtain by
peaceful manœuvre, and the chit-canery of cabinets, those advantages which a nation would otherwise have wrested by force of
arms,—in the same manner as a conscientious highwayman re-
forms and becomes a quiet and praiseworthy citizen, contending
himself with cheating his neighbor out of that property he would
formerly have seized with open violence.

In fact, the only time when two nations can be said to be in a state of perfect amity is, when a negotiation is open, and a treaty pending. Then, when there are no stipulations entered into, no bonds to restrain the will, no specific limits to awaken the captious jealousy of right implanted in our nature, when each party has some advantage to hope and expect from the other, then it is that the two nations are wonderfully gracious and friendly,— their ministers professing the highest mutual regard, exchanging billets-doux, making fine speeches, and indulging in all those little diplomatic flirtations, coquetries, and fondlings, that do so marvellously tickle the good-humor of the respective nations. Thus it may paradoxically be said, that there is never so good an understanding between two nations as when there is a little misunderstanding,—and that so long as they are on no terms at all, they are on the best terms in the world!

I do not by any means pretend to claim the merit of having made the above discovery. It has, in fact, long been secretly acted upon by certain enlightened cabinets, and is, together with divers other notable theories, privately copied out of the commonplace book of an illustrious gentleman, who has been member of congress, and enjoyed the unlimited confidence of heads of departments. To this principle may be ascribed the wonderful ingenuity shown of late years in protracting and interrupting negotiations. Hence the cunning measure of appointing as ambassador some political pettifogger skilled in delays, sophisms, and misapprehensions, and dexterous in the art of baffling argument,—or some blundering statesman, whose errors and misconstructions may be a plea for refusing to ratify his engagements. And hence, too, that most notable expedient, so popular with our government, of sending out a brace of ambassadors,—between whom, having each an individual will to consult, character to establish, and interest to promote, you may as well look for unanimity and concord as between two lovers with one mistress, two dogs with one bone, or two naked rogues with one pair of breeches. This disagreement, therefore, is continually breeding delays and impediments, in consequence of which the negotiation goes on swimmingly—inasmuch as there is no prospect of its ever coming to a close. Noth-

ing is lost by these delays and obstacles but time; and in a negotiation, according to the theory I have exposed, all time lost is in
reality so much time gained:—with what delightful paradoxes does
modern political economy abound!

Now all that I have here advanced is so notoriously true, that I
almost blush to take up the time of my readers with treating of
matters which must many a time have stared them in the face.
But the proposition to which I would most earnestly call their
attention is this, that, though a negotiation be the most harmoniz-
ing of all national transactions, yet a treaty of peace is a great
political evil, and one of the most fruitful sources of war.

I have rarely seen an instance of any special contract between
individuals that did not produce jealousies, bickerings, and often
downright ruptures between them; nor did I ever know of a
treaty between two nations that did not occasion continual mis-
understandings. How many worthy country neighbors have I
known, who, after living in peace and good-fellowship for years,
have been thrown into a state of distrust, cavilling, and animosity,
by some ill-starred agreement about fences, runs of water, and
stray cattle! And how many well-meaning nations, who would
otherwise have remained in the most amicable disposition towards
each other, have been brought to swords' points about the in-
fringement or misconstruction of some treaty, which in an evil
hour they had concluded, by way of making their amity more
sure!

Treaties at best are but complied with so long as interest re-
quires their fulfilment; consequently they are virtualiy binding
on the weaker party only, or, in plain truth, they are not binding
at all. No nation will wantonly go to war with another if it has
nothing to gain thereby, and therefore needs no treaty to restrain
it from violence; and if it have anything to gain, I much question,
from what I have witnessed of the righteous conduct of nations,
whether any treaty could be made so strong that it could not thrust
the sword through,—nay, I would hold ten to one, the treaty itself
would be the very source to which resort would be had to find a
pretext for hostilities.

Thus, therefore, I conclude,—that, though it is the best of all policies for a nation to keep up a constant negotiation with its neighbors, yet it is the summit of folly for it ever to be beguiled into a treaty; for then comes on non-fulfilment and infraction, then remonstrance, then altercation, then retaliation, then recrimination, and finally open war. In a word, negotiation is like courtship, a time of sweet words, gallant speeches, soft looks, and endearing caresses,—but the marriage ceremony is the signal for hostilities.

If my painstaking reader be not somewhat perplexed by the ratiocination of the foregoing passage, he will perceive, at a glance, that the Great Peter, in concluding a treaty with his eastern neighbors, was guilty of lamentable error in policy. In fact, to this unlucky agreement may be traced a world of bickerings and heart-burnings, between the parties, about fancied or pretended infringements of treaty-stipulations; in all which the Yankees were prone to indemnify themselves by a "dig into the sides" of the New Netherlands. But, in sooth, these border feuds, albeit they gave great annoyance to the good burghers of Mannahata, were so pitiful in their nature, that a grave historian like myself, who grudges the time spent in anything less than the revolutions of states and fall of empires, would deem them unworthy of being inscribed on his page. The reader is, therefore, to take it for granted, though I scorn to waste, in the detail, that time which my furrowed brow and trembling hand inform me is invaluable, that all the while the Great Peter was occupied in those tremendous and bloody contests which I shall shortly rehearse; there was a continued series of little, dirty, snivelling scourings, broils, and maraudings, kept up on the eastern frontiers by the moss-troopers of Connecticut. But, like that mirror of chivalry, the sage and valorous Don Quixote, I leave these petty contests for some future Sancho Panza of an historian, while I reserve my prowess and my pen for achievements of higher dignity; for at this moment I hear a direful and portentous note issuing from the bosom of the great council of the league, and resounding throughout the regions of the east, menacing the fame and fortunes of Peter Stuyvesant. I call, therefore, upon the reader to leave behind him all the paltry brawls of the Connecticut

borders, and to press forward with me to the relief of our favorite
hero, who, I foresee, will be wofully beset by the implacable Yankees in the next chapter.

CHAPTER V

How Peter Stuyvesant Was Grievously Belied by the Great Council of the
League; and How He Sent Antony the Trumpeter to Take to the Council
a Piece of His Mind

THAT THE READER MAY be aware of the peril at this moment
menacing Peter Stuyvesant and his capital, I must remind him of
the old charge advanced in the council of the league in the time
of William the Testy, that the Nederlanders were carrying on a
trade "damnable and injurious to the colonists," in furnishing the
savages with "guns, powther and shott." This, as I then suggested,
was a crafty device of the Yankee confederacy to have a snug
cause of war *in petto,* in case any favorable opportunity should
present of attempting the conquest of the New Nederlands: the
great object of Yankee ambition.

Accordingly we now find, when every other ground of complaint had apparently been removed by treaty, this nefarious
charge revived with tenfold virulence, and hurled like a thunderbolt at the very head of Peter Stuyvesant; happily his head, like
that of the great bull of the Wabash, was proof against such mis-
siles.

To be explicit, we are told that, in the year 1651, the great
confederacy of the east accused the immaculate Peter, the soul of
honor and heart of steel, of secretly endeavoring, by gifts and
promises, to instigate the Narroheganset, Mohaque, and Pequot
Indians, to surprise and massacre the Yankee settlements. "For,"
as the grand council observed, "the Indians round about for
divers hundred miles cercute seeme to have drunk deepe of an

intoxicating cupp, att or from the Manhattoes against the English, whoe have sought their good, both in bodily and spirituall respects."

This charge they pretended to support by the evidence of divers Indians, who were probably moved by that spirit of truth which is said to reside in the bottle, and who swore to the fact as sturdily as though they had been so many Christian troopers.

Though descended from a family which suffered much injury from the losel Yankees of those times, my great-grandfather having had a yoke of oxen and his best pacer stolen, and having received a pair of black eyes and a bloody nose in one of these border wars, and my grandfather, when a very little boy tending pigs, having been kidnapped and severely flogged by a long-sided Connecticut schoolmaster,—yet I should have passed over all these wrongs with forgiveness and oblivion,—I could even have suffered them to have broken Everet Ducking's head,—to have kicked the doughty Jacobus Van Curlet and his ragged regiment out of doors,—to have carried every hog into captivity, and depopulated every hen-roost on the face of the earth with perfect impunity,—but this wanton attack upon one of the most gallant and irreproachable heroes of modern times is too much even for me to digest, and has overset, with a single puff, the patience of the historian, and the forbearance of the Dutchman.

Oh, reader, it was false! I swear to thee, it was false!—if thou hast any respect to my word,—if the undeviating character for veracity, which I have endeavored to maintain throughout this work, has its due weight upon thee, thou wilt not give thy faith to this tale of slander; for I pledge my honor and my immortal fame to thee, that the gallant Peter Stuyvesant was not only innocent of this foul conspiracy, but would have suffered his right arm or even his wooden leg to consume with slow and everlasting flames, rather than attempt to destroy his enemies in any other way than open, generous warfare;—be-shrew those caitiff scouts, that conspired to sully his honest name by such an imputation!

Peter Stuyvesant, though haply he may never have heard of a knight-errant, had as true a heart of chivalry as ever beat at the round table of King Arthur. In the honest bosom of this heroic

Dutchman dwelt the seven noble virtues of knighthood, flourishing among his hardy qualities like wild flowers among rocks. He was, in truth, a hero of chivalry struck off by nature at a single heat, and though little care may have been taken to refine her workmanship, he stood forth a miracle of her skill. In all his dealings he was headstrong perhaps, but open and aboveboard; if there was anything in the whole world he most loathed and despised, it was cunning and secret wile; "straight forward" was his motto; and he would at any time rather run his hard head against a stone wall than attempt to get round it.

Such was Peter Stuyvesant; and if my admiration of him has on this occasion transported my style beyond the sober gravity which becomes the philosophic recorder of historic events, I must plead as an apology, that, though a little gray-headed Dutchman, arrived almost at the downhill of life, I still retain a lingering spark of that fire which kindles in the eye of youth when contemplating the virtues of ancient worthies. Blessed, thrice and nine times blessed be the good St. Nicholas, if I have indeed escaped that apathy which chills the sympathies of age and paralyzes every glow of enthusiasm.

The first measure of Peter Stuyvesant, on hearing of this slanderous charge, would have been worthy of a man who had studied for years in the chivalrous library of Don Quixote. Drawing his sword and laying it across the table, to put him in proper tune, he took pen in hand and indited a proud and lofty letter to the council of the league, reproaching them with giving ear to the slanders of heathen savages against a Christian, a soldier, and a cavalier; declaring, that, whoever charged him with the plot in question, lied in his throat; to prove which he offered to meet the president of the council or any of his compeers, or their champion, Captain Alicxsander Partridg, that mighty man of Rhodes, in single combat,—wherein he trusted to vindicate his honor by the prowess of his arm.

This missive was intrusted to his trumpeter and squire, Antony Van Corlear, that man of emergencies, with orders to travel night and day, sparing neither whip nor spur, seeing that he carried the vindication of his patron's fame in his saddle-bags.

The loyal Antony accomplished his mission with great speed and considerable loss of leather. He delivered his missive with becoming ceremony, accompanying it with a flourish of defiance on his trumpet to the whole council, ending with a significant and nasal twang full in the face of Captain Partridg, who nearly jumped out of his skin in an ecstasy of astonishment.

The grand council was composed of men too cool and practical to be put readily in a heat, or to indulge in knight-errantry; and above all to run a tilt with such a fiery hero as Peter the Headstrong. They knew the advantage, however, to have always a snug, justifiable cause of war in reserve with a neighbor, who had territories worth invading; so they devised a reply to Peter Stuyvesant, calculated to keep up the "raw" which they had established.

On receiving this answer, Antony Van Corlear remounted the Flanders mare which he always rode, and trotted merrily back to the Manhattoes, solacing himself by the way according to his wont; twanging his trumpet like a very devil, so that the sweet valleys and banks of the Connecticut resounded with the warlike melody; bringing all the folks to the windows as he passed through Hartford and Pyquag, and Middletown, and all the other border towns, ogling and winking at the women, and making aërial windmills from the end of his nose at their husbands, and stopping occasionally in the villages to eat pumpkin-pies, dance at country frolics, and bundle with the Yankee lasses—whom he rejoiced exceedingly with his soul-stirring instrument.

CHAPTER VI

How Peter Stuyvesant Demanded a Court of Honor—And What the Court of Honor Awarded to Him

THE REPLY OF THE GRAND COUNCIL to Peter Stuyvesant was couched in the coolest and most diplomatic language. They assured him that "his confident denials of the barbarous plot alleged against him would weigh little against the testimony of divers sober and respectable Indians"; that "his guilt was proved to their perfect satisfaction," so that they must still require and seek due *satisfaction and security;* ending with—"so we rest, sir— Yours in ways of righteousness."

I forbear to say how the lion-hearted Peter roared and ramped at finding himself more and more entangled in the meshes thus artfully drawn round him by the knowing Yankees. Impatient, however, of suffering so gross an aspersion to rest upon his honest name, he sent a second messenger to the council, reiterating his denial of the treachery imputed to him, and offering to submit his conduct to the scrutiny of a court of honor. His offer was readily accepted; and now he looked forward with confidence to an august tribunal to be assembled at the Manhattoes, formed of high-minded cavaliers, peradventure governors and commanders of the confederate plantations, when the matter might be investigated by his peers, in a manner befitting his rank and dignity.

While he was awaiting the arrival of such high functionaires, behold, one sunshiny afternoon there rode into the great gate of the Manhattoes two lean, hungry-looking Yankees, mounted on Narragansett pacers, with saddle-bags under their bottoms, and green satchels under their arms, who looked marvellously like two pettifogging attorneys beating the hoof from one county court to another in quest of lawsuits; and, in sooth, though they may have passed under different names at the time, I have reason to suspect they were the identical varlets who had negotiated the worthy Dutch commissioners out of the Connecticut river.

It was a rule with these indefatigable missionaries never to let the grass grow under their feet. Scarce had they, therefore, alighted at the inn and deposited their saddle-bags, than they made their way to the residence of the governor. They found him, according to custom, smoking his afternoon pipe on the "stoop," or bench at the porch of his house, and announced themselves, at once, as commissioners sent by the grand council of the east to investigate the truth of certain charges advanced against him.

The good Peter took his pipe from his mouth, and gazed at them for a moment in mute astonishment. By way of expediting business, they were proceeding on the spot to put some preliminary questions,—asking him, peradventure, whether he pleaded guilty or not guilty, considering him something in the light of a culprit at the bar,—when they were brought to a pause by seeing him lay down his pipe and begin to fumble with his walking-staff. For a moment those present would not have given half a crown for both the crowns of the commissioners; but Peter Stuyvesant repressed his mighty wrath and stayed his hand; he scanned the varlets from head to foot, satchels and all, with a look of ineffable scorn; then strode into the house, slammed the door after him, and commanded that they should never again be admitted to his presence.

The knowing commissioners winked to each other, and made a certificate on the spot that the governor had refused to answer their interrogatories or to submit to their examination. They then proceeded to rummage about the city for two or three days, in quest of what they called evidence, perplexing Indians and old women with their cross-questioning until they had stuffed their satchels and saddle-bags with all kinds of apocryphal tales, rumors, and calumnies; with these they mounted their Narraganset pacers and travelled back to the grand council; neither did the proud-hearted Peter trouble himself to hinder their researches nor impede their departure; he was too mindful of their sacred character as envoys; but I warrant me, had they played the same tricks with William the Testy, he would have had them tucked up by the waistband and treated to an aërial gambol on his patent gallows.

CHAPTER VII

How "Drum Ecclesiastic" Was Beaten Throughout Connecticut for a Crusade against the New Netherlands, and How Peter Stuyvesant Took Measures to Fortify His Capital

THE GRAND COUNCIL of the east held a solemn meeting on the return of their envoys. As no advocate appeared in behalf of Peter Stuyvesant, everything went against him. His haughty refusal to submit to the questioning of the commissioners was construed into a consciousness of guilt. The contents of the satchels and saddle-bags were poured forth before the council and appeared a mountain of evidence. A pale, bilious orator took the floor, and declaimed for hours and in belligerent terms. He was one of those furious zealots who blows the bellows of faction until the whole furnace of politics is red-hot with sparks and cinders. What was it to him if he should set the house on fire, so that he might boil his pot by the blaze. He was from the borders of Connecticut; his constituents lived by marauding their Dutch neighbors, and were the greatest poachers in Christendom, excepting the Scotch border nobles. His eloquence had its effect, and it was dedetermined to set on foot an expedition against the Nieuw Nederlands.

It was necessary, however, to prepare the public mind for this measure. Accordingly the arguments of the orator were echoed from the pulpit for several succeeding Sundays, and a crusade was preached up against Peter Stuyvesant and his devoted city.

This is the first we hear of the "drum ecclesiastic" beating up for recruits in worldly warfare in our country. It has since been called into frequent use. A cunning politician often lurks under the clerical robe; things spiritual and things temporal are strangely jumbled together, like drugs on an apothecary's shelf; and instead of a peaceful sermon, the simple seeker after righteousness has often a political pamphlet thrust down his throat, labelled with a pious text from Scripture.

And now nothing was talked of but an expedition against the Manhattoes. It pleased the populace, who had a vehement prejudice against the Dutch, considering them a vastly inferior race, who had sought the new world for the lucre of gain, not the liberty of conscience; who were mere heretics and infidels, inasmuch as they refused to believe in witches and sea-serpents, and had faith in the virtues of horse-shoes nailed to the door; ate pork without molasses; held pumpkins in contempt, and were in perpetual breach of the eleventh commandment of all true Yankees, "Thou shalt have codfish dinners on Saturdays."

No sooner did Peter Stuyvesant get wind of the storm that was brewing in the east, than he set to work to prepare for it. He was not one of those economical rulers, who postpone the expense of fortifying until the enemy is at the door. There is nothing, he would say, that keeps off enemies and crows more than the smell of gunpowder. He proceeded, therefore, with all diligence, to put the province and its metropolis in a posture of defence.

Among the remnants which remained from the days of William the Testy were the militia laws,—by which the inhabitants were obliged to turn out twice a year, which such military equipments as it pleased God,—and were put under the command of tailors and man-milliners, who, though on ordinary occasions they might have been the meekest, most pippin-hearted little men in the world, were very devils at parade, when they had cocked hats on their heads and swords by their sides. Under the instructions of these periodical warriors, the peaceful burghers of the Manhattoes were schooled in iron war, and became so hardy in the process of time, that they could march through sun and rain, from one end of the town to the other, without flinching,—and so intrepid and adroit, that they could face to the right, wheel to the left, and fire without winking or blinking.

Peter Stuyvesant, like all old soldiers who have seen service and smelt gunpowder, had no great respect for militia troops; however, he determined to give them a trial, and accordingly called for a general muster, inspection, and review. But, oh Mars and Bellona! what a turning-out was here! Here came old Roelant Cuckaburt, with a short blunderbuss on his shoulder, and a long horseman's sword trailing by his side; and Barent Dirkson, with something that looked like a copper kettle turned upsidedown on his head, and a couple of old horse-pistols in his belt; and Dirk Volkertson, with a long duck fowling-piece without any ramrod; and a host more, armed higgledy-piggledy,—with swords, hatchets, snickersnees, crowbars, broomsticks, and what not; the officers distinguished from the rest by having their slouched hats cocked up with pins, and surmounted with cock-tail feathers.

The sturdy Peter eyed this nondescript host with some such rueful aspect as a man would eye the devil, and determined to give his feather-bed soldiers a seasoning. He accordingly put them through their manual exercise over and over again; trudged them backwards and forwards about the streets of New Amsterdam until their short legs ached and their fat sides sweated again; and finally encamped them in the evening on the summit of a hill without the city, to give them a taste of camp-life, intending the next day to renew the toils and perils of the field. But so it came to pass that in the night there fell a great and heavy rain, and melted away the army, so that in the morning, when Gaffer Phœbus shed his first beams upon the camp, scarce a warrior remained except Peter Stuyvesant and his trumpeter Van Corlear.

This awful desolation of a whole army would have appalled a commander of less nerve; but it served to confirm Peter's want of confidence in the militia system, which he thenceforward used to call, in joke,—for he sometimes indulged in a joke,—William the Testy's broken reed. He now took into his service a goodly number of burly, broad-shouldered, broad-bottomed Dutchmen; whom he paid in good silver and gold, and of whom he boasted, that, whether they could stand fire or not, they were at least waterproof. He fortified the city, too, with pickets and palisadoes, extending across the island from river to river, and, above all, cast up mud batteries, or redoubts, on the point of the island where it divided the beautiful bosom of the bay.

These latter redoubts, in process of time, came to be pleasantly overrun by a carpet of grass and clover, and overshadowed by wide-spreading elms and sycamores, among the branches of which the birds would build their nests and rejoice the ear with their melodious notes. Under these trees, too, the old burghers would smoke their afternoon pipe, contemplating the golden sun as he sank in the west, an emblem of the tranquil end toward which they were declining. Here, too, would the young men and maidens of the town take their evening stroll, watching the silver moonbeams as they trembled along the calm bosom of the bay, or lit up the sail of some gliding bark, and peradventure interchanging the soft vows of honest affection,—for to evening strolls in this favored spot were traced most of the marriages in New Amsterdam.

Such was the origin of that renowned promenade, THE BATTERY, which, though ostensibly devoted to the stern purposes of war, has ever been consecrated to the sweet delights of peace. The scene of many a gambol in happy childhood,—of many a tender assignation in riper years,—of many a soothing walk in declining age,—the healthful resort of the feeble invalid,—the Sunday refreshment of the dusty tradesman,—in fine, the ornament and delight of New York, and the pride of the lovely island of Manna-hata.

CHAPTER VIII

How the Yankee Crusade against the New Netherlands Was Baffled by the Sudden Outbreak of Witchcraft among the People of the East

HAVING THUS PROVIDED for the temporary security of New Amsterdam, and guarded it against any sudden surprise, the gallant Peter took a hearty pinch of snuff, and snapping his fingers, set the great council of Amphictyons and their champion, the redoubtable Alicxsander Partridg, at defiance. In the mean time the moss-troopers of Connecticut, the warriors of New Haven and Hartford, and Pyquag, otherwise called Weathersfield, famous for its onions and its witches, and of all the other border-towns, were in a prodigious turmoil, furbishing up their rusty weapons, shouting aloud for war, and anticipating easy conquests, and glorious rummaging of the fat little Dutch villages.

In the midst of these warlike preparations, however, they received the chilling news that the colony of Massachusetts refused to back them in this righteous war. It seems that the gallant conduct of Peter Stuyvesant, the generous warmth of his vindication, and the chivalrous spirit of his defiance, though lost upon the grand council of the league, had carried conviction to the general court of Massachusetts, which nobly refused to believe him guilty of the villanous plot laid at his door.*

The defection of so important a colony paralyzed the councils of the league, some such dissension arose among its members as prevailed of yore in the camp of the brawling warriors of Greece, and in the end the crusade against the Manhattoes was abandoned.

It is said that the moss-troopers of Connecticut were sorely disappointed; but well for them that their belligerent cravings were not gratified: for by my faith, whatever might have been the ultimate result of a conflict with all the powers of the east, in the interim the stomachful heroes of Pyquag would have been choked with their own onions, and all the border-towns of Connecticut would have had such a scouring from the lion-hearted Peter and his robustious myrmidons, that I warrant me they would not have had the stomach to squat on the land or invade the henroost of a Nederlander for a century to come.

But it was not merely the refusal of Massachusetts to join in their unholy crusade that confounded the councils of the league; for about this time broke out in the New-England provinces the awful plague of witchcraft, which spread like pestilence through the land. Such a howling abomination could not be suffered to remain long unnoticed; it soon excited the fiery indignation of those guardians of the commonwealth who whilom had evinced such active benevolence in the conversion of Quakers and Anabaptists. The grand council of the league publicly set their faces against the crime, and bloody laws were enacted against all "Solem conversing or compacting with the divil by way of conjuracion or

* Hazard's State Papers.

the like." * Strict search, too, was made after witches, who were easily detected by devil's pinches,—by being able to weep but three tears, and those out of the left eye,—and by having a most suspicious predilection for black cats and broomsticks! What is particularly worthy of admiration is, that this terrible art, which has baffled the studies and researches of philosophers, astrologers, theurgists, and other sages, was chiefly confined to the most ignorant, decrepit, and ugly old women in the community, with scarce more brains than the broomsticks they rode upon.

When once an alarm is sounded, the public, who dearly love to be in a panic, are always ready to keep it up. Raise but the cry of yellow fever, and immediately every headache, indigestion, and overflowing of the bile is pronounced the terrible epidemic; cry out mad dog, and every unlucky cur in the street is in jeopardy: so in the present instance, whoever was troubled with colic or lumbago was sure to be bewitched,—and woe to any unlucky old woman living in the neighborhood!

It is incredible the number of offences that were detected, "for every one of which," says the reverend Cotton Mather, in that excellent work the History of New England, "we have such a sufficient evidence, that no reasonable man in this whole country ever did question them; *and it will be unreasonable to do it in any other.*" †

Indeed, that authentic and judicious historian John Josselyn, Gent., furnishes us with unquestionable facts on this subject. "There are none," observes he, "that beg in this country, but there be witches too many,—bottle-bellied witches, and others, that produce many strange apparitions, if you will believe report, of a shallop at sea manned with women,—and of a ship and great red horse standing by the main-mast; the ship being in a small cove to the eastward, vanished of a sudden," etc.

The number of delinquents, however, and their magical devices, were not more remarkable than their diabolical obstinacy. Though exhorted in the most solemn, persuasive, and affectionate manner to confess themselves guilty, and be burnt for the good of religion

* New Plymouth record.
† Mather's Hist. New Eng. B. 6, ch. 7.

and the entertainment of the public, yet did they most pertinaciously persist in asserting their innocence. Such incredible obstinacy was in itself deserving of immediate punishment, and was sufficient proof, if proof were necessary, that they were in league with the devil, who is perverseness itself. But their judges were just and merciful, and were determined to punish none that were not convicted on the best of testimony; not that they needed any evidence to satisfy their own minds,—for, like true and experienced judges, their minds were perfectly made up, and they were thoroughly satisfied of the guilt of the prisoners before they proceeded to try them,—but still something was necessary to convince the community at large,—to quiet those prying quidnuncs who should come after them,—in short, the world must be satisfied. Oh, the world—the world!—all the world knows the world of trouble the world is eternally occasioning! The worthy judges, therefore, were driven to the necessity of sifting, detecting, and making evident as noonday, matters which were at the commencement all clearly understood and firmly decided upon in their own pericraniums,—so that it may truly be said, that the witches were burnt to gratify the populace of the day, but were tried for the satisfaction of the whole world that should come after them!

Finding, therefore, that neither exhortation, sound reason, nor friendly entreaty had any avail on these hardened offenders, they resorted to the more urgent arguments of torture; and having thus absolutely wrung the truth from their stubborn lips, they condemned them to undergo the roasting due unto the heinous crimes they had confessed. Some even carried their perverseness so far as to expire under the torture, protesting their innocence to the last; but these were looked upon as thoroughly and absolutely possessed by the devil: and the pious by-standers only lamented that they had not lived a little longer, to have perished in the flames.

In the city of Ephesus, we are told that the plague was expelled by stoning a ragged old beggar to death, whom Apollonius pointed out as being the evil spirit that caused it, and who actually showed himself to be a demon, by changing into a shagged dog. In like manner, and by measures equally sagacious, a salutary check was given to this growing evil. The witches were all burnt, banished, or panic-struck, and in a little while there was not an ugly old woman to be found throughout New England,—which is doubtless one reason why all the young women there are so handsome. Those honest folk who had suffered from their incantations gradually recovered, excepting such as had been afflicted with twitches and aches, which, however, assumed the less alarming aspects of rheumatisms, sciatics and lumbagos; and the good people of New England, abandoning the study of the occult sciences, turned their attention to the more profitable hocus-pocus of trade, and soon became expert in the legerdemain art of turning a penny. Still, however, a tinge of the old leaven is discernible, even unto this day, in their characters: witches occasionally start up among them in different disguises, as physicians, civilians, and divines. The people at large show a keenness, a cleverness, and a profundity of wisdom, that savors strongly of witchcraft; and it has been remarked, that, whenever any stones fall from the moon, the greater part of them is sure to tumble into New England!

CHAPTER IX

Which Records the Rise and Renown of a Military Commander; Showing that a Man, like a Bladder, May Be Puffed Up to Greatness by Mere Wind; Together with the Catastrophe of a Veteran and His Queue

WHEN TREATING OF THESE tempestuous times, the unknown writer of the Stuyvesant manuscript breaks out into an apostrophe in praise of the good St. Nicholas, to whose protecting care he ascribes the dissensions which broke out in the council of the league, and the direful witchcraft which filled all Yankee land as with Egyptian darkness.

A portentous gloom, says he, hung lowering over the fair valleys of the East: the pleasant banks of the Connecticut no longer echoed to the sounds of rustic gayety; grisly phantoms glided about each wild brook and silent glen; fearful apparitions were seen in the air; strange voices were heard in solitary places; and the bordertowns were so occupied in detecting and punishing losel witches, that, for a time, all talk of war was suspended, and New Amsterdam and its inhabitants seemed to be totally forgotten.

I must not conceal the fact that at one time there was some danger of this plague of witchcraft extending into the New Netherlands; and certain witches, mounted on broomsticks, are said to have been seen whisking in the air over some of the Dutch villages near the borders; but the worthy Nederlanders took the precaution to nail horse-shoes to their doors, which it is well known are effectual barriers against all diabolical vermin of the kind. Many of those horse-shoes may be seen at this very day on ancient mansions and barns remaining from the days of the patriarchs; nay, the custom is still kept up among some of our legitimate Dutch yeomanry, who inherit from their forefathers a desire to keep witches and Yankees out of the country.

And now the great Peter, having no immediate hostility to apprehend from the east, turned his face, with characteristic vigilance, to his southern frontiers. The attentive reader will recollect that certain freebooting Swedes had become very troublesome in this quarter in the latter part of the reign of William the Testy, setting at naught the proclamations of that veritable potentate, and putting his admiral, the intrepid Jan Jansen Alpendam, to a perfect non-plus. To check the incursions of these Swedes, Peter Stuyvesant now ordered a force to that frontier, giving the command of it to General Jacobus Van Poffenburgh, an officer who had risen to great importance during the reign of Wilhelmus Kieft. He had, if histories speak true, been second in command to the doughty Van Curlet, when he and his warriors were inhumanly kicked out of Fort Goed Hoop by the Yankees. In that memorable affair Van Poffenburgh is said to have received more kicks in a certain honorable part than any of his comrades, in consequence of which, on the resignation of Van Curlet, he had been promoted to his place, being considered a hero who had seen service, and suffered in his country's cause.

It is tropically observed by honest old Socrates, that heaven infuses into some men at their birth a portion of intellectual gold, into others of intellectual silver, while others are intellectually furnished with iron and brass. Of the last class was General Van Poffenburgh; and it would seem as if dame Nature, who will sometimes be partial, had given him brass enough for a dozen ordinary braziers. All this he had contrived to pass off upon William the Testy for genuine gold; and the little governor would sit for hours and listen to his gunpowder stories of exploits, which left those of Tirante the White, Don Belianis of Greece, or St. George and the Dragon quite in the background. Having been promoted by William Kieft to the command of his whole disposable forces, he gave importance to his station by the grandiloquence of his bulletins, always styling himself Commander-in-chief of the Armies of the New Netherlands, though in sober truth, these armies were nothing more than a handful of hen-stealing, bottle-bruising ragamuffins.

In person he was not very tall, but exceedingly round; neither did his bulk proceed from his being fat, but windy, being blown up by a prodigious conviction of his own importance, until he resembled one of those bags of wind given by Æolus, in an incredible fit of generosity, to that vagabond warrior Ulysses. His windy endowments had long excited the admiration of Anthony Van Corlear, who is said to have hinted more than once to William the Testy, that in making Van Poffenburgh a general he had spoiled an admirable trumpeter.

As it is the practice in ancient story to give the reader a description of the arms and equipments of every noted warrior, I will bestow a word upon the dress of this redoubtable commander. It comported with his character, being so crossed and slashed, and embroidered with lace and tinsel, that he seemed to have as much brass without as nature had stored away within. He was swathed, too, in a crimson sash, of the size and texture of a fishing-net,—doubtless to keep his swelling heart from bursting through his ribs. He face glowed with furnace-heat from between a huge pair of well-powdered whiskers; and his valorous soul seemed ready to bounce out of a pair of large, glassy, blinking eyes, projecting like those of a lobster.

I swear to thee, worthy reader, if history and tradition belie not this warrior, I would give all the money in my pocket to have seen him accoutred *cap-à-pie,*—booted to the middle, sashed to the chin, collared to the ears, whiskered to the teeth, crowned with an overshadowing cocked hat, and girded with a leathern belt ten inches broad, from which trailed a falchion, of a length that I dare not mention. Thus equipped, he strutted about, as bitter-looking a man of war as the far-famed More, of More-hall, when he sallied forth to slay the dragon of Wantley. For what says the ballad?

> "Had you but seen him in this dress,
>   How fierce he looked and how big,
> You would have thought him for to be
>   Some Egyptian porcupig.
> He frighted all—cats, dogs, and all,
>   Each cow, each horse, and each hog;
> For fear they did flee, for they took him to be
>   Some strange outlandish hedge-hog." *

I must confess this general, with all his outward valor and ventosity, was not exactly an officer to Peter Stuyvesant's taste, but he stood foremost in the army list of William the Testy; and it is probable the good Peter, who was conscientious in his dealings with all men, and had his military notions of precedence, thought it but fair to give him a chance of proving his right to his dignities.

To this copper captain, therefore, was confided the command of the troops destined to protect the southern frontier; and scarce had he departed for his station than bulletins began to arrive from him, describing his undaunted march through savage deserts, over insurmountable mountains, across impassable rivers, and through impenetrable forests, conquering vast tracts of uninhabited country, and encountering more perils than did Xenophon in his far-famed retreat with his ten thousand Grecians.

* Ballad of Dragon of Wantley

Peter Stuyvesant read all these grandiloquent despatches with a dubious screwing of the mouth and shaking of the head; but Antony Van Corlear repeated these contents in the streets and market-places with an appropriate flourish upon his trumpet, and the windy victories of the general resounded through the streets of New Amsterdam.

On arriving at the southern frontier, Van Poffenburgh proceeded to erect a fortress, or stronghold, on the South or Delaware river. At first he bethought him to call it Fort Stuyvesant, in honor of the governor,—a lowly kind of homage prevalent in our country among speculators, military commanders, and office-seekers of all kinds, by which our maps come to be studded with the names of political patrons and temporary great men; in the present instance, Van Poffenburgh carried his homage to the most lowly degree, giving his fortress the name of Fort Casimir, in honor, it is said, of a favorite pair of brimstone trunk-breeches of his Excellency.

As this fort will be found to give rise to important events, it may be worth while to notice that it was afterwards called Nieuw Amstel, and was the germ of the present flourishing town of New Castle, or, more properly speaking, No Castle, there being nothing of the kind on the premises.

His fortress being finished, it would have done any man's heart good to behold the swelling dignity with which the general would stride in and out a dozen times a day, surveying it in front and in rear, on this side and on that; how he would strut backwards and forwards, in full regimentals, on the top of the ramparts,—like a vain-glorious cock-pigeon, swelling and vaporing on the top of a dove-cot.

There is a kind of valorous spleen which, like wind, is apt to grow unruly in the stomachs of newly made soldiers, compelling them to box-lobby brawls and broken-headed quarrels, unless there can be found some more harmless way to give it vent. It is recorded in the delectable romance of Pierce Forest, that a young knight, being dubbed by King Alexander, did incontinently gallop into an adjacent forest and belabor the trees with such might and main, that he not merely eased off the sudden effervescence of his valor, but convinced the whole court that he was the most potent and courageous cavalier on the face of the earth. In like manner the commander of Fort Casimir, when he found his martial spirit waxing too hot within him, would sally forth into the fields and lay about him most lustily with his sabre,—decapitating cabbages by platoons, hewing down lofty sunflowers, which he termed gigantic Swedes, and if, perchance, he espied a colony of big-bellied pumpkins quietly basking in the sun,—"Ah! caitiff Yankees?" would he roar, "have I caught ye at last?"— So saying, with one sweep of his sword he would cleave the unhappy vegetables from their chins to their waistbands; by which warlike havoc his choler being in some sort allayed, he would return into the fortress with the full conviction that he was a very miracle of military prowess.

He was a disciplinarian, too, of the first order. Woe to any unlucky soldier who did not hold up his head and turn out his toes when on parade, or who did not salute the general in proper style as he passed. Having one day, in his Bible researches, encountered the history of Absalom and his melancholy end, the general bethought him, that, in a country abounding with forests, his soldiers were in constant risk of a like catastrophe; he therefore, in an evil hour, issued orders for cropping the hair of both officers and men throughout the garrison.

Now, so it happened, that among his officers was a sturdy veteran named Keldermeester, who had cherished, through a long life, a mop of hair not a little resembling the shag of a Newfoundland dog terminating in a queue like the handle of a frying-pan, and queued so tightly to his head that his eyes and mouth generally stood ajar, and his eyebrows were drawn up to the top of his forehead. It may naturally be supposed that the possessor of so goodly an appendage would resist with abhorrence an order condemning it to the shears. On hearing the general orders, he discharged a tempest of veteran, soldier-like oaths, and dunder and blixums,—swore he would break any man's head who attempted to meddle with his tail,—queued it stiffer than ever, and whisked it about the garrison as fiercely as the tail of a crocodile.

The eel-skin queue of old Keldermeester became instantly an

affair of the utmost importance. The commander-in-chief was too enlightened an officer not to perceive that the discipline of the garrison, the subordination and good order of the armies of the Nieuw Nederlands, the consequent safety of the whole province, and ultimately the dignity and prosperity of their High Mightinesses the Lords States General, imperiously demanded the docking of that stubborn queue. He decreed, therefore, that old Keldermeester should be publicly shorn of his glories in presence of the whole garrison; the old man as resolutely stood on the defensive; whereupon he was arrested, and tried by a court-martial for mutiny, desertion, and all the other list of offences noticed in the articles of war, ending with a "videlicet, in wearing an eel-skin queue, three feet long, contrary to orders." Then came on arraignments, and trials, and pleadings; and the whole garrison was in a ferment about this unfortunate queue. As it is well known that the commander of a frontier post has the power of acting pretty much after his own will, there is little doubt but that the veteran would have been hanged or shot at least, had he not luckily fallen ill of a fever, through mere chagrin and mortification,—and deserted from all earthly command, with his beloved locks unviolated. His obstinacy remained unshaken to the very last moment, when he directed that he should be carried to his grave with his eel-skin queue sticking out of a hole in his coffin.

This magnanimous affair obtained the general great credit as a disciplinarian; but it is hinted that he was ever afterwards subject to bad dreams and fearful visitations in the night, when the grizzly spectrum of old Keldermeester would stand sentinel by his bedside, erect as a pump, his enormous queue strutting out like the handle.

THE SKETCH-BOOK

·{❁❀❁}·

THE AUTHOR'S ACCOUNT OF HIMSELF

"I am of this mind with Homer, that as the snaile that crept out of her shel was turned eftsoons into a toad, and thereby was forced to make a stoole to sit on; so the traveller that stragleth from his owne country is in a short time transformed into so monstrous a shape, that he is faine to alter his mansion with his manners, and to live where he can, not where he would."—LYLY's: *Euphues*

I WAS ALWAYS FOND of visiting new scenes, and observing strange characters and manners. Even when a mere child I began my travels, and made many tours of discovery into foreign parts and unknown regions of my native city, to the frequent alarm of my parents, and the emolument of the town-crier. As I grew into boyhood, I extended the range of my observations. My holiday afternoons were spent in rambles about the surrounding country. I made myself familiar with all its places famous in history or fable. I knew every spot where a murder or robbery had been committed, or a ghost seen. I visited the neighboring villages, and added greatly to my stock of knowledge by noting their habits and customs, and conversing with their sages and great men. I even journeyed one long summer's day to the summit of the most distant hill, whence I stretched my eye over many a mile of *terra incognita,* and was astonished to find how vast a globe I inhabited.

This rambling propensity strengthened with my years. Books of voyages and travels became my passion, and in devouring their contents, I neglected the regular exercises of the school. How wistfully would I wander about the pier-heads in fine weather, and watch the parting ships, bound to distant climes; with what longing eyes would I gaze after their lessening sails, and waft myself in imagination to the ends of the earth!

Further reading and thinking, though they brought this vague inclination into more reasonable bounds, only served to make it more decided. I visited various parts of my own country; and had I been merely a lover of fine scenery, I should have felt little desire to seek elsewhere its gratification, for on no country have the charms of nature been more prodigally lavished. Her mighty lakes, like oceans of liquid silver; her mountains, with their bright aërial tints; her valleys, teeming with wild fertility; her tremendous cataracts, thundering in their solitudes; her boundless plains, waving with spontaneous verdure; her broad deep rivers, rolling in solemn silence to the ocean; her trackless forests, where vegetation puts forth all its magnificence; her skies, kindling with the magic of summer clouds and glorious sunshine;—no, never need an American look beyond his own country for the sublime and beautiful of natural scenery.

But Europe held forth the charms of storied and poetical association. There were to be seen the masterpiece of art, the refinements of highly cultivated society, the quaint peculiarities of ancient and local custom. My native country was full of youthful promise: Europe was rich in the accumulated treasures of age. Her very ruins told the history of times gone by, and every mouldering stone was a chronicle. I longed to wander over the scenes of renowned achievement,—to tread, as it were, in the footsteps of antiquity,—to loiter about the ruined castle,—to meditate on the falling tower,—to escape, in short, from the commonplace realities of the present, and lose myself among the shadowy grandeurs of the past.

I had, beside all this, an earnest desire to see the great men of the earth. We have, it is true, our great men in America: not a city but has an ample share of them. I have mingled among them in my time, and been almost withered by the shade into which they cast me; for there is nothing so baleful to a small man as the shade of a great one, particularly the great man of a city. But I was anxious to see the great men of Europe; for I had read in the works of various philosophers, that all animals degenerated in America, and man among the number. A great man of Europe, thought I, must therefore be as superior to a great man of America as a peak of the Alps to a highland of the Hudson; and in this idea I was confirmed by observing the comparative importance and swelling magnitude of many English travellers among us, who, I was assured, were very little people in their own country. I will visit this land of wonders, thought I, and see the gigantic race from which I am degenerated.

It has been either my good or evil lot to have my roving passion gratified. I have wandered through different countries, and witnessed many of the shifting scenes of life. I cannot say that I have studied them with the eye of a philosopher, but rather with the sauntering gaze with which humble lovers of the picturesque stroll from the window of one print-shop to another, caught sometimes by the delineations of beauty, sometimes by the distortions of caricature, and sometimes by the loveliness of landscape. As it is the fashion for modern tourists to travel pencil in hand, and bring home their portfolios filled with sketches, I am disposed to get up a few for the entertainment of my friends. When, however, I look over the hints and memorandums I have taken down for the purpose, my heart almost fails me at finding how my idle humor has led me aside from the great objects studied by every regular traveller who would make a book. I fear I shall give equal disappointment with an unlucky landscape-painter, who had travelled on the continent, but, following the bent of his vagrant inclination, had sketched in nooks, and corners, and by-places. His sketch-book was accordingly crowded with cottages, and landscapes, and obscure ruins; but he had neglected to paint St. Peter's or the Coliseum; the cascade of Terni, or the bay of Naples; and had not a single glacier or volcano in his whole collection.

THE VOYAGE

Ships, ships, I will descrie you
Amidst the main,
I will come and try you,
What you are protecting,
And projecting,
What's your end and aim.
One goes abroad for merchandise and trading,
Another stays to keep his country from invading,
A third is coming home with rich and wealthy lading.
Halloo! my fancie, whither wilt thou go?

Old Poem

To AN AMERICAN visiting Europe, the long voyage he has to make is an excellent preparative. The temporary absence of wordly scenes and employments produces a state of mind peculiarly fitted to receive new and vivid impressions. The vast space of waters that separates the hemispheres is like a blank page in existence. There is no gradual transition, by which, as in Europe, the features and population of one country blend almost imperceptibly with those of another. From the moment you lose sight of the land you have left, all is vacancy until you step on the opposite shore, and are launched at once into the bustle and novelties of another world.

In travelling by land there is a continuity of scene and a connected succession of persons and incidents, that carry on the story of life, and lessen the effect of absence and separation. We drag, it is true, "a lengthening chain" at each remove of our pilgrimage; but the chain is unbroken: we can trace it back link by link; and we feel that the last still grapples us to home. But a wide sea-voyage severs us at once. It makes us conscious of being cast loose from the secure anchorage of settled life, and sent adrift upon a doubtful world. It interposes a gulf, not merely imaginary, but real, between us and our homes,—a gulf subject to tempest, and fear, and uncertainty, rendering distance palpable, and return precarious.

Such, at least, was the case with myself. As I saw the last blue line of my native land fade away like a cloud in the horizon, it seemed as if I had closed one volume of the world and its concerns, and had time for meditation, before I opened another. That land, too, now vanishing from my view, which contained all most dear to me in life; what vicissitudes might occur in it, what changes might take place in me, before I should visit it again! Who can tell, when he sets forth to wander, whither he may be driven by the uncertain currents of existence; or when he may return; or whether it may ever be his lot to revisit the scenes of his childhood?

I said that at sea all is vacancy; I should correct the expression. To one given to day-dreaming, and fond of losing himself in reveries, a sea-voyage is full of subjects for meditation; but then they are the wonders of the deep, and of the air, and rather tend to abstract the mind from worldly themes. I delighted to loll over the quarter-railing, or climb to the main-top, of a calm day, and muse for hours together on the tranquil bosom of a summer's sea; to gaze upon the piles of golden clouds just peering above the horizon, fancy them some fairy realms, and people them with a creation of my own;—to watch the gentle undulating billows, rolling their silver volumes, as if to die away on those happy shores.

There was a delicious sensation of mingled security and awe with which I looked down, from my giddy height, on the monsters of the deep at their uncouth gambols. Shoals of porpoises tumbling about the bow of the ship; the grampus slowly heaving his huge form above the surface; or the ravenous shark, darting, like a spectre, through the blue waters. My imagination would conjure up all that I had heard or read of the watery world beneath me; of the finny herds that roam its fathomless valleys; of the shapeless monsters that lurk among the very foundations of the earth; and of those wild phantasms that swell the tales of fishermen and sailors.

Sometimes a distant sail, gliding along the edge of the ocean, would be another theme of idle speculation. How interesting this fragment of a world, hastening to rejoin the great mass of existence! What a glorious monument of human invention; which has in a manner triumphed over wind and wave; has brought the ends of the world into communion; has established an interchange of blessings, pouring into the sterile regions of the north all the luxuries of the south; has diffused the light of knowledge and the charities of cultivated life; and has thus bound together those scattered portions of the human race, between which nature seemed to have thrown an insurmountable barrier.

We one day descried some shapeless object drifting at a distance. At sea, everything that breaks the monotony of the surrounding expanse attracts attention. It proved to be the mast of a ship that must have been completely wrecked; for there were the remains of handkerchiefs, by which some of the crew had fastened themselves to this spar, to prevent their being washed off by the waves. There was no trace by which the name of the ship could be ascertained. The wreck had evidently drifted about for many months; clusters of shell-fish had fastened about it, and long sea-weeds flaunted at its sides. But where, thought I, is the crew? Their struggle has long been over,—they have gone down amidst the roar of the tempest,—their bones lie whitening among the caverns of the deep. Silence, oblivion, like the waves, have closed over them, and no one can tell the story of their end. What sighs have been wafted after that ship! what prayers offered up at the deserted fireside of home! How often has the mistress, the wife, the mother, pored over the daily news, to catch some casual intelligence of this rover of the deep! How has expectation darkened into anxiety—anxiety into dread—and dread into despair! Alas! not one memento may ever return for love to cherish. All that may ever be known, is, that she sailed from her port, "and was never heard of more!"

The sight of this wreck, as usual, gave rise to many dismal anecdotes. This was particularly the case in the evening, when the weather, which had hitherto been fair, began to look wild and threatening, and gave indications of one of those sudden storms which will sometimes break in upon the serenity of a summer voyage. As we sat round the dull light of a lamp in the cabin, that made the gloom more ghastly, every one had his tale of shipwreck and disaster. I was particularly struck with a short one related by the captain.

"As I was once sailing," said he, "in a fine stout ship across the banks of Newfoundland, one of those heavy fogs which prevail in those parts rendered it impossible for us to see far ahead even in the daytime; but at night the weather was so thick that we could not distinguish any object at twice the length of the ship. I kept lights at the mast-head, and a constant watch forward to look out for fishing-smacks, which are accustomed to lie at anchor on the banks. The wind was blowing a smacking breeze, and we were going at a great rate through the water. Suddenly the watch gave the alarm of 'a sail ahead!'—it was scarcely uttered before we were upon her. She was a small schooner, at anchor, with her broadside towards us. The crew were all asleep, and had neglected to hoist a light. We struck her just amidships. The force, the size, and weight of our vessel bore her down below the waves; we passed over her, and were hurried on our course. As the crashing wreck was sinking beneath us, I had a glimpse of two or three half-naked wretches rushing from her cabin; they just started from their beds to be swallowed shrieking by the waves. I heard their drowning cry mingling with the wind. The blast that bore it to our ears swept us out of all farther hearing. I shall never forget that cry! It was some time before we could put the ship about, she was under such headway. We returned, as nearly as we could guess, to the place where the smack had anchored. We cruised about for several hours in the dense fog. We fired signal-guns, and listened if we might hear the halloo of any survivors; but all was silent—we never saw or heard anything of them more."

I confess these stories, for a time, put an end to all my fine fancies. The storm increased with the night. The sea was lashed into tremendous confusion. There was a fearful, sullen sound of rushing waves, and broken surges. Deep called unto deep. At times the black volume of clouds overhead seemed rent asunder by flashes of lightning which quivered along the foaming billows, and made the succeeding darkness doubly terrible. The thunders bellowed over the wild waste of waters, and were echoed and prolonged by the mountain-waves. As I saw the ship staggering and plunging among these roaring caverns, it seemed miraculous that she regained her balance, or preserved her buoyancy. Her yards would dip into the water: her bow was almost buried beneath the waves. Sometimes an impending surge appeared ready to overwhelm her, and nothing but a dexterous movement of the helm preserved her from the shock.

When I retired to my cabin, the awful scene still followed me. The whistling of the wind through the rigging sounded like funeral wailings. The creaking of the masts, the straining and groaning of bulk-heads, as the ship labored in the weltering sea, were frightful. As I heard the waves rushing along the sides of the ship, and roaring in my very ear, it seemed as if Death were raging round this floating prison, seeking for his prey: the mere starting of a nail, the yawning of a seam, might give him entrance.

A fine day, however, with a tranquil sea and favoring breeze, soon put all these dismal reflections to flight. It is impossible to resist the gladdening influence of fine weather and fair wind at sea. When the ship is decked out in all her canvas, every sail swelled, and careering gayly over the curling waves, how lofty, how gallant she appears—how she seems to lord it over the deep!

I might fill a volume with the reveries of a sea-voyage, for with me it is almost a continual reverie,—but it is time to get to shore.

It was a fine sunny morning when the thrilling cry of "land!" was given from the mast-head. None but those who have experienced it can form an idea of the delicious throng of sensations which rush into an American's bosom, when he first comes in sight of Europe. There is a volume of associations with the very name. It is the land of promise, teeming with everything of which his childhood has heard, or on which his studious years have pondered.

From that time until the moment of arrival, it was all feverish excitement. The ships-of-war, that prowled like guardian giants along the coast; the headlands of Ireland, stretching out into the channel; the Welsh mountains, towering into the clouds; all were objects of intense interest. As we sailed up the Mersey, I reconnoitred the shores with a telescope. My eye dwelt with delight on neat cottages, with their trim shrubberies and green grass plots. I saw the mouldering ruin of an abbey overrun with ivy, and the taper spire of a village church rising from the brow of a neighboring hill;—all were characteristic of England.

The tide and wind were so favorable that the ship was enabled to come at once to the pier. It was thronged with people: some, idle lookers-on; others, eager expectants of friends or relatives. I could distinguish the merchant to whom the ship was consigned. I knew him by his calculating brow and restless air. His hands were thrust into his pockets; he was whistling throughtfully, and walking to and fro, a small space having been accorded him by the crowd, in deference to his temporary importance. There were repeated cheerings and salutations interchanged between the shore and the ship, as friends happened to recognize each other. I particularly noticed one young woman of humble dress, but interesting demeanor. She was leaning forward from among the crowd; her eye hurried over the ship as it neared the shore, to catch some wished-for countenance. She seemed disappointed and agitated; when I heard a faint voice call her name. It was from a poor sailor who had been ill all the voyage, and had excited the sympathy of every one on board. When the weather was fine, his messmates had spread a mattress for him on deck in the shade; but of late his illness had so increased, that he had taken to his hammock, and only breathed a wish that he might see his wife before he died. He had been helped on deck as we came up the river, and was now leaning against the shrouds, with a countenance so wasted, so pale, so ghastly, that it was no wonder even the eye of affection did not recognize him. But at the sound of his voice, her eye darted on his features: it read, at once, a whole volume of sorrow; she clasped her hands, uttered a faint shriek, and stood wringing them in silent agony.

All now was hurry and bustle. The meetings of acquaintances— the greeting of friends—the consultations of men of business. I alone was solitary and idle. I had no friend to meet, no cheering

to receive. I stepped upon the land of my forefathers—but felt
that I was a stranger in the land.

RIP VAN WINKLE

A Posthumous Writing of Diedrich Knickerbocker

> By Woden, God of Saxons,
> From whence comes Wensday, that is Wodensday.
> Truth is a thing that ever I will keep
> Unto thylke day in which I creep into
> My sepulchre——
>
> Cartwright

[The following Tale was found among the papers of the late Diedrich
Knickerbocker, an old gentleman of New York, who was very curious in
the Dutch history of the province, and the manners of the descendants from
its primitive settlers. His historical researches, however, did not lie so much
among books as among men; for the former are lamentably scanty on his
favorite topics; whereas he found the old burghers, and still more their
wives, rich in that legendary lore so invaluable to true history. Whenever,
therefore, he happened upon a genuine Dutch family, snugly shut up in its
low-roofed farmhouse, under a spreading sycamore, he looked upon it as a
little clasped volume of black-letter, and studied it with the zeal of a bookworm.

The result of all these researches was a history of the province during the
reign of the Dutch governors, which he published some years since. There
have been various opinions as to the literary character of his work, and, to
tell the truth, it is not a whit better than it should be. Its chief merit is its
scrupulous accuracy, which indeed was a little questioned on its first appearance, but has since been completely established; and it is now admitted into
all historical collections as a book of unquestionable authority.

The old gentleman died shortly after the publication of his work; and
now that he is dead and gone, it cannot do much harm to his memory to

say that his time might have been much better employed in weightier labors. He, however, was apt to ride his hobby his own way; and though it did now and then kick up the dust a little in the eyes of his neighbors, and grieve the spirit of some friends, for whom he felt the truest deference and affection, yet his errors and follies are remembered "more in sorrow than in anger," and it begins to be suspected that he never intended to injure or offend. But however his memory may be appreciated by critics, it is still held dear by many folk whose good opinion is well worth having; particularly by certain biscuit-bakers, who have gone so far as to imprint his likeness on their New-Year cakes; and have thus given him a chance for immortality, almost equal to the being stamped on a Waterloo Medal, or a Queen Anne's Farthing.]

WHOEVER HAS MADE A VOYAGE up the Hudson must remember the Kaatskill mountains. They are a dismembered branch of the great Appalachian family, and are seen away to the west of the river, swelling up to a noble height, and lording it over the surrounding country. Every change of season, every change of weather, indeed, every hour of the day, produces some change in the magical hues and shapes of these mountains, and they are regarded by all the good wives, far and near, as perfect barometers. When the weather is fair and settled, they are clothed in blue and purple, and print their bold outlines on the clear evening sky; but sometimes, when the rest of the landscape is cloudless, they will gather a hood of gray vapors about their summits, which, in the last rays of the setting sun, will glow and light up like a crown of glory.

At the foot of these fairy mountains, the voyager may have descried the light smoke curling up from a village, whose shingle-roofs gleam among the trees, just where the blue tints of the upland melt away into the fresh green of the nearer landscape. It is a little village, of great antiquity, having been founded by some of the Dutch colonists in the early times of the province, just about the beginning of the government of the good Peter Stuyvesant, (may he rest in peace!) and there were some of the houses of the original settlers standing within a few years, built of small yellow bricks brought from Holland, having latticed windows and gable fronts, surmounted with weathercocks.

In that same village, and in one of these very houses (which, to tell the precise truth, was sadly time-worn and weather-beaten), there lived, many years since, while the country was yet a province of Great Britain, a simple, good-natured fellow, of the name of Rip Van Winkle. He was a descendant of the Van Winkles who figured so gallantly in the chivalrous days of Peter Stuyvesant, and accompanied him to the siege of Fort Christina. He inherited, however, but little of the martial character of his ancestors. I have observed that he was a simple, good-natured man; he was, moreover, a kind neighbor, and an obedient, hen-pecked husband. Indeed, to the latter circumstance might be owing that meekness of spirit which gained him such universal popularity; for those men are most apt to be obsequious and conciliating abroad, who are under the discipline of shrews at home. Their tempers, doubtless, are rendered pliant and malleable in the fiery furnace of domestic tribulation; and a curtain-lecture is worth all the sermons in the world for teaching the virtues of patience and long-suffering. A termagant wife may, therefore, in some respects be considered a tolerable blessing; and if so, Rip Van Winkle was thrice blessed.

Certain it is, that he was a great favorite among all the good wives of the village, who, as usual with the amiable sex, took his part in all family squabbles; and never failed, whenever they talked those matters over in their evening gossipings, to lay all the blame on Dame Van Winkle. The children of the village, too, would shout with joy whenever he approached. He assisted at their sports, made their playthings, taught them to fly kites and shoot marbles, and told them long stories of ghosts, witches, and Indians. Whenever he went dodging about the village, he was surrounded by a troop of them, hanging on his skirts, clambering on his back, and playing a thousand tricks on him with impunity; and not a dog would bark at him throughout the neighborhood.

The great error in Rip's composition was an insuperable aversion to all kinds of profitable labor. It could not be from the want of assiduity or perseverance; for he would sit on a wet rock, with a rod as long and heavy as a Tartar's lance, and fish all day without a murmur, even though he should not be encouraged by a single nibble. He would carry a fowling-piece on his shoulder for hours together, trudging through woods and swamps, and up hill and down dale, to shoot a few squirrels or wild pigeons. He would never refuse to assist a neighbor even in the roughest toil, and was a foremost man at all country frolics for husking Indian corn, or building stone fences; the women of the village, too, used to employ him to run their errands, and to do such little odd jobs as their less obliging husbands would not do for them. In a word, Rip was ready to attend to anybody's business but his own; but as to doing family duty, and keeping his farm in order, he found it impossible.

In fact, he declared it was of no use to work on his farm; it was the most pestilent little piece of ground in the whole country; everything about it went wrong, and would go wrong, in spite of him. His fences were continually falling to pieces; his cow would either go astray, or get among the cabbages; weeds were sure to grow quicker in his fields than anywhere else; the rain always made a point of setting in just as he had some out-door work to do; so that though his patrimonial estate had dwindled away under his management, acre by acre, until there was little more left than a mere patch of Indian corn and potatoes, yet it was the worst conditioned farm in the neighborhood.

His children, too, were as ragged and wild as if they belonged to nobody. His son Rip, an urchin begotten in his own likeness, promised to inherit the habits, with the old clothes, of his father. He was generally seen trooping like a colt at his mother's heels, equipped in a pair of his father's cast-off galligaskins, which he had much ado to hold up with one hand, as a fine lady does her train in bad weather.

Rip Van Winkle, however, was one of those happy mortals, of foolish, well-oiled dispositions, who take the world easy, eat white bread or brown, whichever can be got with least thought or trouble, and would rather starve on a penny than work for a pound. If left to himself, he would have whistled life away in perfect contentment; but his wife kept continually dinning in his ears about his idleness, his carelessness, and the ruin he was bringing on his family. Morning, noon, and night, her tongue was incessantly going, and everything he said or did was sure to produce a torrent of household eloquence. Rip had but one way of replying to all lectures of the kind, and that, by frequent use, had grown into a habit. He shrugged his shoulders, shook his head, cast up his eyes, but said nothing. This, however, always provoked a fresh volley from his wife; so that he was fain to draw off his forces, and take to the outside of the house—the only side which, in truth, belongs to a hen-pecked husband.

Rip's sole domestic adherent was his dog Wolf, who was as much hen-pecked as his master; for Dame Van Winkle regarded them as companions in idleness, and even looked upon Wolf with an evil eye, as the cause of his master's going so often astray. True it is, in all points of spirit befitting an honorable dog, he was as courageous an animal as ever scoured the woods; but what courage can withstand the ever-during and all-besetting terrors of a woman's tongue? The moment Wolf entered the house his crest fell, his tail drooped to the ground, or curled between his legs, he sneaked about with a gallows air, casting many a sidelong glance at Dame Van Winkle, and at the least flourish of a broomstick or ladle he would fly to the door with yelping precipitation.

Times grew worse and worse with Rip Van Winkle as years of matrimony rolled on; a tart temper never mellows with age, and a sharp tongue is the only edged tool that grows keener with constant use. For a long while he used to console himself, when driven from home, by frequenting a kind of perpetual club of the sages, philosophers, and other idle personages of the village, which held its sessions on a bench before a small inn, designated by a rubicund portrait of His Majesty George the Third. Here they used to sit in the shade through a long, lazy summer's day, talking listlessly over village gossip, or telling endless sleepy stories about nothing. But it would have been worth any statesman's money to have heard the profound discussions that sometimes took place, when by chance an old newspaper fell into their hands from some passing traveller. How solemnly they would listen to the contents, as drawled out by Derrick Van Bummel, the schoolmaster, a dapper learned little man, who was not to be daunted by the most gigantic word in the dictionary; and how sagely they would deliberate upon public events some months after they had taken place.

The opinions of this junto were completely controlled by Nicholas Vedder, a patriarch of the village, and landlord of the inn, at the door of which he took his seat from morning till night, just moving sufficiently to avoid the sun and keep in the shade of a large tree; so that the neighbors could tell the hour by his movements as accurately as by a sun-dial. It is true he was rarely heard to speak, but smoked his pipe incessantly. His adherents, however (for every great man has his adherents), perfectly understood him, and knew how to gather his opinions. When anything that was read or related displeased him, he was observed to smoke his pipe vehemently, and to send forth short, frequent, and angry puffs; but when pleased, he would inhale the smoke slowly and tranquilly, and emit it in light and placid clouds; and sometimes, taking the pipe from his mouth, and letting the fragrant vapor curl about his nose, would gravely nod his head in token of perfect approbation.

From even this stronghold the unlucky Rip was at length routed by his termagant wife, who would suddenly break in upon the tranquillity of the assemblage and call the members all to naught; nor was that august personage, Nicholas Vedder himself, sacred from the daring tongue of this terrible virago, who charged him outright with encouraging her husband in habits of idleness.

Poor Rip was at last reduced almost to despair; and his only alternative, to escape from the labor of the farm and clamor of his wife, was to take gun in hand and stroll away into the woods. Here he would sometimes seat himself at the foot of a tree, and share the contents of his wallet with Wolf, with whom he sympathized as a fellow-sufferer in persecution. "Poor Wolf," he would say, "thy mistress leads thee a dog's life of it; but never mind, my lad, whilst I live thou shalt never want a friend to stand by thee!" Wolf would wag his tail, look wistfully in his master's face; and if dogs can feel pity, I verily believe he reciprocated the sentiment with all his heart.

In a long ramble of the kind on a fine autumnal day, Rip had unconsciously scrambled to one of the highest parts of the Kaat-skill mountains. He was after his favorite sport of squirrel-shoot-ing, and the still solitudes had echoed and re-echoed with the re-ports of his gun. Panting and fatigued, he threw himself, late in the afternoon, on a green knoll, covered with mountain herbage, that crowned the brow of a precipice. From an opening between the trees he could overlook all the lower country for many a mile of rich woodland. He saw at a distance the lordly Hudson, far, far below him, moving on its silent but majestic course, with the re-flection of a purple cloud, or the sail of a lagging bark, here and there sleeping on its glassy bosom, and at last losing itself in the blue highlands.

On the other side he looked down into a deep mountain glen, wild, lonely, and shagged, the bottom filled with fragments from the impending cliffs, and scarcely lighted by the reflected rays of the setting sun. For some time Rip lay musing on this scene; eve-ning was gradually advancing; the mountains began to throw their long blue shadows over the valleys; he saw that it would be dark long before he could reach the village, and he heaved a heavy sigh when he thought of encountering the terrors of Dame Van Winkle.

As he was about to descend, he heard a voice from a distance, hallooing, "Rip Van Winkle, Rip Van Winkle!" He looked round, but could see nothing but a crow winging its solitary flight across the mountain. He thought his fancy must have deceived him, and turned again to descend, when he heard the same cry ring through the still evening air: "Rip Van Winkle! Rip Van Winkle!"—at the same time Wolf bristled up his back, and giving a low growl, skulked to his master's side, looking fearfully down into the glen. Rip now felt a vague apprehension stealing over him; he looked anxiously in the same direction, and perceived a strange figure slowly toiling up the rocks, and bending under the weight of something he carried on his back. He was suprised to see any human being in this lonely and unfrequented place; but suppos-ing it to be some one of the neighborhood in need of his assistance, he hastened down to yield it.

On nearer approach he was still more surprised at the singularity of the stranger's appearance. He was a short, square-built old fellow, with thick bushy hair, and a grizzled beard. His dress was of the antique Dutch fashion,—a cloth jerkin strapped round the waist—several pair of breeches, the outer one of ample volume, decorated with rows of buttons down the sides, and bunches at the knees. He bore on his shoulder a stout keg, that seemed full of liquor, and made signs for Rip to approach and assist him with the load. Though rather shy and distrustful of this new acquaintance, Rip complied with his usual alacrity; and mutually relieving one another, they clambered up a narrow gully, apparently the dry bed of a mountain torrent. As they ascended, Rip every now and then heard long, rolling peals, like distant thunder, that seemed to issue out of a deep ravine, or rather cleft, between lofty rocks, toward which their rugged path conducted. He paused for an instant, but supposing it to be the muttering of one of those transient thunder-showers which often take place in mountain heights, he proceeded. Passing through the ravine, they came to a hollow, like a small amphitheatre, surrounded by perpendicular precipices, over the brinks of which impending trees shot their branches, so that you only caught glimpses of the azure sky and the bright evening cloud. During the whole time Rip and his companion had labored on in silence; for though the former marvelled greatly what could be the object of carrying a keg of liquor up this wild mountain, yet there was something strange and incomprehensible about the unknown, that inspired awe and checked familiarity.

On entering the amphitheatre, new objects of wonder presented themselves. On a level spot in the centre was a company of odd-looking personages playing at ninepins. They were dressed in a quaint, outlandish fashion; some wore short doublets, others jerkins, with long knives in their belts, and most of them had enormous breeches, of similar style with that of the guide's. Their visages, too, were peculiar: one had a large beard, broad face, and small piggish eyes; the face of another seemed to consist entirely of nose, and was surmounted by a white sugar-loaf hat, set off with a little red cock's tail. They all had beards, of various shapes and colors. There was one who seemed to be the commander. He was a stout old gentleman, with a weather-beaten countenance; he wore a laced doublet, broad belt and hanger, high crowned hat and feather, red stockings, and high-heeled shoes, with roses in them. The whole group reminded Rip of the figures in an old Flemish painting, in the parlor of Dominie Van Shaick, the village parson, and which had been brought over from Holland at the time of the settlement.

What seemed particularly odd to Rip was, that, though these folks were evidently amusing themselves, yet they maintained the gravest faces, the most mysterious silence, and were, withal, the most melancholy party of pleasure he had ever witnessed. Nothing interrupted the stillness of the scene but the noise of the balls, which, whenever they were rolled, echoed along the mountains like rumbling peals of thunder.

As Rip and his companion approached them, they suddenly desisted from their play, and stared at him with such fixed, statue-like gaze, and such strange, uncouth, lack-lustre countenances, that his heart turned within him, and his knees smote together. His companion now emptied the contents of the keg into large flagons, and made signs to him to wait upon the company. He obeyed with fear and trembling; they quaffed the liquor in profound silence, and then returned to their game.

By degrees Rip's awe and apprehension subsided. He even ventured, when no eye was fixed upon him, to taste the beverage, which he found had much of the flavor of excellent Hollands. He was naturally a thirsty soul, and was soon tempted to repeat the draught. One taste provoked another; and he reiterated his visits to the flagon so often that at length his senses were overpowered, his eyes swam in his head, his head gradually declined, and he fell into a deep sleep.

On waking, he found himself on the green knoll whence he had first seen the old man of the glen. He rubbed his eyes—it was a bright sunny morning. The birds were hopping and twittering among the bushes, and the eagle was wheeling aloft, and breasting the pure mountain breeze. "Surely," thought Rip, "I have not slept here all night." He recalled the occurrences before he fell asleep. The strange man with a keg of liquor—the mountain ravine—the wild retreat among the rocks—the woe-begone party at ninepins—the flagon—"Oh! that flagon! that wicked flagon!" thought Rip,—"what excuse shall I make to Dame Van Winkle?" He looked round for his gun, but in place of the clean, well-oiled fowling-piece, he found an old firelock lying by him, the barrel incrusted with rust, the lock falling off, and the stock worm-eaten. He now suspected that the grave roisters of the mountain had put a trick upon him, and, having dosed him with liquor, had robbed him of his gun. Wolf, too, had disappeared, but he might have strayed away after a squirrel or partridge. He whistled after him, and shouted his name, but all in vain; the echoes repeated his whistle and shout, but no dog was to be seen.

He determined to revisit the scene of the last evening's gambol, and if he met with any of the party, to demand his dog and gun. As he rose to walk, he found himself stiff in the joints, and wanting in his usual activity. "These mountain beds do not agree with me," thought Rip, "and if this frolic should lay me up with a fit of the rheumatism, I shall have a blessed time with Dame Van Winkle." With some difficulty he got down into the glen: he found the gully up which he and his companion had ascended the preceding evening; but to his astonishment a mountain stream was now foaming down it, leaping from rock to rock, and filling the glen with babbling murmurs. He, however, made shift to scramble up its sides, working his toilsome way through thickets of birch, sassafras, and witch-hazel, and sometimes tripped up or entangled by the wild grape-vines that twisted their coils or tendrils from tree to tree, and spread a kind of network in his path.

At length he reached to where the ravine had opened through the cliffs to the amphitheatre; but no traces of such opening remained. The rocks presented a high, impenetrable wall, over which the torrent came tumbling in a sheet of feathery foam, and fell into a broad deep basin, black from the shadows of the surrounding forest. Here, then, poor Rip was brought to a stand. He again called and whistled after his dog; he was only answered by the cawing of a flock of idle crows, sporting high in air about a dry tree that overhung a sunny precipice; and who, secure in their elevation, seemed to look down and scoff at the poor man's perplexities. What was to be done? the morning was passing away, and Rip felt famished for want of his breakfast. He grieved to give up his dog and gun; he dreaded to meet his wife; but it would not do to starve among the mountains. He shook his head, shouldered the rusty firelock, and, with a heart full of trouble and anxiety, turned his steps homeward.

As he approached the village he met a number of people, but none whom he knew, which some what surprised him, for he had thought himself acquainted with every one in the country round. Their dress, too, was of a different fashion from that to which he was accustomed. They all stared at him with equal marks of surprise, and whenever they cast their eyes upon him, invariably stroked their chins. The constant recurrence of this gesture induced Rip, involuntarily, to do the same, when, to his astonishment, he found his beard had grown a foot long!

He had now entered the skirts of the village. A troop of strange children ran at his heels, hooting after him, and pointing at his gray beard. The dogs, too, not one of which he recognized for an old acquaintance, barked at him as he passed. The very village was altered; it was larger and more populous. There were rows of houses which he had never seen before, and those which had been his familiar haunts had disappeared. Strange names were over the doors—strange faces at the windows—everything was strange. His mind now misgave him; he began to doubt whether both he and the world around him were not bewitched. Surely this was his native village, which he had left but the day before. There stood the Kaatskill mountains—there ran the silver Hudson at a distance—there was every hill and dale precisely as it had always been. Rip was sorely perplexed. "That flagon last night," thought he, "has addled my poor head sadly!"

It was with some difficulty that he found the way to his own house, which he approached with silent awe, expecting every moment to hear the shrill voice of Dame Van Winkle. He found the house gone to decay—the roof fallen in, the windows shattered, and the doors off the hinges. A half-starved dog that looked like Wolf was skulking about it. Rip called him by name, but the cur snarled, showed his teeth, and passed on. This was an unkind cut indeed. "My very dog," sighed poor Rip, "has forgotten me!"

He entered the house, which, to tell the truth, Dame Van Winkle had always kept in neat order. It was empty, forlorn, and apparently abandoned. This desolateness overcame all his connubial fears—he called loudly for his wife and children—the lonely chambers rang for a moment with his voice, and then all again was silence.

He now hurried forth, and hastened to his old resort, the village inn—but it too was gone. A large rickety wooden building stood in its place, with great gaping windows, some of them broken and mended with old hats and petticoats, and over the door was painted, "The Union Hotel, by Jonathan Doolittle." Instead of the great tree that used to shelter the quiet little Dutch inn of yore, there now was reared a tall naked pole, with something on the top that looked like a red nightcap, and from it was fluttering a flag, on which was a singular assemblage of stars and stripes;— all this was strange and incomprehensible. He recognized on the sign, however, the ruby face of King George, under which he had smoked so many a peaceful pipe; but even this was singularly metamorphosed. The red coat was changed for one of blue and buff, a sword was held in the hand instead of a sceptre, the head was decorated with a cocked hat, and underneath was painted in large characters, GENERAL WASHINGTON.

There was, as usual, a crowd of folk about the door, but none that Rip recollected. The very character of the people seemed changed. There was a busy, bustling, disputatious tone about it, instead of the accustomed phlegm and drowsy tranquillity. He looked in vain for the sage Nicholas Vedder, with his broad face, double chin, and fair long pipe, uttering clouds of tobacco-smoke instead of idle speeches; or Van Bummel, the schoolmaster, doling forth the contents of an ancient newspaper. In place of these, a lean, bilious-looking fellow, with his pockets full of hand-bills, was haranguing vehemently about rights of citizens—elections— members of congress—liberty—Bunker's Hill—heroes of seventy-six—and other words, which were a perfect Babylonish jargon to the bewildered Van Winkle.

The appearance of Rip, with his long, grizzled beard, his rusty fowling-piece, his uncouth dress, and an army of women and children at his heels, soon attracted the attention of the tavern-politicians. They crowded round him, eying him from head to foot with great curiosity. The orator bustled up to him, and, drawing him partly aside, inquired "On which side he voted?" Rip stared in vacant stupidity. Another short but busy little fellow pulled him by the arm, and, rising on tiptoe, inquired in his ear, "Whether he was Federal or Democrat?" Rip was equally at a loss to comprehend the question; when a knowing, self-important old gentleman, in a sharp cocked hat, made his way through the crowd, putting them to the right and left with his elbows as he passed, and planting himself before Van Winkle, with one arm akimbo, the other resting on his cane, his keen eyes and sharp hat penetrating, as it were, into his very soul, demanded, in an austere tone, "What brought him to the election with a gun on his shoulder, and a mob at his heels; and whether he meant to breed a riot in the village?"—"Alas! gentlemen," cried Rip, somewhat dismayed, "I am a poor quiet man, a native of the place, and a loyal subject of the King, God bless him!"

Here a general shout burst from the by-standers—"A tory! a tory! a spy! a refugee! hustle him! away with him!" It was with great difficulty that the self-important man in the cocked hat restored order; and, having assumed a tenfold austerity of brow, demanded again of the unknown culprit, what he came there for, and whom he was seeking? The poor man humbly assured him that he meant no harm, but merely came there in search of some of his neighbors, who used to keep about the tavern.

"Well—who are they?—name them."

Rip bethought himself a moment, and inquired, "Where's Nicholas Vedder?"

There was a silence for a little while, when an old man replied, in a thin piping voice, "Nicholas Vedder! why, he is dead and gone these eighteen years! There was a wooden tombstone in the churchyard that used to tell all about him, but that's rotten and gone too."

"Where's Brom Dutcher?"

"Oh, he went off to the army in the beginning of the war; some say he was killed at the storming of Stony Point—others say he was drowned in a squall at the foot of Antony's Nose. I don't know—he never came back again."

"Where's Van Bummel, the schoolmaster?"

"He went off to the wars too, was a great militia general, and is now in congress."

Rip's heart died away at hearing of these sad changes in his home and friends, and finding himself thus alone in the world. Every answer puzzled him too, by treating of such enormous lapses of time, and of matters which he could not understand: war—congress—Stony Point;—he had no courage to ask after any more friends, but cried out in despair, "Does nobody here know Rip Van Winkle?"

"Oh, Rip Van Winkle!" exclaimed two or three, "oh, to be sure! that's Rip Van Winkle yonder, leaning against the tree."

Rip looked, and beheld a precise counterpart of himself, as he went up the mountain; apparently as lazy, and certainly as ragged. The poor fellow was now completely confounded. He doubted his own identity, and whether he was himself or another man. In the midst of his bewilderment, the man in the cocked hat demanded who he was, and what was his name.

"God knows," exclaimed he, at his wit's end; "I'm not myself —I'm somebody else—that's me yonder—no—that's somebody else got into my shoes—I was myself last night, but I fell asleep on the mountain, and they've changed my gun, and everything's changed, and I'm changed, and I can't tell what's my name, or who I am!"

The by-standers began now to look at each other nod, wink significantly, and tap their fingers against their foreheads. There was a whisper, also, about securing the gun, and keeping the old fellow from doing mischief, at the very suggestion of which the self-important man in the cocked hat retired with some precipitation. At this critical moment a fresh, comely woman pressed through the throng to get a peep at the gray-bearded man. She had a chubby child in her arms, which, frightened at his looks, began to cry. "Hush, Rip," cried she, "hush, you little fool; the old man won't hurt you." The name of the child, the air of the mother, the tone of her voice, all awakened a train of recollections in his mind. "What is your name, my good woman?" asked he.

"Judith Gardenier."

"And your father's name?"

"Ah, poor man, Rip Van Winkle was his name, but it's twenty years since he went away from home with his gun, and never has been heard of since,—his dog came home without him; but whether he shot himself, or was carried away by the Indians, nobody can tell. I was then but a little girl."

Rip had but one question more to ask; but he put it with a faltering voice:

"Where's your mother?"

"Oh, she too had died but a short time since; she broke a bloodvessel in a fit of passion at a New-England pedler."

There was a drop of comfort, at least, in this intelligence. The honest man could contain himself no longer. He caught his daughter and her child in his arms. "I am your father!" cried he —"Young Rip Van Winkle once—old Rip Van Winkle now!— Does nobody know poor Rip Van Winkle?"

All stood amazed, until an old woman, tottering out from among the crowd, put her hand to her brow, and peering under it in his face for a moment, exclaimed, "Sure enough! it is Rip Van Winkle—it is himself! Welcome home again, old neighbor. Why, where have you been these twenty long years?"

Rip's story was soon told, for the whole twenty years had been to him but as one night. The neighbors stared when they heard it; some were seen to wink at each other, and put their tongues in their cheeks: and the self-important man in the cocked hat, who, when the alarm was over, had returned to the field, screwed down the corners of his mouth, and shook his head—upon which there was a general shaking of the head throughout the assemblage.

It was determined, however, to take the opinion of old Peter

Vanderdonk, who was seen slowly advancing up the road. He was a descendant of the historian of that name, who wrote one of the earliest accounts of the province. Peter was the most ancient inhabitant of the village, and well versed in all the wonderful events and traditions of the neighborhood. He recollected Rip at once, and corroborated his story in the most satisfactory manner. He assured the company that it was a fact, handed down from his ancestor the historian, that the Kaatskill mountains had always been haunted by strange beings. That it was affirmed that the great Hendrick Hudson, the first discoverer of the river and country, kept a kind of vigil there every twenty years, with his crew of the Half-moon; being permitted in this way to revisit the scenes of his enterprise, and keep a guardian eye upon the river and the great city called by his name. That his father had once seen them in their old Dutch dresses playing at ninepins in a hollow of the mountain; and that he himself had heard, one summer afternoon, the sound of their balls, like distant peals of thunder.

To make a long story short, the company broke up and returned to the more important concerns of the election. Rip's daughter took him home to live with her; she had a snug, well-furnished house, and a stout, cheery farmer for a husband, whom Rip recollected for one of the urchins that used to climb upon his back. As to Rip's son and heir, who was the ditto of himself, seen leaning against the tree, he was employed to work on the farm; but evinced an hereditary disposition to attend to anything else but his business.

Rip now resumed his old walks and habits; he soon found many of his former cronies, though all rather the worse for the wear and tear of time; and preferred making friends among the rising generation, with whom he soon grew into great favor.

Having nothing to do at home, and being arrived at that happy age when a man can be idle with impunity, he took his place once more on the bench at the inn-door, and was reverenced as one of the patriarchs of the village, and a chronicle of the old times "before the war." It was some time before he could get into the regular track of gossip, or could be made to comprehend the strange events that had taken place during his torpor. How that there had been a revolutionary war,—that the country had thrown off the yoke of old England,—and that, instead of being a subject of his Majesty George the Third, he was now a free citizen of the United States. Rip, in fact, was no politician; the changes of states and empires made but little impression on him; but there was one species of despotism under which he had long groaned, and that was—petticoat government. Happily that was at an end; he had got his neck out of the yoke of matrimony, and could go in and out whenever he pleased, without dreading the tyranny of Dame Van Winkle. Whenever her name was mentioned, however, he shook his head, shrugged his shoulders, and cast up his eyes; which might pass either for an expression of resignation to his fate, or joy at his deliverance.

He used to tell his story to every stranger that arrived at Mr. Doolittle's hotel. He was observed, at first, to vary on some points every time he told it, which was, doubtless, owing to his having so recently awaked. It at last settled down precisely to the tale I have related, and not a man, woman, or child in the neighborhood but knew it by heart. Some always pretended to doubt the reality of it, and insisted that Rip had been out of his head, and that this was one point on which he always remained flighty. The old Dutch inhabitants, however, almost universally gave it full credit. Even to this day they never hear a thunder-storm of a summer afternoon about the Kaatskill, but they say Hendrick Hudson and his crew are at their game of ninepins; and it is a common wish of all hen-pecked husbands in the neighborhood, when life hangs heavy on their hands, that they might have a quieting draught out of Rip Van Winkle's flagon.

NOTE

The foregoing Tale, one would suspect, had been suggested to Mr. Knickerbocker by a little German superstition about the Emperor Frederick *der Rothbart,* and the Kypphäuser mountain: the subjoined note, however, which he had appended to the tale, shows that it is an absolute fact, narrated with his usual fidelity.

"The story of Rip Van Winkle may seem incredible to many, but nevertheless I give it my full belief, for I know the vicinity of our old Dutch settlements to have been very subject to marvellous events and appearances. Indeed, I have heard many stranger stories than this, in the villages along the Hudson; all of which were too well authenticated to admit of a doubt. I have even talked with Rip Van Winkle myself, who, when last I saw him, was a very venerable old man, and so perfectly rational and consistent on every other point, that I think no conscientious person could refuse to take this into the bargain; nay, I have seen a certificate on the subject taken before a country justice and signed with a cross, in the justice's own handwriting. The story, therefore, is beyond the possibility of doubt.

"D. K."

POSTSCRIPT

The following are travelling notes from a memorandum-book of Mr. Knickerbocker.

The Kaatsberg, or Catskill Mountains, have always been a region full of fable. The Indians considered them the abode of spirits, who influenced the weather, spreading sunshine or clouds over the landscape, and sending good or bad hunting-seasons. They were ruled by an old squaw spirit, said to be their mother. She dwelt on the highest peak of the Catskills, and had charge of the doors of day and night to open and shut them at the proper hour. She hung up the new moons in the skies, and cut up the old ones into stars. In times of drought, if properly propitiated, she would spin light summer clouds out of cobwebs and morning dew, and send them off from the crest of the mountain, flake after flake, like flakes of carded cotton, to float in the air; until, dissolved by the heat of the sun, they would fall in gentle showers, causing the grass to spring, the fruits to ripen, and the corn to grow an inch an hour. If displeased, however, she would brew up clouds black as ink, sitting in the midst of them like a bottle-bellied spider in the midst of its web; and when these clouds broke, woe betide the valleys!

In old times, say the Indian traditions, there was a kind of Manitou or Spirit, who kept about the wildest recesses of the Catskill Mountains, and took a mischievous pleasure in wreaking all kinds of evils and vexations upon the red men. Sometimes he would assume the form of a bear, a panther, or a deer, lead the bewildered hunter a weary chase through tangled forests and among ragged rocks; and then spring off with a loud ho! ho! leaving him aghast on the brink of a beetling precipice or raging torrent.

The favorite abode of this Manitou is still shown. It is a great rock or cliff on the loneliest part of the mountains, and, from the flowering vines which clamber about it, and the wild flowers which abound in its neighborhood, is known by the name of the Garden Rock. Near the foot of it is a small lake, the haunt of the solitary bittern, with water-snakes basking in the sun on the leaves of the pond-lilies which lie on the surface. This place was held in great awe by the Indians, insomuch that the boldest hunter would not pursue his game within its precincts. Once upon a time, however, a hunter who had lost his way, penetrated to the Garden Rock, where he beheld a number of gourds placed in the crotches of trees. One of these he seized and made off with it, but in the hurry of his retreat he let it fall among the rocks, when a great stream gushed forth, which washed him away and swept him down precipices, where he was dashed to pieces, and the stream made its way to the Hudson, and continues to flow to the present day; being the identical stream known by the name of the Kaaters-kill.

THE MUTABILITY OF LITERATURE

A COLLOQUY IN WESTMINSTER ABBEY

I know that all beneath the moon decays,
And what by mortals in this world is brought,
In time's great period shall return to nought.
I know that all the muse's heavenly lays,
With toil of sprite which are so dearly bought,
As idle sounds, of few or none are sought,
That there is nothing lighter than mere praise.

DRUMMOND OF HAWTHORNDEN

THERE ARE CERTAIN half-dreaming moods of mind, in which we naturally steal away from noise and glare, and seek some quiet haunt, where we may indulge our reveries and build our air-castles undisturbed. In such a mood I was loitering about the old gray cloisters of Westminster Abbey, enjoying that luxury of wandering thought which one is apt to dignify with the name of reflection; when suddenly an interruption of madcap boys from Westminster School, playing at football, broke in upon the monastic stillness of the place, making the vaulted passages and mouldering tombs echo with their merriment. I sought to take refuge from their noise by penetrating still deeper into the solitudes of the pile, and applied to one of the vergers for admission to the library. He conducted me through a portal rich with the crumbling sculpture of former ages, which opened upon a gloomy passage leading to the chapter-house and the chamber in which doomsday-book is deposited. Just within the passage is a small door on the left. To this the verger applied a key; it was double locked, and opened with some difficulty, as if seldom used. We now ascended a dark narrow staircase, and, passing through a second door, entered the library.

I found myself in a lofty antique hall, the roof supported by massive joists of old English oak. It was soberly lighted by a row of Gothic windows at a considerable height from the floor, and which apparently opened upon the roofs of the cloisters. An ancient picture of some reverend dignitary of the church in his robes hung over the fireplace. Around the hall and in a small gallery were the books, arranged in carved oaken cases. They consisted principally of old polemical writers, and were much more worn by time than use. In the centre of the library was a solitary table with two or three books on it, an inkstand without ink, and a few pens parched by long disuse. The place seemed fitted for quiet study and profound meditation. It was buried deep among the massive walls of the abbey, and shut up from the tumult of the world. I could only hear now and then the shouts of the school-boys faintly swelling from the cloisters, and the sound of a bell tolling for prayers, echoing soberly along the roofs of the abbey. By degrees the shouts of merriment grew fainter and fainter, and at length died away; the bell ceased to toll, and a profound silence reigned through the dusky hall.

I had taken down a little thick quarto, curiously bound in parchment, with brass clasps, and seated myself at the table in a venerable elbow-chair. Instead of reading, however, I was beguiled by the solemn monastic air, and lifeless quiet of the place, into a train of musing. As I looked around upon the old volumes in their mouldering covers, thus ranged on the shelves, and apparently never disturbed in their repose, I could not but consider the library a kind of literary catacomb, where authors, like mummies, are piously entombed, and left to blacken and moulder in dusty oblivion.

How much, thought I, has each of these volumes, now thrust aside with such indifference, cost some aching head! how many weary days! how many sleepless nights! How have their authors buried themselves in the solitude of cells and cloisters; shut themselves up from the face of man, and the still more blessed face of nature; and devoted themselves to painful research and intense reflection! And all for what? to occupy an inch of dusty shelf,—to have the title of their works read now and then in a future age, by some drowsy churchman or casual straggler like myself; and in another age to be lost, even to remembrance. Such is the amount of this boasted immortality. A mere temporary rumor, a local sound; like the tone of that bell which has just tolled among these towers, filling the ear for a moment—lingering transiently in echo—and then passing away like a thing that was not!

While I sat half murmuring, half meditating these unprofitable speculations, with my head resting on my hand, I was thrumming with the other hand upon the quarto, until I accidentally loosened the clasps; when, to my utter astonishment, the little book gave two or three yawns, like one awaking from a deep sleep; then a husky hem; and at length began to talk. At first its voice was very hoarse and broken, being much troubled by a cobweb which some studious spider had woven across it; and having probably contracted a cold from long exposure to the chills and damps of the abbey. In a short time, however, it became more distinct, and I soon found it an exceedingly fluent, conversable little tome. Its language, to be sure, was rather quaint and obsolete, and its pronunciation, what, in the present day, would be deemed barbarous; but I shall endeavor, as far as I am able, to render it in modern parlance.

It began with railings about the neglect of the world—about merit being suffered to languish in obscurity, and other such commonplace topics of literary repining, and complained bitterly that it had not been opened for more than two centuries. That the dean only looked now and then into the library, sometimes took down a volume or two, trifled with them for a few moments, and then returned them to their shelves. "What a plague do they mean," said the little quarto, which I began to perceive was somewhat choleric, "what a plague do they mean by keeping several thousand volumes of us shut up here, and watched by a set of old vergers, like so many beauties in a harem, merely to be looked at now and then by the dean? Books were written to give pleasure and to be enjoyed; and I would have a rule passed that the dean should pay each of us a visit at least once a year; or, if he is not equal to the task, let them once in a while turn loose the whole School of Westminster among us, that at any rate we may now and then have an airing."

"Softly, my worthy friend," replied I; "you are not aware how much better you are off than most books of your generation. By being stored away in this ancient library, you are like the treasured remains of those saints and monarchs which lie enshrined in the adjoining chapels; while the remains of your contemporary mortals, left to the ordinary course of nature, have long since returned to dust."

"Sir," said the little tome, ruffling his leaves and looking big, "I was written for all the world, not for the bookworms of an abbey. I was intended to circulate from hand to hand, like other great contemporary works; but here have I been clasped up for more than two centuries, and might have silently fallen a prey to these worms that are playing the very vengeance with my intestines, if you had not by chance given me an opportunity of uttering a few last words before I go to pieces."

"My good friend," rejoined I, "had you been left to the circulation of which you speak, you would long ere this have been no more. To judge from your physiognomy, you are now well stricken in years: very few of your contemporaries can be at present in existence; and those few owe their longevity to being immured like yourself in old libraries; which, suffer me to add, instead of likening to harems, you might more properly and gratefully have compared to those infirmaries attached to religious establishments, for the benefit of the old and decrepit, and where, by quiet fostering and no employment, they often endure to an amazingly good-for-nothing old age. You talk of your contemporaries as if in circulation,—where do we meet with their works? What do we hear of Robert Groteste, of Lincoln? No one could have toiled harder than he for immortality. He is said to have written nearly two hundred volumes. He built, as it were, a pyramid of books to perpetuate his name; but, alas! the pyramid has long since fallen, and only a few fragments are scattered in various libraries, where they are scarcely disturbed even by the antiquarian. What do we hear of Giraldus Cambrensis, the historian, antiquary, philosopher, theologian, and poet? He declined two bishoprics, that he might shut himself up and write for posterity: but posterity never inquires after his labors. What of Henry of Huntingdon, who, besides a learned history of England, wrote a

treatise on the contempt of the world, which the world has revenged by forgetting him? What is quoted of Joseph of Exeter,
styled the miracle of his age in classical composition? Of his three
great heroic poems one is lost forever, excepting a mere fragment;
the others are known only to a few of the curious in literature;
and as to his love-verses and epigrams, they have entirely disappeared. What is in current use of John Wallis, the Franciscan,
who acquired the name of the tree of life? Of William of Malms-
bury;—of Simeon of Durham;—of Benedict of Peterborough;—
of John Hanvill of St. Albans;—of——"

"Prithee, friend," cried the quarto, in a testy tone, "how old do
you think me? You are talking of authors that lived long before
my time, and wrote either in Latin or French, so that they in a
manner expatriated themselves, and deserved to be forgotten;*
but I, sir, was ushered into the world from the press of the renowned Wynkyn de Worde. I was written in my own native
tongue, at a time when the language had become fixed; and indeed I was considered a model of pure and elegant English."

(I should observe that these remarks were couched in such
intolerably antiquated terms, that I have had infinite difficulty
in rendering them into modern phraseology.)

"I cry your mercy," said I, "for mistaking your age; but it
matters little: almost all the writers of your time have likewise
passed into forgetfulness; and De Worde's publications are mere
literary rarities among book-collectors. The purity and stability
of language, too, on which you found your claims to perpetuity,
have been the fallacious dependence of authors of every age, even
back to the times of the worthy Robert of Gloucester, who wrote
his history in rhymes of mongrel Saxon.† Even now many talk of

---

* In Latin and French hath many soueraine wittes had great delyte to
endite, and have many noble thinges fulfilde, but certes there ben some that
speaken their poisye in French, of which speche the Frenchmen have as
good a fantasye as we have in hearying of Frenchmen's Englishe.—CHAUCER:
Testament of Love.

† Holinshed, in his Chronicle, observes, "afterwards, also, by deligent travell
of Geffry Chaucer and of John Gowre, in the time of Richard the Second,
and after them of John Scogan and John Lydgate, monke of Berrie, our
said toong was brought to an excellent passe, notwithstanding that it never
came unto the type of perfection until the time of Queen Elizabeth, wherein

Spenser's 'Well of pure English undefiled' as if the language ever sprang from a well or fountain-head, and was not rather a mere confluence of various tongues, perpetually subject to changes and intermixtures. It is this which has made English literature so extremely mutable, and the reputation built upon it so fleeting. Unless thought can be committed to something more permanent and unchangeable than such a medium, even thought must share the fate of everything else, and fall into decay. This should serve as a check upon the vanity and exultation of the most popular writer. He finds the language in which he has embarked his fame gradually altering, and subject to the dilapidations of time and the caprice of fashion. He looks back and beholds the early authors of his country, once the favorites of their day, supplanted by modern writers. A few short ages have covered them with obscurity, and their merits can only be relished by the quaint taste of the bookworm. And such, he anticipates, will be the fate of his own work, which, however it may be admired in its day, and held up as a model of purity, will in the course of years grow antiquated and obsolete; until it shall become almost as unintelligible in its native land as an Egyptian obelisk, or one of those Runic inscriptions said to exist in the deserts of Tartary. I declare," added I, with some emotion, "when I contemplate a modern library, filled with new works, in all the bravery of rich gilding and binding, I feel disposed to sit down and weep; like the good Xerxes when he surveyed his army, pranked out in all the splendor of military array, and reflected that in one hundred years not one of them would be in existence!"

"Ah," said the little quarto, with a heavy sigh, "I see how it is; these modern scribblers have superseded all the good old authors. I suppose nothing is read nowadays but Sir Philip Sydney's 'Arcadia,' Sackville's stately plays, and 'Mirror for Magistrates,' or the fine-spun euphuisms of the 'unparalleled John Lyly.'"

"There you are again mistaken," said I; "the writers whom you suppose in vogue, because they happened to be so when you

---

John Jewell, Bishop of Sarum, John Fox, and sundrie learned and excellent writers, have fully accomplished the ornature of the same, to their great praise and immortal commendation."

were last in circulation, have long since had their day. Sir Philip Sydney's 'Arcadia,' the immortality of which was so fondly predicted by his admirers,* and which, in truth, is full of noble thoughts, delicate images, and graceful turns of language, is now scarcely ever mentioned. Sackville has strutted into obscurity; and even Lyly, though his writings were once the delight of a court, and apparently perpetuated by a proverb, is now scarcely known even by name. A whole crowd of authors who wrote and wrangled at the time, have likewise gone down, with all their writings and their controversies. Wave after wave of succeeding literature has rolled over them, until they are buried so deep, that it is only now and then that some industrious diver after fragments of antiquity brings up a specimen for the gratification of the curious.

"For my part," I continued, "I consider this mutability of language a wise precaution of Providence for the benefit of the world at large, and of authors in particular. To reason from analogy, we daily behold the varied and beautiful tribes of vegetables springing up, flourishing, adorning the fields for a short time, and then fading into dust, to make way for their successors. Were not this the case, the fecundity of nature would be a grievance instead of a blessing. The earth would groan with rank and excessive vegetation, and its surface become a tangled wilderness. In like manner the works of genius and learning decline, and make way for subsequent productions. Language gradually varies, and with it fade away the writings of authors who have flourished their allotted time; otherwise, the creative powers of genius would overstock the world, and the mind would be completely bewildered in the endless mazes of literature. Formerly there were some restraints on this excessive multiplication. Works had to be transcribed by hand, which was a slow and laborious operation;

* Live ever sweete booke; the simple image of his gentle witt, and the golden-pillar of his noble courage; and ever notify unto the world that thy writer was the secretary of eloquence, the breath of the muses, the honeybee of the daintyest flowers of witt and arte, the pith of morale and intellectual virtues, the arme of Bellona in the field, the tonge of Suada in the chamber, the sprite of Practise in esse, and the paragon of excellency in print.—HARVEY PIERCE: *Supererogation.*

they were written either on parchment, which was expensive, so that one work was often erased to make way for another; or on papyrus, which was fragile and extremely perishable. Authorship was a limited and unprofitable craft, pursued chiefly by monks in the leisure and solitude of their cloisters. The accumulation of manuscripts was slow and costly, and confined almost entirely to monasteries. To these circumstances it may, in some measure, be owing that we have not been inundated by the intellect of antiquity; that the fountains of thought have not been broken up, and modern genius drowned in the deluge. But the inventions of paper and the press have put an end to all these restraints. They have made every one a writer, and enabled every mind to pour itself into print, and diffuse itself over the whole intellectual world. The consequences are alarming. The stream of literature has swollen into a torrent—augmented into a river—expanded into a sea. A few centuries since, five or six hundred manuscripts constituted a great library; but what would you say to libraries such as actually exist containing three or four hundred thousand volumes; legions of authors at the same time busy; and the press going on with activity, to double and quadruple the number? Unless some unforeseen mortality should break out among the progeny of the muse, now that she has become so prolific, I tremble for posterity. I fear the mere fluctuation of language will not be sufficient. Criticism may do much. It increases with the increase of literature, and resembles one of those salutary checks on population spoken of by economists. All possible encouragement, therefore, should be given to the growth of critics, good or bad. But I fear all will be in vain; let criticism do what it may, writers will write, printers will print, and the world will inevitably be overstocked with good books. It will soon be the employment of a lifetime merely to learn their names. Many a man of passable information, at the present day, reads scarcely anything but reviews; and before long a man of erudition will be little better than a mere walking catalogue."

"My very good sir," said the little quarto, yawning most drearily in my face, "excuse my interrupting you, but I perceive you are rather given to prose. I would ask the fate of an author who was making some noise just as I left the world. His reputation, however, was considered quite temporary. The learned shook their heads at him, for he was a poor half-educated varlet, that knew little of Latin, and nothing of Greek, and had been obliged to run the country for deer-stealing. I think his name was Shakspeare. I presume he soon sunk into oblivion."

"On the contrary," said I, "it is owing to that very man that the literature of his period has experienced a duration beyond the ordinary term of English literature. There rise authors now and then, who seem proof against the mutability of language, because they have rooted themselves in the unchanging principles of human nature. They are like gigantic trees that we sometimes see on the banks of a stream; which, by their vast and deep roots, penetrating through the mere surface, and laying hold on the very foundations of the earth, preserve the soil around them from being swept away by the ever-flowing current, and hold up many a neighboring plant, and, perhaps, worthless weed, to perpetuity. Such is the case with Shakspeare, whom we behold defying the encroachments of time, retaining in modern use the language and literature of his day, and giving duration to many an indifferent author, merely from having flourished in his vicinity. But even he, I grieve to say, is gradually assuming the tint of age, and his whole form is overrun by a profusion of commentators, who, like clambering vines and creepers, almost bury the noble plant that upholds them."

Here the little quarto began to heave his sides and chuckle, until at length he broke out in a plethoric fit of laughter that had wellnigh choked him, by reason of his excessive corpulency. "Mighty well!" cried he, as soon as he could recover breath, "mighty well! and so you would persuade me that the literature of an age is to be perpetuated by a vagabond deer-stealer! by a man without learning; by a poet, forsooth—a poet!" And here he wheezed forth another fit of laughter.

I confess that I felt somewhat nettled at this rudeness, which, however, I pardoned on account of his having flourished in a less polished age. I determined, nevertheless, not to give up my point.

"Yes," resumed I, positively, "a poet; for of all writers he has the best chance for immortality. Others may write from the head, but he writes from the heart, and the heart will always understand him. He is the faithful portrayer of nature, whose features are always the same, and always interesting. Prose-writers are voluminous and unwieldy; their pages are crowded with commonplaces, and their thoughts expanded into tediousness. But with the true poet everything is terse, touching, or brilliant. He gives the choicest thoughts in the choicest language. He illustrates them by everything that he sees most striking in nature and art. He enriches them by pictures of human life, such as it is passing before him. His writings, therefore, contain the spirit, the aroma, if I may use the phrase, of the age in which he lives. They are caskets which enclose within a small compass the wealth of the language,—its family jewels, which are thus transmitted in a portable form to posterity. The setting may occasionally be antiquated, and require now and then to be renewed, as in the case of Chaucer; but the brilliancy and intrinsic value of the gems continue unaltered. Cast a look back over the long reach of literary history. What vast valleys of dulness, filled with monkish legends and academical controversies! what bogs of theological speculations! what dreary wastes of metaphysics. Here and there only do we behold the heaven-illuminated bards, elevated like beacons on their widely separate heights, to transmit the pure light of poetical intelligence from age to age." *

I was just about to launch forth into eulogiums upon the poets of the day, when the sudden opening of the door caused me to turn my head. It was the verger, who came to inform me that it

* Thorow earth and waters deepe,
   The pen by skill doth passe:
And featly nyps the worldes abuse,
   And shoes us in a glasse,
The vertu and the vice
   Of every wight alyve;
The honey comb that bee doth make
   Is not so sweet in hyve,
As are the golden leves
   That drop from poet's head!
Which doth surmount our common talke
   As farre as dross doth lead.
              Churchyard.

was time to close the library. I sought to have a parting word with the quarto, but the worthy little tome was silent; the clasps were closed; and it looked perfectly unconscious of all that had passed. I have been to the library two or three times since, and have endeavored to draw it into further conversation, but in vain; and whether all this rambling colloquy actually took place, or whether it was another of those odd day-dreams to which I am subject, I have never to this moment been able to discover.

THE SPECTRE BRIDEGROOM

A TRAVELLER'S TALE*

> He that supper for is dight,
> He lyes full cold, I trow, this night!
> Yestreen to chamber I him led,
> This night Gray-Steel has made his bed.
>
> SIR EGER, SIR GRAHAME, AND SIR GRAY-STEEL

ON THE SUMMIT OF ONE of the heights of the Odenwald, a wild and romantic tract of Upper Germany, that lies not far from the confluence of the Main and the Rhine, there stood, many, many years since, the Castle of the Baron Von Landshort. It is now quite fallen to decay, and almost buried among beech-trees and dark firs; above which, however, its old watchtower may still be seen, struggling, like the former possessor I have mentioned, to carry a high head, and look down upon the neighboring country.

The baron was a dry branch of the great family of Katzenellenbogen,† and inherited the relics of the property, and all the pride

---

* The erudite reader, well versed in good-for-nothing lore, will perceive that the above Tale must have been suggested to the old Swiss by a little French anecdote, a circumstance said to have taken place at Paris.

† *I. e.* CAT'S-ELBOW. The name of a family of those parts very powerful in former times. The appellation, we are told, was given in compliment to a peerless dame of the family, celebrated for her fine arm.

of his ancestors. Though the warlike disposition of his predecessors had much impaired the family possessions, yet the baron still endeavored to keep up some show of former state. The times were peaceable, and the German nobles, in general, had abandoned their inconvenient old castles, perched like eagles' nests among the mountains, and had built more convenient residences in the valleys: still the baron remained proudly drawn up in his little fortress, cherishing, with hereditary inveteracy, all the old family feuds; so that he was on ill terms with some of his nearest neighbors, on account of dispute that had happened between their great-great-grandfathers.

The baron had but one child, a daughter; but nature, when she grants but one child, always compensates by making it a prodigy; and so it was with the daughter of the baron. All the nurses, gossips, and country cousins assured her father that she had not her equal for beauty in all Germany; and who should know better than they? She had, moreover, been brought up with great care under the superintendence of two maiden aunts, who had spent some years of their early life at one of the little German courts, and were skilled in all the branches of knowledge necessary to the education of a fine lady. Under their instructions she became a miracle of accomplishments. By the time she was eighteen, she could embroider to admiration, and had worked whole histories of the saints in tapestry, with such strength of expression in their countenances, that they looked like so many souls in purgatory. She could read without great difficulty, and had spelled her way through several church legends, and almost all the chivalric wonders of the Heldenbuch. She had even made considerable proficiency in writing; could sign her own name without missing a letter, and so legibly, that her aunts could read it without spectacles. She excelled in making little elegant good-for-nothing ladylike knickknacks of all kinds; was versed in the most abstruse dancing of the day; played a number of airs on the harp and guitar; and knew all the tender ballads of the Minnelieders by heart.

Her aunts, too, having been great flirts and coquettes in their younger days, were admirably calculated to be vigilant guardians and strict censors of the conduct of their niece; for there is no duenna so rigidly prudent, and inexorably decorous, as a superannuated coquette. She was rarely suffered out of their sight; never went beyond the domains of the castle, unless well attended, or rather well watched; had continual lectures read to her about strict decorum and implicit obedience; and, as to the men—pah!—she was taught to hold them at such a distance, and in such absolute distrust, that, unless properly authorized, she would not have cast a glance upon the handsomest cavalier in the world—no, not if he were even dying at her feet.

The good effects of this system were wonderfully apparent. The young lady was a pattern of docility and correctness. While others were wasting their sweetness in the glare of the world, and liable to be plucked and thrown aside by every hand, she was coyly blooming into fresh and lovely womanhood under the protection of those immaculate spinsters like a rose-bud blushing forth among guardian thorns. Her aunts looked upon her with pride and exultation, and vaunted that though all the other young ladies in the world might go astray, yet, thank Heaven, nothing of the kind could happen to the heiress of Katzenellenbogen.

But, however scantily the Baron Von Landshort might be provided with children, his household was by no means a small one; for Providence had enriched him with abundance of poor relations. They, one and all, possessed the affectionate disposition common to humble relatives; were wonderfully attached to the baron, and took every possible occasion to come in swarms and enliven the castle. All family festivals were commemorated by these good people at the baron's expense; and when they were filled with good cheer, they would declare that there was nothing on earth so delightful as these family meetings, these jubilees of the heart.

The baron, though a small man, had a large soul, and it swelled with satisfaction at the consciousness of being the greatest man in the little world about him. He loved to tell long stories about the dark old warriors whose portraits looked grimly down from the walls around, and he found no listeners equal to those who fed at his expense. He was much given to the marvellous, and a firm believer in all those supernatural tales with which every mountain and valley in Germany abounds. The faith of his guests exceeded even his own: they listened to every tale of wonder with open eyes and mouth, and never failed to be astonished, even though repeated for the hundredth time. Thus lived the Baron Von Landshort, the oracle of his table, the absolute monarch of his little territory, and happy, above all things, in the persuasion that he was the wisest man of the age.

At the time of which my story treats, there was a great family-gathering at the castle, on an affair of the utmost importance: it was to receive the destined bridegroom of the baron's daughter. A negotiation had been carried on between the father and an old nobleman of Bavaria, to unite the dignity of their houses by the marriage of their children. The preliminaries had been conducted with proper punctilio. The young people were betrothed without seeing each other; and the time was appointed for the marriage ceremony. The young Count Von Altenburg had been recalled from the army for the purpose, and was actually on his way to the baron's to receive his bride. Missives had even been received from him, from Würtzburg, where he was accidentally detained, mentioning the day and hour when he might be expected to arrive.

The castle was in a tumult of preparation to give him a suitable welcome. The fair bride had been decked out with uncommon care. The two aunts had superintended her toilet, and quarrelled the whole morning about every article of her dress. The young lady had taken advantage of their contest to follow the bent of her own taste; and fortunately it was a good one. She looked as lovely as youthful bridegroom could desire; and the flutter of expectation heightened the lustre of her charms.

The suffusions that mantled her face and neck, the gentle heaving of the bosom, the eye now and then lost in reverie, all betrayed the soft tumult that was going on in her little heart. The aunts were continually hovering around her; for maiden aunts are apt to take great interest in affairs of this nature. They were giving her a world of staid counsel how to deport herself, what to say, and in what manner to receive the expected lover.

The baron was no less busied in preparations. He had, in truth, nothing exactly to do; but he was naturally a fuming, bustling little man, and could not remain passive when all the world was in a hurry. He worried from top to bottom of the castle with an air of infinite anxiety; he continually called the servants from their work to exhort them to be diligent; and buzzed about every hall and chamber, as idly restless and importunate as a blue-bottle fly on a warm summer's day.

In the mean time the fatted calf had been killed; the forests had rung with the clamor of the huntsmen; the kitchen was crowded with good cheer; the cellars had yielded up whole oceans of *Rheinwein* and *Ferne-wein;* and even the great Heidelberg tun had been laid under contribution. Everything was ready to receive the distinguished guest with *Saus und Braus* in the true spirit of German hospitality;—but the guest delayed to make his appearance. Hour rolled after hour. The sun, that had poured his downward rays upon the rich forest of the Odenwald, now just gleamed along the summits of the mountains. The baron mounted the highest tower, and strained his eyes in hope of catching a distant sight of the count and his attendants. Once he thought he beheld them; the sound of horns came floating from the valley, prolonged by the mountain echoes. A number of horsemen were seen far below, slowly advancing along the road; but when they had nearly reached the foot of the mountain, they suddenly struck off in a different direction. The last ray of sunshine departed,—the bats began to flit by in the twilight,—the road grew dimmer and dimmer to the view, and nothing appeared stirring in it but now and then a peasant lagging homeward from his labor.

While the old castle of Landshort was in this state of perplexity, a very interesting scene was transacting in a different part of the Odenwald.

The young Count Von Altenburg was tranquilly pursuing his route in that sober jog-trot way, in which a man travels toward matrimony when his friends have taken all the trouble and uncertainty of courtship off his hands, and a bride is waiting for him, as certainly as a dinner at the end of his journey. He had encountered at Würtzburg a youthful companion in arms, with whom he had seen some service on the frontiers,—Herman Von Starkenfaust, one of the stoutest hands and worthiest hearts of German chivalry, who was now returning from the army. His father's castle was not far distant from the old fortress of Landshort, although an hereditary feud rendered the families hostile, and strangers to each other.

In the warm-hearted moment of recognition, the young friends related all their past adventures and fortunes, and the count gave the whole history of his intended nuptials with a young lady whom he had never seen, but of whose charms he had received the most enrapturing descriptions.

As the route of the friends lay in the same direction, they agreed to perform the rest of their journey together; and, that they might do it the more leisurely, set off from Würtzburg at an early hour, the count having given directions for his retinue to follow and overtake him.

They beguiled their wayfaring with recollections of their military scenes and adventures; but the count was apt to be a little tedious, now and then, about the reputed charms of his bride, and the felicity that awaited him.

In this way they had entered among the mountains of the Odenwald, and were traversing one of its most lonely and thickly-wooded passes. It is well known that the forests of Germany have always been as much infested by robbers as its castles by spectres; and, at this time, the former were particularly numerous, from the hordes of disbanded soldiers wandering about the country. It will not appear extraordinary, therefore, that the cavaliers were attacked by a gang of these stragglers, in the midst of the forest. They defended themselves with bravery, but were nearly overpowered, when the count's retinue arrived to their assistance. At sight of them the robbers fled, but not until the count had received a mortal wound. He was slowly and carefully conveyed back to the city of Würtzburg, and a friar summoned from a neighboring convent, who was famous for his skill in administering to both soul and body; but half of his skill was superfluous; the moments of the unfortunate count were numbered.

With his dying breath he entreated his friend to repair instantly to the castle of Landshort, and explain the fatal cause of his not keeping his appointment with his bride. Though not the most ardent of lovers, he was one of the most punctilious of men, and appeared earnestly solicitous that his mission should be speedily and courteously executed. "Unless this is done," said he, "I shall not sleep quietly in my grave!" He repeated these last words with peculiar solemnity. A request, at a moment so impressive, admitted no hesitation. Starkenfaust endeavored to soothe him to calmness; promised faithfully to execute his wish, and gave him his hand in solemn pledge. The dying man pressed it in acknowledgment, but soon lapsed into delirium—raved about his bride—his engagements—his plighted word; ordered his horse, that he might ride to the castle of Landshort; and expired in the fancied act of vaulting into the saddle.

Starkenfaust bestowed a sigh and a soldier's tear on the untimely fate of his comrade; and then pondered on the awkward mission he had undertaken. His heart was heavy, and his head perplexed; for he was to present himself an unbidden guest among hostile people, and to damp their festivity with tidings fatal to their hopes. Still there were certain whisperings of curiosity in his bosom to see this far-famed beauty of Katzenellenbogen, so cautiously shut up from the world; for he was a passionate admirer of the sex, and there was a dash of eccentricity and enterprise in his character that made him fond of all singular adventure.

Previous to his departure he made all due arrangements with the holy fraternity of the convent for the funeral solemnities of his friend, who was to be buried in the cathedral of Würtzburg, near some of his illustrious relatives; and the mourning retinue of the count took charge of his remains.

It is now high time that we should return to the ancient family of Katzenellenbogen, who were impatient for their guest, and still more for their dinner; and to the worthy little baron, whom we left airing himself on the watch-tower.

Night closed in, but still no guest arrived. The baron descended from the tower in despair. The banquet, which had been delayed from hour to hour, could no longer be postponed. The meats were already overdone; the cook in an agony; and the whole household had the look of a garrison that had been reduced by famine.

The baron was obliged reluctantly to give orders for the feast without the presence of the guest. All were seated at table, and just on the point of commencing, when the sound of a horn from without the gate gave notice of the approach of a stranger. Another long blast filled the old courts of the castle with its echoes, and was answered by the warder from the walls. The baron hastened to receive his future son-in-law.

The drawbridge had been let down, and the stranger was before the gate. He was a tall, gallant cavalier, mounted on a black steed. His countenance was pale, but he had a beaming, romantic eye, and an air of stately melancholy. The baron was a little mortified that he should have come in this simple, solitary style. His dignity for a moment was ruffled, and he felt disposed to consider it a want of proper respect for the important occasion, and the important family with which he was to be connected. He pacified himself, however, with the conclusion, that it must have been youthful impatience which had induced him thus to spur on sooner than his attendants.

"I am sorry," said the stranger, "to break in upon you thus unseasonably"——

Here the baron interrupted him with a world of compliments and greetings; for, to tell the truth, he prided himself upon his courtesy and eloquence. The stranger attempted, once or twice, to stem the torrent of words, but in vain, so he bowed his head and suffered it to flow on. By the time the baron had come to a pause, they had reached the inner court of the castle; and the stranger was again about to speak, when he was once more interrupted by the appearance of the female part of the family, leading forth the shrinking and blushing bride. He gazed on her for a moment as one entranced; it seemed as if his whole soul beamed forth in the gaze, and rested upon that lovely form. One of the maiden aunts whispered something in her ear; she made an effort to speak; her moist blue eye was timidly raised; gave a shy glance of inquiry on the stranger; and was cast again to the ground. The words died away; but there was a sweet smile playing about her lips, and a soft dimpling of the cheek that showed her glance had not been unsatisfactory. It was impossible for a girl

of the fond age of eighteen, highly predisposed for love and matrimony, not to be pleased with so gallant a cavalier.

The late hour at which the guest had arrived left no time for
parley. The baron was peremptory, and deferred all particular
conversation until the morning, and led the way to the untasted
banquet.

It was served up in the great hall of the castle. Around the walls
hung the hard-favored portaits of the heroes of the house of Katzenellenbogen, and the trophies which they had gained in the field
and in the chase. Hacked corselets, splintered jousting spears,
and tattered banners, were mingled with the spoils of sylvan warfare; the jaws of the wolf, and the tusks of the boar, grinned horribly among cross-bows and battle-axes, and a huge pair of antlers
branched immediately over the head of the youthful bridegroom.

The cavalier took but little notice of the company or the entertainment. He scarcely tasted the banquet, but seemed absorbed
in admiration of his bride. He conversed in a low tone that could
not be overheard—for the language of love is never loud; but
where is the female ear so dull that it cannot catch the softest
whisper of the lover? There was a mingled tenderness and gravity
in his manner, that appeared to have a powerful effect upon the
young lady. Her color came and went as she listened with deep
attention. Now and then she made some blushing reply, and when
his eye was turned away, she would steal a sidelong glance at his
romantic countenance, and heave a gentle sigh of tender happiness.
It was evident that the young couple were completely enamored.
The aunts, who were deeply versed in the mysteries of the heart,
declared that they had fallen in love with each other at first sight.

The feast went on merrily, or at least noisily, for the guests
were all blessed with those keen appetites that attend upon light
purses and mountain-air. The baron told his best and longest stories, and never had he told them so well, or with such great effect.
If there was anything marvellous, his auditors were lost in astonishment; and if anything facetious, they were sure to laugh
exactly in the right place. The baron, it is true, like most great
men, was too dignified to utter any joke but a dull one; it was always enforced, however, by a bumper of excellent Hockheimer;

and even a dull joke, at one's own table, served up with jolly old wine, is irresistible. Many good things were said by poorer and keener wits, that would not bear repeating, except on similar occasions; many sly speeches whispered in ladies' ears, that almost convulsed them with suppressed laughter; and a song or two roared out by a poor, but merry and broad-faced cousin of the baron, that absolutely made the maiden aunts hold up their fans.

Amidst all this revelry, the stranger guest maintained a most singular and unseasonable gravity. His countenance assumed a deeper cast of dejection as the evening advanced; and, strange as it may appear, even the baron's jokes seemed only to render him the more melancholy. At times he was lost in thought, and at times there was a perturbed and restless wandering of the eye that bespoke a mind but ill at ease. His conversations with the bride became more and more earnest and mysterious. Lowering clouds began to steal over the fair serenity of her brow, and tremors to run through her tender frame.

All this could not escape the notice of the company. Their gayety was chilled by the unaccountable gloom of the bridegroom; their spirits were infected; whispers and glances were interchanged, accompanied by shrugs and dubious shakes of the head. The song and the laugh grew less and less frequent; there were dreary pauses in the conversation, which were at length succeeded by wild tales and supernatural legends. One dismal story produced another still more dismal, and the baron nearly frightened some of the ladies into hysterics with the history of the goblin horseman that carried away the fair Leonora; a dreadful story, which has since been put into excellent verse, and is read and believed by all the world.

The bridegroom listened to this tale with profound attention. He kept his eyes steadily fixed on the baron, and, as the story drew to a close, began gradually to rise from his seat, growing taller and taller, until, in the baron's entranced eye, he seemed almost to tower into a giant. The moment the tale was finished, he heaved a deep sigh, and took a solemn farewell of the company. They were all amazement. The baron was perfectly thunderstruck.

"What! going to leave the castle at midnight? why, everything was prepared for his reception; a chamber was ready for him if he wished to retire."

The stranger shook his head mournfully and mysteriously; "I must lay my head in a different chamber to-night!"

There was something in this reply, and the tone in which it was uttered, that made the baron's heart misgive him; but he rallied his forces, and repeated his hospitable entreaties.

The stranger shook his head silently, but positively, at every offer; and, waving his farewell to the company, stalked slowly out of the hall. The maiden aunts were absolutely petrified; the bride hung her head, and a tear stole to her eye.

The baron followed the stranger to the great court of the castle, where the black charger stood pawing the earth, and snorting with impatience.—When they had reached the portal, whose deep archway was dimly lighted by a cresset, the stranger paused, and addressed the baron in a hollow tone of voice, which the vaulted roof rendered still more sepulchral.

"Now that we are alone," said he, "I will impart to you the reason of my going. I have a solemn, an indispensable engagement"—

"Why," said the baron, "cannot you send some one in your place?"

"It admits of no substitute— I must attend it in person— I must away to Würtzburg cathedral"—

"Ay," said the baron, plucking up spirit, "but not until to-morrow—to-morrow you shall take your bride there."

"No! no!" replied the stranger, with tenfold solemnity, "my engagement is with no bride—the worms! the worms expect me! I am a dead man—I have been slain by robbers—my body lies at Würtzburg—at midnight I am to be buried—the grave is waiting for me—I must keep my appointment!"

He sprang on his black charger, dashed over the drawbridge, and the clattering of his horse's hoofs was lost in the whistling of the night-blast.

The baron returned to the hall in the utmost consternation, and related what had passed. Two ladies fainted outright, others sickened at the idea of having banqueted with a spectre. It was the opinion of some, that this might be the wild huntsman, famous in German legend. Some talked of mountain sprites, of wood-demons, and of other supernatural beings, with which the good people of Germany have been so grievously harassed since time immemorial. One of the poor relations ventured to suggest that it might be some sportive evasion of the young cavalier, and that the very gloominess of the caprice seemed to accord with so melancholy a personage. This, however, drew on him the indignation of the whole company, and especially of the baron, who looked upon him as little better than an infidel; so that he was fain to abjure his heresy as speedily as possibly, and come into the faith of the true believers.

But whatever may have been the doubts entertained, they were completely put to an end by the arrival, next day, of regular missives, confirming the intelligence of the young count's murder, and his interment in Würtzburg cathedral.

The dismay at the castle may well be imagined. The baron shut himself up in his chamber. The guests, who had come to rejoice with him, could not think of abandoning him in his distress. They wandered about the courts, or collected in groups in the hall, shaking their heads and shrugging their shoulders, at the troubles of so good a man; and sat longer than ever at table, and ate and drank more stoutly than ever, by way of keeping up their spirits. But the situation of the widowed bride was the most pitiable. To have lost a husband before she had even embraced him—and such a husband! if the very spectre could be so gracious and noble, what must have been the living man. She filled the house with lamentations.

On the night of the second day of her widowhood, she had retired to her chamber, accompanied by one of her aunts, who insisted on sleeping with her. The aunt, who was one of the best tellers of ghost-stories in all Germany, had just been recounting one of her longest, and had fallen asleep in the very midst of it. The chamber was remote, and overlooked a small garden. The niece lay pensively gazing at the beams of the rising moon, as they trembled on the leaves of an aspen-tree before the lattice. The castle-clock had just tolled midnight, when a soft strain of music stole up from the garden. She rose hastily from her bed, and stepped lightly to the window. A tall figure stood among the shadows of the trees. As it raised its head, a beam of moonlight fell upon the countenance. Heaven and earth! she beheld the Spectre Bridegroom! A loud shriek at that moment burst upon her ear, and her aunt, who had been awakened by the music, and had followed her silently to the window, fell into her arms. When she looked again, the spectre had disappeared.

Of the two females, the aunt now required the most soothing, for she was perfectly beside herself with terror. As to the young lady, there was something, even in the spectre of her lover, that seemed endearing. There was still the semblance of manly beauty; and though the shadow of a man is but little calculated to satisfy the affections of a lovesick girl yet, where the substance is not to be had, even that is consoling. The aunt declared she would never sleep in that chamber again; the niece, for once, was refractory, and declared as strongly that she would sleep in no other in the castle: the consequence was, that she had to sleep in it alone; but she drew a promise from her aunt not to relate the story of the spectre, lest she should be denied the only melancholy pleasure left her on earth—that of inhabiting the chamber over which the guardian shade of her lover kept its nightly vigils.

How long the good old lady would have observed this promise is uncertain, for she dearly loved to talk of the marvellous, and there is a triumph in being the first to tell a frightful story; it is, however, still quoted in the neighborhood, as a memorable instance of female secrecy, that she kept it to herself for a whole week; when she was suddenly absolved from all further restraint, by intelligence brought to the breakfast-table one morning that the young lady was not to be found. Her room was empty—the bed had not been slept in—the window was open, and the bird had flown!

The astonishment and concern with which the intelligence was received can only be imagined by those who have witnessed the agitation which the mishaps of a great man cause among his friends. Even the poor relations paused for a moment from the indefatigable labors of the trencher; when the aunt, who had at first been struck speechless, wrung her hands, and shrieked out, "The goblin! the goblin! she's carried away by the goblin!"

In a few words she related the fearful scene of the garden, and concluded that the spectre must have carried off his bride. Two of the domestics corroborated the opinion, for they had heard the clattering of a horse's hoofs down the mountain about midnight, and had no doubt that it was the spectre on his black charger, bearing her away to the tomb. All present were struck with the direful probability; for events of the kind are extremely common in Germany, as many well-authenticated histories bear witness.

What a lamentable situation was that of the poor baron! What a heart-rending dilemma for a fond father, and a member of the great family of Katzenellenbogen! His only daughter had either been rapt away to the grave, or he was to have some wood-demon for a son-in-law, and, perchance, a troop of goblin grandchildren. As usual, he was completely bewildered, and all the castle in an uproar. The men were ordered to take horse, and scour every road and path and glen of the Odenwald. The baron himself had just drawn on his jack-boots, girded on his sword and was about to mount his steed to sally forth on the doubtful quest, when he was brought to a pause by a new apparition. A lady was seen approaching the castle, mounted on a palfrey, attended by a cavalier on horseback. She galloped up to the gate, sprang from her horse, and falling at the baron's feet, embraced his knees. It was his lost daughter, and her companion—the Spectre Bridegroom! The baron was astounded. He looked at his daughter, then at the spectre, and almost doubted the evidence of his senses. The latter, too, was wonderfully improved in his appearance since his visit to the world of spirits. His dress was splendid, and set off a noble figure of manly symmetry. He was no longer pale and melancholy. His fine countenance was flushed with the glow of youth, and joy rioted in his large dark eye.

The mystery was soon cleared up. The cavalier (for, in truth, as you must have known all the while, he was no goblin) announced himself as Sir Herman Von Starkenfaust. He related his adventure with the young count. He told how he had hastened to the castle to deliver the unwelcome tidings, but that the eloquence of the baron had interrupted him in every attempt to tell his tale. How the sight of the bride had completely captivated him, and that to pass a few hours near her, he had tacitly suffered the mistake to continue. How he had been sorely perplexed in what way to make a decent retreat, until the baron's goblin stories had suggested his eccentric exit. How, fearing the feudal hostility of the family, he had repeated his visits by stealth—had haunted the garden beneath the young lady's window—had wooed—had won—had borne away in triumph—and, in a word, had wedded the fair.

Under any other circumstances the baron would have been inflexible, for he was tenacious of paternal authority, and devoutly obstinate in all family feuds; but he loved his daughter; he had lamented her as lost; he rejoiced to find her still alive; and, though her husband was of a hostile house, yet, thank Heaven, he was not a goblin. There was something, it must be acknowledged, that did not exactly accord with his notions of strict veracity, in the joke the knight had passed upon him of his being a dead man; but several old friends present, who had served in the wars, assured him that every stratagem was excusable in love, and that the cavalier was entitled to especial privilege, having lately served as a trooper.

Matters, therefore, were happily arranged. The baron pardoned the young couple on the spot. The revels at the castle were resumed. The poor relations overwhelmed this new member of the family with loving-kindness; he was so gallant, so generous— and so rich. The aunts, it is true, were somewhat scandalized that their system of strict seclusion and passive obedience should be so badly exemplified, but attributed it all to their negligence in not having the windows grated. One of them was particularly mortified at having her marvellous story marred, and that the only spectre she had ever seen should turn out a counterfeit; but the niece seemed perfectly happy at having found him, substantial flesh and blood—and so the story ends.

WESTMINSTER ABBEY

When I behold, with deep astonishment,
To famous Westminster how there resorte
Living in brasse or stoney monument,
The princes and the worthies of all sorte:
Doe not I see reformde nobilitie,
Without contempt, or pride, or ostentation,
And looke upon offenselesse majesty,
Naked of pomp or earthly domination?
And how a play-game of a painted stone
Contents the quiet now and silent sprites,
Whome all the world which late they stood upon
Could not content or quench their appetites.
    Life is a frost of cold felicitie,
    And death the thaw of all our vanitie.

CHRISTOLERO: Epigrams, by T. B., 1598

ON ONE OF THOSE SOBER and rather melancholy days, in the latter part of Autumn, when the shadows of morning and evening almost mingle together, and throw a gloom over the decline of the year, I passed several hours in rambling about Westminster Abbey. There was something congenial to the season in the mournful magnificence of the old pile; and, as I passed its threshold, seemed like stepping back into the regions of antiquity, and losing myself among the shades of former ages.

I entered from the inner court of Westminster School, through a long, low, vaulted passage, that had an almost subterranean look, being dimly lighted in one part by circular perforations in the massive walls. Through this dark avenue I had a distant view of the cloisters, with the figure of an old verger, in his black gown, moving along their shadowy vaults, and seeming like a spectre from one of the neighboring tombs. The approach to the abbey through these gloomy monastic remains prepares the mind for its solemn contemplation. The cloisters still retain something of the quiet and seclusion of former days. The gray walls are discolored by damps, and crumbling with age; a coat of hoary moss has gathered over the inscriptions of the mural monuments, and obscured the death's-heads, and other funereal emblems. The sharp touches of the chisel are gone fom the rich tracery of the arches; the roses which adorned the key-stones have lost their leafy beauty; everything bears marks of the gradual dilapidations of time, which yet has something touching and pleasing in its very decay.

The sun was pouring down a yellow autumnal ray into the square of the cloisters; beaming upon a scanty plot of grass in the centre, and lighting up an angle of the vaulted passage with a kind of dusky splendor. From between the arcades, the eye glanced up to a bit of blue sky or a passing cloud, and beheld the sun-gilt pinnacles of the abbey towering into the azure heaven.

As I paced the cloisters, sometimes contemplating this mingled picture of glory and decay, and sometimes endeavoring to decipher the inscriptions on the tombstones, which formed the pavement beneath my feet, my eye was attracted to three figures, rudely carved in relief, but nearly worn away by the footsteps of many generations. They were the effigies of three of the early abbots; the epitaphs were entirely effaced; the names alone remained, having no doubt been renewed in later times. (Vitalis Abbas. 1082, and Gislebertus Crispinus. Abbas. 1114, and Laurentius. Abbas. 1176.) I remained some little while, musing over these casual relics of antiquity, thus left like wrecks upon this distant shore of time, telling no tale but that such beings had been, and had perished; teaching no moral but the futility of that pride which hopes still to exact homage in its ashes, and to live in an inscription. A little longer, and even these faint records will be obliterated, and the monument will cease to be a memorial. Whilst I was yet looking down upon these gravestones, I was roused by the sound of the abbey clock, reverberating from buttress to buttress, and echoing among the cloisters. It is almost startling to hear this warning of departed time sounding among the tombs, and telling the lapse of the hour, which, like a billow, has rolled us onward towards the grave. I pursued my walk to an arched door opening to the interior of the abbey. On entering here, the magnitude of the building breaks fully upon the mind, contrasted with the vaults of the cloisters. The eyes gaze with wonder at clustered columns of gigantic dimensions, with arches springing from them to such an amazing height; and man wandering about their bases, shrunk into insignificance in comparison with his own handiwork. The spaciousness and gloom of this vast edifice produce a profound and mysterious awe. We step cautiously and softly about, as if fearful of disturbing the hallowed silence of the tomb; while every footfall whispers along the walls, and chatters among the sepulchres, making us more sensible of the quiet we have interrupted.

It seems as if the awful nature of the place presses down upon the soul, and hushes the beholder into noiseless reverence. We feel that we are surrounded by the congregated bones of the great men of past times, who have filled history with their deeds, and the earth with their renown.

And yet it almost provokes a smile at the vanity of human ambition, to see how they are crowded together and jostled in the dust; what parsimony is observed in doling out a scanty nook, a gloomy corner, a little portion of earth, to those, whom, when alive, kingdoms could not satisfy; and how many shapes, and forms, and artifices are devised to catch the casual notice of the passenger, and save from forgetfulness, for a few short years, a name which once aspired to occupy ages of the world's thought and admiration.

I passed some time in Poet's Corner, which occupies an end of one of the transepts or cross aisles of the abbey. The monuments are generally simple; for the lives of literary men afford no striking themes for the sculptor. Shakespeare and Addison have statues erected to their memories; but the greater part have busts, medallions, and sometimes mere inscriptions. Notwithstanding the simplicity of these memorials, I have always observed that the visitors to the abbey remained longest about them. A kinder and fonder feeling takes place of that cold curiosity or vague admiration with which they gaze on the splendid monuments of the great and the heroic. They linger about these as about the tombs of friends and companions; for indeed there is something of companionship between the author and the reader. Other men are known to posterity only through the medium of history, which is continually growing faint and obscure; but the intercourse between the author and his fellowmen is ever new, active, and immediate. He has lived for them more than for himself; he has sacrificed surrounding enjoyments, and shut himself up from the delights of social life, that he might the more intimately commune with distant minds and distant ages. Well may the world cherish his renown; for it has been purchased, not by deeds of violence and blood, but by the diligent dispensation of pleasure. Well may posterity be grateful to his memory; for he has left it an inheritance, not of empty names and sounding actions, but whole treasures of wisdom, bright gems of thought, and golden veins of language.

From Poet's Corner I continued my stroll towards that part of the abbey which contains the sepulchres of the kings. I wandered among what once were chapels, but which are now occupied by the tombs and monuments of the great. At every turn I met with some illustrious name, or the cognizance of some powerful house renowned in history. As the eye darts into these dusky chambers of death, it catches glimpses of quaint effigies; some kneeling in niches, as if in devotion; others stretched upon the tombs, with hands piously pressed together; warriors in armor, as if reposing after battle; prelates with crosiers and mitres; and nobles in robes and coronets, lying as it were in state. In glancing over this scene, so strangely populous, yet where every form is so still and silent, it seems almost as if we were treading a mansion of that fabled city, where every being had been suddenly transmuted into stone.

I paused to contemplate a tomb on which lay the effigy of a knight in complete armor. A large buckler was on one arm; the hands were pressed together in supplication upon the breast; the face was almost covered by the morion; the legs were crossed in token of the warrior's having been engaged in the holy war. It was the tomb of a Crusader; of one of those military enthusiasts who so strangely mingled religion and romance, and whose exploits form the connecting link between fact and fiction; between the history and the fairy tale. There is something extremely picturesque in the tombs of these adventurers, decorated as they are with rude armorial bearings and Gothic sculpture. They comport with the antiquated chapels in which they are generally found; and in considering them, the imagination is apt to kindle with the legendary associations, the romantic fiction, the chivalrous pomp and pageantry, which poetry has spread over the wars for the sepulchre of Christ. They are the relics of times utterly gone by; of beings passed from recollection; of customs and manners with which ours have no affinity. They are like objects from some strange and distant land, of which we have no certain knowledge, and about which all our conceptions are vague and visionary. There is something extremely solemn and awful in those effigies on Gothic tombs, extended as if in the sleep of death, or in the supplication of the dying hour. They have an effect infinitely more impressive on my feelings than the fanciful attitudes, the over-wrought conceits, and allegorical groups, which abound on modern monuments. I have been struck, also, with the superiority of many of the old sepulchral inscriptions. There was a noble way, in former times, of saying things simply, and yet saying them proudly; and I do not know an epitaph that breathes a loftier consciousness of family worth and honorable lineage than one which affirms, of a noble house, that "all the brothers were brave, and all the sisters virtuous."

In the opposite transept to Poet's Corner stands a monument which is among the most renowned achievements of modern art; but which to me appears horrible rather than sublime. It is the tomb of Mrs. Nightingale, by Roubillac. The bottom of the monument is represented as throwing open its marble doors, and a sheeted skeleton is starting forth. The shroud is falling from his fleshless frame as he launches his dart at his victim. She is sinking into her affrighted husband's arms, who strives, with vain and frantic effort, to avert the blow. The whole is executed with terrible truth and spirit; we almost fancy we hear the gibbering yell of triumph bursting from the distended jaws of the spectre.—But why should we thus seek to clothe death with unneccessary terrors, and to spread horrors round the tomb of those we love? The grave should be surrounded by everything that might inspire tenderness and veneration for the dead; or that might win the living to virtue. It is the place, not of disgust and dismay, but of sorrow and meditation.

While wandering about those gloomy vaults and silent aisles, studying the records of the dead, the sound of busy existence from without occasionally reaches the ear;—the rumbling of the passing equipage; the murmur of the multitude; or perhaps the light laugh of pleasure. The contrast is striking with the deathlike repose around: and it has a strange effect upon the feelings, thus to hear the surges of active life hurrying along, and beating against the very walls of the sepulchre.

I continued in this way to move from tomb to tomb, and from chapel to chapel. The day was gradually wearing away; the distant tread of loiterers about the abbey grew less and less frequent; the sweet-tongued bell was summoning to evening prayers; and I saw at a distance the choristers, in their white surplices, crossing the aisle and entering the choir. I stood before the entrance to Henry the Seventh's chapel. A flight of steps lead up to it, through a deep and gloomy, but magnificent arch. Great gates of brass, richly and delicately wrought, turn heavily upon their hinges, as if proudly reluctant to admit the feet of common mortals into this most gorgeous of sepulchres.

On entering, the eye is astonished by the pomp of architecture, and the elaborate beauty of sculptured detail. The very walls are wrought into universal ornament, incrusted with tracery, and scooped into niches, crowded with the statues of saints and martyrs. Stone seems, by the cunning labor of the chisel, to have been robbed of its weight and density, suspended aloft, as if by magic, and the fretted roof achieved with the wonderful minuteness and airy security of a cobweb.

Along the sides of the chapel are the lofty stalls of the Knights of the Bath, richly carved of oak, though with the grotesque decorations of Gothic architecture. On the pinnacles of the stalls are affixed the helmets and crests of the knights, with their scarfs and swords; and above them are suspended their banners, emblazoned with armorial bearings, and contrasting the splendor of gold and purple and crimson with the cold gray fretwork of the roof. In the midst of this grand mausoleum stands the sepulchre of its founder,—his effigy, with that of his queen, extended on a sumptuous tomb, and the whole surrounded by a superbly wrought brazen railing.

There is a sad dreariness in this magnificence, this strange mixture of tombs and trophies; these emblems of living and aspiring ambition, close beside mementos which show the dust and oblivion in which all must sooner or later terminate. Nothing impresses the mind with a deeper feeling of loneliness than to tread the silent and deserted scene of former throng and pageant. On looking round on the vacant stalls of the knights and their esquires, and on the rows of dusty but gorgeous banners that were once borne before them, my imagination conjured up the scene when this hall was bright with the valor and beauty of the land; glittering with the splendor of jewelled rank and military array; alive with the tread of many feet and the hum of an admiring multitude. All had passed away; the silence of death had settled again upon the place, interrupted only by the casual chirping of birds, which had found their way into the chapel, and built their nests among its friezes and pendants—sure signs of solitariness and desertion.

When I read the names inscribed on the banners, they were those of men scattered far and wide about the world; some tossing upon distant seas; some under arms in distant lands; some mingling in the busy intrigues of courts and cabinets; all seeking to deserve one more distinction in this mansion of shadowy honors: the melancholy reward of a monument.

Two small aisles on each side of this chapel present a touching instance of the equality of the grave; which brings down the oppressor to a level with the oppressed, and mingles the dust of the bitterest enemies together. In one is the sepulchre of the haughty Elizabeth; in the other is that of her victim, the lovely and unfortunate Mary. Not an hour in the day but some ejaculation of pity is uttered over the fate of the latter, mingled with indignation at her oppressor. The walls of Elizabeth's sepulchre continually echo with the sighs of sympathy heaved at the grave of her rival.

A peculiar melancholy reigns over the aisle where Mary lies buried. The light struggles dimly through windows darkened by dust. The greater part of the place is in deep shadow, and the walls are stained and tinted by time and weather. A marble figure of Mary is stretched upon the tomb, round which is an iron railing, much corroded, bearing her national emblem—the thistle. I was weary with wandering, and sat down to rest myself by the monument, revolving in my mind the checkered and disastrous story of poor Mary.

The sound of casual footsteps had ceased from the abbey. I could only hear, now and then, the distant voice of the priest repeating the evening service, and the faint responses of the choir; these paused for a time, and all was hushed. The stillness, the desertion and obscurity that were gradually prevailing around, gave a deeper and more solemn interest to the place.

> For in the silent grave no conversation,
> No joyful tread of friends, no voice of lovers.
> No careful father's counsel—nothing's heard,
> For nothing is, but all oblivion,
> Dust, and an endless darkness.

Suddenly the notes of the deep-laboring organ burst upon the ear, falling with doubled and redoubled intensity, and rolling, as it were, huge billows of sound. How well do their volume and grandeur accord with this mighty building! With what pomp do they swell through its vast vaults, and breathe their awful harmony through these caves of death, and make the silent sepulchre vocal!—And now they rise in triumph and acclamation, heaving higher and higher their accordant notes, and piling sound on sound.—And now they pause, and the soft voices of the choir break out into sweet gushes of melody; they soar aloft, and warble along the roof, and seem to play about these lofty vaults like the pure airs of heaven. Again the pealing organ heaves its thrilling thunders, compressing air into music, and rolling it forth upon the soul. What long-drawn cadences! What solemn sweeping concords! It grows more and more dense and powerful—it fills the vast pile, and seems to jar the very walls—the ear is stunned—the senses are overwhelmed. And now it is winding up in full jubilee —it is rising from the earth to heaven—the very soul seems rapt away and floated upwards on this swelling tide of harmony!

I sat for some time lost in that kind of reverie which a strain of music is apt sometimes to inspire: the shadows of evening were gradually thickening round me; the monuments began to cast deeper and deeper gloom; and the distant clock again gave token of the slowly waning day.

I rose and prepared to leave the abbey. As I descended the flight of steps which lead into the body of the building, my eye was caught by the shrine of Edward the Confessor, and I ascended the small staircase that conducts to it, to take from thence a general survey of this wilderness of tombs. The shrine is elevated upon a kind of platform, and close around it are the sepulchres of various kings and queens. From this eminence the eye looks down between pillars and funeral trophies to the chapels and chambers below, crowded with tombs,—where warriors, prelates, courtiers, and statesmen lie mouldering in their "beds of darkness." Close by me stood the great chair of coronation, rudely carved of oak, in the barbarous taste of a remote and Gothic age. The scene seemed almost as if contrived, with theatrical artifice, to produce an effect upon the beholder. Here was a type of the beginning and the end of human pomp and power; here it was literally but a step from the throne to the sepulchre. Would not one think that these incongruous mementos had been gathered together as a lesson to living greatness?—to show it, even in the moment of its proudest exaltation, the neglect and dishonor to which it must soon arrive; how soon that crown which encircles its brow must pass away, and it must lie down in the dust and disgraces of the tomb, and be trampled upon by the feet of the meanest of the multitude. For, strange to tell, even the grave is here no longer a sanctuary. There is a shocking levity in some natures, which leads them to sport with awful and hallowed things; and there are base minds, which delight to revenge on the illustrious dead the abject homage and grovelling servility which they pay to the living. The coffin of Edward the Confessor has been broken open, and his remains despoiled of their funereal ornaments; the sceptre has been stolen from the hand of the imperious Elizabeth, and the effigy of Henry the Fifth lies headless. Not a royal monument but bears some proof how false and fugitive is the homage of mankind. Some are plundered; some mutilated; some covered with ribaldry and insult,—all more or less outraged and dishonored!

The last beams of day were now faintly streaming through the painted windows in high vaults above me; the lower parts of the abbey were already wrapped in the obscurity of twilight. The chapels and aisles grew darker and darker. The effigies of the kings faded into shadows; the marble figures of the monuments assumed strange shapes in the uncertain light; the evening breeze crept through the aisles like the cold breath of the grave; and even the distant footfall of a verger, traversing the Poet's Corner, had something strange and dreary in its sound. I slowly retraced my morning's walk, and as I passed out at the portal of the cloisters, the door, closing with a jarring noise behind me, filled the whole building with echoes.

I endeavored to form some arrangement in my mind of the objects I had been contemplating, but found they were already fallen into indistinctness and confusion. Names, inscriptions, trophies, had all become confounded in my recollection, though I had scarcely taken my foot from off the threshold. What, thought I, is this vast assemblage of sepulchres but a treasury of humiliation; a huge pile of reiterated homilies on the emptiness of renown, and the certainty of oblivion! It is, indeed, the empire of death—his great shadowy palace, where he sits in state, mocking at the relics of human glory, and spreading dust and forgetfulness on the monuments of princes. How idle a boast, after all, is the immortality of a name. Time is ever silently turning over his pages; we are too much engrossed by the story of the present, to think of the characters and anecdotes that gave interest to the past; and each age is a volume thrown aside to the speedily forgotten. The idol of to-day pushes the hero of yesterday out of our recollection; and will, in turn, be supplanted by his successor of to-morrow. "Our fathers," says Sir Thomas Browne, "find their graves in our short memories, and sadly tell us how we may be buried in our survivors." History fades into fable; fact becomes clouded with doubt and controversy; the inscription moulders from the tablet; the statue falls from the pedestal. Columns, arches, pyramids, what are they but heaps of sand; and their epitaphs, but characters written in the dust? What is the security of a tomb, or the perpetuity of an embalmment? The remains of Alexander the Great have been scattered to the wind, and his empty sarcophagus is now the mere curiosity of a museum. "The Egyptian mummies, which Cambyses or time hath spared, avarice now consumeth; Mizraim cures wounds, and Pharaoh is sold for balsams." *

What then is to insure this pile which now towers above me from sharing the fate of mightier mausoleums? The time must come when its gilded vaults, which now spring so loftily, shall lie in rubbish beneath the feet; when, instead of the sound of melody and praise, the wind shall whistle through the broken arches, and the owl hoot from the shattered tower,—when the gairish sunbeam shall break into these gloomy mansions of death, and the ivy twine round the fallen column; and the foxglove hang its blossoms about the nameless urn, as if in mockery of the dead. Thus man passes away; his name perishes from record and recollection; his history is as a tale that is told, and his very monument becomes a ruin.

* Sir T. Browne.

STRATFORD-ON-AVON

Thou soft-flowing Avon, by thy silver stream
Of things more than mortal sweet Shakspeare would dream;
The fairies by moonlight dance round his green bed,
For hallow'd the turf is which pillow'd his head.

GARRICK

To a homeless man, who has no spot on this wide world which he can truly call his own, there is a momentary feeling of something like independence and territorial consequence, when, after a weary day's travel, he kicks off his boots, thrusts his feet into slippers, and stretches himself before an inn fire. Let the world without go as it may; let kingdoms rise or fall, so long as he has the wherewithal to pay his bill, he is, for the time being, the very monarch of all he surveys. The arm-chair is his throne, the poker his sceptre, and the little parlor, some twelve feet square, his undisputed empire. It is a morsel of certainty, snatched from the midst of the uncertainties of life; it is a sunny moment gleaming out kindly on a cloudy day; and he who has advanced some way on a pilgrimage of existence, knows the importance of husbanding even morsels and moments of enjoyment. "Shall I not take mine ease in mine inn?" thought I, as I gave the fire a stir, lolled back in my elbow-chair, and cast a complacent look about the little parlor of the Red Horse, at Stratford-on-Avon.

The words of sweet Shakspeare were just passing through my mind as the clock struck midnight from the tower of the church in which he lies buried. There was a gentle tap at the door, and a pretty chambermaid, putting in her smiling face, inquired, with a hesitating air, whether I had rung. I understood it as a modest hint that it was time to retire. My dream of absolute dominion was at an end; so abdicating my throne, like a prudent potentate, to avoid being deposed, and putting the Stratford Guide-Book under my arm, as a pillow companion, I went to bed, and dreamt all night of Shakspeare, the jubilee, and David Garrick.

The next morning was one of those quickening mornings which we sometimes have in early spring; for it was about the middle of March. The chills of a long winter had suddenly given way; the north wind had spent its last gasp; and a mild air came stealing from the west, breathing the breath of life into nature, and wooing every bud and flower to burst forth into fragrance and beauty.

I had come to Stratford on a poetical pilgrimage. My first visit was to the house where Shakspeare was born, and where, according to tradition, he was brought up to his father's craft of wool-combing. It is a small, mean-looking edifice of wood and plaster, a true nestling-place of genius, which seems to delight in hatching its offspring in by-corners. The walls of its squalid chambers are covered with names and inscriptions in every language, by pilgrims of all nations, ranks, and conditions, from the prince to the peasant; and present a simple, but striking instance of the spontaneous and universal homage of mankind to the great poet of nature.

The house is shown by a garrulous old lady, in a frosty red face, lighted up by a cold blue anxious eye, and garnished with artificial locks of flaxen hair, curling from under an exceedingly dirty cap. She was peculiarly assiduous in exhibiting the relics with which ,this, like all other celebrated shrines, abounds. There was the shattered stock of the very matchlock with which Shakspeare shot the deer, on his poaching exploits. There, too, was his tobacco-box; which proves that he was a rival smoker of Sir Walter Raleigh; the sword also with which he played Hamlet; and the identical lantern with which Friar Laurence discovered Romeo and Juliet at the tomb! There was an ample supply also of Shakspeare's mulberry-tree, which seems to have as extraordinary powers of self-multiplication as the wood of the true cross; of which there is enough extant to build a ship of the line.

The most favorite object of curiosity, however, is Shakspeare's chair. It stands in the chimney nook of a small gloomy chamber, just behind what was his father's shop. Here he may many a time have sat when a boy, watching the slowly revolving spit with all the longing of an urchin; or of an evening, listening to the cronies and gossips of Stratford, dealing forth churchyard tales and legendary anecdotes of the troublesome times of England. In this chair it is the custom of every one that visits the house to sit: whether this be done with the hope of imbibing any of the inspiration of the bard I am at a loss to say, I merely mention the fact; and mine hostess privately assured me, that, though built of solid oak, such was the fervent zeal of devotees, that the chair had to be new bottomed at least once in three years. It is worthy of notice also, in the history of this extraordinary chair, that it partakes something of the volatile nature of the Santa Casa of Loretto, or the flying chair of the Arabian enchanter; for though sold some few years since to a northern princess, yet, strange to tell, it has found its way back again to the old chimney corner.

I am always of easy faith in such matters, and am ever willing to be deceived, where the deceit is pleasant and costs nothing. I am therefore a ready believer in relics, legends, and local anecdotes of goblins and great men; and would advise all travellers who travel for their gratification to be the same. What is it to us, whether these stories be true or false, so long as we can persuade ourselves into the belief of them, and enjoy all the charm of the reality? There is nothing like resolute good-humored credulity in these matters; and on this occasion I went even so far as willingly to believe the claims of mine hostess to a lineal descent from the poet, when, luckily for my faith, she put into my hands a play of her own composition, which set all belief in her consanguinity at defiance.

From the birthplace of Shakspeare a few paces brought me to his grave. He lies buried in the chancel of the parish church, a large and venerable pile, mouldering with age, but richly ornamented. It stands on the banks of the Avon, on an embowered point, and separated by adjoining gardens from the suburbs of the town. Its situation is quiet and retired; the river runs murmuring at the foot of the churchyard, and the elms which grow upon its banks droop their branches into its clear bosom. An avenue of limes, the boughs of which are curiously interlaced, so as to form in summer an arched way of foliage, leads up from the gate of the yard to the church porch. The graves are overgrown with grass; the gray tombstones, some of them nearly sunk into the earth, are half covered with moss, which has likewise tinted the reverend old building. Small birds have built their nests among the cornices and fissures of the walls, and keep up a continual flutter and chirping; and rooks are sailing and cawing about its lofty gray spire.

In the course of my rambles I met with the gray-headed sexton, Edmonds, and accompanied him home to get the key of the church. He had lived in Stratford, man and boy, for eighty years, and seemed still to consider himself a vigorous man, with the trivial exception that he had nearly lost the use of his legs for a few years past. His dwelling was a cottage, looking out upon the Avon and its bordering meadows; and was a picture of that neatness, order, and comfort, which pervade the humblest dwellings in this country. A low white-washed room, with a stone floor carefully scrubbed, served for parlor, kitchen, and hall. Rows of pewter and earthen dishes glittered along the dresser. On an old oaken table, well rubbed and polished, lay the family Bible and prayer-book, and the drawer contained the family library, composed of about half a score of well-thumbed volumes. An ancient clock, that important article of cottage furniture, ticked on the opposite side of the room; with a bright warming-pan hanging on one side of it, and the old man's horn-handled Sunday cane on the other. The fireplace, as usual, was wide and deep enough to admit a gossip knot within its jambs. In one corner sat the old man's grand-daughter sewing, a pretty blue-eyed girl,—and in the opposite corner was a superannuated crony, whom he addressed by the name of John Ange, and who, I found, had been his companion from childhood. They had played together in infancy; they had worked together in manhood; they were now tottering about and gossiping away the evening of life; and in a short time they will probably be buried together in the neighboring churchyard. It is not often that we see two streams of existence running thus evenly and tranquilly side by side; it is only in such quiet "bosom scenes" of life that they are to be met with.

I had hoped to gather some traditionary anecdotes of the bard from these ancient chroniclers; but they had nothing new to impart. The long interval during which Shakspeare's writing lay in comparative neglect has spread its shadow over his history; and it is his good or evil lot that scarcely anything remains to his biographers but a scanty handful of conjectures.

The sexton and his companion had been employed as carpenters on the preparations for the celebrated Stratford jubilee, and they remembered Garrick, the prime mover of the fête, who superintended the arrangements, and who, according to the sexton, was "a short punch man, very lively and bustling." John Ange had assisted also in cutting down Shakspeare's mulberry-tree, of which he had a morsel in his pocket for sale; no doubt a sovereign quickener of literary conception.

I was grieved to hear these two worthy wights speak very dubiously of the eloquent dame who shows the Shakspeare house. John Ange shook his head when I mentioned her valuable collection of relics, particularly her remains of the mulberry-tree; and the old sexton even expressed a doubt as to Shakspeare having been born in her house. I soon discovered that he looked upon her mansion with an evil eye, as a rival to the poet's tomb: the latter having comparatively but few visitors. Thus it is that historians differ at the very outset, and mere pebbles make the stream of truth diverge into different channels even at the fountain-head.

We approached the church through the avenue of limes, and entered by a Gothic porch, highly ornamented, with carved doors of massive oak. The interior is spacious, and the architecture and embellishments superior to those of most country churches. There are several ancient monuments of nobility and gentry, over some of which hang funeral escutcheons, and banners dropping piecemeal from the walls. The tomb of Shakspeare is in the chancel. The place is solemn and sepulchral. Tall elms wave before the pointed windows, and the Avon, which runs at a short distance from the walls, keeps up a low perpetual murmur. A flat stone marks the spot where the bard is buried. There are four lines inscribed on it, said to have been written by himself, and which have in them something extremely awful. If they are indeed his own, they show that solicitude about the quiet of the grave, which seems natural to fine sensibilities and thoughtful minds.

Good friend, for Jesus' sake forbeare
To dig the dust enclosed here.
Blessed be he that spares these stones,
And curst be he that moves my bones.

Just over the grave, in a niche of the wall, is a bust of Shakspeare, put up shortly after his death, and considered as a resemblance. The aspect is pleasant and serene, with a finely arched forehead, and I thought I could read in it clear indications of that cheerful, social disposition, by which he was as much characterized among his contemporaries as by the vastness of his genius. The inscription mentions his age at the time of his decease—fifty-three years; an untimely death for the world: for what fruit might not have been expected from the golden autumn of such a mind, sheltered as it was from the stormy vicissitudes of life, and flourishing in the sunshine of popular and royal favor.

The inscription on the tombstone has not been without its effect. It has prevented the removal of his remains from the bosom of his native place to Westminster Abbey, which was at one time contemplated. A few years since also, as some laborers were digging to make an adjoining vault, the earth caved in, so as to leave a vacant space almost like an arch, through which one might have reached into his grave. No one, however, presumed to meddle with his remains so awfully guarded by a malediction; and lest any of the idle or the curious, or any collector of relics, should be tempted to commit depredations, the old sexton kept watch over the place for two days, until the vault was finished and the aperture closed again. He told me that he had made bold to look in at the hole, but could see neither coffin nor bones; nothing but dust. It was something, I thought, to have seen the dust of Shakspeare.

Next to this grave are those of his wife, his favorite daughter, Mrs. Hall, and others of his family. On a tomb close by, also, is a full-length effigy of his old friend John Combe of usurious memory; on whom he is said to have written a ludicrous epitaph. There are other monuments around, but the mind refuses to dwell on anything that is not connected with Shakspeare. His idea pervades the place; the whole pile seems but as his mausoleum. The feelings, no longer checked and thwarted by doubt, here indulge in perfect confidence: other traces of him may be false or dubious, but here is palpable evidence and absolute certainty. As I trod the sounding pavement, there was something intense and thrilling in the idea, that, in very truth, the remains of Shakspeare were mouldering beneath my feet. It was a long time before I could prevail upon myself to leave the place; and as I passed through the churchyard, I plucked a branch from one of the yew-trees, the only relic that I have brought from Stratford.

I had now visited the usual objects of a pilgrim's devotion, but I had a desire to see the old family seat of the Lucys, at Charlecot, and to ramble through the park where Shakspeare, in company with some of the roysters of Stratford, committed his youthful offence of deer-stealing. In this hare-brained exploit we are told that he was taken prisoner, and carried to the keeper's lodge, where he remained all night in doleful captivity. When brought into the presence of Sir Thomas Lucy, his treatment must have been galling and humiliating; for it so wrought upon his spirit as to produce a rough pasquinade, which was affixed to the park gate at Charlecot.*

This flagitious attack upon the dignity of the knight so incensed him, that he applied to a lawyer at Warwick to put the severity of the laws in force against the rhyming deer-stalker. Shakspeare did not wait to brave the united puissance of a knight of the shire and a country attorney. He forthwith abandoned the pleasant banks of the Avon and his paternal trade; wandered away to London; became a hanger-on to the theatres; then an actor; and, finally, wrote for the stage; and thus, through the persecution of Sir Thomas Lucy, Stratford lost an indifferent wool-comber, and

---

* The following is the only stanza extant of this lampoon:—

A parliament member, a justice of peace,
At home a poor scarecrow, at London an asse,
If lowsie is Lucy, as some volke miscalle it,
Then Lucy is lowsie, whatever befall it.
    He thinks himself great;
    Yet an asse in his state,
We allow by his ears but with asses to mate,
If Lucy is lowsie, as some volke miscalle it,
Then sing lowsie Lucy whatever befall it.

the world gained an immortal poet. He retained, however, for a long time, a sense of the harsh treatment of the Lord of Charlecot, and revenged himself in his writings; but in the sportive way of a good-natured mind. Sir Thomas is said to be the original Justice Shallow, and the satire is slyly fixed upon him by the justice's armorial bearings, which, like those of the knight, had white luces* in the quarterings.

Various attempts have been made by his biographers to soften and explain away this early transgression of the poet; but I look upon it as one of those thoughtless exploits natural to his situation and turn of mind. Shakspeare, when young, had doubtless all the wildness and irregularity of an ardent, undisciplined, and undirected genius. The poetic temperament has naturally something in it of the vagabond. When left to itself it runs loosely and wildly, and delights in everything eccentric and licentious. It is often a turn-up of a die, in the gambling freaks of fate, whether a natural genius shall turn out a great rogue or a great poet; and had not Shakspeare's mind fortunately taken a literary bias, he might have as daringly transcended all civil, as he has all dramatic laws.

I have little doubt that, in early life, when running, like an unbroken colt, about the neighborhood of Stratford, he was to be found in the company of all kinds of odd anomalous characters; that he associated with all the madcaps of the place, and was one of those unlucky urchins, at mention of whom old men shake their heads, and predict that they will one day come to the gallows. To him the poaching in Sir Thomas Lucy's park was doubtless like a foray to a Scottish knight, and struck his eager, and, as yet untamed, imagination, as something delightfully adventurous.†

---

* The luce is a pike or jack, and abounds in the Avon about Charlecot.
† A proof of Shakspeare's random habits and associates in his youthful days may be found in a traditionary anecdote, picked up at Stratford by the elder Ireland, and mentioned in his "Picturesque Views on the Avon."

About seven miles from Stratford lies the thirsty little market-town of Bedford, famous for its ale. Two societies of the village yeomanry used to meet, under the appellation of the Bedford topers, and to challenge the lovers of good ale of the neighboring villages to a contest of drinking. Among others, the people of Stratford were called out to prove the strength

The old mansion of Charlecot and its surrounding park still remain in the possession of the Lucy family, and are peculiarly interesting, from being connected with this whimsical but eventful circumstance in the scanty history of the bard. As the house stood but little more than three miles' distance from Stratford, I resolved to pay it a pedestrian visit, that I might stroll leisurely through some of those scenes from which Shakspeare must have derived his earliest ideas of rural imagery.

The country was yet naked and leafless; but English scenery is always verdant, and the sudden change in the temperature of the weather was surprising in its quickening effects upon the landscape. It was inspiring and animating to witness this first awakening of spring; to feel its warm breath stealing over the senses; to see the moist mellow earth beginning to put forth the green sprout and the tender blade; and the trees and shrubs, in their reviving tints and bursting buds, giving the promise of returning foliage and flower. The cold snowdrop, that little borderer on the skirts of winter, was to be seen with its chaste white blossoms in the small gardens before the cottages. The bleating of the new-dropt lambs was faintly heard from the fields. The sparrow twittered about the thatched eaves and budding hedges; the robin threw a livelier note into his late querulous wintry strain; and the lark, springing up from the reeking bosom of the meadow,

---

of their heads; and in the number of the champions was Shakspeare, who, in spite of the proverb that "they who drink beer will think beer," was as true to his ale as Falstaff to his sack. The chivalry of Stratford was staggered at the first onset, and sounded a retreat while they had yet legs to carry them off the field. They had scarcely marched a mile when, their legs failing them, they were forced to lie down under a crab-tree, where they passed the night. It is still standing, and goes by the name of Shakspeare's tree.

In the morning his companions awaked the bard, and proposed returning to Bedford, but he declined, saying he had had enough, having drank with

> Piping Pebworth, Dancing Marston,
> Haunted Hilbro', Hungry Grafton,
> Dudging Exhall, Papist Wicksford,
> Beggarly Broom, and Drunken Bedford.

"The villages here alluded to," says Ireland, "still bear the epithets thus given them: the people of Pebworth are still famed for their skill on the pipe and tabor; Hilborough is now called Haunted Hilborough; and Grafton is famous for the poverty of its soil."

towered away into the bright fleecy cloud, pouring forth torrents of melody. As I watched the little songster, mounting up higher and higher, until his body was a mere speck on the white bosom of the cloud, while the ear was still filled with his music, it called to mind Shakspeare's exquisite little song in Cymbeline:—

> Hark! hark! the lark at heaven's gate sings,
>   And Phœbus 'gins arise,
> His steeds to water at those springs,
>   On chaliced flowers that lies.

> And winking mary-buds begin
>   To ope their golden eyes;
> With everything that pretty bin,
>   My lady sweet arise!

Indeed the whole country about here is poetic ground: everything is associated with the idea of Shakspeare. Every old cottage that I saw, I fancied into some resort of his boyhood, where he had acquired his intimate knowledge of rustic life and manners, and heard those legendary tales and wild superstitions which he has woven like witchcraft into his dramas. For in his time, we are told, it was a popular amusement in winter evenings "to sit round the fire, and tell merry tales of errant knights, queens, lovers, lords, ladies, giants, dwarfs, thieves, cheaters, witches, fairies, goblins, and friars." *

My route for a part of the way lay in sight of the Avon, which made a variety of the most fancy doublings and windings through a wide and fertile valley; sometimes glittering from among willows, which fringed its borders; sometimes disappearing among

---

* Scot, in his "Discoverie of Witchcraft," enumerates a host of these fireside fancies. "And they have so fraid us with bull-beggars, spirits, witches, urchins, elves, hags, fairies, satyrs, pans, faunes, syrens, kit with the can sticke, tritons, centaurs, dwarfes, giantes, imps, calcars, conjurors, nymphes, changelings, incubus, Robin-good-fellow, the spoorne, the mare, the man in the oke, the hell-waine, the fier drake, the puckle, Tom Thombe, hobgoblins, Tom Tumbler, boneless, and such other bugs, that we were afraid of our own shadowes."

groves, or beneath green banks; and sometimes rambling out into full view, and making an azure sweep round a slope of meadow land. This beautiful bosom of country is called the Vale of the Red Horse. A distant line of undulating blue hills seems to be its boundary, whilst all the soft intervening landscape lies in a manner enchained in the silver links of the Avon.

After pursuing the road for about three miles, I turned off into a footpath, which led along the borders of fields, and under hedgerows to a private gate of the park; there was a stile, however, for the benefit of the pedestrian; there being a public right of way through the grounds. I delight in these hospitable estates, in which every one has a kind of property—at least as far as the footpath is concerned. It in some measure reconciles a poor man to his lot, and, what is more, to the better lot of his neighbor, thus to have parks and pleasure-grounds thrown open for his recreation. He breathes the pure air as freely, and lolls as luxuriously under the shade, as the lord of the soil; and if he has not the privilege of calling all that he sees his own, he has not, at the same time, the trouble of paying for it, and keeping it in order.

I now found myself among noble avenues of oaks and elms, whose vast size bespoke the growth of centuries. The wind sounded solemnly among their branches, and the rooks cawed from their hereditary nests in the tree-tops. The eye ranged through a long lessening vista, with nothing to interrupt the view but a distant statue; and a vagrant deer stalking like a shadow across the opening.

There is something about these stately old avenues that has the effect of Gothic architecture, not merely from the pretended similarity of form, but from their bearing the evidence of long duration, and of having had their origin in a period of time with which we associate ideas of romantic grandeur. They betoken also the long-settled dignity, and proudly concentrated independence of an ancient family; and I have heard a worthy but aristocratic old friend observe, when speaking of the sumptuous palaces of modern gentry, that "money could do much with stone and mortar, but, thank Heaven, there was no such thing as suddenly building up an avenue of oaks."

It was from wandering in early life among this rich scenery, and about the romantic solitudes of the adjoining park of Fullbroke, which then formed a part of the Lucy estate, that some of Shakspeare's commentators have supposed he derived his noble forest meditations of Jaques, and the enchanting woodland pictures in "As You Like It." It is in lonely wanderings through such scenes, that the mind drinks deep but quiet draughts of inspiration, and becomes intensely sensible of the beauty and majesty of nature. The imagination kindles into revery and rapture; vague but exquisite images and ideas keep breaking upon it; and we revel in a mute and almost incommunicable luxury of thought. It was in some such mood, and perhaps under one of those very trees before me, which threw their broad shades over the grassy banks and quivering waters of the Avon, that the poet's fancy may have sallied forth into that little song which breathes the very soul of a rural voluptuary.

> Under the green wood tree,
> Who loves to lie with me,
> And tune his merry throat
> Unto the sweet bird's note,
> Come hither, come hither, come hither.
> Here shall he see
> No enemy,
> But winter and rough weather.

I had now come in sight of the house. It is a large building of brick, with stone quoins, and is in the Gothic style of Queen Elizabeth's day, having been built in the first year of her reign. The exterior remains very nearly in its original state, and may be considered a fair specimen of the residence of a wealthy country gentleman of those days. A great gateway opens from the park into a kind of courtyard in front of the house, ornamented with a grass-plot, shrubs, and flower-beds. The gateway is in imitation of the ancient barbacan; being a kind of outpost, and flanked by towers; though evidently for mere ornament, instead of defence. The front of the house is completely in the old style; with stone-shafted casements, a great bow-window of heavy stone-work, and a portal with armorial bearings over it, carved in stone. At each corner of the building is an octagon tower, surmounted by a gilt ball and weathercock.

The Avon, which winds through the park, makes a bend just at the foot of a gently sloping bank, which sweeps down from the rear of the house. Large herds of deer were feeding or reposing upon its borders; and swans were sailing majestically upon its bosom. As I contemplated the venerable old mansion, I called to mind Falstaff's encomium on Justice Shallow's abode, and the affected indifference and real vanity of the latter.

"*Falstaff.* You have a goodly dwelling and a rich.

"*Shallow.* Barren, barren, barren; beggars all, beggars all, Sir John:—marry, good air."

Whatever may have been the joviality of the old mansion in the days of Shakspeare, it had now an air of stillness and solitude. The great iron gateway that opened into the courtyard was locked; there was no show of servants bustling about the place; the deer gazed quietly at me as I passed, being no longer harried by the moss-troopers of Stratford. The only sign of domestic life that I met with was a white cat, stealing with wary look and stealthy pace towards the stables, as if on some nefarious expedition. I must not omit to mention the carcass of a scoundrel crow which I saw suspended against the barn wall, as it shows that the Lucys still inherit that lordly abhorrence of poachers, and maintain that rigorous exercise of territorial power which was so strenuously manifested in the case of the bard.

After prowling about for some time, I at length found my way to a lateral portal, which was the every-day entrance to the mansion. I was courteously received by a worthy old housekeeper, who, with the civility and communicativeness of her order, showed me the interior of the house. The greater part has undergone alterations, and been adapted to modern tastes and modes of living: there is a fine old oaken staircase; and the great hall, that noble feature in an ancient manor-house, still retains much of the appearance it must have had in the days of Shakspeare. The ceiling is arched and lofty; and at one end is a gallery in which stands an organ. The weapons and trophies of the chase, which formerly adorned the hall of a country gentleman, have made way for family portraits. There is a wide hospitable fireplace, calculated for an ample old-fashioned wood fire, formerly the rallying-place of winter festivity. On the opposite side of the hall is the huge Gothic bow-window, with stone shafts, which looks out upon the courtyard. Here are emblazoned in stained glass the armorial bearings of the Lucy family for many generations, some being dated in 1558. I was delighted to observe in the quarterings the three *white luces*, by which the character of Sir Thomas was first identified with that of Justice Shallow. They are mentioned in the first scene of the "Merry Wives of Windsor," where the Justice is in a rage with Falstaff for having "beaten his men, killed his deer, and broken into his lodge." The poet had no doubt the offences of himself and his comrades in mind at the time, and we may suppose the family pride and vindictive threats of the puissant Shallow to be a caricature of the pompous indignation of Sir Thomas.

"*Shallow*. Sir Hugh, persuade me not; I will make a Star-Chamber matter of it; if he were twenty John Falstaffs, he shall not abuse Sir Robert Shallow, Esq.

Slender. In the county of Gloster, justice of peace, and *coram*.

Shallow. Ay, cousin Slender, and *custalorum*.

Slender. Ay, and *ratalorum* too, and a gentleman born, master parson; who writes himself *Armigero* in any bill, warrant, quittance, or obligation, *Armigero*.

Shallow. Ay, that I do; and have done any time these three hundred years.

Slender. All his successors gone before him have done 't, and all his ancestors that come after him may; they may give the dozen *white luces* in their coat.*****

Shallow. The council shall hear it; it is a riot.

Evans. It is not meet the council hear of a riot; there is no fear of Got in a riot; the council, hear you, shall desire to hear the fear of Got, and not to hear a riot; take your vizaments in that.

Shallow. Ha! o' my life, if I were young again, the sword should end it!"

Near the window thus emblazoned hung a portrait by Sir Peter Lely, of one of the Lucy family, a great beauty of the time of Charles the Second: the old housekeeper shook her head as she pointed to the picture, and informed me that this lady had been sadly addicted to cards, and had gambled away a great portion of the family estate, among which was that part of the park where Shakspeare and his comrades had killed the deer. The lands thus lost had not been entirely regained by the family even at the present day. It is but justice to this recreant dame to confess that she had a surpassingly fine hand and arm.

The picture which most attracted my attention was a great painting over the fireplace, containing likenesses of Sir Thomas Lucy and his family, who inhabited the hall in the latter part of Shakspeare's lifetime. I at first thought that it was the vindictive knight himself, but the housekeeper assured me that it was his son; the only likeness extant of the former being an effigy upon his tomb in the church of the neighboring hamlet of Charlecot.* The picture gives a lively idea of the costume and manners of the time. Sir Thomas is dressed in ruff and doublet; white shoes with

* This effigy is in white marble, and represents the Knight in complete armor. Near him lies the effigy of his wife, and on her tomb is the following inscription; which, if really composed by her husband, places him quite above the intellectual level of Master Shallow:
Here lyeth the Lady Joyce Lucy wife of Sir Thomas Lucy of Charlecot in ye county of Warwick, Knight, Daughter and heir of Thomas Acton of Sutton in ye county of Worcester Esquire who departed out of this wretched world to her heavenly kingdom ye 10 day of February in ye yeare of our Lord God 1595 and of her age 60 and three. All the time of her lyfe a true and faythful servant of her good God, never detected of any cryme or vice. In religion most sounde, in love to her husband most faythful and true. In friendship most constant; to what in trust was committed unto her most secret. In wisdom excelling. In governing of her house, bringing up of youth in ye fear of God that did converse with her moste rare and singular. A great maintayner of hospitality. Greatly esteemed of her betters; misliked of none unless of the envyous. When all is spoken that can be saide a woman so garnished with virtue as not to be bettered and hardly to be equalled by any. As shee lived most virtuously so shee died most Godly. Set downe by him yt best did knowe what hath byn written to be true.
                                                              Thomas Lucye.

roses in them; and has a peaked yellow, or, as Master Slender would say, "a cane-colored beard." His lady is seated on the opposite side of the picture, in wide ruff and long stomacher, and the children have a most venerable stiffness and formality of dress. Hounds and spaniels are mingled in the family group; a hawk is seated on his perch in the foreground, and one of the children holds a bow;—all intimating the knight's skill in hunting, hawking, and archery—so indispensable to an accomplished gentleman in those days.*

I regretted to find that the ancient furniture of the hall, had disappeared; for I had hoped to meet with the stately elbow-chair of carved oak, in which the country squire of former days was wont to sway the sceptre of empire over his rural domains; and in which it might be presumed the redoubted Sir Thomas sat enthroned in awful state when the recreant Shakspeare was brought before him. As I like to deck out pictures for my own entertainment, I pleased myself with the idea that this very hall had been the scene of the unlucky bard's examination on the morning after his captivity in the lodge. I fancied to myself the rural potentate, surrounded by his body-guard of butler, pages, and blue-coated serving-men, with their badges; while the luckless culprit was brought in, forlorn and chopfallen, in the custody of gamekeepers, huntsmen, and whippers-in, and followed by a rabble rout of country clowns. I fancied bright faces of curious housemaids peeping from the half-opened doors; while from the gallery the fair daughters of the knight leaned gracefully forward, eying the youthful prisoner with that pity "that dwells in womanhood."— Who would have thought that this poor varlet, thus trembling

---

* Bishop Earle, speaking of the country gentleman of his time, observes, "his housekeeping is seen much in the different families of dogs, and serving-men attendant on their kennels; and the deepness of their throats is the depth of his discourse. A hawk he esteems the true burden of nobility, and is exceedingly ambitious to seem delighted with the sport, and have his fist gloved with his jesses." And Gilpin, in his description of a Mr. Hastings, remarks, "he kept all sorts of hounds that run buck, fox, hare, otter, and badger, and had hawks of all kinds both long and short winged. His great hall was commonly strewed with marrow-bones, and full of hawk, perches, hounds, spaniels, and terriers. On a broad hearth, paved with brick, lay some of the choicest terriers, hounds, and spaniels."

before the brief authority of a country squire, and the sport of
rustic boors, was soon to become the delight of princes, the theme
of all tongues and ages, the dictator to the human mind, and was
to confer immortality on his oppressor by a caricature and a lampoon!

I was now invited by the butler to walk into the garden, and I
felt inclined to visit the orchard and arbor where the justice
treated Sir John Falstaff and Cousin Silence "to a last year's pip-
pin of his own grafting, with a dish of caraways;" but I had already spent so much of the day in my ramblings that I was
obliged to give up any further investigations. When about to take
my leave I was gratified by the civil entreaties of the housekeeper
and butler, that I would take some refreshment: an instance of
good old hospitality which, I grieve to say, we castle-hunters seldom meet with in modern days. I make no doubt it is a virtue
which the present representative of the Lucys inherits from his
ancestors; for Shakspeare, even in his caricature, makes Justice
Shallow importunate in this respect, as witness his pressing instances to Falstaff.

"By cock and pye, sir, you shall not away to-night . . . I will
not excuse you; you shall not be excused; excuses shall not be
admitted; there is no excuse shall serve; you shall not be
excused. . . . Some pigeons, Davy; a couple of short-legged
hens; a joint of mutton; and any pretty little tiny kickshaws, tell
William Cook."

I now bade a reluctant farewell to the old hall. My mind had
become so completely possessed by the imaginary scenes and characters connected with it, that I seemed to be actually living among
them. Everything brought them as it were before my eyes; and
as the door of the dining-room opened, I almost expected to hear
the feeble voice of Master Silence quavering forth his favorite
ditty:—

> " 'T is merry in hall, when beards wag all,
>   And welcome merry shrove-tide!"

On returning to my inn, I could not but reflect on the singular gift of the poet; to be able thus to spread the magic of his mind over the very face of nature; to give to things and places a charm and character not their own, and to turn this "working-day world" into a perfect fairy land. He is indeed the true enchanter, whose spell operates, not upon the senses, but upon the imagination and the heart. Under the wizard influence of Shakspeare I had been walking all day in a complete delusion. I had surveyed the landscape through the prism of poetry, which tinged every object with the hues of the rainbow. I had been surrounded with fancied beings; with mere airy nothings, conjured up by poetic power; yet which, to me, had all the charm of reality. I had heard Jaques soliloquize beneath his oak: had beheld the fair Rosalind and her companion adventuring through the woodlands; and, above all, had been once more present in spirit with fat Jack Falstaff and his contemporaries, from the august Justice Shallow, down to the gentle Master Slender and the sweet Anne Page. Ten thousand honors and blessings on the bard who has thus gilded the dull realities of life with innocent illusions; who has spread exquisite and unbought pleasures in my checkered path; and beguiled my spirit in many a lonely hour, with all the cordial and cheerful sympathies of social life!

As I crossed the bridge over the Avon on my return, I paused to contemplate the distant church in which the poet lies buried, and could not but exult in the malediction, which has kept his ashes undisturbed in its quiet and hallowed vaults. What honor could his name have derived from being mingled in dusty companionship with the epitaphs and escutcheons and venal eulogiums of a titled multitude? What would a crowded corner in Westminster Abbey have been, compared with this reverend pile, which seems to stand in beautiful loneliness as his sole mausoleum! The solicitude about the grave may be but the offspring of an overwrought sensibility; but human nature is made up of foibles and prejudices; and its best and tenderest affections are mingled with these factitious feelings. He who has sought renown about the world, and has reaped a full harvest of worldly favor, will find, after all, that there is no love, no admiration, no applause, so sweet to the soul as that which springs up in his native place. It is there that he seeks to be gathered in peace and honor among his kindred and his early friends. And when the weary heart and failing head begin to warn him that the evening of life is drawing on, he turns as fondly as does the infant to the mother's arms, to sink to sleep in the bosom of the scene of his childhood.

How would it have cheered the spirit of the youthful bard when, wandering forth in disgrace upon a doubtful world, he cast back a heavy look upon his paternal home, could he have foreseen that, before many years, he should return to it covered with renown; that his name should become the boast and glory of his native place: that his ashes should be religiously guarded as its most precious treasure; and that its lessening spire, on which his eyes were fixed in tearful contemplation, should one day become the beacon, towering amidst the gentle landscape, to guide the literary pilgrim of every nation to his tomb!

THE LEGEND OF SLEEPY HOLLOW

Found among the Papers of the Late Diedrich Knickerbocker

A pleasing land of drowsy head it was,
Of dreams that wave before the half-shut eye;
And of gay castles in the clouds that pass,
For ever flushing round a summer sky.

Castle of Indolence

In the bosom of one of those spacious coves which indent the eastern shore of the Hudson, at that broad expansion of the river denominated by the ancient Dutch navigators the Tappan Zee, and where they always prudently shortened sail, and implored the protection of St. Nicholas when they crossed, there lies a small market-town or rural port, which by some is called Greensburgh,

but which is more generally and properly known by the name of
Tarry Town. This name was given, we are told, in former days, by
the good housewives of the adjacent country, from the inveterate
propensity of their husbands to linger about the village tavern on
market-days. Be that as it may, I do not vouch for the fact, but
merely advert to it for the sake of being precise and authentic.
Not far from this village, perhaps about two miles, there is a little
valley, or rather lap of land, among high hills, which is one of the
quietest places in the whole world. A small brook glides through
it, with just murmur enough to lull one to repose; and the occasional whistle of a quail, or tapping of a woodpecker, is almost the
only sound that ever breaks in upon the uniform tranquillity.

I recollect that, when a stripling, my first exploit in squirrel-
shooting was in a grove of tall walnut-trees that shades one side
of the valley. I had wandered into it at noon-time, when all nature
is peculiarly quiet, and was startled by the roar of my own gun, as
it broke the Sabbath stillness around, and was prolonged and reverberated by the angry echoes. If ever I should wish for a retreat,
whither I might steal from the world and its distractions, and
dream quietly away the remnant of a troubled life, I know of none
more promising than this little valley.

From the listless repose of the place, and the peculiar character
of its inhabitants, who are descendants from the original Dutch
settlers, this sequestered glen has long been known by the name
of SLEEPY HOLLOW, and its rustic lads are called the Sleepy Hollow Boys throughout all the neighboring country. A drowsy,
dreamy influence seems to hang over the land, and to pervade the
very atmosphere. Some say that the place was bewitched by a
high German doctor, during the early days of the settlement; others, that an old Indian chief, the prophet or wizard of his tribe,
held his pow-wows there before the country was discovered by
Master Hendrick Hudson. Certain it is, the place still continues
under the sway of some witching power, that holds a spell over
the minds of the good people, causing them to walk in a continual
reverie. They are given to all kinds of marvellous beliefs; are subject to trances and visions; and frequently see strange sights, and
hear music and voices in the air. The whole neighborhood abounds

with local tales, haunted spots, and twilight superstitions; stars shoot and meteors glare oftener across the valley than in any other part of the country, and the nightmare, with her whole ninefold, seems to make it the favorite scene of her gambols.

The dominant spirit, however, that haunts this enchanted region, and seems to be commander-in-chief of all the powers of the air, is the apparition of a figure on horseback without a head. It is said by some to be the ghost of a Hessian trooper, whose head had been carried away by a cannonball, in some nameless battle during the Revolutionary War, and who is ever and anon seen by the country folk, hurrying along in the gloom of night, as if on the wings of the wind. His haunts are not confined to the valley, but extend at times to the adjacent roads, and especially to the vicinity of a church at no great distance. Indeed certain of the most authentic historians of those parts, who have been careful in collecting and collating the floating facts concerning this spectre, allege that the body of the trooper, having been buried in the churchyard, the ghost rides forth to the scene of battle in nightly quest of his head; and that the rushing speed with which he sometimes passes along the Hollow, like a midnight blast, is owing to his being belated, and in a hurry to get back to the church yard before daybreak.

Such is the general purport of this legendary superstition, which has furnished materials for many a wild story in that region of shadows; and the spectre is known, at all the country firesides, by the name of the Headless Horseman of Sleepy Hollow.

It is remarkable that the visionary propensity I have mentioned is not confined to the native inhabitants of the valley, but is unconsciously imbibed by every one who resides there for a time. However wide awake they may have been before they entered that sleepy region, they are sure, in a little time, to inhale the witching influence of the air, and begin to grow imaginative, to dream dreams, and see apparitions.

I mention this peaceful spot with all possible laud; for it is in such little retired Dutch valleys, found here and there embosomed in the great State of New York, that population, manners, and customs remain fixed; while the great torrent of migration and improvement, which is making such incessant changes in other parts of this restless country, sweeps by them unobserved. They are like those little nooks of still water which border a rapid stream; where we may see the straw and bubble riding quietly at anchor, or slowly revolving in their mimic harbor, undisturbed by the rush of the passing current. Though many years have elapsed since I trod the drowsy shades of Sleepy Hollow, yet I question whether I should not still find the same trees and the same families vegetating in its sheltered bosom.

In this by-place of nature, there abode, in a remote period of American history, that is to say, some thirty years since, a worthy wight of the name of Ichabod Crane; who sojourned, or, as he expressed it, "tarried," in Sleepy Hollow, for the purpose of instructing the children of the vicinity. He was a native of Connecticut, a State which supplies the Union with pioneers for the mind as well as for the forest, and sends forth yearly its legions of frontier woodsmen and country schoolmasters. The cognomen of Crane was not inapplicable to his person. He was tall, but exceedingly lank, with narrow shoulders, long arms and legs, hands that dangled a mile out of his sleeves, feet that might have served for shovels, and his whole frame most loosely hung together. His head was small, and flat at top, with huge ears, large green glassy eyes, and a long snipe nose, so that it looked like a weathercock perched upon his spindle neck, to tell which way the wind blew. To see him striding along the profile of a hill on a windy day, with his clothes bagging and fluttering about him, one might have mistaken him for the genius of famine descending upon the earth, or some scarecrow eloped from a cornfield.

His school-house was a low building of one large room, rudely constructed of logs; the windows partly glazed, and partly patched with leaves of old copy-books. It was most ingeniously secured at vacant hours by a withe twisted in the handle of the door, and stakes set against the window-shutters; so that, though a thief might get in with perfect ease, he would find some embarrassment in getting out: an idea most probably borrowed by the architect, Yost Van Houten, from the mystery of an eel-pot. The schoolhouse stood in a rather lonely but pleasant situation, just at the foot of a woody hill, with a brook running close by, and a formidable birch-tree growing at one end of it. From hence the low murmur of his pupils' voices, conning over their lessons, might be heard in a drowsy summer's day, like the hum of a bee-hive; interrupted now and then by the authoritative voice of the master, in the tone of menace or command; or, peradventure, by the appalling sound of the birch, as he urged some tardy loiterer along the flowery path of knowledge. Truth to say, he was a conscientious man, and ever bore in mind the golden maxim, "Spare the rod and spoil the child."—Ichabod Crane's scholars certainly were not spoiled.

I would not have it imagined, however, that he was one of those cruel potentates of the school, who joy in the smart of their subjects; on the contrary, he administered justice with discrimination rather than severity, taking the burden off the backs of the weak, and laying it on those of the strong. Your mere puny stripling, that winced at the least flourish of the rod, was passed by with indulgence; but the claims of justice were satisfied by inflicting a double portion on some little, tough, wrong-headed, broad-skirted Dutch urchin, who sulked and swelled and grew dogged and sullen beneath the birch. All this he called "doing his duty" by their parents; and he never inflicted a chastisement without following it by the assurance, so consolatory to the smarting urchin, that "he would remember it, and thank him for it the longest day he had to live."

When school-hours were over, he was even the companion and playmate of the larger boys; and on holiday afternoons would convoy some of the smaller ones home, who happened to have pretty sisters, or good housewives for mothers, noted for the comforts of the cupboard. Indeed it behooved him to keep on good terms with his pupils. The revenue arising from his school was small, and would have been scarcely sufficient to furnish him with daily bread, for he was a huge feeder, and, though lank, had the dilating powers of an anaconda; but to help out his maintenance, he was, according to country custom in those parts, boarded and lodged at the houses of the farmers, whose children he instructed. With these he lived successively a week at a time; thus going the rounds of the neighborhood, with all his worldly effects tied up in a cotten handkerchief.

That all this might not be too onerous on the purses of his rustic patrons, who are apt to consider the costs of schooling a grievous burden, and schoolmasters as mere drones, he had various ways of rendering himself both useful and agreeable. He assisted the farmers occasionally in the lighter labors of their farms; helped to make hay; mended the fences; took the horses to water; drove the cows from pasture; and cut wood for the winter fire. He laid aside, too, all the dominant dignity and absolute sway with which he lorded it in his little empire, the school, and became wonderfully gentle and ingratiating. He found favor in the eyes of the mothers, by petting the children, particularly the youngest; and like the lion bold, which whilom so magnanimously the lamb did hold, he would sit with a child on one knee, and rock a cradle with his foot for whole hours together.

In addition to his other vocations, he was the singing-master of the neighborhood, and picked up many bright shillings by instructing the young folks in psalmody. It was a matter of no little vanity to him, on Sundays, to take his station in front of the church-gallery, with a band of chosen singers; where, in his own mind, he completely carried away the palm from the parson. Certain it is, his voice resounded far above all the rest of the congregation; and there are peculiar quavers still to be heard in that church, and which may even be heard half a mile off, quite to the opposite side of the mill-pond, on a still Sunday morning, which are said to be legitimately descended from the nose of Ichabod Crane. Thus, by divers little makeshifts in that ingenious way which is commonly denominated "by hook and by crook," the worthy pedagogue got on tolerably enough, and was thought, by all who understood nothing of the labor of headwork, to have a wonderfully easy life of it.

The schoolmaster is generally a man of some importance in the female circle of a rural neighborhood; being considered a kind of idle, gentleman-like personage, of vastly superior taste and accomplishments to the rough country swains, and, indeed, inferior in learning only to the parson. His appearance, therefore, is apt to occasion some little stir at the tea-table of a farm-house, and the addition of a supernumerary dish of cakes or sweetmeats, or, peradventure, the parade of a silver teapot. Our man of letters, therefore, was peculiarly happy in the smiles of all the country damsels. How he would figure among them in the churchyard, between services on Sundays! gathering grapes for them from the wild vines that overrun the surrounding trees; reciting for their amusement all the epitaphs on the tombstones; or sauntering, with a whole bevy of them, along the banks of the adjacent mill-pond; while the more bashful country bumpkins hung sheepishly back, envying his superior elegance and address.

From his half itinerant life, also, he was a kind of travelling gazette, carrying the whole budget of local gossip from house to house: so that his appearance was always greeted with satisfaction. He was, moreover, esteemed by the women as a man of great erudition, for he had read several books quite through, and was a perfect master of Cotton Mather's "History of New England Witchcraft," in which, by the way, he most firmly and potently believed.

He was, in fact, an odd mixture of small shrewdness and simple credulity. His appetite for the marvellous, and his powers of digesting it, were equally extraordinary; and both had been increased by his residence in this spellbound region. No tale was too gross or monstrous for his capacious swallow. It was often his delight, after his school was dismissed in the afternoon, to stretch himself on the rich bed of clover bordering the little brook that whimpered by his school-house, and there con over old Mather's direful tales, until the gathering dusk of the evening made the printed page a mere mist before his eyes. Then, as he wended his way, by swamp and stream, and awful woodland, to the farmhouse where he happened to be quartered, every sound of nature, at that witching hour, fluttered his excited imagination; the moan of the whippoorwill* from the hill-side; the boding cry of the tree-toad, that harbinger of storm; the dreary hooting of the screech-owl, or the sudden rustling in the thicket of birds frightened from

---

* The whippoorwill is a bird which is only heard at night. It receives its name from its note, which is thought to resemble those words.

their roost. The fire-flies, too, which sparkled most vividly in the darkest places, now and then startled him, as one of uncommon brightness would stream across his path; and if, by chance, a huge blockhead of a beetle came winging his blundering flight against him, the poor varlet was ready to give up the ghost, with the idea that he was struck with a witch's token. His only resource on such occasions, either to drown thought or drive away evil spirits, was to sing psalm-tunes; and the good people of Sleepy Hollow, as they sat by their doors of an evening, were often filled with awe, at hearing his nasal melody, "in linked sweetness long drawn out," floating from the distant hill, or along the dusky road.

Another of his sources of fearful pleasure was, to pass long winter evenings with the old Dutch wives, as they sat spinning by the fire, with a row of apples roasting and spluttering along the hearth, and listen to their marvellous tales of ghosts and goblins, and haunted fields, and haunted brooks, and haunted bridges, and haunted houses, and particularly of the headless horseman, or Galloping Hessian of the Hollow, as they sometimes called him. He would delight them equally by his anecdotes of witchcraft, and of the direful omens and portentous sights and sounds in the air, which prevailed in the earlier times of Connecticut; and would frighten them wofully with speculations upon comets and shooting stars, and with the alarming fact that the world did absolutely turn round, and that they were half the time topsy-turvy!

But if there was a pleasure in all this, while snugly cuddling in the chimney-corner of a chamber that was all of a ruddy glow from the crackling wood-fire, and where, of course, no spectre dared to show his face, it was dearly purchased by the terrors of his subsequent walk homewards. What fearful shapes and shadows beset his path amidst the dim and ghastly glare of a snowy night! —With what wistful look did he eye every trembling ray of light streaming across the waste fields from some distant window!— How often was he appalled by some shrub covered with snow, which, like a sheeted spectre, beset his very path!—How often did he shrink with curdling awe at the sound of his own steps on the frosty crust beneath his feet; and dread to look over his shoulder, lest he should behold some uncouth being tramping close behind him!—and how often was he thrown into complete dismay by some rushing blast, howling among the trees, in the idea that it was the Galloping Hessian on one of his nightly scourings!

All these, however, were mere terrors of the night, phantoms of the mind that walk in darkness; and though he had seen many spectres in his time, and been more than once beset by Satan in divers shapes, in his lonely perambulations, yet daylight put an end to all these evils; and he would have passed a pleasant life of it, in despite of the devil and all his works, if his path had not been crossed by a being that causes more perplexity to mortal man than ghosts, goblins, and the whole race of witches put together, and that was—a woman.

Among the musical disciples who assembled, one evening in each week, to receive his instructions in psalmody, was Katrina Van Tassel, the daughter and only child of a substantial Dutch farmer. She was a blooming lass of fresh eighteen; plump as a partridge; ripe and melting and rosy-cheeked as one of her father's peaches, and universally famed, not merely for her beauty, but her vast expectations. She was withal a little of a coquette, as might be perceived even in her dress, which was a mixture of ancient and modern fashions, as most suited to set off her charms. She wore the ornaments of pure yellow gold, which her great-great-grandmother had brought over from Saardam; the tempting stomacher of the olden time; and withal a provokingly short petticoat, to display the prettiest foot and ankle in the country round.

Ichabod Crane had a soft and foolish heart towards the sex; and it is not to be wondered at that so tempting a morsel soon found favor in his eyes; more especially after he had visited her in her paternal mansion. Old Baltus Van Tassel was a perfect picture of a thriving, contented, liberal-hearted farmer. He seldom, it is true, sent either his eyes or his thoughts beyond the boundaries of his own farm; but within those everything was snug, happy, and well-conditioned. He was satisfied with his wealth, but not proud of it; and piqued himself upon the hearty abundance rather than the style in which he lived. His stronghold was situated on the banks of the Hudson, in one of those green, sheltered, fertile nooks in which the Dutch farmers are so fond of nestling. A great

elm-tree spread its broad branches over it; at the foot of which
bubbled up a spring of the softest and sweetest water, in a little
well, formed of a barrel; and then stole sparkling away through
the grass, to a neighboring brook, that bubbled along among al-
ders and dwarf willows. Hard by the farm-house was a vast barn,
that might have served for a church; every window and crevice of
which seemed bursting forth with the treasures of the farm; the
flail was busily resounding within it from morning till night; swallows and martins skimmed twittering about the eaves; and rows of
pigeons, some with one eye turned up, as if watching the weather,
some with their heads under their wings, or buried in their bosoms,
and others swelling, and cooing, and bowing about their dames,
were enjoying the sunshine on the roof. Sleek unwieldly porkers
were grunting in the repose and abundance of their pens; whence
sallied forth, now and then, troops of sucking pigs, as if to snuff
the air. A stately squadron of snowy geese were riding in an adjoining pond, convoying whole fleets of ducks; regiments of turkeys were gobbling through the farm-yard, and guinea fowls fret-
ting about it, like ill-tempered housewives, with their peevish
discontented cry. Before the barn-door strutted the gallant cock,
that pattern of a husband, a warrior, and a fine gentleman, clap-
ping his burnished wings, and crowing in the pride and gladness
of his heart—sometimes tearing up the earth with his feet, and
then generously calling his ever-hungry family of wives and children to enjoy the rich morsel which he had discovered.

The pedagogue's mouth watered, as he looked upon this sumptuous promise of luxurious winter fare. In his devouring mind's
eye he pictured to himself every roasting-pig running about with
a pudding in his belly, and an apple in his mouth; the pigeons
were snugly put to bed in a comfortable pie, and tucked in with a
coverlet of crust; the geese were swimming in their own gravy;
and the ducks pairing cosily in dishes, like snug married couples,
with a decent competency of onion-sauce. In the porkers he saw
carved out the future sleek side of bacon, and juicy relishing ham;
not a turkey but he beheld daintily trussed up, with its gizzard
under its wing, and, peradventure, a necklace of savory sausages;
and even bright chanticleer himself lay sprawling on his back, in

a side-dish, with uplifted claws, as if craving that quarter which his chivalrous spirit disdained to ask while living.

As the enraptured Ichabod fancied all this, and as he rolled his great green eyes over the fat meadow-lands, the rich fields of wheat, of rye, of buckwheat, and Indian corn, and the orchard burdened with ruddy fruit, which surrounded the warm tenement of Van Tassel, his heart yearned after the damsel who was to inherit these domains, and his imagination expanded with the idea how they might be readily turned into cash, and the money invested in immense tracts of wild land, and shingle palaces in the wilderness. Nay, his busy fancy already realized his hopes, and presented to him the blooming Katrina, with a whole family of children, mounted on the top of a wagon loaded with household trumpery, with pots and kettles dangling beneath; and he beheld himself bestriding a pacing mare, with a colt at her heels, setting out for Kentucky, Tennessee, or the Lord knows where.

When he entered the house, the conquest of his heart was complete. It was one of those spacious farm-houses, with high-ridged, but lowly-sloping roofs, built in the style handed down from the first Dutch settlers; the low projecting eaves forming a piazza along the front, capable of being closed up in bad weather. Under this were hung flails, harness, various utensils of husbandry, and nets for fishing in the neighboring river. Benches were built along the sides for summer use; and a great spinning-wheel at one end, and a churn at the other, showed the various uses to which this important porch might be devoted. From this piazza the wondering Ichabod entered the hall, which formed the centre of the mansion and the place of usual residence. Here, rows of resplendent pewter, ranged on a long dresser, dazzled his eyes. In one corner stood a huge bag of wool ready to be spun; in another a quantity of linsey-woolsey just from the loom; ears of Indian corn, and strings of dried apples and peaches, hung in gay festoons along the walls, mingled with the gaud of red peppers; and a door left ajar gave him a peep into the best parlor, where the claw-footed chairs and dark mahogany tables shone like mirrors; and irons, with their accompanying shovel and tongs, glistened from their covert of asparagus tops; mock-oranges and conch-shells decorated the mantel-piece; strings of various colored birds' eggs were suspended above it; a great ostrich egg was hung from the centre of the room, and a corner-cupboard, knowingly left open, displayed immense treasures of old silver and well-mended china.

From the moment Ichabod laid his eyes upon these regions of delight, the peace of his mind was at an end, and his only study was how to gain the affections of the peerless daughter of Van Tassel. In this enterprise, however, he had more real difficulties than generally fell to the lot of a knight-errant of yore, who seldom had anything but giants, enchanters, fiery dragons, and such like easily conquered adversaries, to contend with; and had to make his way merely through gates of iron and brass, and walls of adamant, to the castle-keep, where the lady of his heart was confined; all which he achieved as easily as a man would carve his way to the centre of a Christmas pie; and then the lady gave him her hand as a matter of course. Ichabod, on the contrary, had to win his way to the heart of a country coquette, beset with a labyrinth of whims and caprices, which were forever presenting new difficulties and impediments; and he had to encounter a host of fearful adversaries of real flesh and blood, the numerous rustic admirers, who beset every portal to her heart; keeping a watchful and angry eye upon each other, but ready to fly out in the common cause against any new competitor.

Among these the most formidable was a burly, roaring, roistering blade, of the name of Abraham, or, according to the Dutch abbreviation, Brom Van Brunt, the hero of the country round, which rang with his feats of strength and hardihood. He was broad-shouldered, and double-jointed, with short curly black hair, and a bluff but not unpleasant countenance, having a mingled air of fun and arrogance. From his Herculean frame and great powers of limb, he had received the nickname of BROM BONES, by which he was universally known. He was famed for great knowledge and skill in horsemanship, being as dexterous on horseback as a Tartar. He was foremost at all races and cockfights; and, with the ascendency which bodily strength acquires in rustic life, was the umpire in all disputes, setting his hat on one side, and giving his decisions with an air and tone admitting of no gainsay or appeal.

He was always ready for either a fight or a frolic; but had more mischief than ill-will in his composition; and, with all his overbearing roughness, there was a strong dash of waggish good-humor at bottom. He had three or four boon companions, who regarded him as their model, and at the head of whom he scoured the country, attending every scene of feud or merriment for miles round. In cold weather he was distinguished by a fur cap, surmounted with a flaunting fox's tail; and when the folks at a country gathering descried this well-known crest at a distance, whisking about among a squad of hard riders, they always stood by for a squall. Sometimes his crew would be heard dashing along past the farmhouses at midnight, with whoop and halloo, like a troop of Don Cossacks; and the old dames, startled out of their sleep, would listen for a moment till the hurry-scurry had clattered by, and then exclaim, "Ay, there goes Brom Bones and his gang!" The neighbors looked upon him with a mixture of awe, admiration, and good-will; and when any madcap prank, or rustic brawl, occurred in the vicinity, always shook their heads, and warranted Brom Bones was at the bottom of it.

This rantipole hero had for some time singled out the blooming Katrina for the object of his uncouth gallantries; and though his amorous toyings were something like the gentle caresses and endearments of a bear, yet it was whispered that she did not altogether discourage his hopes. Certain it is, his advances were signals for rival candidates to retire, who felt no inclination to cross a lion in his amours; insomuch, that, when his horse was seen tied to Van Tassel's paling, on a Sunday night, a sure sign that his master was courting, or, as it is termed, "sparking," within, all other suitors passed by in despair, and carried the war into other quarters.

Such was the formidable rival with whom Ichabod Crane had to contend, and, considering all things, a stouter man than he would have shrunk from the competition, and a wiser man would have despaired. He had, however, a happy mixture of pliability and perseverance in his nature; he was in form and spirit like a supplejack—yielding, but tough; though he bent, he never broke; and though he bowed beneath the slightest pressure, yet, the moment it was away—jerk! he was as erect, and carried his head as high as ever.

To have taken the field openly against his rival would have been madness; for he was not a man to be thwarted in his amours, any more than that stormy lover, Achilles. Ichabod, therefore, made his advances in a quiet and gently insinuating manner. Under cover of his character of singing-master, he had made frequent visits at the farm-house; not that he had anything to apprehend from the meddlesome interference of parents, which is so often a stumbling-block in the path of lovers. Balt Van Tassel was an easy, indulgent soul; he loved his daughter better even than his pipe, and, like a reasonable man and an excellent father, let her have her way in everything. His notable little wife, too, had enough to do to attend to her housekeeping and manage her poultry; for, as she sagely observed, ducks and geese are foolish things, and must be looked after, but girls can take care of themselves. Thus while the busy dame bustled about the house, or plied her spinning-wheel at one end of the piazza, honest Balt would sit smoking his evening pipe at the other, watching the achievements of a little wooden warrior, who, armed with a sword in each hand, was most valiantly fighting the wind on the pinnacle of the barn. In the mean time, Ichabod would carry on his suit with the daughter by the side of the spring under the great elm, or sauntering along in the twilight,—that hour so favorable to the lover's eloquence.

I profess not to know how women's hearts are wooed and won. To me they have always been matters of riddle and admiration. Some seem to have but one vulnerable point, or door of access; while others have a thousand avenues, and may be captured in a thousand different ways. It is a great triumph of skill to gain the former, but a still greater proof of generalship to maintain possession of the latter, for the man must battle for his fortress at every door and window. He who wins a thousand common hearts is therefore entitled to some renown; but he who keeps undisputed sway over the heart of a coquette, is indeed a hero. Certain it is, this was not the case with the redoubtable Brom Bones; and from the moment Ichabod Crane made his advances, the interests of the former evidently declined; his horse was no longer seen tied at the palings on Sunday nights, and a deadly feud gradually arose between him and the preceptor of Sleepy Hollow.

Brom, who had a degree of rough chivalry in his nature, would fain have carried matters to open warfare, and have settled their pretensions to the lady according to the mode of those most concise and simple reasoners, the knights-errant of yore—by single combat; but Ichabod was too conscious of the superior might of his adversary to enter the lists against him: he had overheard a boast of Bones, that he would "double the schoolmaster up, and lay him on a shelf of his own school-house;" and he was too wary to give him an opportunity. There was something extremely provoking in this obstinately pacific system; it left Brom no alternative but to draw upon the funds of rustic waggery in his disposition, and to play off boorish practical jokes upon his rival. Ichabod became the object of whimsical persecution to Bones and his gang of rough riders. They harried his hitherto peaceful domains; smoked out his singing-school, by stopping up the chimney; broke into the school-house at night, in spite of its formidable fastenings of withe and window-stakes, and turned everything topsy-turvy: so that the poor schoolmaster began to think all the witches in the country held their meetings there. But what was still more annoying, Brom took opportunities of turning him into ridicule in presence of his mistress, and had a scoundrel dog whom he taught to whine in the most ludicrous manner, and introduced as a rival of Ichabod's to instruct her in psalmody.

In this way matters went on for some time, without producing any material effect on the relative situation of the contending powers. On a fine autumnal afternoon, Ichabod, in pensive mood, sat enthroned on the lofty stool whence he usually watched all the concerns of his little literary realm. In his hand he swayed a ferule, that sceptre of despotic power; the birch of justice reposed on three nails, behind the throne, a constant terror to evil-doers; while on the desk before him might be seen sundry contraband articles and prohibited weapons, detected upon the persons of idle urchins; such as half-munched apples, popguns, whirligigs, flycages, and whole legions of rampant little paper game-cocks. Apparently there had been some appalling act of justice recently inflicted, for his scholars were all busily intent upon their books, or slyly whispering behind them with one eye kept upon the master; and a kind of buzzing stillness reigned throughout the school-room. It was suddenly interrupted by the appearance of a negro, in tow-cloth jacket and trousers, a round-crowned fragment of a hat, like the cap of Mercury, and mounted on the back of a ragged, wild, half-broken colt, which he managed with a rope by way of halter. He came clattering up to the school-door with an invitation to Ichabod to attend a merry-making or "quilting frolic," to be held that evening at Mynheer Van Tassel's; and having delivered his message with that air of importance, and effort at fine language, which a negro is apt to display on petty embassies of the kind, he dashed over the brook, and was seen scampering away up the Hollow, full of the importance and hurry of his mission.

All was now bustle and hubbub in the late quiet school-room. The scholars were hurried through their lessons, without stopping at trifles; those who were nimble skipped over half with impunity, and those who were tardy had a smart application now and then in the rear, to quicken their speed, or help them over a tall word. Books were flung aside without being put away on the shelves, inkstands were overturned, benches thrown down, and the whole school was turned loose an hour before the usual time, bursting forth like a legion of young imps, yelping and racketing about the green, in joy at their early emancipation.

The gallant Ichabod now spent at least an extra half-hour at his toilet, brushing and furbishing up his best and indeed only suit of rusty black, and arranging his looks by a bit of broken looking-glass, that hung up in the school-house. That he might make his appearance before his mistress in the true style of a cavalier, he borrowed a horse from the farmer with whom he was domiciliated, a choleric old Dutchman, of the name of Hans Van Ripper, and, thus gallantly mounted, issued forth, like a knight-errant in quest of adventures. But it is meet I should, in the true spirit of romantic story, give some account of the looks and equipments of my hero and his steed. The animal he bestrode was a broken-down plough-horse, that had outlived almost everything but his viciousness. He was gaunt and shagged, with a ewe neck and a head like a hammer; his rusty mane and tail were tangled and knotted with burrs; one eye had lost its pupil, and was glaring and spectral; but the other had the gleam of a genuine devil in it. Still he must have had fire and mettle in his day, if we may judge from the name he bore of Gunpowder. He had, in fact, been a favorite steed of his master's, the choleric Van Ripper, who was a furious rider, and had infused, very probably, some of his own spirit into the animal; for, old and broken-down as he looked, there was more of the lurking devil in him than in any young filly in the country.

Ichabod was a suitable figure for such a steed. He rode with short stirrups, which brought his knees nearly up to the pommel of the saddle; his sharp elbows stuck out like grasshoppers'; he carried his whip perpendicularly in his hand, like a sceptre, and, as his horse jogged on, the motion of his arms was not unlike the flapping of a pair of wings. A small wool hat rested on the top of his nose, for so his scanty strip of forehead might be called; and the skirts of his black coat fluttered out almost to the horse's tail. Such was the appearance of Ichabod and his steed, as they shambled out of the gate of Hans Van Ripper, and it was altogether such an apparition as is seldom to be met with in broad daylight.

It was, as I have said, a fine autumnal day, the sky was clear and serene, and nature wore that rich and golden livery which we always associate with the idea of abundance. The forests had put on their sober brown and yellow, while some trees of the tenderer kind had been nipped by the frosts into brilliant dyes of orange, purple, and scarlet. Streaming files of wild ducks began to make their appearance high in the air; the bark of the squirrel might be heard from the groves of beech and hickory nuts, and the pensive whistle of the quail at intervals from the neighboring stubble-field.

The small birds were taking their farewell banquets. In the fulness of their revelry, they fluttered, chirping and frolicking, from bush to bush, and tree to tree, capricious from the very profusion and variety around them. There was the honest cockrobin, the favorite game of stripling sportsmen, with its loud querulous notes; and the twittering blackbirds flying in sable clouds; and the golden-winged woodpecker, with his crimson crest, his broad black gorget, and splendid plumage; and the cedar-bird, with its red-tipt wings and yellow-tipt tail, and its little monteiro cap of feathers; and the blue jay, that noisy coxcomb, in his gay light-blue coat and white under-clothes, screaming and chattering, nodding and bobbing and bowing, and pretending to be on good terms with every songster of the grove.

As Ichabod jogged slowly on his way, his eye, ever open to every symptom of culinary abundance, ranged with delight over the treasures of jolly autumn. On all sides he beheld vast store of apples; some hanging in oppressive opulence on the trees; some gathered into baskets and barrels for the market; others heaped up in rich piles for the cider-press. Farther on he beheld great fields of Indian corn, with its golden ears peeping from their leafy coverts, and holding out the promise of cakes and hasty-pudding; and the yellow pumpkins lying beneath them, turning up their fair round bellies to the sun, and giving ample prospects of the most luxurious of pies; and anon he passed the fragrant buckwheat fields, breathing the odor of the bee-hive, and as he beheld them, soft anticipations stole over his mind of dainty slapjacks, well buttered, and garnished with honey or treacle, by the delicate little dimpled hand of Katrina Van Tassel.

Thus feeding his mind with many sweet thoughts and "sugared suppositions," he journeyed along the sides of a range of hills which look out upon some of the goodliest scenes of the mighty Hudson. The sun gradually wheeled his broad disk down into the west. The wide bosom of the Tappan Zee lay motionless and glossy, excepting that here and there a gentle undulation waved and prolonged the blue shadow of the distant mountain. A few amber clouds floated in the sky, without a breath of air to move them. The horizon was of a fine golden tint, changing gradually into a pure apple-green, and from that into the deep blue of the mid-heaven. A slanting ray lingered on the woody crests of the precipices that overhung some parts of the river, giving greater depth to the dark-gray and purple of their rocky sides. A sloop was loitering in the distance, dropping slowly down with the tide, her sail hanging uselessly against the mast; and as the reflection of the sky gleamed along the still water, it seemed as if the vessel was suspended in the air.

It was toward evening that Ichabod arrived at the castle of the Heer Van Tassel, which he found thronged with the pride and flower of the adjacent country. Old farmers, a spare leathern-faced race, in homespun coats and breeches, blue stockings, huge shoes, and magnificent pewter buckles. Their brisk withered little dames, in close crimped caps, long-waisted shortgowns, homespun petticoats, with scissors and pincushions, and gay calico pockets hanging on the outside. Buxom lasses, almost as antiquated as their mothers, excepting where a straw hat, a fine ribbon, or perhaps a white frock, gave symptoms of city innovation. The sons, in short square-skirted coats with rows of stupendous brass buttons, and their hair generally queued in the fashion of the times, especially if they could procure an eel-skin for the purpose, it being esteemed, throughout the country, as a potent nourisher and strengthener of the hair.

Brom Bones, however, was the hero of the scene, having come to the gathering on his favorite steed, Daredevil, a creature, like himself, full of mettle and mischief, and which no one but himself could manage. He was, in fact, noted for preferring vicious animals, given to all kinds of tricks, which kept the rider in constant risk of his neck, for he held a tractable well-broken horse as unworthy of a lad of spirit.

Fain would I pause to dwell upon the world of charms that burst upon the enraptured gaze of my hero, as he entered the state parlor of Van Tassel's mansion. Not those of the bevy of buxom lasses, with their luxurious display of red and white; but the ample charms of a genuine Dutch country tea-table, in the sumptuous time of autumn. Such heaped-up platters of cakes of various and almost indescribable kinds, known only to experienced Dutch housewives! There was the doughty doughnut, the tenderer oly koek, and the crisp and crumbling cruller; sweet cakes and short cakes, ginger-cakes and honey-cakes, and the whole family of cakes. And then there were apple-pies and peach-pies and pumpkin-pies; besides slices of ham and smoked beef; and moreover delectable dishes of preserved plums, and peaches, and pears, and quinces; not to mention broiled shad and roasted chickens; together with bowls of milk and cream, all mingled higgledy-piggledy, pretty much as I have enumerated them, with the motherly tea-pot sending up its clouds of vapor from the midst—Heaven bless the mark! I want breath and time to discuss this banquet as it deserves, and am too eager to get on with my story. Happily, Ichabod Crane was not in so great a hurry as his historian, but did ample justice to every dainty.

He was a kind and thankful creature, whose heart dilated in proportion as his skin was filled with good cheer; and whose spirits rose with eating as some men's do with drink. He could not help, too, rolling his large eyes round him as he ate, and chuckling with the possibility that he might one day be lord of all this scene of almost unimaginable luxury and splendor. Then, he thought, how soon he'd turn his back upon the old school-house; snap his fingers in the face of Hans Van Ripper, and every other niggardly patron, and kick any itinerant pedagogue out-of-doors that should dare to call him comrade!

Old Baltus Van Tassel moved about among his guests with a face dilated with content and good-humor, round and jolly as the harvest-moon. His hospitable attentions were brief, but expressive, being confined to a shake of the hand, a slap on the shoulder, a loud laugh, and a pressing invitation to "fall to, and help themselves."

And now the sound of the music from the common room, or hall, summoned to the dance. The musician was an old gray-headed negro, who had been the itinerant orchestra of the neighborhood for more than half a century. His instrument was as old and battered as himself. The greater part of the time he scraped on two or three strings accompanying every movement of the bow with a motion of the head; bowing almost to the ground and stamping with his foot whenever a fresh couple were to start.

Ichabod prided himself upon his dancing as much as upon his vocal powers. Not a limb, not a fibre about him was idle; and to have seen his loosely hung frame in full motion, and clattering about the room, you would have thought Saint Vitus himself, that blessed patron of the dance, was figuring before you in person. He was the admiration of all the negroes; who, having gathered, of all ages and sizes, from the farm and the neighborhood, stood forming a pyramid of shining black faces at every door and window, gazing with delight at the scene, rolling their white eyeballs, and showing grinning rows of ivory from ear to ear. How could the flogger of urchins be otherwise than animated and joyous? the lady of his heart was his partner in the dance, and smiling graciously in reply to all his amorous oglings; while Brom Bones, sorely smitten with love and jealousy, sat brooding by himself in one corner.

When the dance was at an end, Ichabod was attracted to a knot of the sager folks, who, with old Van Tassel, sat smoking at one end of the piazza, gossiping over former times, and drawing out long stories about the war.

This neighborhood, at the time of which I am speaking, was one of those highly favored places which abound with chronicle and great men. The British and American line had run near it during the war; it had, therefore, been the scene of marauding, and infested with refugees, cow-boys, and all kinds of border chivalry. Just sufficient time had elapsed to enable each story-teller to dress up his tale with a little becoming fiction, and, in the indistinctness of his recollection, to make himself the hero of every exploit.

There was the story of Doffue Martling, a large blue-bearded Dutchman, who had nearly taken a British frigate with an old iron nine-pounder from a mud breastwork, only that his gun burst at the sixth discharge. And there was an old gentleman who shall be nameless, being too rich a mynheer to be lightly mentioned, who, in the battle of Whiteplains, being an excellent master of defence, parried a musket-ball with a small sword, insomuch that he absolutely felt it whiz round the blade, and glance off at the hilt; in proof of which he was ready at any time to show the sword, with the hilt a little bent. There were several more that had been equally great in the field, not one of whom but was persuaded that he had a considerable hand in bringing the war to a happy termination.

But all these were nothing to the tales of ghosts and apparitions that succeeded. The neighborhood is rich in legendary treasures of the kind. Local tales and superstitions thrive best in these sheltered long-settled retreats; but are trampled underfoot by the shifting throng that forms the population of most of our country places. Besides, there is no encouragement for ghosts in most of our villages, for they have scarcely had time to finish their first nap, and turn themselves in their graves, before their surviving friends have travelled away from the neighborhood; so that when they turn out at night to walk their rounds, they have no acquaintance left to call upon. This is perhaps the reason why we so seldom hear of ghosts, except in our long-established Dutch communities.

The immediate cause, however, of the prevalence of supernatural stories in these parts was doubtless owing to the vicinity of Sleepy Hollow. There was a contagion in the very air that blew from that haunted region; it breathed forth an atmosphere of dreams and fancies infecting all the land. Several of the Sleepy Hollow people were present at Van Tassel's, and, as usual, were doling out their wild and wonderful legends. Many dismal tales were told about funeral trains, and mourning cries and wailings heard and seen about the great tree where the unfortunate Major André was taken, and which stood in the neighborhood. Some mention was made also of the woman in white, that haunted the dark glen at Raven Rock, and was often heard to shriek on winter nights before a storm, having perished there in the snow. The chief part of the stories, however, turned upon the favorite spectre of Sleepy Hollow, the headless horseman, who had been heard several times of late, patrolling the country; and, it was said, tethered his horse nightly among the graves in the churchyard.

The sequestered situation of this church seems always to have made it a favorite haunt of troubled spirits. It stands on a knoll, surrounded by locust-trees and lofty elms, from among which its decent whitewashed walls shine modestly forth, like Christian purity beaming through the shades of retirement. A gentle slope descends from it to a silver sheet of water, bordered by high trees, between which, peeps may be caught at the blue hills of the Hudson. To look upon its grass-grown yard, where the sunbeams seem to sleep so quietly, one would think that there at least the dead might rest in peace. On one side of the church extends a wide woody dell, along which raves a large brook among broken rocks and trunks of fallen trees. Over a deep black part of the stream, not far from the church, was formerly thrown a wooden bridge; the road that led to it, and the bridge itself, were thickly shaded by overhanging trees, which cast a gloom about it, even in the daytime, but occasioned a fearful darkness at night. This was one of the favorite haunts of the headless horseman; and the place where he was most frequently encountered. The tale was told of old Brouwer, a most heretical disbeliever in ghosts, how he met the horseman returning from his foray into Sleepy Hollow, and was obliged to get up behind him; how they galloped over bush and brake, over hill and swamp, until they reached the bridge; when the horseman suddenly turned into a skeleton, threw old Brouwer into the brook, and sprang away over the tree-tops with a clap of thunder.

This story was immediately matched by a thrice marvellous adventure of Brom Bones, who made light of the galloping Hessian as an arrant jockey. He affirmed that, on returning one night from the neighboring village of Sing Sing, he had been overtaken by this midnight trooper; that he had offered to race with him for a bowl of punch, and should have won it too, for Daredevil beat the goblin horse all hollow, but, just as they came to the church-bridge, the Hessian bolted, and vanished in a flash of fire.

All these tales, told in that drowsy undertone with which men talk in the dark, the countenances of the listeners only now and then receiving a casual gleam from the glare of a pipe, sank deep in the mind of Ichabod. He repaid them in kind with large extracts from his invaluable author, Cotton Mather, and added many marvellous events that had taken place in his native State of Connecticut, and fearful sights which he had seen in his nightly walks about the Sleepy Hollow.

The revel now gradually broke up. The old farmers gathered together their families in their wagons, and were heard for some time rattling along the hollow roads, and over the distant hills. Some of the damsels mounted on pillions behind their favorite swains, and their light-hearted laughter, mingling with the clatter of hoofs, echoed along the silent woodlands, sounding fainter and fainter until they gradually died away—and the late scene of noise and frolic was all silent and deserted. Ichabod only lingered behind, according to the custom of country lovers, to have a tête-à-tête with the heiress, fully convinced that he was now on the high road to success. What passed at this interview I will not pretend to say, for in fact I do not know. Something, however, I fear me, must have gone wrong, for he certainly sallied forth, after no very great interval, with an air quite desolate and chopfallen. —Oh, these women! these women! Could that girl have been playing off any of her coquettish tricks?—Was her encouragement of the poor pedagogue all a mere sham to secure her conquest of his rival?—Heaven only knows, not I!—Let it suffice to say, Ichabod stole forth with the air of one who had been sacking a hen-roost, rather than a fair lady's heart. Without looking to the right or left to notice the scene of rural wealth on which he had so often gloated, he went straight to the stable, and with several hearty cuffs and kicks, roused his steed most uncourteously from the comfortable quarters in which he was soundly sleeping, dreaming of mountains of corn and oats, and whole valleys of timothy and clover.

It was the very witching time of night that Ichabod, heavy-hearted and crestfallen, pursued his travel homewards, along the sides of the lofty hills which rise above Tarry Town, and which he had traversed so cheerily in the afternoon. The hour was as dismal as himself. Far below him, the Tappan Zee spread its dusky and indistinct waste of waters, with here and there the tall mast of a sloop riding quietly at anchor under the land. In the dead hush of midnight he could even hear the barking of the watch-dog from the opposite shore of the Hudson; but it was so vague and faint as only to give an idea of his distance from this faithful companion of man. Now and then, too, the long-drawn crowing of a cock, accidentally awakened, would sound far, far off, from some farm-house away among the hills—but it was like a dreaming sound in his ear. No signs of life occurred near him, but occasionally the melancholy chirp of a cricket, or perhaps the guttural twang of a bull-frog, from a neighboring marsh, as if sleeping uncomfortably, and turning suddenly in his bed.

All the stories of ghosts and goblins that he had heard in the afternoon, now came crowding upon his recollection. The night grew darker and darker; the stars seemed to sink deeper in the sky, and driving clouds occasionally hid them from his sight. He had never felt so lonely and dismal. He was, moreover, approaching the very place where many of the scenes of the ghost-stories had been laid. In the centre of the road stood an enormous tulip-tree, which towered like a giant above all the other trees of the neighborhood, and formed a kind of landmark. Its limbs were gnarled, and fantastic, large enough to form trunks for ordinary trees, twisting down almost to the earth, and rising again into the air. It was connected with the tragical story of the unfortunate André, who had been taken prisoner hard by; and was universally known by the name of Major André's tree. The common people regarded it with a mixture of respect and superstition, partly out of sympathy for the fate of its ill-starred namesake, and partly from the tales of strange sights and doleful lamentations told concerning it.

As Ichabod approached this fearful tree, he began to whistle: he thought his whistle was answered,—it was but a blast sweeping sharply through the dry branches. As he approached a little nearer, he thought he saw something white, hanging in the midst of the tree,—he paused and ceased whistling; but on looking more narrowly, perceived that it was a place where the tree had been scathed by lightning, and the white wood laid bare. Suddenly he heard a groan,—his teeth chattered and his knees smote against the saddle: it was but the rubbing of one huge bough upon another, as they were swayed about by the breeze. He passed the tree in safety; but new perils lay before him.

About two hundred yards from the tree a small brook crossed the road, and ran into a marshy and thickly wooded glen, known by the name of Wiley's swamp. A few rough logs, laid side by side, served for a bridge over this stream. On that side of the road where the brook entered the wood, a group of oaks and chestnuts, matted thick with wild grape-vines, threw a cavernous gloom over it. To pass this bridge was the severest trial. It was at this identical spot that the unfortunate André was captured, and under the covert of those chestnuts and vines were the sturdy yeomen concealed who surprised him. This has ever since been considered a haunted stream, and fearful are the feelings of the school boy who has to pass it alone after dark.

As he approached the stream, his heart began to thump; he summoned up, however, all his resolution, gave his horse half a score of kicks in the ribs, and attempted to dash briskly across the bridge; but instead of starting forward, the perverse old animal made a lateral movement, and ran broadside against the fence. Ichabod, whose fears increased with the delay, jerked the reins on the other side, and kicked lustily with the contrary foot: it was all in vain; his steed started, it is true, but it was only to plunge to the opposite side of the road into a thicket of brambles and alder bushes. The schoolmaster now bestowed both whip and heel upon the starveling ribs of old Gunpowder, who dashed forward, snuffling and snorting, but came to a stand just by the bridge, with a suddenness that had nearly sent his rider sprawling over his head. Just at this moment a plashy tramp by the side of the bridge caught the sensitive ear of Ichabod. In the dark shadow of the grove, on the margin of the brook, he beheld something huge, misshapen, black, and towering. It stirred not, but seemed gathered up in the gloom, like some gigantic monster ready to spring upon the traveller.

The hair of the affrighted pedagogue rose upon his head with terror. What was to be done? To turn and fly was not too late; and besides, what chance was there of escaping ghost or goblin, if such it was, which could ride upon the wings of the wind? Summoning up, therefore, a show of courage, he demanded in stammering accents—"Who are you?" He received no reply. He repeated his demand in a still more agitated voice. Still there was no answer. Once more he cudgelled the sides of the inflexible Gunpowder, and, shutting his eyes, broke forth with involuntary fervor into a psalm-tune. Just then the shadowy object of alarm put itself in motion, and, with a scramble and a bound, stood at once in the middle of the road. Though the night was dark and dismal, yet the form of the unknown might now in some degree be ascertained. He appeared to be a horseman of large dimensions, and mounted on a black horse of powerful frame. He made no offer of molestation or sociability, but kept aloof on one side of the road, jogging along on the blind side of old Gunpowder, who had now got over his fright and waywardness.

Ichabod, who had no relish for this strange midnight companion, and bethought himself of the adventure of Brom Bones with the Galloping Hessian, now quickened his steed, in hopes of leaving him behind. The stranger, however, quickened his horse to an equal pace. Ichabod pulled up, and fell into a walk, thinking to lag behind,—the other did the same. His heart began to sink within him; he endeavored to resume his psalm-tune, but his parched tongue clove to the roof of his mouth, and he could not utter a stave. There was something in the moody and dogged silence of this pertinacious companion, that was mysterious and appalling. It was soon fearfully accounted for. On mounting a rising ground, which brought the figure of his fellow-traveller in relief against the sky, gigantic in height, and muffled in a cloak, Ichabod was horror-struck, on perceiving that he was headless! —but his horror was still more increased, on observing that the head, which should have rested on his shoulders, was carried before him on the pommel of the saddle: his terror rose to desperation; he rained a shower of kicks and blows upon Gunpowder, hoping, by a sudden movement, to give his companion the slip,— but the spectre started full jump with him. Away then they dashed, through thick and thin; stones flying, and sparks flashing at every bound. Ichabod's flimsy garments fluttered in the air, as he stretched his long lank body away over his horse's head, in the eagerness of his flight.

They had now reached the road which turns off to Sleepy Hollow; but Gunpowder, who seemed possessed with a demon, instead of keeping up it, made an opposite turn, and plunged headlong downhill to the left. This road leads through a sandy hollow, shaded by trees for about a quarter of a mile, where it crosses the bridge famous in goblin story, and just beyond swells the green knoll on which stands the whitewashed church.

As yet the panic of the steed had given his unskilful rider an apparent advantage in the chase; but just as he had got half-way through the hollow, the girths of the saddle gave way, and he felt it slipping from under him. He seized it by the pommel, and endeavored to hold it firm, but in vain; and had just time to save himself by clasping old Gunpowder round the neck, when the saddle fell to the earth, and he heard it trampled underfoot by his pursuer. For a moment the terror of Hans Van Ripper's wrath passed across his mind—for it was his Sunday saddle; but this was no time for petty fears; the goblin was hard on his haunches; and (unskilful rider that he was!) he had much ado to maintain his seat; sometimes slipping on one side, sometimes on another, and sometimes jolted on the high ridge of his horse's backbone, with a violence that he verily feared would cleave him asunder.

An opening in the trees now cheered him with the hopes that the church-bridge was at hand. The wavering reflection of a silver star in the bosom of the brook told him that he was not mistaken. He saw the walls of the church dimly glaring under the trees beyond. He recollected the place where Brom Bones's ghostly competitor had disappeared. "If I can but reach that bridge," thought Ichabod, "I am safe." Just then he heard the black steed panting and blowing close behind him; he even fancied that he felt his hot breath. Another convulsive kick in the ribs, and old Gunpowder sprang upon the bridge; he thundered over the resounding planks; he gained the opposite side; and now Ichabod cast a look behind to see if his pursuer should vanish, according to rule, in a flash of fire and brimstone. Just then he saw the goblin rising in his stirrups, and in the very act of hurling his head at him. Ichabod endeavored to dodge the horrible missile, but too late. It encountered his cranium with a tremendous crash,—he was tumbled headlong into the dust, and Gunpowder, the black steed, and the goblin rider, passed by like a whirlwind.

The next morning the old horse was found without his saddle, and with the bridle under his feet, soberly cropping the grass at his master's gate. Ichabod did not make his appearance at breakfast;—dinner-hour came, but no Ichabod. The boys assembled at the school-house, and strolled idly about the banks of the brook; but no schoolmaster. Hans Van Ripper now began to feel some uneasiness about the fate of poor Ichabod, and his saddle. An inquiry was set on foot, and after diligent investigation they came upon his traces. In one part of the road leading to the church was found the saddle trampled in the dirt; the tracks of horses' hoofs deeply dented in the road, and evidently at furious speed, were traced to the bridge, beyond which, on the bank of a broad part of the brook, where the water ran deep and black, was found the hat of the unfortunate Ichabod, and close beside it a shattered pumpkin.

The brook was searched, but the body of the schoolmaster was not to be discovered. Hans Van Ripper, as executor of his estate, examined the bundle which contained all his worldly effects. They consisted of two shirts and a half; two stocks for the neck; a pair or two of worsted stockings; an old pair of corduroy small-clothes; a rusty razor; a book of psalm-tunes, full of dogs' ears, and a broken pitchpipe. As to the books and furniture of the school-house, they belonged to the community, excepting Cotton Mather's "History of Witchcraft," a "New England Almanac," and a book of dreams and fortune-telling; in which last was a sheet of foolscap much scribbled and blotted in several fruitless attempts to make a copy of verses in honor of the heiress of Van Tassel. These magic books and the poetic scrawl were forthwith consigned to the flames by Hans Van Ripper; who from that time forward determined to send his children no more to school; observing, that he never knew any good come of this same reading and writing. Whatever money the schoolmaster possessed, and he had received his quarter's pay but a day or two before, he must have had about his person at the time of his disappearance.

The mysterious event caused much speculation at the church on the following Sunday. Knots of gazers and gossips were collected in the churchyard, at the bridge, and at the spot where the hat and pumpkin had been found. The stories of Brouwer, of Bones, and a whole budget of others, were called to mind; and when they had diligently considered them all, and compared them with the symptoms of the present case, they shook their heads, and came to the conclusion that Ichabod had been carried off by the Galloping Hessian. As he was a bachelor, and in nobody's debt, nobody troubled his head any more about him. The school was removed to a different quarter of the Hollow, and another pedagogue reigned in his stead.

It is true, an old farmer, who had been down to New York on a visit several years after, and from whom this account of the ghostly adventure was received, brought home the intelligence that Ichabod Crane was still alive; that he had left the neighborhood, partly through fear of the goblin and Hans Van Ripper, and partly in mortification at having been suddenly dismissed by the heiress; that he had changed his quarters to a distant part of the country; had kept school and studied law at the same time, had been admitted to the bar, turned politician, electioneered, written for the newspapers, and finally had been made a justice of the Ten Pound Court. Brom Bones too, who shortly after his rival's disappearance conducted the blooming Katrina in triumph to the altar, was observed to look exceeding knowing whenever the story of Ichabod was related, and always burst into a hearty laugh at the mention of the pumpkin; which led some to suspect that he knew more about the matter than he chose to tell.

The old country wives, however, who are the best judges of these matters, maintain to this day that Ichabod was spirited away by supernatural means; and it is a favorite story often told about the neighborhood round the winter evening fire. The bridge became more than ever an object of superstitious awe, and that may be the reason why the road has been altered of late years, so as to approach the church by the border of the mill-pond. The school-house, being deserted, soon fell to decay, and was reported to be haunted by the ghost of the unfortunate pedagogue; and the ploughboy, loitering homeward of a still summer evening, has often fancied his voice at a distance, chanting a melancholy psalm-tune among the tranquil solitudes of Sleepy Hollow.

POSTSCRIPT,
Found in the Handwriting of Mr. Knickerbocker

THE preceding Tale is given, almost in the precise words in which I heard it related at a Corporation meeting of the ancient city of Manhattoes, at which were present many of its sagest and most illustrious burghers. The narrator was a pleasant, shabby, gentlemanly old fellow, in pepper-and-salt clothes, with a sadly humorous face; and one whom I strongly suspected of being poor,—he made such efforts to be entertaining. When his story was concluded, there was much laughter and approbation, particularly from two or three deputy aldermen, who had been asleep the greater part of the time. There was, however, one tall, dry-looking old gentleman, with beetling eyebrows, who maintained a grave and rather severe face throughout: now and then folding his arms, inclining his head, and looking down upon the floor, as if turning a doubt over in his mind. He was one of your wary men, who never laugh, but upon good grounds—when they have reason and the law on their side. When the mirth of the rest of the company had subsided and silence was restored, he leaned one arm on the elbow of his chair, and, sticking the other akimbo, demanded, with a slight but exceedingly sage motion of the head, and contraction of the brow, what was the moral of the story, and what it went to prove?

The story-teller, who was just putting a glass of wine to his lips, as a refreshment after his toils, paused for a moment, looked at his inquirer with an air of infinite deference, and, lowering the glass slowly to the table, observed, that the story was intended most logically to prove:—

"That there is no situation in life but has its advantages and pleasures—provided we will but take a joke as we find it:

"That, therefore, he that runs races with goblin troopers is likely to have rough riding of it.

"Ergo, for a country schoolmaster to be refused the hand of a Dutch heiress, is a certain step to high preferment in the state."

The cautious old gentleman knit his brows tenfold closer after this explanation, being sorely puzzled by the ratiocination of the syllogism; while, methought, the one in pepper-and-salt eyed him with something of a triumphant leer. At length he observed, that all this was very well, but still he thought the story a little on the extravagant—there were one or two points on which he had his doubts.

"Faith, sir," replied the story-teller, "as to that matter, I don't believe one half of it myself."

D. K.

BRACEBRIDGE HALL

·{❀❀❀}·

THE HALL

The ancient house, and the best for housekeeping, in this county or the next; and though the master of it write but squire, I know no lord like him.

Merry Beggars

THE READER, IF HE has perused the volumes of the "Sketch-Book," will probably recollect something of the Bracebridge family, with which I once passed a Christmas. I am now on another visit at the Hall, having been invited to a wedding which is shortly to take place. The Squire's second son, Guy, a fine, spirited young captain in the army, is about to be married to his father's ward, the fair Julia Templeton. A gathering of relations and friends has already commenced, to celebrate the joyful occasion; for the old gentleman is an enemy to quiet, private weddings. "There is nothing," he says, "like launching a young couple gayly, and cheering them from the shore; a good outset is half the voyage."

Before proceeding any farther, I would beg that the Squire might not be confounded with that class of hard-riding, fox-hunting gentlemen, so often described, and, in fact, so nearly extinct in England. I used this rural title partly because it is his universal appellation throughout the neighborhood, and partly because it saves me the frequent repetition of his name, which is one of those rough old English names at which Frenchmen exclaim in despair.

The Squire is, in fact, a lingering specimen of the old English country gentleman; rusticated a little by living almost entirely on his estate, and something of a humorist, as Englishmen are apt to become when they have an opportunity of living in their own way. I like his hobby passing well, however, which is, a bigoted devotion to old English manners and customs; it jumps a little with my own humor, having as yet a lively and unsated curiosity about the ancient and genuine characteristics of my "father-land."

There are some traits about the Squire's family, also, which appear to me to be national. It is one of those old aristocratical families which, I believe, are peculiar to England, and scarcely understood in other countries; that is to say, families of the ancient gentry, who, though destitute of titled rank, maintain a high ancestral pride: who look down upon all nobility of recent creation, and would consider it a sacrifice of dignity to merge the venerable name of their house in a modern title.

This feeling is very much fostered by the importance which they enjoy on their hereditary domains. The family mansion is an old manor-house, standing in a retired and beautiful part of Yorkshire. Its inhabitants have been always regarded, through the surrounding country, as "the great ones of the earth"; and the little village near the Hall looks up to the Squire with almost feudal homage. An old manor-house, and an old family of this kind, are rarely to be met with at the present day; and it is probably the peculiar humor of the Squire that has retained this secluded specimen of English housekeeping in something like the genuine old style.

I am again quartered in the panelled chamber, in the antique wing of the house. The prospect from my window, however, has quite a different aspect from that which it wore on my winter visit. Though early in the month of April, yet a few warm, sunshiny days have drawn forth the beauties of the spring, which, I think, are always most captivating on their first opening. The parterres of the old-fashioned garden are gay with flowers; and the gardener has brought out his exotics, and placed them along the stone balustrades. The trees are clothed with green buds and tender leaves. When I throw open my jingling casement, I smell the odor of mignonette, and hear the hum of the bees from the flowers against the sunny wall, with the varied song of the throstle, and the cheerful notes of the tuneful little wren.

While sojourning in this stronghold of old fashions, it is my intention to make occasional sketches of the scenes and characters before me. I would have it understood, however, that I am not writing a novel, and have nothing of intricate plot nor marvellous adventure to promise the reader. The Hall of which I treat has, for aught I know, neither trap-door, nor sliding-panel, nor lonjon-keep; and indeed appears to have no mystery about it. The family is a worthy, well-meaning family, that, in all probability, will eat and drink, and go to bed, and get up regularly, from one end of my work to the other; and the Squire is so kind-hearted, that I see no likelihood of his throwing any kind of distress in the way of the approaching nuptials. In a word, I cannot foresee a single extraordinary event that is likely to occur in the whole term of my sojourn at the Hall.

I tell this honestly to the reader, lest, when he finds me dally-ing along, through every-day English scenes, he may hurry ahead, in hopes of meeting with some marvellous adventure further on. I invite him, on the contrary, to ramble gently on with me, as he would saunter out into the fields, stopping occasionally to gather a flower, or listen to a bird, or admire a prospect, without any anxiety to arrive at the end of his career. Should I, however, in the course of my wanderings about this old mansion, see or hear any-thing curious, that might serve to vary the monotony of this every-day life, I shall not fail to report it for the reader's entertainment:

> For freshest wits I know will soon be wearie,
> Of any book, how grave soe'er it be,
> Except it have odd matter, strange and merrie,
> Well sauc'd with lies, and glared all with glee.*

* *Mirror for Magistrates.*

FAMILY SERVANTS

Verily old servants are the vouchers of worthy housekeeping. They are like rats in a mansion, or mites in a cheese, bespeaking the antiquity and fatness of their abode.

IN MY CASUAL ANECDOTES of the Hall, I may often be tempted to dwell upon circumstances of a trite and ordinary nature, from their appearing to me illustrative of genuine national character. It seems to me to be the study of the Squire to adhere, as much as possible, to what he considers the old landmarks of English manners. His servants all understand his ways, and for the most part have been accustomed to them from infancy; so that, upon the whole, his household presents one of the few tolerable specimens that can now be met with, of the establishment of an English country gentleman of the old school.

By the by, the servants are not the least characteristic part of the household: the housekeeper, for instance, has been born and brought up at the Hall, and has never been twenty miles from it; yet she has a stately air that would not disgrace a lady that had figured at the court of Queen Elizabeth.

I am half inclined to think she has caught it from living so much among the old family pictures. It may, however, be owing to a consciousness of her importance in the sphere in which she has always moved; for she is greatly respected in the neighboring village, and among the farmers' wives, and has high authority in the household, ruling over the servants with quiet but undisputed sway.

She is a thin old lady, with blue eyes and pointed nose and chin. Her dress is always the same as to fashion. She wears a small, well-starched ruff, a laced stomacher, full petticoats, and a gown festooned and open in front, which, on particular occasions, is of ancient silk, the legacy of some former dame of the family, or an inheritance from her mother, who was housekeeper before her. I have a reverence for these old garments, as I make no doubt they have figured about these apartments in days long past, when they have set off the charms of some peerless family beauty; and I have sometimes looked from the old housekeeper to the neighboring portraits, to see whether I could not recognize her antiquated brocade in the dress of some one of those long-waisted dames that smile on me from the walls.

Her hair, which is quite white, is frizzed out in front, and she wears over it a small cap, nicely plaited, and brought down under the chin. Her manners are simple and primitive, heightened a little by a proper dignity of station.

The Hall is her world, and the history of the family the only history she knows, excepting that which she has read in the Bible. She can give a biography of every portrait in the picture gallery, and is a complete family chronicle.

She is treated with great consideration by the Squire. Indeed, Master Simon tells me that there is a traditional anecdote current among the servants, of the Squire's having been seen kissing her in the picture gallery, when they were both young. As, however, nothing further was ever noticed between them, the circumstance caused no great scandal; only she was observed to take to reading Pamela shortly afterwards, and refused the hand of the village innkeeper, whom she had previously smiled on.

The old butler, who was formerly footman, and a rejected admirer of hers, used to tell the anecdote now and then, at those little cabals which will occasionally take place among the most orderly servants, arising from the common propensity of the governed to talk against administration; but he has left it off, of late years, since he has risen into place, and shakes his head rebukingly when it is mentioned.

It is certain that the old lady will, to this day, dwell upon the looks of the Squire when he was a young man at college; and she maintains that none of his sons can compare with their father when he was of their age, and was dressed out in his full suit of scarlet, with his hair craped and powdered, and his three-cornered hat.

She has an orphan niece, a pretty, soft-hearted baggage, named Phoebe Wilkins, who has been transplanted to the hall within a year or two, and been nearly spoiled for any condition of life. She is a kind of attendant and companion of the fair Julia's; and from loitering about the young lady's apartments, reading scraps of novels, and inheriting second-hand finery, has become something between a waiting-maid and a slipshod fine lady.

She is considered a kind of heiress among the servants, as she will inherit all her aunt's property; which, if report be true, must be a round sum of good golden guineas, the accumulated wealth of two housekeepers' savings; not to mention the hereditary wardrobe, and the many little valuables and knick-knacks treasured up in the housekeepers' room. Indeed, the old housekeeper has the reputation among the servants and the villagers of being passing rich; and there is a japanned chest of drawers and a large iron-bound coffer in her room, which are supposed, by the housemaids, to hold treasures of wealth.

The old lady is a great friend of Master Simon, who, indeed, pays a little court to her, as to a person high in authority; and they have many discussions on points of family history, in which, notwithstanding his extensive information and pride of knowledge, he commonly admits her superior accuracy. He seldom returns to the Hall, after one of his visits to the other branches of the family, without bringing Mrs. Wilkins some remembrance from the ladies of the house where he has been staying.

Indeed, all the children of the house look up to the old lady with habitual respect and attachment, and she seems almost to consider them as her own, from their having grown up under her eye. The Oxonian, however, is her favorite, probably from being the youngest, though he is the most mischievous, and has been apt to play tricks upon her from boyhood.

I cannot help mentioning one little ceremony, which, I believe, is peculiar to the Hall. After the cloth is removed at dinner, the old housekeeper sails into the room, and stands behind the Squire's chair, when he fills her a glass of wine with his own hands, in which she drinks the health of the company in a truly respectful yet dignified manner, and then retires. The Squire received the custom from his father, and has always continued it.

There is a peculiar character about the servants of old English families, that reside principally in the country. They have a quiet, orderly, respectful mode of doing their duties. They are always neat in their persons, and appropriately, and, if I may use the phrase, technically dressed; they move about the house without hurry or noise; there is nothing of the bustle of employment, or the voice of command; nothing of that obtrusive housewifery which amounts to a torment. You are not persecuted by the process of making you comfortable; yet everything is done, and is done well. The work of the house is performed as if by magic, but it is the magic of system. Nothing is done by fits and starts, nor at awkward seasons; the whole goes on like well-oiled clock-work, where there is no noise nor jarring in its operations.

English servants, in general, are not treated with great indulgence, nor rewarded by many commendations; for the English are laconic and reserved toward their domestics; but an approving nod and a kind word from master or mistress goes as far here as an excess of praise or indulgence elsewhere. Neither do servants often exhibit any animated marks of affection to their employers; yet, though quiet, they are strong in their attachments; and the reciprocal regard of masters and servants, though not ardently expressed, is powerful and lasting in old English families.

The title of "an old family servant" carries with it a thousand kind associations, in all parts of the world; and there is no claim upon the homebred charities of the heart more irresistible than that of having been "born in the house." It is common to see gray-headed domestics of this kind attached to an English family of the "old school," who continue in it to the day of their death, in the enjoyment of steady, unaffected kindness, and the performance of faithful, unofficious duty. I think such instances of attachment speak well for both master and servant, and the frequency of them speaks well for national character.

These observations, however, hold good only with families of the description I have mentioned, and with such as are somewhat retired, and pass the greater part of their time in the country. As to the powdered menials that throng the halls of fashionable town residences, they equally reflect the character of the establishments to which they belong; and I know no more complete epitome of dissolute heartlessness, and pampered inutility.

But the good "old family servant,"—the one who has always been linked, in idea, with the home of our heart; who has led us to school in the days of prattling childhood; who has been the confidant of our boyish cares, and schemes, and enterprises; who has hailed us as we came home at vacations, and been the promoter of all our holiday sports; who, when we, in wandering manhood, have left the paternal roof, and only return thither at intervals, will welcome us with a joy inferior only to that of our parents; who, now grown gray and infirm with age, still totters about the house of our fathers, in fond and faithful servitude; who claims us, in a manner, as his own; and hastens with querulous eagerness to anticipate his fellow-domestics in waiting upon us at table; and who, when we retire at night to the chamber that still goes by our name, will linger about the room to have one more kind look, and one more pleasant word about times that are past, —who does not experience towards such a being a feeling of almost filial affection?

I have met with several instances of epitaphs on the gravestones of such valuable domestics, recorded with the simple truth of natural feeling. I have two before me at this moment; one copied from a tombstone of a church in Warwickshire:

"Here lieth the body of Joseph Batte, confidential servant to George Birch, Esq., of Hamstead Hall. His grateful friend and master caused this inscription to be written in memory of his discretion, fidelity, diligence, and continence. He died (a bachelor) aged 84, having lived 44 years in the same family."

The other was taken from a tombstone in Eltham church-yard:

"Here lie the remains of Mr. James Tappy, who departed this life on the 8th of September, 1818, aged 84, after a faithful service of 60 years in one family; by each individual of which he lived respected, and died lamented by the sole survivor."

Few monuments, even of the illustrious, have given me the glow about the heart that I felt while copying this honest epitaph in the church-yard of Eltham. I sympathized with this "sole sur-

vivor" of a family mourning over the grave of the faithful follower
of his race, who had been, no doubt, a living memento of times
and friends that had passed away; and in considering this record
of long and devoted service, I call to mind the touching speech of
Old Adam, in "As You Like It," when tottering after the youthful
son of his ancient master:

> "Master, go on, and I will follow thee
> To the last gasp, with love and loyalty."

NOTE

I cannot but mention a tablet which I have seen somewhere in the
chapel of Windsor Castle, put up by the late king to the memory of a family
servant, who had been a faithful attendant of his lamented daughter, the
Princess Amelia. George III. possessed much of the strong, domestic feeling
of the old English country gentleman; and it is an incident curious in monumental history, and creditable to the human heart, a monarch erecting a
monument in honor of the humble virtues of a menial.

READY-MONEY JACK

> My purse, it is my privy wyfe,
> This song I dare both syng and say,
> It keepeth men from grievous stryfe
> When every man for hymself shall pay
> As I ryde in ryche array
> For gold and silver men wyll me floryshe;
> By thys matter I dare well saye,
> Ever gramercy myne owne purse.
>
> *Book of Hunting*

ON THE SKIRTS of the neighboring village there lives a kind of
small potentate, who, for aught I know, is a representative of one
of the most ancient legitimate lines of the present day; for the

empire over which he reigns has belonged to his family time out of mind. His territories comprise a considerable number of good fat acres; and his seat of power is in an old farm-house, where he enjoys, unmolested, the stout oaken chair of his ancestors. The personage to whom I allude is a sturdy old yeoman of the name of John Tibbets, or rather Ready-Money Jack Tibbets, as he is called throughout the neighborhood.

The first place where he attracted my attention was in the church-yard on Sunday; where he sat on a tombstone after the service, with his hat a little on one side, holding forth to a small circle of auditors; and, as I presumed, expounding the law and the prophets; until, on drawing a little nearer, I found he was only expatiating on the merits of a brown horse. He presented so faithful a picture of a substantial English yeoman, such as he is often described in books, heightened, indeed, by some little finery peculiar to himself, that I could not but take note of his whole appearance.

He was between fifty and sixty, of a strong, muscular frame, and at least six feet high, with a physiognomy as grave as a lion's, and set off with short, curling, iron-gray locks. His shirt-collar was turned down, and displayed a neck covered with the same short, curling, gray hair; and he wore a colored silk neck-cloth, tied very loosely, and tucked in at the bosom, with a green paste brooch on the knot. His coat was of dark-green cloth, with silver buttons, on each of which was engraved a stag, with his own name, John Tibbets, underneath. He had an inner waistcoat of figured chintz, between which and his coat was another of scarlet cloth, unbuttoned. His breeches were also left unbuttoned at the knees, not from any slovenliness, but to show a broad pair of scarlet garters. His stockings were blue, with white clocks; he wore large silver shoe-buckles; a broad paste buckle in his hatband; his sleeve-buttons were gold seven-shilling pieces; and he had two or three guineas hanging as ornaments to his watch-chain.

On making some inquiries about him, I gathered, that he was descended from a line of farmers that had always lived on the same spot, and owned the same property; and that half of the church-yard was taken up with the tombstones of his race. He has all his life been an important character in the place. When a youngster he was one of the most roaring blades of the neighborhood. No one could match him at wrestling, pitching the bar, cudgel play, and other athletic exercises. Like the renowned Pinner of Wakefield, he was the village champion; carried off the prize at all the fairs, and threw his gauntlet at the country round. Even to this day the old people talk of his prowess, and undervalue, in comparison, all heroes of the green that have succeeded him; nay, they say, that if Ready-Money Jack were to take the field even now, there is no one could stand before him.

When Jack's father died, the neighbors shook their heads, and predicted that young hopeful would soon make way with the old homestead; but Jack falsified all their predictions. The moment he succeeded to the paternal farm, he assumed a new character: took a wife; attended resolutely to his affairs, and became an industrious, thrifty farmer. With the family property he inherited a set of old family maxims, to which he steadily adhered. He saw to everything himself; put his own hand to the plough; worked hard; ate heartily; slept soundly; paid for everything in cash down; and never danced except he could do it to the music of his own money in both pockets. He has never been without a hundred or two pounds in gold by him, and never allows a debt to stand unpaid. This has gained him his current name, of which, by the by, he is a little proud; and has caused him to be looked upon as a very wealthy man by all the village.

Notwithstanding his thrift, however, he has never denied himself the amusements of life, but has taken a share in every passing pleasure. It is his maxim, that "he that works hard can afford to play." He is, therefore, an attendant at all the country fairs and wakes, and has signalized himself by feats of strength and prowess on every village green in the shire. He often makes his appearance at horse-races, and sports his half-guinea, and even his guinea at a time; keeps a good horse for his own riding, and to this day is fond of following the hounds, and is generally in at the death. He keeps up the rustic revels, and hospitalities too, for which his paternal farm-house has always been noted; has plenty of good cheer and dancing at harvest-home, and, above all, keeps the "merry night," * as it is termed, at Christmas.

With all his love of amusement, however, Jack is by no means a boisterous jovial companion. He is seldom known to laugh even in the midst of his gayety; but maintains the same grave, lion-like demeanor. He is very slow at comprehending a joke; and is apt to sit puzzling at it, with a perplexed look, while the rest of the company is in a roar. This gravity has, perhaps, grown on him with the growing weight of his character; for he is gradually rising into patriarchal dignity in his native place. Though he no longer takes an active part in athletic sports, he always presides at them, and is appealed to on all occasions as umpire. He maintains the peace on the village green at holiday games, and quells all brawls and quarrels by collaring the parties and shaking them heartily, if refractory. No one ever pretends to raise a hand against him, or to contend against his decisions; the young men have grown up in habitual awe of his prowess, and in implicit deference to him as the champion and lord of the green.

He is a regular frequenter of the village inn, the landlady having been a sweetheart of his in early life, and he having always continued on kind terms with her. He seldom, however, drinks anything but a draught of ale; smokes his pipe, and pays his reckoning before leaving the tap-room. Here he "gives his little senate laws"; decides bets, which are very generally referred to him; determines upon the characters and qualities of horses; and, indeed, plays now and then the part of a judge, in settling petty disputes between neighbors, which otherwise might have been nursed by country attorneys into tolerable law-suits. Jack is very candid and impartial in his decisions, but he has not a head to carry a long argument, and is very apt to get perplexed and out of patience if there is much pleading. He generally breaks through the argument with a strong voice, and brings matters to a summary conclusion by pronouncing what he calls the "upshot of the

---

* MERRY NIGHT. A rustic merry-making in a farm-house about Christmas, common in some parts of Yorkshire. There is abundance of homely fare, tea, cakes, fruit, and ale; various feats of agility, amusing games, romping, dancing, and kissing withal. They commonly break up at midnight.

business," or, in other words, "the long and the short of the matter."

Jack made a journey to London a great many years since, which has furnished him with topics of conversation ever since. He saw the old king on the terrace at Windsor, who stopped, and pointed him out to one of the princesses, being probably struck with Jack's truly yeomanlike appearance. This is a favorite anecdote with him, and has no doubt had a great effect in making him a most loyal subject ever since, in spite of taxes and poors' rates. He was also at Bartholomew fair, where he had half the buttons cut off his coat; and a gang of pickpockets, attracted by his external show of gold and silver, made a regular attempt to hustle him as he was gazing at a show; but for once they caught a tartar, for Jack enacted as great wonders among the gang as Samson did among the Philistines. One of his neighbors, who had accompanied him to town, and was with him at the fair, brought back an account of his exploits, which raised the pride of the whole village; who considered their champion as having subdued all London, and eclipsed the achievements of Friar Tuck, or even the renowned Robin Hood himself.

Of late years the old fellow has begun to take the world easily; he works less, and indulges in greater leisure, his son having grown up, and succeeded to him both in the labors of the farm and the exploits of the green. Like all sons of distinguished men, however, his father's renown is a disadvantage to him, for he can never come up to public expectation. Though a fine active fellow of three-and-twenty, and quite the "cock of the walk," yet the old people declare he is nothing like what Ready-Money Jack was at his time of life. The youngster himself acknowledges his inferiority, and has a wonderful opinion of the old man, who indeed taught him all his athletic accomplishments, and holds such a sway over him, that, I am told, even to this day, he would have no hesitation to take him in hands, if he rebelled against paternal government.

The Squire holds Jack in very high esteem, and shows him to all his visitors, as a specimen of old English "heart of oak." He frequently calls at his house, and tastes some of his home-brewed, which is excellent. He made Jack a present of old Tusser's "Hundred Points of good Husbandrie," which has furnished him with reading ever since, and is his text-book and manual in all agricultural and domestic concerns. He has made dog's ears at the most favorite passages, and knows many of the poetical maxims by heart.

Tibbets, though not a man to be daunted or fluttered by high acquaintances, and though he cherishes a sturdy independence of mind and manner, yet is evidently gratified by the attentions of the Squire, whom he has known from boyhood, and pronounces "a true gentleman every inch of him." He is, also, on excellent terms with Master Simon, who is a kind of privy counsellor to the family; but his great favorite is the Oxonian, whom he taught to wrestle and play at quarter-staff when a boy, and considers the most promising young gentleman in the whole county.

STORY-TELLING

A FAVORITE EVENING pastime at the Hall, and one which the worthy Squire is fond of promoting, is story-telling, "a good old-fashioned fireside amusement," as he terms it. Indeed, I believe he promotes it chiefly because it was one of the choice recreations in those days of yore when ladies and gentlemen were not much in the habit of reading. Be this as it may, he will often, at supper-table, when conversation flags, call on some one or other of the company for a story, as it was formerly the custom to call for a song; and it is edifying to see the exemplary patience, and even satisfaction, with which the good old gentleman will sit and listen to some hackneyed tale that he has heard for at least a hundred times.

In this way one evening the current of anecdotes and stories ran upon mysterious personages that have figured at different times, and filled the world with doubts and conjecture; such as the Wandering Jew, the Man with the Iron Mask, who tormented the curiosity of all Europe; the Invisible Girl, and last, though not least, the Pig-faced Lady.

At length one of the company was called upon who had the most unpromising physiognomy for a story-teller that ever I had seen. He was a thin, pale, weazen-faced man, extremely nervous, who had sat at one corner of the table, shrunk up, as it were, into himself, and almost swallowed up in the cape of his coat, as a turtle in its shell. The very demand seemed to throw him into a nervous agitation, yet he did not refuse. He emerged his head out of his shell, made a few odd grimaces and gesticulations, before he could get his muscles into order, or his voice under command, and then offered to give some account of a mysterious personage whom he had recently encountered in the course of his travels, and one whom he thought fully entitled of being classed with the Man with the Iron Mask.

I was so much struck with his extraordinary narrative, that I have written it out to the best of my recollection, for the amusement of the reader. I think it has in it all the elements of that mysterious and romantic narrative so greedily sought after at the present day.

THE STOUT GENTLEMAN

A Stage-coach Romance

I'll cross it, though it blast me!

Hamlet

It was a rainy Sunday in the gloomy month of November. I had been detained, in the course of a journey, by a slight indipsosition, from which I was recovering; but was still feverish, and obliged to keep within doors all day, in an inn of the small town of Derby.

A wet Sunday in a country inn!—whoever has had the luck to experience one can alone judge of my situation. The rain pattered against the casements; the bells tolled for church with a melancholy sound. I went to the windows in quest of something to amuse the eye; but it seemed as if I had been placed completely out of the reach of all amusement. The windows of my bedroom looked out among tiled roofs and stacks of chimneys, while those of my sitting-room commanded a full view of the stable-yard. I know of nothing more calculated to make a man sick of this world than a stable-yard on a rainy day. The place was littered with wet straw that had been kicked about by travellers and stable-boys. In one corner was a stagnant pool of water, surrounding an island of muck; there were several half-drowned fowls crowded together under a cart, among which was a miserable, crestfallen cock, drenched out of all life and spirit; his drooping tail matted, as it were, into a single feather, along which the water trickled from his back; near the cart was a half-dozing cow, chewing the cud, and standing patiently to be rained on, with wreaths of vapor rising from her reeking hide; a wall-eyed horse, tired of the loneliness of the stable, was poking his spectral head out of a window, with the rain dripping on it from the eaves; an unhappy cur, chained to a dog-house hard by, uttered something, every now and then, between a bark and a yelp; a drab of a kitchen-wench tramped backwards and forwards through the yard in pattens, looking as sulky as the weather itself; everything, in short, was comfortless and forlorn, excepting a crew of hardened ducks, assembled like boon companions round a puddle, and making a riotous noise over their liquor.

I was lonely and listless, and wanted amusement. My room soon became insupportable. I abandoned it, and sought what is technically called the travellers'-room. This is a public room set apart at most inns for the accommodation of a class of wayfarers called travellers, or riders; a kind of commercial knights-errant, who are incessantly scouring the kingdom in gigs, on horseback, or by coach. They are the only successors that I know of at the present day to the knights-errant of yore. They lead the same kind of roving, adventurous life, only changing the lance for a driving-whip, the buckler for a pattern-card, and the coat of mail for an upper Benjamin. Instead of vindicating the charms of peerless beauty, they rove about, spreading the fame and standing of some substantial tradesman, or manufacturer, and are ready at any time to bargain in his name; it being the fashion nowadays to trade, instead of fight, with one another. As the room of the hostel, in the good old fighting-times, would be hung round at night with the armor of way-worn warriors, such as coats of mail, falchions, and yawning helmets, so the travellers'-room is garnished with the harnessing of their successors, with box-coats, whips of all kinds, spurs, gaiters, and oil-cloth covered hats.

I was in hopes of finding some of these worthies to talk with, but was disappointed. There were, indeed, two or three in the room; but I could make nothing of them. One was just finishing his breakfast, quarrelling with his bread and butter, and huffing the waiter; another buttoned on a pair of gaiters, with many execrations at Boots for not having cleaned his shoes well; a third sat drumming on the table with his fingers and looking at the rain as it streamed down the window-glass; they all appeared infected by the weather, and disappeared, one after the other, without exchanging a word.

I sauntered to the window, and stood gazing at the people, picking their way to church, with petticoats hoisted midleg high, and dripping umbrellas. The bell ceased to toll, and the streets became silent. I then amused myself with watching the daughters of a tradesman opposite; who, being confined to the house for fear of wetting their Sunday finery, played off their charms at the front windows, to fascinate the chance tenants of the inn. They at length were summoned away by a vigilant vinegar-faced mother, and I had nothing further from without to amuse me.

What was I to do to pass away the long-lived day? I was sadly nervous and lonely; and everything about an inn seems calculated to make a dull day ten times duller. Old newspapers, smelling of beer and tobacco-smoke, and which I had already read half a dozen times. Good-for-nothing books, that were worse than rainy weather. I bored myself to death with an old volume of the Lady's Magazine. I read all the commonplace names of ambitious travellers scrawled on the panes of glass; the eternal families of the Smiths, and the Browns, and the Jacksons, and the Johnsons, and all the other sons; and I deciphered several scraps of fatiguing inn-window poetry which I have met with in all parts of the world.

The day continued lowering and gloomy; the slovenly, ragged, spongy cloud drifted heavily along; there was no variety even in the rain: it was one dull, continued, monotonous patter—patter—patter, excepting that now and then I was enlivened by the idea of a brisk shower, from the rattling of the drops upon a passing umbrella.

It was quite *refreshing* (if I may be allowed a hackneyed phrase of the day) when, in the course of the morning, a horn blew, and a stage-coach whirled through the street, with outside passengers stuck all over it, cowering under cotton umbrellas, and seethed together, and reeking with the steams of wet box-coats and upper Benjamins.

The sound brought out from their lurking-places a crew of vagabond boys, and vagabond dogs, and the carroty-headed hostler, and that nondescript animal ycleped Boots, and all the other vagabond race that infest the purlieus of an inn; but the bustle was transient; the coach again whirled on its way; and boy and dog, and hostler and Boots, all slunk back again to their holes; the street again became silent, and the rain continued to rain on. In fact, there was no hope of its clearing up; the barometer pointed to rainy weather; mine hostess's tortoise-shell cat sat by the fire washing her face, and rubbing her paws over her ears; and, on referring to the Almanac, I found a direful prediction stretching from the top of the page to the bottom through the whole month, "expect—much—rain—about—this—time!"

I was dreadfully hipped. The hours seemed as if they would never creep by. The very ticking of the clock became irksome. At length the stillness of the house was interrupted by the ringing of a bell. Shortly after I heard the voice of a waiter at the bar: "The stout gentleman in No. 13 wants his breakfast. Tea and bread and butter, with ham and eggs; the eggs not to be too much done."

In such a situation as mine, every incident is of importance.

Here was a subject of speculation presented to my mind, and ample exercise for my imagination. I am prone to paint pictures to myself, and on this occasion I had some materials to work upon. Had the guest up-stairs been mentioned as Mr. Smith, or Mr. Brown, or Mr. Jackson, or Mr. Johnson, or merely as "the gentleman in No. 13," it would have been a perfect blank to me. I should have thought nothing of it; but "The stout gentleman!"— the very name had something in it of the picturesque. It at once gave the size; it embodied the personage to my mind's eye, and my fancy did the rest.

He was stout, or, as some term it, lusty; in all probability, therefore, he was advanced in life, some people expanding as they grow old. By his breakfasting rather late, and in his own room, he must be a man accustomed to live at his ease, and above the necessity of early rising; no doubt a round, rosy, lusty old gentleman.

There was another violent ringing. The stout gentleman was impatient for his breakfast. He was evidently a man of importance; "well to do in the world;" accustomed to be promptly waited upon; of a keen appetite, and a little cross when hungry; "perhaps," thought I, "he may be some London Alderman; or who knows but he may be a Member of Parliament?"

The breakfast was sent up, and there was a short interval of silence; he was, doubtless, making the tea. Presently there was a violent ringing; and before it could be answered, another ringing still more violent. "Bless me! what a choleric old gentleman!" The waiter came down in a huff. The butter was rancid, the eggs were overdone, the ham was too salt;—the stout gentleman was evidently nice in his eating; one of those who eat and growl, and keep the waiter on the trot, and live in a state militant with the household.

The hostess got into a fume. I should observe that she was a brisk, coquettish woman; a little of a shrew, and something of a slammerkin, but very pretty withal; with a nincompoop for a husband, as shrews are apt to have. She rated the servants roundly for their negligence in sending up so bad a breakfast, but said not a word against the stout gentleman; by which I clearly perceived that he must be a man of consequence, entitled to make a noise and to give trouble at a country inn. Other eggs, and ham, and bread and butter were sent up. They appeared to be more graciously received; at least there was no further complaint.

I had not made many turns about the travellers'-room, when there was another ringing. Shortly afterwards there was a stir and an inquest about the house. The stout gentleman wanted the Times or the Chronicle newspaper. I set him down, therefore, for a Whig; or rather, from his being so absolute and lordly where he had a chance, I suspected him of being a Radical. Hunt, I had heard, was a large man; "who knows," thought I, "but it is Hunt himself!"

My curiosity began to be awakened. I inquired of the waiter who was this stout gentleman that was making all this stir; but I could get no information: nobody seemed to know his name. The landlords of bustling inns seldom trouble their heads about the names or occupations of their transient guests. The color of a coat, the shape or size of the person, is enough to suggest a travelling name. It is either the tall gentleman, or the short gentleman, or the gentleman in black, or the gentleman in snuff-color; or, as in the present instance, the stout gentleman. A designation of the kind once hit on, answers every purpose, and saves all further inquiry.

Rain—rain—rain! pitiless, ceaseless rain! No such thing as putting a foot out of doors, and no occupation nor amusement within. By and by I heard some one walking overhead. It was in the stout gentleman's room. He evidently was a large man by the heaviness of his tread; and an old man from his wearing such creaking soles. "He is doubtless," thought I, "some rich old square-toes of regular habits, and is now taking exercise after breakfast."

I now read all the advertisements of coaches and hotels that were stuck about the mantelpiece. The Lady's Magazine had become an abomination to me; it was as tedious as the day itself. I wandered out, not knowing what to do, and ascended again to my room. I had not been there long, when there was a squall from a neighboring bedroom. A door opened and slammed violently; a chamber-maid, that I had remarked for having a ruddy, good-humored face, went down stairs in a violent flurry. The stout gentleman had been rude to her!

This sent a whole host of my deductions to the deuce in a moment. This unknown personage could not be an old gentleman; for old gentlemen are not apt to be so obstreperous to chamber-maids. He could not be a young gentleman; for young gentlemen are not apt to inspire such indignation. He must be a middle-aged man, and confounded ugly into the bargain, or the girl would not have taken the matter in such terrible dudgeon. I confess I was sorely puzzled.

In a few minutes I heard the voice of my landlady. I caught a glance of her as she came tramping up-stairs,—her face glowing, her cap flaring, her tongue wagging the whole way. "She'd have no such doings in her house, she'd warrant. If gentlemen did spend money freely, it was no rule. She'd have no servant-maids of hers treated in that way, when they were about their work, that's what she wouldn't."

As I hate squabbles, particularly with women, and above all with pretty women, I slunk back into my room, and partly closed the door; but my curiosity was too much excited not to listen. The landlady marched intrepidly to the enemy's citadel, and entered it with a storm: the door closed after her. I heard her voice in high windy clamor for a moment or two. Then it gradually subsided, like a gust of wind in a garret; then there was a laugh; then I heard nothing more.

After a little while my landlady came out with an odd smile on her face, adjusting her cap, which was a little on one side. As she went down stairs, I heard the landlord ask her what was the matter; she said, "Nothing at all, only the girl's a fool."—I was more than ever perplexed what to make of this unaccountable personage, who could put a good-natured chamber-maid in a passion, and send away a termagant landlady in smiles. He could not be so old, nor cross, nor ugly either.

I had to go to work at his picture again, and to paint him entirely different. I now set him down for one of those stout gentlemen that are frequently met with swaggering about the doors of country inns. Moist, merry fellows, in Belcher handkerchiefs, whose bulk is a little assisted by malt-liquors. Men who have seen the world, and been sworn at Highgate; who are used to tavern-life; up to all the tricks of tapsters, and knowing in the ways of sinful publicans. Free-livers on a small scale; who are prodigal within the compass of a guinea; who call all the waiters by name, tousle the maids, gossip with the landlady at the bar, and prose over a pint of port, or a glass of negus, after dinner.

The morning wore away in forming these and similar surmises. As fast as I wove one system of belief, some movement of the unknown would completely overturn it, and throw all my thoughts again into confusion. Such are the solitary operations of a feverish mind. I was, as I have said, extremely nervous; and the continual meditation on the concerns of this invisible personage began to have its effect:—I was getting a fit of the fidgets.

Dinner-time came. I hoped the stout gentleman might dine in the travellers'-room, and that I might at length get a view of his person; but no—he had dinner served in his own room. What could be the meaning of this solitude and mystery? He could not be a radical; there was something too aristocratical in thus keeping himself apart from the rest of the world, and condemning himself to his own dull company throughout a rainy day. And then, too, he lived too well for a discontented politician. He seemed to expatiate on a variety of dishes, and to sit over his wine like a jolly friend of good living. Indeed, my doubts on this head were soon at an end; for he could not have finished his first bottle before I could faintly hear him humming a tune; and on listening I found it to be "God save the King." 'T was plain, then, he was no radical, but a faithful subject; one who grew loyal over his bottle, and was ready to stand by king and constitution, when he could stand by nothing else. But who could he be? My conjectures began to run wild. Was he not some personage of distinction travelling incog.? "God knows!" said I, at my wit's end; "it may be one of the royal family for aught I know, for they are all stout gentlemen!"

The weather continued rainy. The mysterious unknown kept his room, and, as far as I could judge, his chair, for I did not hear him move. In the mean time, as the day advanced, the travellers' room began to be frequented. Some, who had just arrived, came in buttoned up in box-coats; others came home who had been dispersed about the town; some took their dinners, and some their tea. Had I been in a different mood, I should have found entertainment in studying this peculiar class of men. There were two especially, who were regular wags of the road, and up to all the standing jokes of travellers. They had a thousand sly things to say to the waiting-maid, whom they called Louisa, and Ethelinda, and a dozen other fine names, changing the name every time, and chuckling amazingly at their own waggery. My mind, however, had been completely engrossed by the stout gentleman. He had kept my fancy in chase during a long day, and it was not now to be diverted from the scent.

The evening gradually wore away. The travellers read the papers two or three times over. Some drew round the fire and told long stories about their horses, about their adventures, their overturns, and breakings-down. They discussed the credit of different merchants and different inns; and the two wags told several choice anecdotes of pretty chamber-maids and kind landladies. All this passed as they were quietly taking what they called their night-caps, that is to say, strong glasses of brandy and water and sugar, or some other mixture of the kind; after which they one after another rang for "Boots" and the chamber-maid, and walked off to bed in old shoes cut down into marvellously uncomfortable slippers.

There was now only one man left: a short-legged, long-bodied, plethoric fellow, with a very large, sandy head. He sat by himself, with a glass of port-wine negus, and a spoon; sipping and stirring, and meditating and sipping, until nothing was left but the spoon. He gradually fell asleep bolt upright in his chair, with the empty glass standing before him; and the candle seemed to fall asleep too, for the wick grew long, and black, and cabbaged at the end, and dimmed the little light that remained in the chamber. The gloom that now prevailed was contagious. Around hung the shapeless, and almost spectral, box-coats of departed travellers, long since buried in deep sleep. I only heard the ticking of the clock, with the deep-drawn breathings of the sleeping topers, and the drippings of the rain, drop—drop—drop, from the eaves of the house. The church-bells chimed midnight. All at once the stout gentleman began to walk overhead, pacing slowly backwards and forwards. There was something extremely awful in all this, especially to one in my state of nerves. These ghastly great-coats, these guttural breathings, and the creaking footsteps of this mysterious being. His steps grew fainter and fainter, and at length died away. I could bear it no longer. I was wound up to the desperation of a hero of romance. "Be he who or what he may," said I to myself, "I'll have a sight of him!" I seized a chamber-candle, and hurried up to No. 13. The door stood ajar. I hesitated—I entered: the room was deserted. There stood a large, broad-bottomed elbow-chair at a table, on which was an empty tumbler, and a "Times," newspaper, and the room smelt powerfully of Stilton cheese.

The mysterious stranger had evidently but just retired. I turned off, sorely disappointed, to my room, which had been changed to the front of the house. As I went along the corridor, I saw a large pair of boots, with dirty, waxed tops, standing at the door of a bedchamber. They doubtless belonged to the unknown; but it would not do to disturb so redoubtable a personage in his den: he might discharge a pistol, or something worse, at my head. I went to bed, therefore, and lay awake half the night in a terribly nervous state; and even when I fell asleep, I was still haunted in my dreams by the idea of the stout gentleman and his wax-topped boots.

I slept rather late the next morning, and was awakened by some stir and bustle in the house, which I could not at first comprehend; until getting more awake, I found there was a mail-coach starting from the door. Suddenly there was a cry from below, "The gentleman has forgot his umbrella! Look for the gentleman's umbrella in No. 13!" I heard an immediate scampering of a chamber-maid along the passage, and a shrill reply as she ran, "Here it is! here's the gentleman's umbrella!"

The mysterious stranger then was on the point of setting off. This was the only chance I should ever have of knowing him. I sprang out of bed, scrambled to the window, snatched aside the curtains, and just caught a glimpse of the rear of a person getting in at the coach-door. The skirts of a brown coat parted behind, and gave me a full view of the broad disk of a pair of drab breeches. The door closed—"all right!" was the word—the coach whirled off;—and that was all I ever saw of the stout gentleman!

TALES OF A TRAVELLER

·{❀❀❀}·

TO THE READER

WORTHY AND DEAR READER!—Hast thou ever been waylaid in the midst of a pleasant tour by some treacherous malady: thy heels tripped up, and thou left to count the tedious minutes as they passed, in the solitude of an inn-chamber? If thou hast, thou wilt be able to pity me. Behold me, interrupted in the course of my journeying up the fair banks of the Rhine, and laid up by indisposition in this old frontier town of Mentz. I have worn out every source of amusement. I know the sound of every clock that strikes, and bell that rings, in the place. I know to a second when to listen for the first tap of the Prussian drum, as it summons the garrison to parade, or at what hour to expect the distant sound of the Austrian military band. All these have grown wearisome to me; and even the well-known step of my doctor, as he slowly paces the corridor, with healing in the creak of his shoes, no longer affords an agreeable interruption to the monotony of my apartment.

For a time I attempted to beguile the weary hours by studying German under the tuition of mine host's pretty little daughter, Katrine; but I soon found even German had not power to charm a languid ear, and that the conjugating of *ich liebe* might be powerless, however rosy the lips which uttered it.

I tried to read, but my mind would not fix itself. I turned over volume after volume, but threw them by with distaste: "Well, then," said I at length, in despair, "if I cannot read a book, I will write one." Never was there a more lucky idea; it at once gave me occupation and amusement. The writing of a book was considered in old times as an enterprise of toil and difficulty, insomuch that the most trifling lucubration was denominated a "work," and the world talked with awe and reverence of "the labors of the learned." These matters are better understood nowadays.

Thanks to the improvements in all kind of manufactures, the art of book-making has been made familiar to the meanest capacity. Everybody is an author. The scribbling of a quarto is the mere pastime of the idle; the young gentleman throws off his brace of duodecimos in the intervals of the sporting-season, and the young lady produces her set of volumes with the same facility that her great-grandmother worked a set of chair-bottoms.

The idea having struck me, therefore, to write a book, the reader will easily perceive that the execution of it was no difficult matter. I rummaged my portfolio, and cast about, in my recollection, for those floating materials which a man naturally collects in travelling; and here I have arranged them in this little work.

As I know this to be a story-telling and a story-reading age, and that the world is fond of being taught by apologue, I have digested the instruction I would convey into a number of tales. They may not possess the power of amusement which the tales told by many of my contemporaries possess; but then I value myself on the sound moral which each of them contains. This may not be apparent at first, but the reader will be sure to find it out in the end. I am for curing the world by gentle alternatives, not by violent doses; indeed, the patient should never be conscious that he is taking a dose. I have learnt this much from experience under the hands of the worthy Hippocrates of Mentz.

I am not, therefore, for those barefaced tales which carry their moral on the surface, staring one in the face; they are enough to deter the squeamish reader. On the contrary, I have often hid my moral from sight, and disguised it as much as possible by sweets and spices, so that while the simple reader is listening with open mouth to a ghost or a love story, he may have a bolus of sound morality popped down his throat, and be never the wiser for the fraud.

As the public is apt to be curious about the sources whence an author draws his stories, doubtless that it may know how far to put faith in them, I would observe, that the Adventure of the German Student, or rather the latter part of it, is founded on an anecdote related to me as existing somewhere in French; and, indeed, I have been told, since writing it, that an ingenious tale has been founded on it by an English writer; but I have never met with either the former or the latter in print. Some of the circumstances in the Adventure of the Mysterious Picture, and in the Story of the Young Italian, are vague recollections of anecdotes related to me some years since; but from what source derived, I do not know. The Adventure of the Young Painter among the banditti is taken almost entirely from an authentic narrative in manuscript.

As to the other tales contained in this work, and indeed to my tales generally, I can make but one observation: I am an old traveller; I have read somewhat, heard and seen more, and dreamt more than all. My brain is filled, therefore, with all kinds of odds and ends. In travelling, these heterogeneous matters have become shaken up in my mind, as the articles are apt to be in an ill-packed travelling-trunk; so that when I attempt to draw forth a fact, I cannot determine whether I have read, heard, or dreamt it; and I am always at a loss to know how much to believe of my own stories.

These matters being premised, fall to, worthy reader, with good appetite; and, above all, with good-humor, to what is here set before thee. If the tales I have furnished should prove to be bad, they will at least be found short; so that no one will be wearied long on the same theme. "Variety is charming," as some poet observes.

There is a certain relief in change, even though it be from bad to worse! As I have often found in travelling in a stage-coach, that it is often a comfort to shift one's position, and be bruised in a new place.

Ever thine,
GEOFFREY CRAYON.

Dated from the HOTEL DE DARMSTADT,
  ci-devant HOTEL DE PARIS,
    MENTZ, *otherwise called* MAYENCE.

THE GREAT UNKNOWN

THE FOLLOWING ADVENTURES were related to me by the same nervous gentleman who told me the romantic tale of the Stout Gentleman, published in "Bracebridge Hall." It is very singular, that, although I expressly stated that story to have been told to me, and described the very person who told it, still it has been received as an adventure that happened to myself. Now I protest I never met with any adventure of the kind. I should not have grieved at this, had it not been intimated by the author of "Waverley," in an introduction to his novel of "Peveril of the Peak," that he was himself the stout gentleman alluded to. I have ever since been importuned by questions and letters from gentlemen, and particularly from ladies without number, touching what I had seen of the Great Unknown.

Now all this is extremely tantalizing. It is like being congratulated on the high prize when one has drawn a blank; for I have just as great a desire as any one of the public to penetrate the mystery of that very singular personage, whose voice fills every corner of the world, without any one being able to tell whence it comes.

My friend, the nervous gentleman, also, who is a man of very shy, retired habits, complains that he has been excessively annoyed in consequence of its getting about in his neighborhood that he is the fortunate personage. Insomuch, that he has become a character of considerable notoriety in two or three country-towns, and has been repeatedly teased to exhibit himself at blue-stocking parties, for no other reason than that of being "the gentleman who has had a glimpse of the author of 'Waverley.' "

Indeed the poor man has grown ten times as nervous as ever since he has discovered, on such good authority, who the stout gentleman was; and will never forgive himself for not having made a more resolute effort to get a full sight of him. He has anxiously endeavored to call up a recollection of what he saw of that portly personage; and has ever since kept a curious eye on all gentlemen of more than ordinary dimensions, whom he has seen getting into stage-coaches. All in vain! The features he had caught a glimpse of seem common to the whole race of stout gentlemen, and the Great Unknown remains as great as unknown as ever.

Having premised these circumstances, I will now let the nervous gentleman proceed with his stories.

THE HUNTING-DINNER

I WAS ONCE AT a hunting-dinner, given by a worthy fox-hunting old Baronet, who kept bachelor's hall in jovial style in an ancient rook-haunted family-mansion, in one of the middle counties. He had been a devoted admirer of the fair sex in his younger days; but, having travelled much, studied the sex in various countries with distinguished success, and returned home profoundly instructed, as he supposed, in the ways of woman, and a perfect master of the art of pleasing, had the mortification of being jilted by a little boarding-school girl, who was scarcely versed in the accidence of love.

The Baronet was completely overcome by such an incredible defeat; retired from the world in disgust; put himself under the government of his housekeeper; and took to fox-hunting like a perfect Nimrod. Whatever poets may say to the contrary, a man will grow out of love as he grows old; and a pack of fox-hounds may chase out of his heart even the memory of a boarding-school goddess. The Baronet was, when I saw him, as merry and mellow an old bachelor as ever followed a hound; and the love he had once felt for one woman had spread itself over the whole sex; so that there was not a pretty face in the whole country round but came in for a share.

The dinner was prolonged till a late hour; for our host having no ladies in his household to summon us to the drawing-room, the bottle maintained its true bachelor sway, unrivalled by its potent enemy, the tea-kettle. The old hall in which we dined echoed to bursts of robustious fox-hunting merriment, that made the ancient antlers shake on the walls. By degrees, however, the wine and the wassail of mine host began to operate upon bodies already a little jaded by the chase. The choice spirits which flashed up at the beginning of the dinner, sparkled for a time, then gradually went out one after another, or only emitted now and then a faint gleam from the socket. Some of the briskest talkers, who had given tongue so bravely at the first burst, fell fast asleep; and none kept on their way but certain of those long-winded prosers, who, like short-legged hounds, worry on unnoticed at the bottom of conversation, but are sure to be in at the death. Even these at length subsided into silence; and scarcely anything was heard but the nasal communications of two or three veteran masticators, who having been silent while awake, were indemnifying the company in their sleep.

At length the announcement of tea and coffee in the cedar-parlor roused all hands from this temporary torpor. Every one awoke marvellously renovated, and while sipping the refreshing beverage out of the Baronet's old-fashioned hereditary china, began to think of departing for their several homes. But here a sudden difficulty arose. While we had been prolonging our repast, a heavy winter storm had set in, with snow, rain, and sleet, driven by such bitter blasts of wind, that they threatened to penetrate to the very bone.

"It's all in vain," said our hospitable host, "to think of putting one's head out of doors in such weather. So, gentlemen, I hold you my guests for this night at least, and will have your quarters prepared accordingly."

The unruly weather, which became more and more tempestuous, rendered the hospitable suggestion unanswerable. The only question was, whether such an unexpected accession of company to an already crowded house would not put the housekeeper to her trumps to accommodate them.

"Pshaw," cried mine host; "did you ever know a bachelor's hall that was not elastic. and able to accommodate twice as many as it could hold?" So, out of a good-humored pique, the house-keeper was summoned to a consultation before us all. The old lady appeared in her gala suit of faded brocade, which rustled with flurry and agitation; for, in spite of our host's bravado, she was a little perplexed. But in a bachelor's house, and with bache-lor guests, these matters are readily managed. There is no lady of the house to stand upon squeamish points about lodging gen-tlemen in odd holes and corners, and exposing the shabby parts of the establishment. A bachelor's housekeeper is used to shifts and emergencies; so, after much worrying to and fro, and divers con-sultations about the red-room, and the blue-room, and the chintz-room, and the damask-room, and the little room with the bow-window, the matter was finally arranged.

When all this was done, we were once more summoned to the standing rural amusement of eating. The time that had been con-sumed in dozing after dinner, and in the refreshment and consul-tation of the cedar-parlor, was sufficient, in the opinion of the rosy-faced butler, to engender a reasonable appetite for supper. A slight repast had, therefore, been tricked up from the residue of dinner, consisting of a cold sirloin of beef, hashed venison, a devilled leg of a turkey or so, and a few other of those light articles taken by country gentlemen to insure sound sleep and heavy snoring.

The nap after dinner had brightened up every one's wit; and a great deal of excellent humor was expanded upon the perplexities of mine host and his housekeeper, by certain married gentlemen of the company, who considered themselves privileged in joking with a bachelor's establishment. From this the banter turned as to what quarters each would find, on being thus suddenly billeted in so antiquated a mansion.

"By my soul," said an Irish captain of dragoons, one of the most merry and boisterous of the party, "by my soul, but I should not be surprised if some of those good-looking gentlefolks that hang along the walls should walk about the rooms of this stormy night; or if I should find the ghosts of one of those long-waisted ladies turning into my bed in mistake for her grave in the church-yard."

"Do you believe in ghosts, then?" said a thin, hatchet-faced gentleman, with projecting eyes like a lobster.

I had remarked this last personage during dinner-time for one of those incessant questioners, who have a craving, unhealthy appetite in conversation. He never seemed satisfied with the whole of a story; never laughed when others laughed; but always put the joke to the question. He never could enjoy the kernel of the nut, but pestered himself to get more out of the shell. "Do you believe in ghosts, then?" said the inquisitive gentleman.

"Faith, but I do," replied the jovial Irishman. "I was brought up in the fear and belief of them. We had a Benshee in our own family, honey."

"A Benshee, and what's that?" cried the questioner.

"Why, an old lady ghost that tends upon your real Milesian families, and waits at their window to let them know when some of them are to die."

"A mighty pleasant piece of information!" cried an elderly gentleman with a knowing look, and with a flexible nose, to which he could give a whimsical twist when he wished to be waggish.

"By my soul, but I'd have you to know it's a piece of distinction to be waited on by a Benshee. It's a proof that one has pure blood in one's veins. But i' faith, now we are talking of ghosts, there never was a house or a night better fitted than the present for a ghost adventure. Pray, Sir John, haven't you such a thing as a haunted chamber to put a guest in?"

"Perhaps," said the Baronet, smiling, "I might accommodate you even on that point."

"Oh, I should like it of all things, my jewel. Some dark oaken room, with ugly woe-begone portraits, that stare dismally at one; and about which the housekeeper has a power of delightful stories of love and murder. And then a dim lamp, a table with a rusty sword across it, and a spectre all in white, to draw aside one's curtains at midnight"—

"In truth," said an old gentleman at one end of the table, "you put me in mind of an anecdote"—

"Oh, a ghost-story! a ghost-story!" was vociferated round the board, every one edging his chair a little nearer.

The attention of the whole company was now turned upon the speaker. He was an old gentleman, one side of whose face was no match for the other. The eye-lid drooped and hung down like an unhinged window-shutter. Indeed, the whole side of his head was dilapidated, and seemed like the wing of a house shut up and haunted. I'll warrant that side was well stuffed with ghost-stories. There was a universal demand for the tale.

"Nay," said the old gentleman, "it's a mere anecdote, and a very commonplace one; but such as it is you shall have it. It is a story that I once heard my uncle tell as having happened to himself. He was a man very apt to meet with strange adventures. I have heard him tell of others much more singular."

"What kind of a man was your uncle?" said the questioning gentleman.

"Why, he was rather a dry, shrewd kind of body; a great traveller, and fond of telling his adventures."

"Pray, how old might he have been when that happened?"

"When what happened?" cried the gentleman with the flexible nose, impatiently. "Egad, you have not given anything a chance to happen. Come, never mind our uncle's age; let us have his adventures."

The inquisitive gentleman being for the moment silenced, the old gentleman with the haunted head proceeded.

THE BOLD DRAGOON

OR

The Adventure of My Grandfather

My grandfather was a bold dragoon, for it's a profession, d'ye see, that has run in the family. All my forefathers have been dragoons, and died on the field of honor, except myself, and I hope

my posterity may be able to say the same; however, I don't mean
to be vainglorious. Well, my grandfather, as I said, was a bold
dragoon, and had served in the Low Countries. In fact, he was
one of that very army, which, according to my uncle Toby, swore
so terribly in Flanders. He could swear a good stick himself; and
moreover was the very man that introduced the doctrine Corporal
Trim mentions of radical heat and radical moisture, or, in other
words, the mode of keeping out the damps of ditch-water by burnt
brandy. Be that as it may, it's nothing to the purport of my story.
I only tell it to show you that my grandfather was a man not
easily to be humbugged. He had seen service, or, according to his
own phrase, he had seen the devil—and that's saying everything.

Well, gentlemen, my grandfather was on his way to England,
for which he intended to embark from Ostend—bad luck to the
place! for one where I was kept by storms and head-winds for
three long days, and the devil of a jolly companion or pretty girl
to comfort me. Well, as I was saying, my grandfather was on his
way to England, or rather to Ostend—no matter which, it's all the
same. So one evening, towards nightfall, he rode jollily into
Bruges.—Very like you all know Bruges, gentlemen; a queer, old-
fashioned Flemish town, once, they say, a great place for trade
and money-making in old times, when the Mynheers were in their
glory; but almost as large and as empty as an Irishman's pocket
at the present day.—Well, gentlemen, it was at the time of the
annual fair. All Bruges was crowded; and the canals swarmed
with Dutch boats, and the streets swarmed with Dutch merchants; and there was hardly any getting along for goods, wares,
and merchandises, and peasants in big breeches, and women in
half a score of petticoats.

My grandfather rode jollily along, in his easy, slashing way, for
he was a saucy, sunshiny fellow—staring about him at the motley
crowd, and the old houses with gable ends to the street, and storks'
nests in the chimneys; winking at the yafrows who showed their
faces at the windows, and joking the women right and left in the
street; all of whom laughed, and took it in amazing good part; for

though he did not know a word of the language, yet he had always a knack of making himself understood among the women.

Well, gentlemen, it being the time of the annual fair, all the town was crowded, every inn and tavern full, and my grandfather applied in vain from one to the other for admittance. At length he rode up to an old rickety inn, that looked ready to fall to pieces, and which all the rats would have run away from, if they could have found room in any other house to put their heads. It was just such a queer building as you see in Dutch pictures, with a tall roof that reached up into the clouds, and as many garrets, one over the other, as the seven heavens of Mahomet. Nothing had saved it from tumbling down but a stork's nest on the chimney, which always brings good luck to a house in the Low Countries; and at the very time of my grandfather's arrival, there were two of these long-legged birds of grace standing like ghosts on the chimney-top. Faith, but they've kept the house on its legs to this very day, for you may see it any time you pass through Bruges, as it stands there yet, only it is turned into a brewery of strong Flemish beer,—at least it was so when I came that way after the battle of Waterloo.

My grandfather eyed the house curiously as he approached. It might not have altogether struck his fancy, had he not seen in large letters over the door,

HEER VERKOOPT MAN GOEDEN DRANK

My grandfather had learnt enough of the language to know that the sign promised good liquor. "This is the house for me," said he, stopping short before the door.

The sudden appearance of a dashing dragoon was an event in an old inn frequented only by the peaceful sons of traffic. A rich burgher of Antwerp, a stately ample man in a broad Flemish hat, and who was the great man and great patron of the establishment, sat smoking a clean long pipe on one side of the door; a fat little distiller of Geneva, from Schiedam, sat smoking on the other; and the bottled-nosed host stood in the door, and the comely hostess, in crimped cap, beside him; and the hostess's daughter, a plump Flanders lass, with long gold pendants in her ears, was at a side-window.

"Humph!" said the rich burgher of Antwerp, with a sulky glance at the stranger.

"De duyvel!" said the fat little distiller of Schiedam.

The landlord saw, with the quick glance of a publican, that the new guest was not at all to the taste of the old ones; and, to tell the truth, he did not like my grandfather's saucy eye. He shook his head. "Not a garret in the house but was full."

"Not a garret!" echoed the landlady.

"Not a garret!" echoed the daughter.

The burgher of Antwerp, and the little distiller of Schiedam, continued to smoke their pipes sullenly, eying the enemy askance from under their broad hats, but said nothing.

My grandfather was not a man to be brow-beaten. He threw the reins on his horse's neck, cocked his head on one side, stuck one arm akimbo,—"Faith and troth!" said he, "but I'll sleep in this house this very night."—As he said this he gave a slap on his thigh, by way of emphasis—the slap went to the landlady's heart.

He followed up the vow by jumping off his horse, and making his way past the staring Mynheers into the public room.—Maybe you've been in the bar-room of an old Flemish inn—faith, but a handsome chamber it was as you'd wish to see; with a brick floor, and a great fireplace, with the whole Bible history in glazed tiles; and then the mantelpiece, pitching itself head foremost out of the wall, with a whole regiment of cracked tea-pots and earthen jugs paraded on it; not to mention half a dozen great Delft platters, hung about the room by way of pictures; and the little bar in one corner, and the bouncing bar-maid inside of it, with a red calico cap, and yellow ear-drops.

My grandfather snapped his fingers over his head, as he cast an eye round the room,—"Faith, this is the very house I've been looking after," said he.

There was was some further show of resistance on the part of the garrison; but my grandfather was an old soldier, and an Irishman to boot, and not easily repulsed, especially after he had got into the fortress. So he blarneyed the landlord, kissed the land-lord's wife, tickled the landlord's daughter, chucked the bar-maid under the chin; and it was agreed on all hands that it would be a thousand pities, and a burning shame into the bargain, to turn such a bold dragoon into the streets. So they laid their heads together, that is to say, my grandfather and the landlady, and it was at length agreed to accommodate him with an old chamber, that had been for some time shut up.

"Some say it's haunted," whispered the landlord's daughter; "but you are a bold dragoon, and I dare say don't fear ghosts."

"The devil a bit!" said my grandfather, pinching her plump cheek. "But if I should be troubled by ghosts, I've been to the Red Sea in my time, and have a pleasant way of laying them, my darling."

And then he whispered something to the girl which made her laugh, and give him a good-humored box on the ear. In short, there was nobody knew better how to make his way among the petticoats than my grandfather.

In a little while, as was his usual way, he took complete posses-sion of the house, swaggering all over it; into the stable to look after his horse, into the kitchen to look after his supper. He had something to say or do with every one; smoked with the Dutch-men, drank with the Germans, slapped the landlord on the shoul-der, romped with his daughter and the bar-maid:—never, since the days of Alley Croaker, had such a rattling blade been seen. The landlord stared at him with astonishment; the landlord's daughter hung her head and giggled whenever he came near; and as he swaggered along the corridor, with his sword trailing by his side, the maids looked after him, and whispered to one another, "What a proper man!"

At supper, my grandfather took command of the table-d'hôte as though he had been at home; helped everybody, not forgetting himself; talked with every one, whether he understood their language or not; and made his way into the intimacy of the rich burgher of Antwerp, who had never been known to be sociable with any one during his life. In fact, he revolutionized the whole establishment, and gave it such a rouse, that the very house reeled with it. He outsat every one at table, excepting the little fat distiller of Schiedam, who sat soaking a long time before he broke forth; but when he did, he was a very devil incarnate. He took a violent affection for my grandfather; so they sat drinking and smoking, and telling stories, and singing Dutch and Irish songs, without understanding a word each other said, until the little Hollander was fairly swamped with his own gin and water, and carried off to bed, whooping and hickuping, and trolling the burden of a Low Dutch love-song.

Well, gentlemen, my grandfather was shown to his quarters up a large staircase, composed of loads of hewn timber; and through long rigmarole passages, hung with blackened paintings of fish, and fruit, and game, and country frolics, and huge kitchens, and portly burgomasters, such as you see about old-fashioned Flemish inns, till at length he arrived at his room.

An old-times chamber it was, sure enough, and crowded with all kinds of trumpery. It looked like an infirmary for decayed and superannuated furniture, where everything diseased or disabled was sent to nurse or to be forgotten. Or rather it might be taken for a general congress of old legitimate movables, where every kind and country had a representative. No two chairs were alike. Such high backs and low backs, and leather bottoms, and worsted bottoms, and straw bottoms, and no bottoms; and cracked marble tables with curiously carved legs, holding balls in their claws, as though they were going to play at ninepins.

My grandfather made a bow to the motley assemblage as he entered, and, having undressed himself, placed his light in the fireplace, asking pardon of the tongs, which seemed to be making love to the shovel in the chimney-corner, and whispering soft nonsense in its ear.

The rest of the guests were by this time sound asleep, for your Mynheers are huge sleepers. The housemaids, one by one, crept up yawning to their attics; and not a female head in the inn was laid on a pillow that night without dreaming of the bold dragoon.

My grandfather, for his part, got into bed, and drew over him one of those great bags of down, under which they smother a man in the Low Countries; and there he lay, melting between two feather beds, like an anchovy sandwich between two slices of toast and butter. He was a warm-complexioned man, and this smothering played the very deuce with him. So, sure enough, in a little time it seemed as if a legion of imps were twitching at him, and all the blood in his veins was in a fever-heat.

He lay still, however, until all the house was quiet, excepting the snoring of the Mynheers from the different chambers; who answered one another in all kinds of tones and cadences, like so many bull-frogs in a swamp. The quieter the house became, the more unquiet became my grandfather. He waxed warmer and warmer, until at length the bed became too hot to hold him.

"Maybe the maid had warmed it too much?" said the curious gentleman, inquiringly.

"I rather think the contrary," replied the Irishman. "But, be that as it may, it grew too hot for my grandfather."

"Faith, there's no standing this any longer," says he. So he jumped out of bed, and went strolling about the house.

"What for?" said the inquisitive gentleman.

"Why, to cool himself, to be sure—or perhaps to find a more comfortable bed—or perhaps— But no matter what he went for— he never mentioned—and there's no use in taking up our time in conjecturing."

Well, my grandfather had been for some time absent from his room, and was returning, perfectly cool, when just as he reached the door, he heard a strange noise within. He paused and listened. It seemed as if some one were trying to hum a tune in defiance of the asthma. He recollected the report of the room being haunted; but he was no believer in ghosts, so he pushed the door gently open and peeped in.

Egad, gentlemen, there was a gambol carrying on within enough to have astonished St. Anthony himself. By the light of the fire he saw a pale weazen-faced fellow, in a long flannel gown and a tall white night-cap with a tassel to it, who sat by the fire with a bellows under his arm by way of bagpipe, from which he forced the asthmatical music that had bothered my grandfather.

As he played, too, he kept twitching about with a thousand queer contortions, nodding his head, and bobbing about his tasselled night-cap.

My grandfather thought this very odd and mighty presumptuous, and was about to demand what business he had to play his wind-instrument in another gentleman's quarters, when a new cause of astonishment met his eye. From the opposite side of the room a long-backed, bandy-legged chair, covered with leather, and studded all over in a coxcombical fashion with little brass nails, got suddenly into motion, thrust out first a claw-foot, then a crooked arm, and at length, making a leg, slided gracefully up to an easy-chair of tarnished brocade, with a hole in its bottom, and led it gallantly out in a ghostly minuet about the floor.

The musician now played fiercer and fiercer, and bobbed his head and his night-cap about like mad. By degrees the dancing mania seemed to seize upon all the other pieces of furniture. The antique, long-bodied chairs paired off in couples and led down a country-dance; a three-legged stool danced a hornpipe, though horribly puzzled by its supernumerary limb; while the amorous tongs seized the shovel round the waist, and whirled it about the room in a German waltz. In short, all the movables got in motion: pirouetting hands across, right and left, like so many devils; all except a great clothes-press, which kept courtesying and courtesying in a corner, like a dowager, in exquisite time to the music; being rather too corpulent to dance, or perhaps at a loss for a partner.

My grandfather concluded the latter to be the reason; so being, like a true Irishman, devoted to the sex, and at all times ready for a frolic, he bounced into the room, called to the musician to strike up Paddy O'Rafferty, capered up to the clothes-press, and seized upon the two handles to lead her out:——when—whirr! the whole revel was at an end. The chairs, tables, tongs and shovel, slunk in an instant as quietly into their places as if nothing had happened, and the musician vanished up the chimney, leaving the bellows behind him in his hurry. My grandfather found himself seated in the middle of the floor with the clothes-press sprawling before him, and the two handles jerked off, and in his hands.

"Then, after all, this was a mere dream!" said the inquisitive gentleman.

"The divil a bit of a dream!" replied the Irishman. "There never was a truer fact in this world. Faith, I should have liked to see any man tell my grandfather it was a dream."

Well, gentlemen, as the clothes-press was a mighty heavy body, and my grandfather likewise, particularly in rear, you may easily suppose that two such heavy bodies coming to the ground would make a bit of a noise. Faith, the old mansion shook as though it had mistaken it for an earthquake. The whole garrison was alarmed. The landlord, who slept below, hurried up with a candle to inquire the cause, but with all his haste his daughter had arrived at the scene of uproar before him. The landlord was followed by the landlady, who was followed by the bouncing barmaid, who was followed by the simpering chambermaids, all holding together, as well as they could, such garments as they first laid hands on; but all in a terrible hurry to see what the deuce was to pay in the chamber of the bold dragoon.

My grandfather related the marvellous scene he had witnessed, and the broken handles of the prostrate clothes-press bore testimony to the fact. There was no contesting such evidence; particularly with a lad of my grandfather's complexion, who seemed able to make good every word either with sword or sheillelah. So the landlord scratched his head and looked silly, as he was apt to do when puzzled. The landlady scratched—no, she did not scratch her head, but she knit her brow, and did not seem half pleased with the explanation. But the landlady's daughter corroborated it by recollecting that the last person who had dwelt in that chamber was a famous juggler who died of St. Vitus's dance, and had no doubt infected all the furniture.

This set all things to rights, particularly when the chambermaids declared that they had all witnessed strange carryings on in that room; and as they declared this "upon their honors," there could not remain a doubt upon this subject.

"And did your grandfather go to bed again in that room?" said the inquisitive gentleman.

"That's more than I can tell. Where he passed the rest of the night was a secret he never disclosed. In fact, though he had seen much service, he was but indifferently acquainted with geography, and apt to make blunders in his travels about inns at night, which it would have puzzled him sadly to account for in the morning."

"Was he ever apt to walk in his sleep?" said the knowing old gentleman.

"Never that I heard of."

There was a little pause after this rigmarole Irish romance, when the old gentleman with the haunted head observed, that the stories hitherto related had rather a burlesque tendency. "I recollect an adventure, however," added he, "which I heard of during a residence at Paris, for the truth of which I can undertake to vouch, and which is of a very grave and singular nature."

ADVENTURE OF THE
GERMAN STUDENT

ON A STORMY NIGHT, in the tempestuous times of the French revolution, a young German was returning to his lodgings, at a late hour, across the old part of Paris. The lightning gleamed, and the loud claps of thunder rattled through the lofty narrow streets —but I should first tell you something about this young German.

Gottfried Wolfgang was a young man of good family. He had studied for some time at Göttingen, but being of a visionary and enthusiastic character, he had wandered into those wild and speculative doctrines which have so often bewildered German students. His secluded life, his intense application, and the singular nature of his studies, had an effect on both mind and body. His health was impaired; his imagination diseased. He had been indulging in fanciful speculations on spiritual essences, until, like Swedenborg, he had an ideal world of his own around him. He took up a notion, I do not know from what cause, that there was an evil influence hanging over him; an evil genius or spirit seeking to ensnare him and ensure his perdition. Such an idea working on his melancholy temperament, produced the most gloomy effects. He became haggard and desponding. His friends discovered the mental malady preying upon him, and determined that the best cure was a change of scene; he was sent, therefore, to finish his studies amidst the splendors and gayeties of Paris.

Wolfgang arrived at Paris at the breaking out of the revolution. The popular delirium at first caught his enthusiastic mind, and he was captivated by the political and philosophical theories of the day: but the scenes of blood which followed shocked his sensitive nature, disgusted him with society and the world, and made him more than ever a recluse. He shut himself up in a solitary apartment in the *Pays Latin,* the quarter of students. There, in a gloomy street not far from the monastic walls of the Sorbonne, he pursued his favorite speculations. Sometimes he spent hours together in the great libraries of Paris, those catacombs of departed authors, rummaging among their hoards of dusty and obsolete works in quest of food for his unhealthy appetite. He was, in a manner, a literary ghoul, feeding in the charnel-house of decayed literature.

Wolfgang, though solitary and recluse, was of an ardent temperament, but for a time it operated merely upon his imagination. He was too shy and ignorant of the world to make any advances to the fair, but he was a passionate admirer of female beauty, and in his lonely chamber would often lose himself in reveries on forms and faces which he had seen, and his fancy would deck out images of loveliness far surpassing the reality.

While his mind was in this excited and sublimated state, a dream produced an extraordinary effect upon him. It was of a female face of transcendent beauty. So strong was the impression made, that he dreamt of it again and again. It haunted his thoughts by day, his slumbers by night; in fine, he became passionately enamoured of this shadow of a dream. This lasted so long that it became one of those fixed ideas which haunt the minds of melancholy men, and are at times mistaken for madness.

Such was Gottfried Wolfgang, and such his situation at the time I mentioned. He was returning home late one stormy night, through some of the old and gloomy streets of the *Marais*, the ancient part of Paris. The loud claps of thunder rattled among the high houses of the narrow streets. He came to the Place de Grève, the square where public executions are performed. The lightning quivered about the pinnacles of the ancient Hôtel de Ville, and shed flickering gleams over the open space in front. As Wolfgang was crossing the square, he shrank back with horror at finding himself close by the guillotine. It was the height of the reign of terror, when this dreadful instrument of death stood ever ready, and its scaffold was continually running with the blood of the virtuous and the brave. It had that very day been actively employed in the work of carnage, and there it stood in grim array, amidst a silent and sleeping city, waiting for fresh victims.

Wolfgang's heart sickened within him, and he was turning shuddering from the horrible engine, when he beheld a shadowy form, cowering as it were at the foot of the steps which led up to the scaffold. A succession of vivid flashes of lightning revealed it more distinctly. It was a female figure, dressed in black. She was seated on one of the lower steps of the scaffold, leaning forward, her face hid in her lap; and her long dishevelled tresses hanging to the ground, streaming with the rain which fell in torrents. Wolfgang paused. There was something awful in this solitary monument of woe. The female had the appearance of being above the common order. He knew the times to be full of vicissitude, and that many a fair head, which had once been pillowed on down, now wandered houseless. Perhaps this was some poor mourner whom the dreadful axe had rendered desolate, and who sat here heart-broken on the strand of existence, from which all that was dear to her had been launched into eternity.

He approached, and addressed her in the accents of sympathy. She raised her head and gazed wildly at him. What was his astonishment at beholding, by the bright glare of the lightning, the very face which had haunted him in his dreams. It was pale and disconsolate, but ravishingly beautiful.

Trembling with violent and conflicting emotions, Wolfgang again accosted her. He spoke something of her being exposed at such an hour of the night, and to the fury of such a storm, and offered to conduct her to her friends. She pointed to the guillotine with a gesture of dreadful signification.

"I have no friend on earth!" said she.

"But you have a home," said Wolfgang.

"Yes—in the grave!"

The heart of the student melted at the words.

"If a stranger dare make an offer," said he, "without danger of being misunderstood, I would offer my humble dwelling as a shelter; myself as a devoted friend. I am friendless myself in Paris, and a stranger in the land; but if my life could be of service, it is at your disposal, and should be sacrificed before harm or indignity should come to you."

There was an honest earnestness in the young man's manner that had its effect. His foreign accent, too, was in his favor; it showed him not to be a hackneyed inhabitant of Paris. Indeed, there is an eloquence in true enthusiasm that is not to be doubted. The homeless stranger confided herself implicitly to the protection of the student.

He supported her faltering steps across the Pont Neuf, and by the place where the statue of Henry the Fourth had been overthrown by the populace. The storm had abated, and the thunder rumbled at a distance. All Paris was quiet; that great volcano of human passion slumbered for a while, to gather fresh strength for the next day's eruption. The student conducted his charge through the ancient streets of the *Pays Latin,* and by the dusky walls of the Sorbonne, to the great dingy hotel which he inhabited. The old portress who admitted them stared with surprise at the unusual sight of the melancholy Wolfgang with a female companion.

On entering his apartment, the student, for the first time, blushed at the scantiness and indifference of his dwelling. He had but one chamber—an old-fashioned saloon—heavily carved, and fantastically furnished with the remains of former magnificence, for it was one of those hotels in the quarter of the Luxembourg palace, which had once belonged to nobility. It was lumbered with books and papers, and all the usual apparatus of a student, and his bed stood in a recess at one end.

When lights were brought, and Wolfgang had a better opportunity of contemplating the stranger, he was more than ever intoxicated by her beauty. Her face was pale, but of a dazzling fairness, set off by a profusion of raven hair that hung clustering about it. Her eyes were large and brilliant, with a singular expression approaching almost to wildness. As far as her black dress permitted her shape to be seen, it was of perfect symmetry. Her whole appearance was highly striking, though she was dressed in the simplest style. The only thing approaching to an ornament which she wore, was a broad black band round her neck, clasped by diamonds.

The perplexity now commenced with the student how to dispose of the helpless being thus thrown upon his protection. He thought of abandoning his chamber to her, and seeking shelter for himself elsewhere. Still he was so fascinated by her charms, there seemed to be such a spell upon his thoughts and senses, that he could not tear himself from her presence. Her manner, too, was singular and unaccountable. She spoke no more of the guillotine. Her grief had abated. The attentions of the student had first won her confidence, and then, apparently, her heart. She was evidently an enthusiast like himself, and enthusiasts soon understand each other.

In the infatuation of the moment, Wolfgang avowed his passion for her. He told her the story of his mysterious dream, and how she had possessed his heart before he had even seen her. She was strangely affected by his recital, and acknowledged to have felt an impulse towards him equally unaccountable. It was the time for wild theory and wild actions. Old prejudices and superstitions were done away; everything was under the sway of the "Goddess of Reason." Among other rubbish of the old times, the forms and ceremonies of marriage began to be considered superfluous bonds for honorable minds. Social compacts were the vogue. Wolfgang was too much of a theorist not to be tainted by the liberal doctrines of the day.

"Why should we separate?" said he: "our hearts are united; in the eye of reason and honor we are as one. What need is there of sordid forms to bind high souls together?"

The stranger listened with emotion: she had evidently received illumination at the same school.

"You have no home nor family," continued he; "let me be everything to you, or rather let us be everything to one another. If form is necessary, form shall be observed—there is my hand. I pledge myself to you forever."

"Forever?" said the stranger, solemnly.

"Forever!" repeated Wolfgang.

The stranger clasped the hand extended to her: "Then I am yours," murmured she, and sank upon his bosom.

The next morning the student left his bride sleeping, and sallied forth at an early hour to seek more spacious apartments suitable to the change in his situation. When he returned, he found the stranger lying with her head hanging over the bed, and one arm thrown over it. He spoke to her, but received no reply. He advanced to awaken her from her uneasy posture. On taking her hand, it was cold—there was no pulsation—her face was pallid and ghastly. In a word, she was a corpse.

Horrified and frantic, he alarmed the house. A scene of confusion ensued. The police was summoned. As the officer of police entered the room, he started back on beholding the corpse.

"Great heaven!" cried he, "how did this woman come here?"

"Do you know anything about her?" said Wolfgang eagerly.

"Do I?" exclaimed the officer: "she was guillotined yesterday."

He stepped forward; undid the black collar round the neck of the corpse, and the head rolled on the floor!

The student burst into a frenzy. "The fiend! the fiend has gained possession of me!" shrieked he: "I am lost forever."

They tried to soothe him, but in vain. He was possessed with the frightful belief that an evil spirit had reanimated the dead body to ensnare him. He went distracted, and died in a madhouse.

Here the old gentleman with the haunted head finished his narrative.

"And is this really a fact?" said the inquisitive gentleman.

"A fact not to be doubted," replied the other. "I had it from the best authority. The student told it me himself. I saw him in a mad-house in Paris."

BOOK III

CHAPTER II

Continuation of the Voyage—First Notice of the Variation of the Needle

[1492]

EARLY IN THE MORNING of the 6th of September, Columbus set sail from the island of Gomera, and now might be said first to strike into the region of discovery; taking leave of these frontier islands of the old world, and steering westward for the unknown parts of the Atlantic. For three days, however, a profound calm kept the vessels loitering with flagging sails, within a short distance of the land. This was a tantalizing delay to Columbus, who was impatient to find himself far out of sight of either land or sail; which, in the pure atmospheres of these latitudes, may be descried at an immense distance. On the following Sunday, the 9th of September, at daybreak, he beheld Ferro, the last of the Canary Islands, about nine leagues distant. This was the island whence the Portuguese caravels had been seen; he was therefore in the very neighborhood of danger. Fortunately a breeze sprang up with the sun, their sails were once more filled, and in the course of the day the heights of Ferro gradually faded from the horizon.

On losing sight of this last trace of land, the hearts of the crews failed them. They seemed literally to have taken leave of the world. Behind them was everything dear to the heart of man; country, family, friends, life itself: before them everything was chaos, mystery, and peril. In the perturbation of the moment, they despaired of ever more seeing their homes. Many of the rugged seamen shed tears, and some broke into loud lamentations. The admiral tried in every way to soothe their distress, and to inspire them with his own glorious anticipations. He described to them the magnificent countries to which he was about to conduct them: the islands of the Indian seas teeming with gold and precious stones; the regions of Mangi and Cathay, with their cities of unrivalled wealth and splendor. He promised them land and riches, and everything that could arouse their cupidity, or inflame their imaginations, nor were these promises made for purposes of mere deception; he certainly believed that he should realize them all.

He now issued orders to the commanders of the other vessels, that, in the event of separation by any accident, they should continue directly westward; but that after sailing seven hundred leagues, they should lay by from midnight until daylight, as at about that distance he confidently expected to find land. In the mean time, as he thought it possible he might not discover land within the distance thus assigned, and as he foresaw that the vague terrors already awakened among the seamen would increase with the space which intervened between them and their homes, he commenced a stratagem which he continued throughout the voyage. He kept two reckonings; one correct, in which the true way of the ship was noted, and which was retained in secret for his own government; in the other, which was open to general inspection, a number of leagues was daily subtracted from the sailing of the ship, so that the crews were kept in ignorance of the real distance they had advanced.*

On the 11th of September, when about one hundred and fifty leagues west of Ferro, they fell in with part of a mast, which from its size appeared to have belonged to a vessel of about a hundred and twenty tons burthen, and which had evidently been a long

* It has been erroneously stated that Columbus kept two journals. It was merely in the reckoning, or log-book, that he deceived the crew. His journal was entirely private, and intended for his own use and the perusal of the sovereigns. In a letter written from Granada, in 1503, to Pope Alexander VII., he says that he had kept an account of his voyages, in the style of the Commentaries of Cæsar, which he intended to submit to his Holiness.

time in the water. The crews, tremblingly alive to everything that could excite their hopes or fears, looked with rueful eye upon this wreck of some unfortunate voyager, drifting ominously at the entrance of those unknown seas.

On the 13th of September, in the evening, being about two hundred leagues from the island of Ferro, Columbus, for the first time, noticed the variation of the needle; a phenomenon which had never before been remarked. He perceived, about nightfall, that the needle, instead of pointing to the north star, varied about half a point, or between five and six degrees, to the northwest, and still more on the following morning. Struck with this curcumstance, he observed it attentively for three days, and found that the variation increased as he advanced. He at first made no mention of this phenomenon, knowing how ready his people were to take alarm, but it soon attracted the attention of the pilots, and filled them with consternation. It seemed as if the very laws of nature were changing as they advanced, and that they were entering another world, subject to unknown influences.* They apprehended that the compass was about to lose its mysterious virtues, and, without this guide, what was to become of them in a vast and trackless ocean?

Columbus tasked his science and ingenuity for reasons with which to allay their terror. He observed that the direction of the needle was not to the polar star, but to some fixed and invisible point. The variation, therefore, was not caused by any fallacy in the compass, but by the movement of the north star itself, which, like the other heavenly bodies, had its changes and revolutions, and every day described a circle round the pole. The high opinion which the pilots entertained of Columbus as a profound astronomer gave weight to this theory, and their alarm subsided. As yet the solar system of Copernicus was unknown: the explanation of Columbus, therefore, was highly plausible and ingenious, and it shows the vivacity of his mind, ever ready to meet the emergency of the moment. The theory may at first have been advanced merely to satisfy the minds of others, but Columbus appears subsequently to have remained satisfied with it himself. The phenomenon has

* Las Casas, Hist. Ind., lib. i. cap. 6.

now become familiar to us, but we still continue ignorant of its cause. It is one of those mysteries of nature, open to daily observation and experiment, and apparently simple from their familiarity, but which on investigation make the human mind conscious of its limits; baffling the experience of the practical, and humbling the pride of science.

CHAPTER III

Continuation of the Voyage—Various Terrors of the Seamen

[1492]

ON THE 14TH OF SEPTEMBER, the voyagers were rejoiced by the sight of what they considered harbingers of land. A heron, and a tropical bird called the Rabo de Junco,* neither of which are supposed to venture far to sea, hovered about the ships. On the following night they were struck with awe at beholding a meteor, or, as Columbus calls it in his journal, a great flame of fire, which seemed to fall from the sky into the sea, about four or five leagues distant. These meteors, common in warm climates, and especially under the tropics, are always seen in the serene azure sky of those latitudes, falling as it were from the heavens; but never beneath a cloud. In the transparent atmosphere of one of those beautiful nights, where every star shines with the purest lustre, they often leave a luminous train behind them which lasts for twelve or fifteen seconds, and may well be compared to a flame.

The wind had hitherto been favorable, with occasional, though transient, clouds and showers. They had made great progress each day, though Columbus, according to his secret plan, contrived to suppress several leagues in the daily reckoning left open to the crew.

* The water-wagtail

They had now arrived within the influence of the trade wind, which, following the sun, blows steadily from east to west between the tropics, and sweeps over a few adjoining degrees of ocean. With this propitious breeze directly aft, they were wafted gently but speedily over a tranquil sea, so that for many days they did not shift a sail. Columbus perpetually recurs to the bland and temperate serenity of the weather, which in this tract of the ocean is soft and refreshing without being cool. In his artless and expressive language he compares the pure and balmy mornings to those of April in Andalusia, and observes that they wanted but the song of the nightingale to complete the illusion. "He had reason to say so," observes the venerable Las Casas; "for it is marvellous the suavity which we experience when half way towards these Indies; and the more the ships approach the lands, so much more do they perceive the temperance and softness of the air, the clearness of the sky, and the amenity and fragrance sent forth from the groves and forests; much more certainly than in April in Andalusia." *

They now began to see large patches of herbs and weeds drifting from the west, and increasing in quantity as they advanced. Some of these weeds were such as grow about rocks, others such as are produced in rivers; some were yellow and withered, others so green as to have apparently been recently washed from land. On one of these patches was a live crab, which Columbus carefully preserved. They saw also a white tropical bird, of a kind which never sleeps upon the sea. Tunny fish also played about the ships, one of which was killed by the crew of the Niña. Columbus now called to mind the account given by Aristotle of certain ships of Cadiz, which, coasting the shores outside of the straits of Gibraltar, were driven westward by an impetuous east wind, until they reached a part of the ocean covered with vast fields of weeds, resembling sunken islands, among which they beheld many tunny fish. He supposed himself arrived in this weedy sea, as it had been called, from which the ancient mariners had turned back in dismay, but which he regarded with animated hope, as indicating the vicinity of land. Not that he had yet any idea of

* Las Casas, Hist. Ind., lib. i. cap. 36, MS.

reaching the object of his search, the eastern end of Asia; for, according to his computation, he had come but three hundred and sixty leagues* since leaving the Canary Islands, and he placed the main land of India much farther on.

On the 18th of September the same weather continued; a soft steady breeze from the east filled every sail, while, to use the words of Columbus, the sea was as calm as the Guadalquiver at Seville. He fancied that the water of the sea grew fresher as he advanced, and noticed this as proof of the superior sweetness and purity of the air.†

The crews were all in high spirits; each ship strove to get in the advance, and every seaman was eagerly on the lookout; for the sovereigns had promised a pension of ten thousand maravedis to him who should first discover land. Martin Alonzo Pinzon crowded all canvas, and as the Pinta was a fast sailor, he generally kept the lead. In the afternoon he hailed the admiral and informed him, that, from the flight of a great number of birds, and from the appearance of the northern horizon, he thought there was land in that direction.

There was in fact a cloudiness in the north, such as often hangs over land; and at sunset it assumed such shapes and masses that many fancied they beheld islands. There was a universal wish, therefore, to steer for that quarter. Columbus, however, was persuaded that they were mere illusions. Every one who has made a sea voyage must have witnessed the deceptions caused by clouds resting upon the horizon, especially about sunset and sunrise; which the eye, assisted by the imagination and desire, easily converts into the wished-for land. This is particularly the case within the tropics, where the clouds at sunset assume the most singular appearances.

On the following day there were drizzling showers, unaccompanied by wind, which Columbus considered favorable signs; two boobies also flew on board the ships, birds which, he observed,

---

* Of twenty to the degree of latitude, the unity of distance used throughout this work.
† Las Casas, Hist. Ind., lib. i. cap. 36.

seldom fly twenty leagues from land. He sounded, therefore, with a line of two hundred fathoms, but found no bottom. He supposed he might be passing between islands, lying to the north and south; but was unwilling to waste the present favoring breeze by going in search of them; beside, he had confidently affirmed that land was to be found by keeping steadfastly to the west; his whole expedition had been founded on such a presumption; he should, therefore, risk all credit and authority with his people were he to appear to doubt and waver, and to go groping blindly from point to point of the compass. He resolved, therefore, to keep one bold course always westward, until he should reach the coast of India; and afterwards, if advisable, to seek these islands on his return.*

Notwithstanding his precaution to keep the people ignorant of the distance they had sailed, they were now growing extremely uneasy at the length of the voyage. They had advanced much farther west than ever man had sailed before, and though already beyond the reach of succor, still they continued daily leaving vast tracts of ocean behind them, and pressing onward and onward into that apparently boundless abyss. It is true they had been flattered by various indications of land, and still others were occurring; but all mocked them with vain hopes: after being hailed with a transient joy, they passed away, one after another, and the same interminable expanse of sea and sky continued to extend before them. Even the bland and gentle breeze, uniformly aft, was now conjured by their ingenious fears into a cause of alarm; for they began to imagine that the wind, in these seas, might always prevail from the east, and if so, would never permit their return to Spain.

Columbus endeavored to dispel these gloomy presages, sometimes by argument and expostulation, sometimes by awakening fresh hopes, and pointing out new signs of land. On the 20th of September the wind veered, with light breezes from the southwest. These, though adverse to their progress, had a cheering

* Hist. del Almirante, cap. 20. Extracts from Journal of Columb. Navarrete,, T. i. p. 16.

effect upon the people, as they proved that the wind did not always prevail from the east.* Several birds also visited the ships; three, of a small kind which keep about groves and orchards, came singing in the morning, and flew away again in the evening. Their song cheered the hearts of the dismayed mariners, who hailed it as the voice of land. The larger fowl, they observed, were strong of wing, and might venture far to sea; but such small birds were too feeble to fly far, and their singing showed that they were not exhausted by their flight.

On the following day there was either a profound calm, or light winds from the south-west. The sea, as far as the eye could reach, was covered with weeds; a phenomenon often observed in this part of the ocean, which has sometimes the appearance of a vast inundated meadow. This has been attributed to immense quantities of submarine plants, which grow at the bottom of the sea until ripe, when they are detached by the motion of the waves and currents, and rise to the surface.† These fields of weeds were at first regarded with great satisfaction, but at length they became, in many places, so dense and matted, as in some degree to impede the sailing of the ships, which must have been under very little headway. The crews now called to mind some tale about the frozen ocean, where ships were said to be sometimes fixed immovable. They endeavored, therefore, to avoid as much as possible these floating masses, lest some disaster of the kind might happen to themselves.‡ Others considered these weeds as proofs that the sea was growing shallower, and began to talk of lurking rocks, and shoals, and treacherous quicksands; and of the danger of running aground, as it were, in the midst of the ocean, where their vessels might rot and fall to pieces, far out of the track of human aid, and without any shore where the crews might take refuge. They had evidently some confused notion of the ancient story of the sunken island of Atalantis, and feared that they were arriving at that part

---

* Mucho me fue necesario este viento contrario, porque mi gente andaban muy estimulados, que pensaban que no ventaban estos mares vientos para volver á España. Primer Viage de Colon. Navarrete, tom. i. p. 12.

† Humboldt, Personal Narrative, book i. cap. 1.

‡ Hist. del Almirante, cap. 18.

of the ocean where navigation was said to be obstructed by drowned lands, and the ruins of an ingulfed country.

To dispel these fears, the admiral had frequent recourse to the lead; but though he sounded with a deep sea line, he still found no bottom. The minds of the crews, however, had gradually become diseased. They were full of vague terrors and superstitious fancies: they construed everything into a cause of alarm, and harassed their commander by incessant murmurs.

For three days there was a continuance of light summer airs from the southward and westward, and the sea was as smooth as a mirror. A whale was seen heaving up its huge form at a distance, which Columbus immediately pointed out as a favorable indication, affirming that these fish were generally in the neighborhood of land. The crews, however, became uneasy at the calmness of the weather. They observed that the contrary winds which they experienced were transient and unsteady, and so light as not to ruffle the surface of the sea, which maintained a sluggish calm like a lake of dead water. Everything differed, they said, in these strange regions from the world to which they had been accustomed. The only winds which prevailed with any constancy and force, were from the east, and they had not power to disturb the torpid stillness of the ocean; there was a risk, therefore, either of perishing amidst stagnant and shoreless waters, or of being prevented, by contrary winds, from ever returning to their native country.

Columbus continued with admirable patience to reason with these fancies; observing that the calmness of the sea must undoubtedly be caused by the vicinity of land in the quarter whence the wind blew, which, therefore, had not space sufficient to act upon the surface, and heave up large waves. Terror, however, multiplies and varies the forms of ideal danger, a thousand times faster than the most active wisdom can dispel them. The more Columbus argued, the more boisterous became the murmurs of his crew, until, on Sunday, the 25th of September, there came on a heavy swell of the sea, unaccompanied by wind. This phenomenon often occurs in the broad ocean; being either the expiring undulations of some past gale, or the movement given to the sea by some distant current of wind; it was, nevertheless, regarded with astonishment by the mariners, and dispelled the imaginary terrors occasioned by the calm.

Columbus, who as usual considered himself under the immediate eye and guardianship of Heaven in this solemn enterprise, intimates in his journal that this swelling of the sea seemed providentially ordered to allay the rising clamors of his crew; comparing it to that which so miraculously aided Moses when conducting the children of Israel out of the captivity of Egypt.*

CHAPTER IV

Continuation of the Voyage—Discovery of Land

[1492]

THE SITUATION OF COLUMBUS was daily becoming more and more critical. In proportion as he approached the regions where he expected to find land, the impatience of his crews augmented. The favorable signs which increased his confidence, were derided by them as delusive; and there was danger of their rebelling, and obliging him to turn back, when on the point of realizing the object of all his labors. They beheld themselves with dismay still wafted onward, over the boundless wastes of what appeared to them a mere watery desert, surrounding the habitable world. What was to become of them should their provisions fail? Their ships were too weak and defective even for the great voyage they had already made, but if they were still to press forward, adding

* "Como la mar estuviese mansa y llana murmuraba la gente diciendo que, pues por alli no habia mar grande que nunca ventaria para volver á España; pero despues alzóse mucho la mar y sin viento, que los asombraba; por lo cual dice aqui el Almirante; *asi que muy necesario me fué la mar alta, que no pareció, salvo el tiempo de los Judios cuando salieron de Egipto contra Moyses que los sacaba de captiverio.*"—Journal of Columb. Navarrete, tom i. p. 12.

at every moment to the immense expanse behind them, how should they ever be able to return, having no intervening port where they might victual and refit?

In this way they fed each other's discontents, gathering together in little knots, and fomenting a spirit of mutinous opposition: and when we consider the natural fire of the Spanish temperament and its impatience of control; and that a great part of these men were sailing on compulsion; we cannot wonder that there was imminent danger of their breaking forth into open rebellion and compelling Columbus to turn back. In their secret conferences they exclaimed against him as a desperado, bent, in a mad fantasy, upon doing something extravagant to render himself notorious. What were their sufferings and dangers to one evidently content to sacrifice his own life for the chance of distinction? What obligations bound them to continue on with him; or when were the terms of their agreement to be considered as fulfilled? They had already penetrated unknown seas, untraversed by a sail, far beyond where man had ever before ventured. They had done enough to gain themselves a character for courage and hardihood in undertaking such an enterprise and persisting in it so far. How much further were they to go in quest of a merely conjectured land? Were they to sail on until they perished, or until all return became impossible? In such case they would be the authors of their own destruction.

On the other hand, should they consult their safety, and turn back before too late, who would blame them? Any complaints made by Columbus would be of no weight; he was a foreigner without friends or influence; his schemes had been condemned by the learned, and discountenanced by people of all ranks. He had no party to uphold him, and a host of opponents whose pride of opinion would be gratified by his failure. Or, as an effectual means of preventing his complaints, they might throw him into the sea, and give out that he had fallen overboard while busy with his instruments contemplating the stars; a report which no one would have either the inclination or the means to controvert.

Columbus was not ignorant of the mutinous disposition of his crew; but he still maintained a serene and steady countenance, soothing some with gentle words, endeavoring to stimulate the pride or avarice of others, and openly menacing the refractory with signal punishment, should they do anything to impede the voyage.*

On the 25th of September, the wind again became favorable, and they were able to resume their course directly to the west. The airs being light, and the sea calm, the vessels sailed near to each other, and Columbus had much conversation with Martin Alonzo Pinzon on the subject of a chart, which the former had sent three days before on board of the Pinta. Pinzon thought that, according to the indications of the map, they ought to be in the neighborhood of Cipango, and the other islands which the admiral had therein delineated. Columbus partly entertained the same idea, but thought it possible that the ships might have been borne out of their track by the prevalent currents, or that they had not come so far as the pilots had reckoned. He desired that the chart might be returned, and Pinzon tying it to the end of a cord, flung it on board to him. While Columbus, his pilot, and several of his experienced mariners were studying the map, and endeavoring to make out from it their actual position, they heard a shout from the Pinta, and looking up, beheld Martin Alonzo Pinzon mounted on the stern of his vessel, crying "Land! land! Señor, I claim my reward!" He pointed at the same time to the south-west, where there was indeed an appearance of land at about twenty-five leagues' distance. Upon this Columbus threw himself on his knees and returned thanks to God; and Martin Alonzo repeated the *Gloria in excelsis,* in which he was joined by his own crew and that of the admiral.†

The seamen now mounted to the mast-head or climbed about the rigging, straining their eyes in the direction pointed out. The conviction became so general of land in that quarter, and the joy of the people so ungovernable, that Columbus found it necessary to vary from his usual course, and stand all night to the south-west. The morning light, however, put an end to all their hopes, as to a dream. The fancied land proved to be nothing but an eve-

* Hist. del Almirante, cap. 19. Herrera, Hist. Ind., decad. i. lib. i. cap. 10.
† Journal of Columb., Primer Viage, Navarrete, tom. i.

ning cloud, and had vanished in the night. With dejected hearts they once more resumed their western course, from which Columbus would never have varied, but in compliance with their clamorous wishes.

For several days they continued on with the same propitious breeze, tranquil sea, and mild, delightful weather. The water was so calm that the sailors amused themselves with swimming about the vessel. Dolphins began to abound, and flying fish, darting into the air, fell upon the decks. The continued signs of land diverted the attention of the crews, and insensibly beguiled them onward.

On the 1st of October, according to the reckoning of the pilot of the admiral's ship, they had come five hundred and eighty leagues west since leaving the Canary Islands. The reckoning which Columbus showed the crew, was five hundred and eighty-four, but the reckoning which he kept privately, was seven hundred and seven.* On the following day, the weeds floated from east to west; and on the third day no birds were to be seen.

The crews now began to fear that they had passed between islands, from one to the other of which the birds had been flying. Columbus had also some doubts of the kind, but refused to alter his westward course. The people again uttered murmurs and menaces; but on the following day they were visited by such flights of birds, and the various indications of land became so numerous, that from a state of despondency they passed to one of confident expectation.

Eager to obtain the promised pension, the seamen were continually giving the cry of land, on the least appearance of the kind. To put a stop to these false alarms, which produced continual disappointments, Columbus declared that should any one give such notice, and land not be discovered within three days afterwards, he should thenceforth forfeit all claim to the reward.

On the evening of the 6th of October, Martin Alonzo Pinzon began to lose confidence in their present course, and proposed that they should stand more to the southward. Columbus, however, still persisted in steering directly west.† Observing this difference

---

* Navarrete, tom. i. p. 16.
† Journ. of Columbus, Navarrete, tom. i. p. 17.

of opinion in a person so important in his squadron as Pinzon, and fearing that chance or design might scatter the ships, he ordered that, should either of the caravels be separated from him, it should stand to the west, and endeavor as soon as possible to join company again: he directed, also, that the vessels should keep near to him at sunrise and sunset, as at these times the state of the atmosphere is most favorable to the discovery of distant land.

On the morning of the 7th of October, at sunrise, several of the admiral's crew thought they beheld land in the west, but so indistinctly that no one ventured to proclaim it, lest he should be mistaken, and forfeit all chance of the reward: the Niña, however, being a good sailor, pressed forward to ascertain the fact. In a little while a flag was hoisted at her mast-head, and a gun discharged, being the preconcerted signals for land. New joy was awakened throughout the little squadron, and every eye was turned to the west. As they advanced, however, their cloud-built hopes faded away, and before evening the fancied land had again melted into air.*

The crews now sank into a degree of dejection proportioned to their recent excitement; but new circumstances occurred to arouse them. Columbus, having observed great flights of small field-birds going towards the south-west, concluded they must be secure of some neighboring land, where they would find food and a resting-place. He knew the importance which the Portuguese voyagers attached to the flight of birds, by following which they had discovered most of their islands. He had now come seven hundred and fifty leagues, the distance at which he had computed to find the island of Cipango; as there was no appearance of it, he might have missed it through some mistake in the latitude. He determined, therefore, on the evening of the 7th of October to alter his course to the west-south-west, the direction in which the birds generally flew, and continue that direction for at least two days. After all, it was no great deviation from his main course, and would meet the wishes of the Pinzons, as well as be inspiriting to his followers generally.

For three days they stood in this direction, and the further they

* Hist. del Almirante, cap. 20. Journ. of Columbus, Navarrete, tom. i.

went the more frequent and encouraging were the signs of land. Flights of small birds of various colors, some of them such as sing in the fields, came flying about the ships, and then continued towards the south-west, and others were heard also flying by in the night. Tunny fish played about the smooth sea, and a heron, a pelican, and a duck, were seen, all bound in the same direction. The herbage which floated by was fresh and green, as if recently from land, and the air, Columbus observes, was sweet and fragrant as April breezes in Seville.

All these, however, were regarded by the crews as so many delusions beguiling them on to destruction; and when on the evening of the third day they beheld the sun go down upon a shoreless ocean, they broke forth into turbulent clamor. They exclaimed against this obstinacy in tempting fate by continuing on into a boundless sea. They insisted upon turning homeward, and abandoning the voyage as hopeless. Columbus endeavored to pacify them by gentle words and promises of large rewards; but finding that they only increased in clamor, he assumed a decided tone. He told them it was useless to murmur; the expedition had been sent by the sovereigns to seek the Indies, and, happen what might, he was determined to persevere, until, by the blessing of God, he should accomplish the enterprise.*

* Hist. del Almirante, cap. 20. Las Casas, lib. i., Journal of Columb., Navarrete, Colec. tom. i. p. 19.

It has been asserted by various historians, that Columbus, a day or two previous to coming in sight of the New World, capitulated with his mutinous crew, promising, if he did not discover land within three days, to abandon the voyage. There is no authority for such an assertion, either in the history of his son Fernando or that of the Bishop Las Casas, each of whom had the admiral's papers before him. There is no mention of such a circumstance in the extracts made from the journal by Las Casas, which have recently been brought to light, nor is it asserted by either Peter Martyr or the Curate of Los Palacios, both contemporaries and acquaintances of Columbus, and who could scarcely have failed to mention so striking a fact, if true. It rests merely upon the authority of Oviedo, who is of inferior credit to either of the authors above cited, and was grossly misled as to many of the particulars of this voyage by a pilot of the name of Hernan Perez Matheo, who was hostile to Columbus. In the manuscript process of the memorable lawsuit between Don Diego, son of the admiral, and the fiscal of the crown, is the evidence of one Pedro de Bilbao, who testifies that he heard many times that some of the pilots and mariners wished to turn back, but that the admiral promised them presents, and entreated them

Columbus was now at open defiance with his crew, and his situation became desperate. Fortunately the manifestations of the vicinity of land were such on the following day as no longer to admit a doubt. Beside a quantity of fresh weeds, such as grow in rivers, they saw a green fish of a kind which keeps about rocks; then a branch of thorn with berries on it, and recently separated from the tree, floated by them; then they picked up a reed, a small board, and, above all, a staff artificially carved. All gloom and mutiny now gave way to sanguine expectation; and throughout the day each one was eagerly on the watch, in hopes of being the first to discover the long-sought-for land.

In the evening, when, according to invariable custom on board of the admiral's ship, the mariners had sung the *salve regina,* or vesper hymn to the Virgin, he made an impressive address to his crew. He pointed out the goodness of God in thus conducting them by soft and favoring breezes across a tranquil ocean, cheering their hopes continually with fresh signs, increasing as their fears augmented, and thus leading and guiding them to a promised land. He now reminded them of the orders he had given on leaving the Canaries, that, after sailing westward seven hundred leagues, they should not make sail after midnight. Present appearances authorized such a precaution. He thought it probable they

---

to wait two or three days, before which time he should discover land. ("Pedro de Bilbao oyo muchas veces que algunos pilotos y marineros querian volverse sino fuera por el Almirante que les prometio donos, les rogō esperasen dos o tres dias i que antes del termino descubriera tierra.") This, if true, implies no capitulation to relinquish the enterprise.

On the other hand, it was asserted by some of the witnesses in the above-mentioned suit, that Columbus, after having proceeded some few hundred leagues without finding land, lost confidence and wished to turn back; but was persuaded and even piqued to continue by the Pinzons. This assertion carries falsehood on its very face. It is in total contradiction to that persevering constancy and undaunted resolution displayed by Columbus, not merely in the present voyage, but from first to last of his difficult and dangerous career. This testimony was given by some of the mutinous men, anxious to exaggerate the merits of the Pinzons, and to depreciate that of Columbus. Fortunately, the extracts from the journal of the latter, written from day to day with guileless simplicity, and all the air of truth, disprove these fables, and show that on the very day previous to his discovery, he expressed a peremptory determination to persevere, in defiance of all dangers and difficulties.

would make land that very night; he ordered, therefore, a vigilant lookout to be kept from the forecastle, promising to whomsoever should make the discovery, a doublet of velvet, in addition to the pension to be given by the sovereigns.*

The breeze had been fresh all day, with more sea than usual, and they had made great progress. At sunset they had stood again to the west, and were ploughing the waves at a rapid rate, the Pinta keeping the lead, from her superior sailing. The greatest animation prevailed throughout the ships; not an eye was closed that night. As the evening darkened, Columbus took his station on the top of the castle or cabin on the high poop of his vessel, ranging his eye along the dusky horizon, and maintaining an intense and unremitting watch. About ten o'clock, he thought he beheld a light glimmering at a great distance. Fearing his eager hopes might deceive him, he called to Pedro Gutierrez, gentleman of the king's bed-chamber, and inquired whether he saw such a light; the latter replied in the affirmative. Doubtful whether it might not yet be some delusion of the fancy, Columbus called Rodrigo Sanchez of Segovia, and made the same inquiry. By the time the latter had ascended the round-house, the light had disappeared. They saw it once or twice afterwards in sudden and passing gleams; as if it were a torch in the bark of a fisherman, rising and sinking with the waves; or in the hand of some person on shore, borne up and down as he walked from house to house. So transient and uncertain were these gleams, that few attached any importance to them; Columbus, however, considered them as certain signs of land, and, moreover, that the land was inhabited.

They continued their course until two in the morning, when a gun from the Pinta gave the joyful signal of land. It was first descried by a mariner named Rodrigo de Triana; but the reward was afterwards adjudged to the admiral, for having previously perceived the light. The land was now clearly seen about two leagues distant, whereupon they took in sail, and laid to, waiting impatiently for the dawn.

The thoughts and feelings of Columbus in this little space of time must have been tumultuous and intense. At length in spite

* Hist. del. Almirante, cap. 21.

of every difficulty and danger, he had accomplished his object. The great mystery of the ocean was revealed; his theory, which had been the scoff of sages, was triumphantly established; he had secured to himself a glory durable as the world itself.

It is difficult to conceive the feelings of such a man, at such a moment; or the conjectures which must have thronged upon his mind, as to the land before him, covered with darkness. That it was fruitful, was evident from the vegetables which floated from its shores. He thought, too, that he perceived the fragrance of aromatic groves. The moving light he had beheld proved it the residence of man. But what were its inhabitants? Were they like those of the other parts of the globe; or were they some strange and monstrous race, such as the imagination was prone in those times to give to all remote and unknown regions? Had he come upon some wild island far in the Indian sea; or was this the famed Cipango itself, the object of his golden fancies? A thousand speculations of the kind must have swarmed upon him, as, with his anxious crews, he waited for the night to pass away; wondering whether the morning light would reveal a savage wilderness, or dawn upon spicy groves, and glittering fanes, and gilded cities, and all the splendor of Oriental civilization.

BOOK IV

CHAPTER I

First Landing of Columbus in the New World

IT WAS ON FRIDAY MORNING, the 12th of October, that Columbus first beheld the New World. As the day dawned he saw before him a level island, several leagues in extent, and covered with trees like a continual orchard. Though apparently uncultivated, it was populous, for the inhabitants were seen issuing from all parts of the woods and running to the shore. They were perfectly naked, and as they stood gazing at the ships, appeared by their attitudes and gestures to be lost in astonishment. Columbus made signal for the ships to cast anchor, and the boats to be manned and armed. He entered his own boat, richly attired in scarlet, and holding the royal standard; whilst Martin Alonzo Pinzon, and Vincent Jañez his brother, put off in company in their boats, each with a banner of the enterprise emblazoned with a green cross, having on either side the letters F. and Y., the initials of the Castilian monarchs Fernando and Ysabel, surmounted by crowns.

As he approached the shore, Columbus, who was disposed for all kinds of agreeable impressions, was delighted with the purity and suavity of the atmosphere, the crystal transparency of the sea, and the extraordinary beauty of the vegetation. He beheld, also, fruits of an unknown kind upon the trees which overhung the shores. On landing, he threw himself on his knees, kissed the earth, and returned thanks to God with tears of joy. His example was followed by the rest, whose hearts indeed overflowed with the same feelings of gratitude. Columbus then rising drew his sword, displayed the royal standard, and assembling around him the two captains, with Rodrigo de Escobedo, notary of the armament, Rodrigo Sanchez, and the rest who had landed, he took solemn possession in the name of the Castilian sovereigns, giving the island the name of San Salvador. Having complied with the requisite forms and ceremonies, he called upon all present to take the oath of obedience to him, as admiral and viceroy, representing the persons of the sovereigns.*

The feelings of the crew now burst forth in the most extravagant transports. They had recently considered themselves devoted men,

---

* In the Tablas Chronologicas, of Padre Claudio Clemente, is conserved a form of prayer, said to have been used by Columbus on this occasion, and which, by order of the Castilian sovereigns, was afterwards used by Balboa, Cortez, and Pizarro in their discoveries. "Domine Deus æterne et omnipotens, sacro tuo verbo cœlum, et terram, et mare creâsti; benedicatur et glorificetur nomen tuum, laudetur tua majestas, quæ dignita est per humilem servum tuum, ut ejus sacrum nomen agnoscatur, et prædicetur in hac altera mundi parte." Tab. Chron. de los Descub., decad. i. Valencia, 1689.

hurrying forward to destruction; they now looked upon themselves as favorites of fortune, and gave themselves up to the most unbounded joy. They thronged around the admiral with overflowing zeal, some embracing him, others kissing his hands. Those who had been most mutinous and turbulent during the voyage, were now most devoted and enthusiastic. Some begged favors of him, as if he had already wealth and honors in his gift. Many abject spirits, who had outraged him by their insolence, now crouched at his feet, begging pardon for all the trouble they had caused him, and promising the blindest obedience for the future.*

The natives of the island, when, at the dawn of day, they had beheld the ships hovering on their coast, had supposed them monsters which had issued from the deep during the night. They had crowded to the beach, and watched their movements with awful anxiety. Their veering about, apparently without effort, and the shifting and furling of their sails, resembling huge wings, filled them with astonishment. When they beheld their boats approach the shore, and a number of strange beings clad in glittering steel, or raiment of various colors, landing upon the beach, they fled in affright to the woods. Finding, however, that there was no attempt to pursue nor molest them, they gradually recovered from their terror, and approached the Spaniards with great awe; frequently prostrating themselves on the earth, and making signs of adoration. During the ceremonies of taking possession, they remained gazing in timid admiration at the complexion, the beards, the shining armor, and splendid dress of the Spaniards. The admiral particularly attracted their attention, from his commanding height, his air of authority, his dress of scarlet, and the deference which was paid him by his companions; all which pointed him out to be the commander.† When they had still further recovered from their fears, they approached the Spaniards, touched their beards, and examined their hands and faces, admiring their whiteness. Columbus was pleased with their gentleness and confiding simplicity, and suffered their scrutiny with perfect acquiescence, winning them by his benignity. They now supposed that the ships had

* Oviedo, lib. i. cap. 6. Las Casas, Hist. Ind., lib. i. cap. 40.
† Las Casas, ubi sup.

sailed out of the crystal firmament which bounded their horizon, or had descended from above on their ample wings, and that these marvelous beings were inhabitants of the skies.*

The natives of the island were no less objects of curiosity to the Spaniards, differing, as they did, from any race of men they had ever seen. Their appearance gave no promise of either wealth or civilization, for they were entirely naked, and painted with a variety of colors. With some it was confined merely to a part of the face, the nose, or around the eyes; with others it extended to the whole body, and gave them a wild and fantastic appearance. Their complexion was of a tawny or copper hue, and they were entirely destitute of beards. Their hair was not crisped, like the recently-discovered tribes of the African coast, under the same latitude, but straight and coarse, partly cut short above the ears, but some locks were left long behind and falling upon their shoulders. Their features, though obscured and disfigured by paint, were agreeable; they had lofty foreheads and remarkably fine eyes. They were of moderate stature and well shaped; most of them appeared to be under thirty years of age: there was but one female with them, quite young, naked like her companions, and beautifully formed.

As Columbus supposed himself to have landed on an island at the extremity of India, he called the natives by the general appellation of Indians, which was universally adopted before the true nature of his discovery was known, and has since been extended to all the aboriginals of the New World.

The islanders were friendly and gentle. Their only arms were lances, hardened at the end by fire, or pointed with a flint, or the teeth or bone of a fish. There was no iron to be seen, nor did they appear acquainted with its properties; for, when a drawn sword was presented to them, they unguardedly took it by the edge.

Columbus distributed among them colored caps, glass beads, hawks' bells, and other trifles, such as the Portuguese were ac-

* The idea that the white men came from heaven was universally entertained by the inhabitants of the New World. When, in the course of subsequent voyages, the Spaniards conversed with the cacique Nicaragua, he inquired how they came down from the skies, whether flying, or whether they descended on clouds. Herrera, decad. iii. lib. iv. cap. 5.

customed to trade with among the nations of the gold coast of Africa. They received them eagerly, hung the beads round their necks, and were wonderfully pleased with their finery, and with the sound of the bells. The Spaniards remained all day on shore refreshing themselves after their anxious voyage amidst the beautiful groves of the island, and returned on board late in the evening, delighted with all they had seen.

On the following morning, at break of day the shore was thronged with the natives; some swam off to the ships, others came in light barks which they called canoes, formed of a single tree, hollowed, and capable of holding from one man to the number of forty or fifty. These they managed dexterously with paddles, and, if overturned, swam about in the water with perfect unconcern, as if in their natural element, righting their canoes with great facility, and baling them with calabashes.*

They were eager to procure more toys and trinkets, not, apparently, from any idea of their intrinsic value, but because everything from the hands of the strangers possessed a supernatural virtue in their eyes, as having been brought from heaven; they even picked up fragments of glass and earthenware as valuable prizes. They had but few objects to offer in return, except parrots, of which great numbers were domesticated among them, and cotton yarn, of which they had abundance, and would exchange large balls of five and twenty pounds' weight for the merest trifle. They brought also cakes of a kind of bread called cassava, which constituted a principal part of their food, and was afterwards an important article of provisions with the Spaniards. It was formed from a great root called yuca, which they cultivated in fields. This they cut into small morsels, which they grated or scraped, and strained in a press, making a broad thin cake, which was afterwards dried hard, and would keep for a long time, being steeped in water when eaten. It was insipid, but nourishing, though the water strained from it in the preparation was a deadly poison.

---

* The calabashes of the Indians, which served the purposes of glass and earthenware, supplying them with all sorts of domestic utensils, were produced on stately trees of the size of elms.

There was another kind of yuca destitute of this poisonous quality, which was eaten in the root, either boiled or roasted.*

The avarice of the discoverers was quickly excited by the sight of small ornaments of gold, worn by some of the natives in their noses. These the latter gladly exchanged for glass beads and hawks' bells; and both parties exulted in the bargain, no doubt admiring each other's simplicity. As gold, however, was an object of royal monopoly in all enterprises of discovery, Columbus forbade any traffic in it without his express sanction; and he put the same prohibition on the traffic for cotton, reserving to the crown all trade for it, wherever it should be found in any quantity.

He inquired of the natives where this gold was procured. They answered him by signs, pointing to the south, where, he understood them, dwelt a king of such wealth that he was served in vessels of wrought gold. He understood, also, that there was land to the south, the south-west and the north-west; and that the people from the last mentioned quarter frequently proceeded to the south-west in quest of gold and precious stones, making in their way descents upon the islands, and carrying off the inhabitants. Several of the natives showed him scars of wounds received in battles with these invaders. It is evident that a great part of this fancied intelligence was self-delusion on the part of Columbus; for he was under a spell of the imagination, which gave its own shapes and colors to every object. He was persuaded that he had arrived among the islands described by Marco Polo, as lying opposite to Cathay, in the Chinese sea, and he construed everything to accord with the account given of those opulent regions. Thus the enemies which the natives spoke of as coming from the north-west, he concluded to be the people of the mainland of Asia, the subjects of the great Khan of Tartary, who were represented by the Venetian traveller as accustomed to make war upon the islands, and to enslave their inhabitants. The country to the south, abounding in gold, could be no other than the famous island of Cipango; and the king who was served out of vessels of gold, must be the monarch whose magnificent city and gorgeous palace, cov-

* Acosta, Hist. Ind., lib. iv. cap. 17.

ered with plates of gold, had been extolled in such splendid terms by Marco Polo.

The island where Columbus had thus, for the first time, set his foot upon the New World, was called by the natives, Guanahanè. It still retains the name of San Salvador, which he gave to it, though called by the English, Cat Island.* The light which he had seen the evening previous to his making land, may have been on Watling's Island, which lies a few leagues to the east. San Salvador is one of the great cluster of the Lucayos, or Bahama Islands, which stretch south-east and north-west, from the coast of Florida to Hispaniola, covering the northern coast of Cuba.

On the morning of the 14th of October, the admiral set off at daybreak with the boats of the ships to reconnoitre the island, directing his course to the north-east. The coast was surrounded by a reef of rocks, within which there was depth of water and sufficient harbor to receive all the ships in Christendom. The entrance was very narrow; within there were several sand-banks, but the water was as still as in a pool.†

The island appeared throughout to be well wooded, with streams of water, and a large lake in the centre. As the boats proceeded, they passed two or three villages, the inhabitants of which, men as well as women, ran to the shores, throwing themselves on the ground, lifting up their hands and eyes, either giving thanks to Heaven, or worshipping the Spaniards as supernatural beings. They ran along parallel to the boats, calling after the Spaniards, and inviting them by signs to land, offering them various fruits and vessels of water. Finding, however, that the boats continued on their course, many threw themselves into the sea and swam after them, and others followed in canoes. The admiral received them all with kindness, giving them glass beads and other trifles, which were received with transport as celestial presents, for the invariable idea of the savages was, that the white men had come from the skies.

---

* Some dispute having recently arisen as to the island on which Columbus first landed, the reader is referred for a discussion of this question to the Illustrations of this work, article "First Landing of Columbus."
† Primer Viage de Colon. Navarrete, tom. I.

In this way they pursued their course, until they came to a small peninsula, which, with two or three days' labor, might be separated from the mainland and surrounded with water, and was therefore specified by Columbus as an excellent situation for a fortress. On this were six Indian cabins, surrounded by groves and gardens as beautiful as those of Castile. The sailors being wearied with rowing, and the island not appearing to the admiral of sufficient importance to induce colonization, he returned to the ships, taking seven of the natives with him, that they might acquire the Spanish language and serve as interpreters.

Having taken in a supply of wood and water, they left the island of San Salvador the same evening, the admiral being impatient to arrive at the wealthy country to the south, which he flattered himself would prove the famous island of Cipango.

CONQUEST OF GRANADA

CHAPTER XC

Preparations of Granada for a Desperate Defense

How is thy strength departed, O Granada! how is thy beauty withered and despoiled, O city of groves and fountains! The commerce that once thronged thy streets is at an end; the merchant no longer hastens to thy gates, with the luxuries of foreign lands. The cities which once paid thee tribute are wrested from thy sway; the chivalry which filled thy Vivarrambla with sumptuous pageantry, have fallen in many battles. The Alhambra still rears its ruddy towers from the midst of groves, but melancholy reigns in its marble halls; and the monarch looks down from his lofty balconies upon a naked waste, where once extended the blooming glories of the vega!

Such is the lament of the Moorish writers, over the lamentable state of Granada, now a mere phantom of former greatness. The two ravages of the vega, following so closely upon each other, had swept off all the produce of the year; and the husbandman had no longer the heart to till the field, seeing the ripening harvest only brought the spoiler to his door.

During the winter season, Ferdinand made diligent preparations for the campaign, that was to decide the fate of Granada. As this war was waged purely for the promotion of the Christian faith, he thought it meet that its enemies should bear the expenses. He levied, therefore, a general contribution upon the Jews throughout his kingdom, by synagogues and districts: and obliged them to render in the proceeds, at the city of Seville.*

On the 11th of April, Ferdinand and Isabella departed for the Moorish frontier, with the solemn determination to lay close siege

* Garibay, lib. 18, c. 39.

to Granada, and never quit its walls until they had planted the standard of the faith on the towers of the Alhambra. Many of the nobles of the kingdom, particularly those from parts remote from the scene of action, wearied by the toils of war, and foreseeing that this would be a tedious siege, requiring patience and vigilance rather than hardy deeds of arms, contented themselves with sending their vassals, while they staid at home, to attend to their domains. Many cities furnished soldiers at their cost, and the king took the field with an army of forty thousand infantry and ten thousand horse. The principal captains who followed him in this campaign, were Roderigo Ponce de Leon, the marques of Cadiz, the master of Santiago, the marques of Villena, the counts of Tendilla, Cifuentes, Cabra, and Urena, and Don Alonzo de Aguilar.

Queen Isabella, accompanied by her son, the prince Juan, and the princesses Juana, Maria, and Cathalina, her daughters, proceeded to Alcala la Real, the mountain fortress and stronghold of the count de Tendilla. Here she remained, to forward supplies to the army, and to be ready to repair to the camp, whenever her presence might be required.

The army of Ferdinand poured into the vega, by various defiles of the mountains; and, on the 23d of April, the royal tent was pitched at a village called Los Ojos de Huescar, about a league and a half from Granada. At the approach of this formidable force, the harassed inhabitants turned pale, and even many of the warriors trembled; for they felt that the last desperate struggle was at hand.

Boabdil el Chico assembled his council in the Alhambra, from the windows of which they could behold the Christian squadrons glistening through clouds of dust, as they poured along the vega. The utmost confusion and consternation reigned in the council. Many of the members, terrified with the horrors impending over their families, advised Boabdil to throw himself upon the generosity of the Christian monarch: even several of the bravest suggested the possibility of obtaining honorable terms.

The wazir of the city, Abul Casim Abdel Melic, was called upon to report the state of the public means for sustenance and defense. There were sufficient provisions, he said, for a few months' supply, independent of what might exist in the possession of merchants and other rich inhabitants. "But of what avail," said he, "is a supply for a few months, against the sieges of the Castilian monarch, which are interminable?"

He produced, also, the lists of men capable of bearing arms. "The number," said he, "is great; but what can be expected from mere citizen-soldiers? They vaunt and menace, in time of safety; none are so arrogant, when the enemy is at a distance—but when the din of war thunders at the gates, they hide themselves in terror."

When Muza heard these words, he rose with generous warmth: "What reason have we," said he, "to despair? The blood of those illustrious Moors, the conquerors of Spain, still flows in our veins. Let us be true to ourselves, and fortune will again be with us. We have a veteran force, both horse and foot, the flower of our chivalry, seasoned in war and scarred in a thousand battles. As to the multitude of our citizens, spoken of so slightly, why should we doubt their valor? There are twenty thousand young men, in the fire of youth, whom I will engage, that in the defense of their homes they will rival the most valiant veterans. Do we want provisions? Our horses are fleet, and our horsemen daring in the foray. Let them scour and scourge the country of those apostate Moslems who have surrendered to the Christians. Let them make inroads into the lands of our enemies. We shall soon see them returning with cavalgadas to our gates; and, to a soldier, there is no morsel so sweet as that wrested with hard fighting from the foe."

Boabdil, though he wanted firm and durable courage, was readily excited to sudden emotions of bravery. He caught a glow of resolution from the noble ardor of Muza. "Do what is needful," said he to his commanders; "into your hands I confide the common safety. You are the protectors of the kingdom, and with the aid of Allah, will revenge the insults of our religion, the deaths of our friends and relations, and the sorrows and sufferings heaped upon our land." *

To every one was now assigned his separate duty. The wazir had charge of the arms and provisions, and the enrolling of the
* Conde.

people. Muza was to command the cavalry, to defend the gates, and to take the lead in all sallies and skirmishings. Naim Reduan, and Muhamed Aben Zayde, were his adjutants. Abdel Kerim Zegri, and the other captains, were to guard the walls; and the alcaydes of the Alcazaba, and of the Red Towers, had command of the fortresses.

Nothing now was heard but the din of arms, and the bustle of preparation. The Moorish spirit, quick to catch fire, was immediately in a flame; and the populace, in the excitement of the moment, set at naught the power of the Christians. Muza was in all parts of the city, infusing his own generous zeal into the bosoms of the soldiery. The young cavaliers rallied round him as their model; the veteran warriors regarded him with a soldier's admiration; the vulgar throng followed him with shouts, and the helpless part of the inhabitants, the old men and the women, hailed him with blessings as their protector.

On the first appearance of the Christian army the principal gates of the city had been closed, and secured with bars and bolts and heavy chains: Muza now ordered them to be thrown open; "To me and my cavaliers," said he, "is intrusted the defense of the gates; our bodies shall be their barriers." He stationed at each gate a strong guard, chosen from his bravest men. His horse-men were always completely armed, and ready to mount at a moment's warning; their steeds stood saddled and caparisoned in the stables, with lance and buckler beside them. On the least approach of the enemy, a squadron of horse gathered within the gate, ready to launch forth like the bolt from the thunder-cloud. Muza made no empty bravado nor haughty threat; he was more terrible in deeds than in words, and executed daring exploits, beyond even the vaunt of the vainglorious. Such was the present champion of the Moors. Had they possessed many such warriors, or had Muza risen to power at an earlier period of the war, the fate of Granada might have been deferred, and the Moor for a long time have maintained his throne within the walls of the Alhambra.

CHAPTER XCI

How King Ferdinand Conducted the Siege Cautiously; and How Queen Isabella Arrived at the Camp

THOUGH GRANADA WAS SHORN of its glories, and nearly cut off from all external aid, still its mighty castles and massive bulwarks seemed to set all attack at defiance. Being the last retreat of Moorish power, it had assembled within its walls the remnants of the armies which had contended, step by step, with the invaders, in their gradual conquest of the land. All that remained of high-born and high-bred chivalry, was here; all that was loyal and patriotic was roused to activity by the common danger; and Granada, so long lulled into inaction by vain hopes of security, now assumed a formidable aspect in the hour of its despair.

Ferdinand saw that any attempt to subdue the city by main force would be perilous and bloody. Cautious in his policy, and fond of conquests gained by art rather than valor, he resorted to the plan so successful with Baza, and determined to reduce the place by famine. For this purpose, his armies penetrated into the very heart of the Alpuxarras, and ravaged the valleys, and sacked and burnt the towns, upon which the city depended for its supplies. Scouting parties, also, ranged the mountains behind Granada, and captured every casual convoy of provisions. The Moors became more daring, as their situation became more hopeless. Never had Ferdinand experienced such vigorous sallies and assaults. Muza, at the head of his cavalry, harassed the borders of the camp, and even penetrated into the interior, making sudden spoil and ravage, and leaving his course to be traced by the slain and wounded. To protect his camp from these assaults, Ferdinand fortified it with deep trenches and strong bulwarks. It was of a quadrangular form, divided into streets like a city, the troops being quartered in tents, and in booths constructed of bushes and branches of trees. When it was completed, Queen Isabella came in state, with all her court, and the prince and princesses, to be present at the siege. This was intended, as on former occasions, to reduce the besieged to despair, by showing the determination of the sovereigns to reside in the camp until the city should surrender. Immediately after her arrival, the queen rode forth, to survey the camp and its environs: wherever she went, she was attended by a splendid retinue; and all the commanders vied with each other, in the pomp and ceremony with which they received her. Nothing was heard, from morning until night, but shouts and acclamations, and bursts of martial music; so that it appeared to the Moors as if a continual festival and triumph reigned in the Christian camp.

The arrival of the queen, however, and the menaced obstinacy of the siege, had no effect in damping the fire of the Moorish chivalry. Muza inspired the youthful warriors with the most devoted heroism: "We have nothing left to fight for," said he, "but the ground we stand on; when this is lost, we cease to have a country and a name."

Finding the Christian king forbore to make an attack, Muza incited his cavaliers to challenge the youthful chivalry of the Christian army to single combat, or partial skirmishes. Scarce a day passed without gallant conflicts of the kind, in sight of the city and the camp. The combatants rivaled each other in the splendor of their armor and array, as well as in the prowess of their deeds. Their contests were more like the stately ceremonials of tilts and tournaments, than the rude conflicts of the field. Ferdinand soon perceived that they animated the fiery Moors with fresh zeal and courage, while they cost the lives of many of his bravest cavaliers: he again, therefore, forbade the acceptance of any individual challenges, and ordered that all partial encounters should be avoided. The cool and stern policy of the Catholic sovereign bore hard upon the generous spirits of either army, but roused the indignation of the Moors, when they found that they were to be subdued in this inglorious manner: "Of what avail," said they, "are chivalry and heroic valor? the crafty monarch of the Christians has no magnanimity in warfare; he seeks to subdue us through the weakness of our bodies, but shuns to encounter the courage of our souls."

CHAPTER XCII

Of the Insolent Defiance of Tarfe the Moor, and the Daring Exploit of Hernan Perez del Pulgar

WHEN THE MOORISH KNIGHTS beheld that all courteous challenges were unavailing, they sought various means to provoke the Christian warriors to the field. Sometimes a body of them, fleetly mounted, would gallop up to the skirts of the camp, and try who should hurl his lance farthest within the barriers, having his name inscribed upon it, or a label affixed, containing some taunting defiance. These bravadoes caused great irritation; still the Spanish warriors were restrained by the prohibition of the king.

Among the Moorish cavaliers was one named Tarfe, renowned for strength and daring spirit; but whose courage partook of fierce audacity, rather than chivalric heroism. In one of these sallies, when skirting the Christian camp, this arrogant Moor outstripped his companions, overleaped the barriers, and, galloping close to the royal quarters, launched his lance so far within, that it remained quivering in the earth close by the pavilions of the sovereigns. The royal guards rushed forth in pursuit, but the Moorish horsemen were already beyond the camp, and scouring in a cloud of dust for the city. Upon wresting the lance from the earth, a label was found upon it, importing that it was intended for the queen.

Nothing could equal the indignation of the Christian warriors at the insolence of the bravado, and the discourteous insult offered to the queen. Hernan Perez del Pulgar, surnamed "he of the exploits," was present, and resolved not to be outbraved by this daring infidel: "Who will stand by me," said he, "in an enterprise of desperate peril?" The Christian cavaliers well knew the harebrained valor of Hernan, yet not one hesitated to step forward. He chose fifteen companions, all of powerful arm and dauntless heart.

His project was to penetrate Granada in the dead of the night, by a secret pass, made known to him by a Moorish renegade of the city, whom he had christened Pedro Pulgar, and who was to act as guide. They were to set fire to the Alcaiceria and other principal edifices, and then effect their retreat as best they might. At the hour appointed, the adventurous troop set forth provided with combustibles. The renegade led them silently to a drain or channel of the river Darro, up which they proceeded cautiously, single file, until they halted under a bridge near the royal gate. Here dismounting, Pulgar stationed six of his companions to remain silent and motionless and keep guard, while followed by the rest, and still guided by the renegade, he continued up the drain or channel of the Darro, which passes under a part of the city, and was thus enabled to make his way undiscovered into the streets. All was dark and silent. At the command of Pulgar, the renegade led him to the principal mosque. Here the cavalier, pious as brave, threw himself on his knees, and drawing forth a parchment scroll on which was inscribed in large letters AVE MARIA, nailed it to the door of the mosque, thus converting the heathen edifice into a Christian chapel and dedicating it to the blessed Virgin. This done, he hastened to the Alcaiceria to set it in a blaze. The combustibles were all placed, but Tristan de Montemayor, who had charge of the firebrand, had carelessly left it at the door of the mosque. It was too late to return there. Pulgar was endeavoring to strike fire with flint and steel into the raveled end of a cord, when he was startled by the approach of the Moorish guard going the rounds. His hand was on his sword in an instant. Seconded by his brave companions, he assailed the astonished Moors and put them to flight. In a little while the whole city resounded with alarms, soldiers were hurrying through the streets in every direction; but Pulgar, guided by the renegade, made good his retreat by the channel of the Darro, to his companions at the bridge, and all mounting their horses, spurred back to the camp. The Moors were at a loss to imagine the meaning of this wild and apparently fruitless assault; but great was their exasperation, on the following day, when the trophy of hardihood and prowess, the "AVE MARIA," was discovered thus elevated in bravado in the very centre of the city. The mosque thus boldly sanctified by Hernan del

Pulgar was actually consecrated into a cathedral, after the capture of Granada.*

CHAPTER XCIII

How Queen Isabella Took a View of the City of Granada—and How Her Curiosity Cost the Lives of Many Christians and Moors

THE ROYAL ENCAMPMENT lay so distant from Granada, that the general aspect of the city only could be seen, as it rose gracefully from the vega, covering the sides of the hills with palaces and towers. Queen Isabella had expressed an earnest desire to behold, nearer at hand, a city whose beauty was so renowned throughout the world; and the marques of Cadiz, with his accustomed courtesy, prepared a great military escort and guard, to protect her and the ladies of the court, while they enjoyed this perilous gratification.

On the morning of June the 18th, a magnificent and powerful train issued from the Christian camp. The advanced guard was composed of legions of cavalry, heavily armed, looking like moving masses of polished steel. Then came the king and queen, with

* The account here given of the exploit of Hernan del Pulgar, differs from that given in the first edition, and is conformable to the record of the fact in a manuscript called *"The House of Salar,"* existing in the library of Salazar, and cited by Alcantara in his *History of Granada.*

In commemoration of this daring feat of Pulgar, the Emperor Charles V., in after years, conferred on that cavalier, and on his descendants, the marquesies of Salar, the privilege of sitting in the choir during high mass, and assigned as the place of sepulture of Pulgar himself, the identical spot where he kneeled to affix the sacred scroll; and his tomb is still held in great veneration. This Hernan Perez del Pulgar was a man of letters, as well as arms, and inscribed to Charles V. a summary of the achievements of Gonsalvo of Cordova, surnamed the Great Captain, who had been one of his comrades in arms. He is often confounded with Hernando del Pulgar, historian and secretary to Queen Isabella.—See note to Pulgar's *Chron. of the Catholic Sovereigns,* part 3, c. iii. edit. Valencia, 1780.

the prince and princesses, and the ladies of the court, surrounded by the royal body-guard, sumptuously arrayed, composed of the sons of the most illustrious houses of Spain; after these was the rear-guard, a powerful force of horse and foot; for the flower of the army sallied forth that day. The Moors gazed with fearful admiration at this glorious pageant, wherein the pomp of the court was mingled with the terrors of the camp. It moved along in radiant line, across the vega, to the melodious thunders of martial music; while banner and plume, and silken scarf, and rich brocade, gave a gay and gorgeous relief to the grim visage of iron war, that lurked beneath.

The army moved towards the hamlet of Zubia, built on the skirts of the mountain to the left of Granada, and commanding a view of the Alhambra, and the most beautiful quarter of the city. As they approached the hamlet, the marques of Villena, the count Ureña, and Don Alonzo de Aguilar filed off with their battalions, and were soon seen glittering along the side of the mountain above the village. In the mean time the marques of Cadiz, the count de Tendilla, the count de Cabra, and Don Alonzo Fernandez, senior of Alcaudrete and Montemayor, drew up their forces in battle array on the plain below the hamlet, presenting a living barrier of loyal chivalry between the sovereigns and the city.

Thus securely guarded, the royal party alighted, and, entering one of the houses of the hamlet, which had been prepared for their reception, enjoyed a full view of the city from its terraced roof. The ladies of the court gazed with delight at the red towers of the Alhambra, rising from amid shady groves, anticipating the time when the Catholic sovereigns should be enthroned within its walls, and its courts shine with the splendor of Spanish chivalry. "The reverend prelates and holy friars, who always surrounded the queen, looked with serene satisfaction," says Fray Antonio Agapida, "at this modern Babylon, enjoying the triumph that awaited them, when those mosques and minarets should be converted into churches, and goodly priests and bishops should succeed to the infidel alfaquis."

When the Moors beheld the Christians thus drawn forth in full array in the plain, they supposed it was to offer battle, and hesitated not to accept it. In a little while the queen beheld a body of Moorish cavalry pouring into the vega, the riders managing their fleet and fiery steeds with admirable address. They were richly armed, and clothed in the most brilliant colors, and the caparisons of their steeds flamed with gold and embroidery. This was the favorite squadron of Muza, composed of the flower of the youthful cavaliers of Granada. Others succeeded, some heavily armed, others *à la gineta*, with lance and buckler; and lastly came the legions of foot-soldiers, with arquebus and cross-bow, and spear and scimetar.

When the queen saw this army issuing from the city, she sent to the marques of Cadiz, and forbade any attack upon the enemy, or the acceptance of any challenge to a skirmish; for she was loth that her curiosity should cost the life of a single human being.

The marques promised to obey, though sorely against his will; and it grieved the spirit of the Spanish cavaliers to be obliged to remain with sheathed swords while bearded by the foe. The Moors could not comprehend the meaning of this inaction of the Christians, after having apparently invited a battle. They sallied several times from their ranks, and approached near enough to discharge their arrows; but the Christians were immovable. Many of the Moorish horsemen galloped close to the Christian ranks, brandishing their lances and scimetars, and defying various cavaliers to single combat; but Ferdinand had rigorously prohibited all duels of the kind, and they dared not transgress his orders under his very eye.

Here, however, the worthy Fray Antonio Agapida, in his enthusiasm for the triumphs of the faith, records the following incident, which we fear is not sustained by any grave chronicler of the times, but rests merely on tradition, or the authority of certain poets and dramatic writers, who have perpetuated the tradition in their works. While this grim and reluctant tranquillity prevailed along the Christian line, says Agapida, there rose a mingled shout and sound of laughter near the gate of the city. A Moorish horseman, armed at all points, issued forth, followed by a rabble, who drew back as he approached the scene of danger. The Moor was more robust and brawny than was common with his country-men. His visor was closed; he bore a huge buckler and a ponderous lance; his scimetar was of a Damascus blade, and his richly ornamented dagger was wrought by an artificer of Fez. He was known by his device to be Tarfe, the most insolent, yet valiant, of the Moslem warriors—the same who had hurled into the royal camp his lance, inscribed to the queen. As he rode slowly along in front of the army, his very steed, prancing with fiery eye and distended nostril, seemed to breathe defiance to the Christians.

But what were the feelings of the Spanish cavaliers, when they beheld, tied to the tail of his steed, and dragged in the dust, the very inscription, "AVE MARIA," which Hernan Perez del Pulgar had affixed to the door of the mosque! A burst of horror and indignation broke forth from the army. Hernan was not at hand, to maintain his previous achievement; but one of his young companions in arms, Garcilasso de la Vega by name, putting spurs to his horse, galloped to the hamlet of Zubia, threw himself on his knees before the king, and besought permission to accept the defiance of this insolent infidel, and to revenge the insult offered to our blessed Lady. The request was too pious to be refused: Garcilasso remounted his steed; closed his helmet, graced by four sable plumes, grasped his buckler of Flemish workmanship, and his lance of matchless temper, and defied the haughty Moor in the midst of his career. A combat took place, in view of the two armies and of the Castilian court. The Moor was powerful in wielding his weapons, and dexterous in managing his steed. He was of larger frame than Garcilasso, and more completely armed; and the Christians trembled for their champion. The shock of their encounter was dreadful; their lances were shivered, and sent up splinters in the air. Garcilasso was thrown back in his saddle—his horse made a wide career before he could recover, gather up the reins, and return to the conflict. They now encountered each other with swords. The Moor circled round his opponent, as a hawk circles whereabout to make a swoop; his steed obeyed his rider with matchless quickness; at every attack of the infidel, it seemed as if the Christian knight must sink beneath his flashing scimetar. But if Garcilasso was inferior to him in power, he was superior in agility; many of his blows he parried; others he received upon his Flemish shield, which was proof against the Damascus blade. The blood streamed from numerous wounds received by either warrior. The Moor, seeing his antagonist exhausted, availed himself of his superior force, and, grappling, endeavored to wrest him from his saddle. They both fell to earth; the Moor placed his knee upon the breast of his victim, and, brandishing his dagger, aimed a blow at his throat. A cry of despair was uttered by the Christian warriors, when suddenly they beheld the Moor rolling lifeless in the dust. Garcilasso had shortened his sword, and, as his adversary raised his arm to strike, had pierced him to the heart. "It was a singular and miraculous victory," says Fray Antonio Agapida; "but the Christian knight was armed by the sacred nature of his cause, and the holy Virgin gave him strength, like another David, to slay this gigantic champion of the Gentiles."

The laws of chivalry were observed throughout the combat—no one interfered on either side. Garcilasso now despoiled his adversary; then, rescuing the holy inscription of "Ave Maria" from its degrading situation, he elevated it on the point of his sword, and bore it off as a signal of triumph, amidst the rapturous shouts of the Christian army.*

The sun had now reached the meridian; and the hot blood of the Moors was inflamed by its rays, and by the sight of the defeat of their champion. Muza ordered two pieces of ordnance to open a fire upon the Christians. A confusion was produced in one part of their ranks: Muza called to the chiefs of the army, "Let us waste no more time in empty challenges—let us charge upon the enemy: he who assaults has always an advantage in the combat." So saying, he rushed forward, followed by a large body of horse and foot, and charged so furiously upon the advance guard of the Christians, that he drove it in upon the battalion of the marques of Cadiz.

The gallant marques now considered himself absolved from all further obedience to the queen's commands. He gave the signal

---

* The above incident has been commemorated in old Spanish ballads, and made the subject of a scene in an old Spanish drama, ascribed by some to Lope de Vega.

to attack. "Santiago!" was shouted along the line; and he pressed forward to the encounter, with his battalion of twelve hundred lances. The other cavaliers followed his example, and the battle instantly became general.

When the king and queen beheld the armies thus rushing to the combat, they threw themselves on their knees, and implored the holy Virgin to protect her faithful warriors. The prince and princess, the ladies of the court, and the prelates and friars who were present, did the same; and the effect of the prayers of these illustrious and saintly persons, was immediately apparent. The fierceness with which the Moors had rushed to the attack was suddenly cooled; they were bold and adroit for a skirmish, but unequal to the veteran Spaniards in the open field. A panic seized upon the foot-soldiers—they turned, and took to flight. Muza and his cavaliers in vain endeavored to rally them. Some took refuge in the mountains; but the greater part fled to the city, in such confusion that they overturned and trampled upon each other. The Christians pursued them to the very gates. Upwards of two thousand were either killed, wounded, or taken prisoners; and the two pieces of ordnance were brought off as trophies of the victory. Not a Christian lance but was bathed that day in the blood of an infidel.*

Such was the brief but bloody action, which was known among the Christian warriors by the name of "the queen's skirmish;" for when the marques of Cadiz waited upon her majesty to apologize for breaking her commands, he attributed the victory entirely to her presence. The queen, however, insisted that it was all owing to her troops being led on by so valiant a commander. Her majesty had not yet recovered from her agitation at beholding so terrible a scene of bloodshed; though certain veterans present pronounced it as gay and gentle a skirmish as they had ever witnessed.

The gayety of this gentle pass at arms, however, was somewhat marred by a rough reverse in the evening. Certain of the Christian cavaliers, among whom were the count de Ureña, Don Alonzo Aguilar, his brother Gonsalvo of Cordova, Diego Castrillo, com-

* *Cura de los Palacios,* cap. 101. Zurita, lib. 20, cap. 88.

mander of Calatrava, and others to the number of fifty, remained
in ambush near Armilla, expecting the Moors would sally forth
at night to visit the scene of battle and to bury their dead. They
were discovered by a Moor, who had climbed an elm-tree to
reconnoiter, and hastened into the city to give notice of their ambush. Scarce had night fallen when the cavaliers found themselves
surrounded by a host which in the darkness seemed innumerable.
The Moors attacked them with sanguinary fury, to revenge the
disgrace of the morning. The cavaliers fought to every disadvantage, overwhelmed by numbers, ignorant of the ground, perplexed
by thickets and by the water-courses of the gardens, the sluices of
which were all thrown open. Even retreat was difficult. The count
de Ureña was surrounded and in imminent peril, from which he
was saved by two of his faithful followers at the sacrifice of their
lives. Several cavaliers lost their horses, and were themselves put
to death in the water-courses. Gonsalvo of Cordova came near
having his own illustrious career cut short in this obscure skirmish. He had fallen into a water-course, whence he extricated
himself, covered with mud, and so encumbered with his armor,
that he could not retreat. Inigo de Mendoza, a relative of his
brother Alonzo, seeing his peril, offered him his horse: "Take it
Señor," said he, "for you cannot save yourself on foot, and I can:
but should I fall, take care of my wife and daughters."

Gonsalvo accepted the devoted offer, mounted the horse, and
had made but few paces, when a lamentable cry caused him to
turn his head, and he beheld the faithful Mendoza transfixed by
Moorish lances. The four principal cavaliers already named, with
several of their followers, effected their retreat and reached the
camp in safety; but this nocturnal reverse obscured the morning's
triumph. Gonsalvo remembered the last words of the devoted
Mendoza, and bestowed a pension on his widow and marriage
portions on his daughters.*

To commemorate the victory of which she had been an eye-

* The account of this nocturnal affair, is from Peter Martyr, lib. 4, *Epist.*
90, and Pulgar, *Hazanas del Gran. Captain,* page 188, as cited by Alcantara,
Hist. Granada, tom. 4, cap. 18.

witness, Queen Isabella afterwards erected a monastery in the village of Zubia, dedicated to St. Francisco, which still exists, and in its garden is a laurel planted by her hands.*

CHAPTER XCIV

The Last Ravage before Granada

THE RAVAGES OF WAR had as yet spared a little portion of the vega of Granada. A green belt of gardens and orchards still flourished round the city, extending along the banks of the Xenil and the Darro. They had been the solace and delight of the inhabitants in their happier days, and contributed to their sustenance in this time of scarcity. Ferdinand determined to make a final and exterminating ravage to the very walls of the city, so that there should not remain a single green thing for the sustenance of man or beast. The eighth of July was the day appointed for this act of desolation. Boabdil was informed by his spies of the intention of the Christian king, and prepared to make a desperate defense. Hernando de Baeza, a Christian, who resided with the royal family in the Alhambra as interpreter, gives in a manuscript memoir an account of the parting of Boabdil from his family as he went forth to battle. At an early hour of the appointed day, the eighth of July, he bathed and perfumed himself as the Moors of high rank were accustomed to do when they went forth to peril their lives. Arrayed in complete armor he took leave of his mother, his wife, and his sister, in the ante-chamber of the tower of Comares. Ayxa la Horra, with her usual dignity, bestowed on him her

* The house whence the king and queen contemplated the battle, is likewise to be seen at the present day. It is the first street to the right on entering the village from the vega; and the royal arms are painted on the ceilings. It is inhabited by a worthy farmer, Francisco Garcia, who in showing the house to the writer, refused all compensation, with true Spanish pride; offering, on the contrary, the hospitalities of his mansion. His children are versed in the old Spanish ballads, about the exploits of Hernan Perez del Pulgar and Garcilasso de la Vega.

benediction, and gave him her hand to kiss. It was a harder parting with his son and his daughter, who hung round him with sobs
and tears; the dueñas and doncellas too, of the royal household,
made the halls of the Alhambra resound with their lamentations.
He then mounted his horse and put himself in front of his squadrons.*

The Christian army approached close to the city, and were laying waste the gardens and orchards, when Boabdil sallied forth,
surrounded by all that was left of the flower and chivalry of Granada. There is one place where even the coward becomes brave—
that sacred spot called home. What then must have been the valor
of the Moors, a people always of chivalrous spirit, when the war
was thus brought to their thresholds! They fought among the
scenes of their loves and pleasures, the scenes of their infancy,
and the haunts of their domestic life. They fought under the eyes
of their wives and children, their old men and their maidens, of
all that was helpless and all that was dear to them; for all Granada, crowded on tower and battlement, watched with trembling
heart the fate of this eventful day.

There was not so much one battle, as a variety of battles; every
garden and orchard became a scene of deadly contest; every inch
of ground was disputed, with an agony of grief and valor, by the
Moors; every inch of ground that the Christians advanced, they
valiantly maintained; but never did they advance with severer
fighting, or greater loss of blood.

The cavalry of Muza was in every part of the field; wherever it
came, it gave fresh ardor to the fight. The Moorish soldier, faint-
ing with heat, fatigue, and wounds, was roused to new life at the
approach of Muza; and even he who lay gasping in the agonies of
death, turned his face towards him, and faintly uttered cheers and
blessings as he passed.

The Christians had by this time gained possession of various
towers near the city, whence they had been annoyed by cross-
bows and arquebuses. The Moors, scattered in various actions,
were severely pressed. Boabdil, at the head of the cavaliers of
his guard, mingling in the fight in various parts of the field, en-

* Hernando de Baeza, as cited by Alcantara, *Hist. Granada*, tom. 4, cap. 18.

deavored to inspirit the foot-soldiers to the combat. But the Moorish infantry was never to be depended upon. In the heat of the action, a panic seized upon them; they fled, leaving their sovereign exposed with his handful of cavaliers to an overwhelming force. Boabdil was on the point of falling into the hands of the Christians, when, wheeling round, he and his followers threw the reins on the necks of their steeds, and took refuge by dint of hoof within the walls of the city.*

Muza endeavored to retrieve the fortune of the field. He threw himself before the retreating infantry, calling upon them to turn and fight for their homes, their families, for everything sacred and dear to them. All in vain: totally broken and dismayed, they fled tumultuously for the gates. Muza would fain have kept the field with his cavalry; but this devoted band, having stood the brunt of war throughout this desperate campaign, was fearfully reduced in numbers, and many of the survivors were crippled and enfeebled by their wounds. Slowly and reluctantly, therefore, he retreated to the city, his bosom swelling with indignation and despair. Entering the gates, he ordered them to be closed, and secured with bolts and bars: for he refused to place any further confidence in the archers and arquebusiers stationed to defend them, and vowed never more to sally with foot soldiers to the field.

In the mean time the artillery thundered from the walls, and checked all further advance of the Christians. King Ferdinand, therefore, called off his troops, and returned in triumph to the ruins of his camp, leaving the beautiful city of Granada wrapped in the smoke of her fields and gardens, and surrounded by the bodies of her slaughtered children.

Such was the last sally of the Moors, in defense of their favorite city. The French ambassador, who witnessed it, was filled with wonder, at the prowess, the dexterity, and daring of the Moslems.

In truth, this whole war was an instance, memorable in history, of the most persevering resolution. For nearly ten years had the war endured—an almost uninterrupted series of disasters to the Moorish arms. Their towns had been taken, one after another, and

* Zurita, lib. 20, cap. 88.

their brethren slain or led into captivity. Yet they disputed every city and town, and fortress and castle, nay every rock itself, as if they had been inspirited by victories. Wherever they could plant foot to fight, or find wall or cliff whence to launch an arrow, they disputed their beloved country; and now, when their capital was cut off from all relief, and a whole nation thundered at its gates, they still maintained defense, as if they hoped some miracle to interpose in their behalf. Their obstinate resistance (says an ancient chronicler) shows the grief with which they yielded up the vega, which was to them a paradise and heaven. Exerting all the strength of their arms, they embraced, as it were, that most beloved soil, from which neither wounds, nor defeats, nor death itself, could part them. They stood firm, battling for it with the united force of love and grief, never drawing back the foot while they had hands to fight, or fortune to befriend them.*

CHAPTER XCV

Conflagration of the Christian Camp.—Building of Santa Fé

THE MOORS NOW SHUT themselves up gloomily within their walls; there were no longer any daring sallies from their gates; and even the martial clangor of the drum and trumpet, which had continually resounded within that warrior city, was now seldom heard from its battlements. In the midst of this deep despondency, a signal disaster in the Christian camp, for a moment lit up a ray of hope in the bosom of the Moors.

The setting sun of a hot summer's day, on the 10th of July, shone splendidly upon the Christian camp, which was in a bustle of preparation for the next day's service, when an attack was meditated on the city. The camp made a glorious appearance. The various tents of the royal family and the attendant nobles

* Abarca, *Reyes de Aragon,* R. 30. cap. 3.

were adorned with rich hangings, and sumptuous devices, and costly furniture; forming as it were, a little city of silk and brocade, where the pinnacles of pavilions of various gay colors, surmounted with waving standards and fluttering pennons, might vie with the domes and minarets of the capital they were besieging.

In the midst of this little gaudy metropolis, the lofty tent of the queen domineered over the rest like a stately palace. The marques of Cadiz had courteously surrendered his own tent to the queen. It was the most complete and sumptuous in Christendom, and had been carried about with him throughout the war. In the centre rose a stately alfaneque or pavilion, in oriental taste, the rich hangings being supported by columns of lances, and ornamented with martial devices. This central pavilion, or silken tower, was surrounded by other compartments, some of painted linen lined with silk, and all separated from each other by curtains. It was one of those camp palaces which are raised and demolished in an instant, like the city of canvas which surrounds them.

As the evening advanced, the bustle in the camp subsided. Every one sought repose, preparatory to the next day's trial. The king retired early, that he might be up with the crowing of the cock, to head the destroying army in person. All stir of military preparation was hushed in the royal quarters; the very sound of minstrelsy was mute, and not the tinkling of a guitar was to be heard from the tents of the fair ladies of the court.

The queen had retired to the innermost part of her pavilion, where she was performing her orisons before a private altar; perhaps the peril to which the king might be exposed in the next day's foray, inspired her with more than usual devotion. While thus at her prayers, she was suddenly aroused by a glare of light, and wreaths of suffocating smoke. In an instant, the whole tent was in a blaze; there was a high gusty wind, which whirled the light flames tent to tent, and wrapped the whole in one conflagration.

Isabella had barely time to save herself by instant flight. Her first thought, on being extricated from her tent, was for the safety of the king. She rushed to his tent, but the vigilant Ferdinand was already at the entrance of it. Starting from bed on the first alarm, and fancying it an assault of the enemy, he had seized his sword and buckler, and sallied forth undressed, with his cuirass upon his arm.

The late gorgeous camp was now a scene of wild confusion. The flames kept spreading from one pavilion to another, glaring upon the rich armor, and golden and silver vessels, which seemed melting in the fervent heat. Many of the soldiers had erected booths and bowers of branches, which, being dry, crackled and blazed, and added to the rapid conflagration. The ladies of the court fled, shrieking and half-dressed, from their tents. There was an alarm of drum and trumpet, and a distracted hurry about the camp of men half armed. The prince Juan had been snatched out of bed by an attendant, and conveyed to the quarters of the count de Cabra, which were at the entrance of the camp. The loyal count immediately summoned his people, and those of his cousin Don Alonzo de Montemayor, and formed a guard round the tent in which the prince was sheltered.

The idea that this was a stratagem of the Moors, soon subsided; but it was feared they might take advantage of it, to assault the camp. The marques of Cadiz, therefore, sallied forth with three thousand horse, to check any advance from the city. As they passed along, the whole camp was a scene of hurry and consternation—some hastening to their posts, at the call of drum and trumpet; some attempting to save rich effects and glittering armor from the tents, others dragging along terrified and restive horses.

When they emerged from the camp, they found the whole firmament illuminated. The flames whirled up in long light spires, and the air was filled with sparks and cinders. A bright glare was thrown upon the city, revealing every battlement and tower. Turbaned heads were seen gazing from every roof, and armor gleamed along the walls; yet not a single warrior sallied from the gates: the Moors suspected some stratagem on the part of the Christians, and kept quietly within their walls. By degrees, the flames expired; the city faded from sight; all again became dark and quiet, and the marques of Cadiz returned with his cavalry to the camp.

When the day dawned on the Christian camp, nothing remained

of that beautiful assemblage of stately pavilions, but heaps of smouldering rubbish, with helms and corselets and other furniture of war, and masses of melted gold and silver glittering among the ashes. The wardrobe of the queen was entirely destroyed, and there was an immense loss in plate, jewels, costly stuffs, and sumptuous armor of the luxurious nobles. The fire at first had been attributed to treachery, but on investigation it proved to be entirely accidental. The queen, on retiring to her prayers, had ordered her lady in attendance to remove a light burning near her couch, lest it should prevent her sleeping. Through heedlessness, the taper was placed in another part of the tent, near the hangings, which being blown against it by a gust of wind, immediately took fire.

The wary Ferdinand knew the sanguine temperament of the Moors, and hastened to prevent their deriving confidence from the night's disaster. At break of day, the drums and trumpets sounded to arms, and the Christian army issued forth from among the smoking ruins of their camp, in shining squadrons, with flaunting banners and bursts of martial melody, as though the preceding night had been a time of high festivity, instead of terror.

The Moors had beheld the conflagration with wonder and perplexity. When the day broke, and they looked towards the Christian camp, they saw nothing but a dark, smoking mass. Their scouts came in with the joyful intelligence that the whole camp was a scene of ruin. In the exultation of the moment, they flattered themselves with hopes that the catastrophe would discourage the besiegers; that as in former years, their invasion would end with the summer and they would withdraw before the autumnal rains.

The measures of Ferdinand and Isabella soon crushed these hopes. They gave orders to build a regular city upon the site of their camp, to convince the Moors that the siege was to endure until the surrender of Granada. Nine of the principal cities of Spain were charged with this stupendous undertaking; and they emulated each other, with a zeal worthy of the cause. "It verily seems," says Fray Antonio Agapida, "as though some miracle operated to aid this pious work, so rapidly did arise a formidable city, with solid edifices, and powerful walls, and mighty towers, where lately had been seen nothing but tents and light pavilions. The city was traversed by two principal streets in form of a cross, terminating in four gates facing the four winds; and in the centre was a vast square, where the whole army might be assembled. To this city it was proposed to give the name of Isabella, so dear to the army and the nation; "but that pious princess," adds Antonio Agapida, "calling to mind the holy cause in which it was erected, gave it the name of Santa Fé (or the City of the Holy Faith); and it remains to this day, a monument of the piety and glory of the Catholic sovereigns."

Hither the merchants soon resorted, from all points. Long trains of mules were seen every day entering and departing from its gates; the streets were crowded with magazines, filled with all kinds of costly and luxurious merchandise; a scene of bustling commerce and prosperity took place, while unhappy Granada remained shut up and desolate.

CHAPTER XCVI

Famine and Discord in the City

THE BESIEGED CITY now began to suffer the distress of famine. Its supplies were all cut off; a cavalgada of flocks and herds, and mules laden with money, coming to the relief of the city from the mountains of the Alpuxarras, was taken by the marques of Cadiz, and led in triumph to the camp, in sight of the suffering Moors. Autumn arrived; but the harvests had been swept from the face of the country; a rigorous winter was approaching, and the city was almost destitute of provisions. The people sank into deep despondency. They called to mind all that had been predicted by astrologers at the birth of their ill-starred sovereign, and all that had been foretold of the fate of Granada at the time of the capture of Zahara.

Boabdil was alarmed by the gathering dangers from without, and by the clamors of his starving people. He summoned a council, composed of the principal officers of the army, the alcaydes of the fortresses, the xequis or sages of the city, and the alfaquis or doctors of the faith. They assembled in the great hall of audience of the Alhambra, and despair was painted in their countenances. Boabdil demanded of them, what was to be done in the present extremity; and their answer was, "Surrender." The venerable Abul Cazim, governor of the city, represented its unhappy state: "Our granaries are nearly exhausted, and no further supplies are to be expected. The provender for the war-horses is required as sustenance for the soldiery; the very horses themselves are killed for food; of seven thousand steeds which once could be sent into the field, three hundred only remain. Our city contains two hundred thousand inhabitants, old and young, with each a mouth that calls piteously for bread."

The xequis and principal citizens declared that the people could no longer sustain the labors and sufferings of a defense: "And of what avail is our defense," said they, "when the enemy is determined to persist in the siege?—what alternative remains, but to surrender or to die?"

The heart of Boabdil was touched by this appeal, and he maintained a gloomy silence. He had cherished some faint hope of relief from the soldan of Egypt or the Barbary powers; but it was now at an end; even if such assistance were to be sent, he had no longer a seaport where it might debark. The counselors saw that the resolution of the king was shaken and they united their voices in urging him to capitulate.

Muza alone rose in opposition: "It is yet too early," said he, "to talk of a surrender. Our means are not exhausted; we have yet one source of strength remaining, terrible in its effects, and which often has achieved the most signal victories—it is our despair. Let us rouse the mass of the people; let us put weapons in their hands; let us fight the enemy to the very utmost, until we rush upon the points of their lances. I am ready to lead the way into the thickest of their squadrons; and much rather would I be numbered among those who fell in the defense of Granada, than of those who survived to capitulate for her surrender!"

The words of Muza were without effect, for they were addressed to broken-spirited and heartless men, or men, perhaps, to whom sad experience had taught discretion. They were arrived at that state of public depression, when heroes and heroism are no longer regarded, and when old men and their counsels rise into importance. Boabdil el Chico yielded to the general voice; it was determined to capitulate with the Christian sovereigns; and the venerable Abul Cazim was sent forth to the camp, empowered to treat for terms.

CHAPTER XCVII

Capitulation of Granada

THE OLD GOVERNOR Abul Cazim was received with great courtesy by Ferdinand and Isabella, who being informed of the purport of his embassy, granted the besieged a truce of sixty days from the 5th of October, and appointed Gonsalvo of Cordova, and Fernando de Zafra, the secretary of the king, to treat about the terms of surrender with such commissioners as might be named by Boabdil. The latter on his part named Abul Cazim, Aben Comixa the vizier, and the grand cadi. As a pledge of good faith, Boabdil gave his son in hostage, who was taken to Moclin, where he was treated with the greatest respect and attention by the good count de Tendilla, as general of the frontier.

The commissioners on both parts held repeated conferences in secret in the dead of the night, at the village of Churriana—those who first arrived at the place of meeting giving notice to the others by signal-fires, or by means of spies. After many debates and much difficulty, the capitulation was signed on the 25th of November. According to this, the city was to be delivered up, with all its gates, towers, and fortresses, within sixty days.

All Christian captives should be liberated, without ransom.

Boabdil and his principal cavaliers should perform the act of homage, and take an oath of fealty to the Castilian crown.

The Moors of Granada should become subjects of the Spanish sovereigns, retaining their possessions, their arms and horses, and yielding up nothing but their artillery. They should be protected in the exercise of their religion, and governed by their own laws, administered by cadis of their own faith, under governors appointed by the sovereigns. They should be exempted from tribute for three years, after which term they should pay the same that they had been accustomed to render to their native monarchs.

Those who chose to depart for Africa within three years, should be provided with a passage for themselves and their effects, free of charge, from whatever port they should prefer.

For the fulfillment of these articles, five hundred hostages from the principal families were required, previous to the surrender, who should be treated with great respect and distinction by the Christians, and subsequently restored. The son of the king of Granada, and all other hostages in possession of the Castilian sovereigns, were to be restored at the same time.

Such are the main articles affecting the public weal, which were agreed upon after much discussion by the mixed commission. There were other articles, however, secretly arranged, which concerned the royal family. These secured to Boabdil, to his wife Morayma, his mother Ayxa, his brothers, and to Zoraya, the widow of Muley Abul Hassan, all the landed possessions, houses, mills, baths, and other hereditaments which formed the royal patrimony, with the power of selling them, personally or by agent, at any and all times. To Boabdil was secured, moreover, his wealthy estates, both in and out of Granada, and to him and his descendants in perpetuity, the lordships of various towns and lands and fertile valleys in the Alpuxarras, forming a petty sovereignty. In addition to all which it was stipulated, that, on the day of surrender, he should receive thirty thousand castellanos of gold.*

* Alcantara, tom. 4, cap. 18.

The conditions of the surrender being finally agreed upon by the commissioners, Abul Cazim proceeded to the royal camp at Santa Fé, where they were signed by Ferdinand and Isabella; he then returned to Granada, accompanied by Fernando de Zafra, the royal secretary, to have the same ratified also by the Moorish king. Boabdil assembled his council, and with a dejected countenance laid before it the articles of capitulation as the best that could be obtained from the besieging foe.

When the members of the council found the awful moment arrived when they were to sign and seal the perdition of their empire, and blot themselves out as a nation, all firmness deserted them, and many gave way to tears. Muza alone retained an unaltered mien: "Leave, seniors," cried he, "this idle lamentation to helpless women and children: we are men—we have hearts, not to shed tender tears, but drops of blood. I see the spirit of the people so cast down, that it is impossible to save the kingdom. Yet there still remains an alternative for noble minds—a glorious death! Let us die defending our liberty, and avenging the woes of Granada. Our mother earth will receive her children into her bosom, safe from the chains and oppressions of the conqueror; or, should any fail a sepulchre to hide his remains, he will not want a sky to cover him. Allah forbid it should be said the nobles of Granada feared to die in her defense!"

Muza ceased to speak, and a dead silence reigned in the assembly. Boabdil looked anxiously round, and scanned every face; but he read in all the anxiety of care-worn men, in whose hearts enthusiasm was dead, and who had grown callous to every chivalrous appeal. "Allah Achbar!" exclaimed he; "there is no God but God, and Mahomet is his prophet! We have no longer forces in the city and the kingdom to resist our powerful enemies. It is in vain to struggle against the will of Heaven. Too surely was it written in the book of fate, that I should be unfortunate, and the kingdom expire under my rule."

"Allah Achbar!" echoed the viziers and alfaquis; "the will of God be done!" So they all agreed with the king, that these evils were preordained; that it was hopeless to contend with them;

and that the terms offered by the Castilian monarchs were as favorable as could be expected.

When Muza heard them assent to the treaty of surrender, he rose in violent indignation: "Do not deceive yourselves," cried he, "nor think the Christians will be faithful to their promises, or their king as magnanimous in conquest as he has been victorious in war. Death is the least we have to fear. It is the plundering and sacking of our city, the profanation of our mosques, the ruin of our homes, the violation of our wives and daughters, cruel oppression, bigoted intolerance, whips and chains, the dungeon, the fagot, and the stake—such are the miseries and indignities we shall see and suffer; at least, those groveling souls will see and suffer them, who now shrink from an honorable death. For my part, by Allah, I will never witness them!"

With these words he left the council-chamber, and passed gloomily through the Court of Lions, and the outer halls of the Alhambra, without deigning to speak to the obsequious courtiers who attended in them. He repaired to his dwelling, armed himself at all points, mounted his favorite war-horse, and, issuing from the city by the gate of Elvira, was never seen or heard of more.*

CHAPTER XCVIII

Commotions in Granada

THE CAPITULATION FOR the surrender of Granada was signed on the 25th of November, 1491, and produced a sudden cessation of those hostilities which had raged for so many years. Christian and Moor might now be seen mingling courteously on the banks of the Xenil and the Darrow, where to have met a few days previous would have produced a scene of sanguinary contest.

* Conde, pt. 4.

Still, as the Moors might be suddenly roused to defense, if, within the allotted term of sixty days, succors should arrive from abroad; and as they were at all times a rash, inflammable people, the wary Ferdinand maintained a vigilant watch upon the city, and permitted no supplies of any kind to enter. His garrisons in the seaports, and his cruisers in the Straits of Gibraltar, were ordered likewise to guard against any relief from the grand soldan of Egypt or the princes of Barbary. There was no need of such precautions. Those powers were either too much engrossed by their own wars, or too much daunted by the success of the Spanish arms, to interfere in a desperate cause; and the unfortunate Moors of Granada were abandoned to their fate.

The month of December had nearly passed away; the famine became extreme, and there was no hope of any favorable event within the term specified in the capitulation. Boabdil saw, that to hold out to the end of the allotted time would but be to protract the miseries of his people. With the consent of his council, he determined to surrender the city on the sixth of January. He accordingly sent his grand vizier, Yusef Aben Comixa, to King Ferdinand, to make known his intention; bearing him, at the same time, a present of a magnificent scimetar, and two Arabian steeds superbly caparisoned.

The unfortunate Boabdil was doomed to meet with trouble, to the end of his career. The very next day, the santon or dervise, Hamet Aben Zarrax, the same who had uttered prophecies and excited commotion on former occasions, suddenly made his appearance. Whence he came no one knew; it was rumored that he had been in the mountains of the Alpuxarras, and on the coast of Barbary, endeavoring to rouse the Moslems to the relief of Granada. He was reduced to a skeleton; his eyes glowed like coals in their sockets, and his speech was little better than frantic raving. He harangued the populace, in the streets and squares; inveighed against the capitulation, denounced the king and nobles as Moslems only in name, and called upon the people to sally forth against the unbelievers, for that Allah had decreed them a signal victory.

Upwards of twenty thousand of the populace seized their

arms, and paraded the streets with shouts and outcries. The shops and houses were shut up; the king himself did not dare to venture forth, but remained a kind of prisoner in the Alhambra.

The turbulent multitude continued roaming and shouting and howling about the city, during the day and a part of the night. Hunger, and a wintry tempest, tamed their frenzy; and when morning came, the enthusiast who had led them on had disappeared. Whether he had been disposed of by the emissaries of the king, or by the leading men of the city, is not known: his disappearance remains a mystery.*

Boabdil now issued forth from the Alhambra, attended by his principal nobles, and harangued the populace. He set forth the necessity of complying with the capitulation, from the famine that reigned in the city, the futility of defense, and from the hostages having already been delivered into the hands of the besiegers.

In the dejection of his spirits, the unfortunate Boabdil attributed to himself the miseries of the country. "It was my crime in ascending the throne in rebellion against my father," said he mournfully, "which has brought these woes upon the kingdom; but Allah has grievously visited my sins upon my head. For your sake, my people, I have now made this treaty, to protect you from the sword, your little ones from famine, your wives and daughters from outrage; and to secure you in the enjoyment of your properties, your liberties, your laws, and your religion, under a sovereign of happier destinies than the illstarred Boabdil."

The versatile population were touched by the humility of their sovereign—they agreed to adhere to the capitulation, and there was even a faint shout of "Long live Boabdil the Unfortunate!" and they all returned to their homes in perfect tranquillity.

Boabdil immediately sent missives to King Ferdinand, apprising him of these events, and of his fears lest further delay should produce new tumults. The vizier Yusef Aben Comixa was again the agent between the monarchs. He was received with unusual courtesy and attention by Ferdinand and Isabella, and

* Mariana.

it was arranged between them that the surrender should take place on the second day of January instead of the sixth. A new difficulty now arose in regard to the ceremonial of surrender. The haughty Ayxa la Horra, whose pride rose with the decline of her fortunes, declared that, as sultana mother, she would never consent that her son should stoop to the humiliation of kissing the hand of his conquerors, and, unless this part of the ceremonial were modified, she would find means to resist a surrender accompanied by such indignities.

Aben Comixa was sorely troubled by this opposition. He knew the high spirit of the indomitable Ayxa, and her influence over her less heroic son, and wrote an urgent letter on the subject to his friend, the count de Tendilla. The latter imparted the circumstance to the Christian sovereigns; a council was called on the matter. Spanish pride and etiquette were obliged to bend in some degree to the haughty spirit of a woman. It was agreed that Boabdil should sally forth on horseback, that on approaching the Spanish sovereigns he should make a slight movement as if about to draw his foot from the stirrup and dismount, but would be prevented from doing so by Ferdinand, who should treat him with a respect due to his dignity and elevated birth. The count de Tendilla dispatched a messenger with this arrangement; and the haughty scruples of Ayxa la Horra were satisfied.*

CHAPTER XCIX

Surrender of Granada

THE NIGHT PRECEDING the surrender was a night of doleful lamentings, within the walls of the Alhambra; for the household of Boabdil were preparing to take a last farewell of that delight-

* Salazar de Mendoza. *Chron. del Gran. Cardinal,* lib. 1, cap. 69, p. 1, Mondajar, *His.* MS. as cited by Alcantara, tom. 4, cap. 18.

ful abode. All the royal treasures and most precious effects were hastily packed upon mules; the beautiful apartments were despoiled, with tears and wailings, by their own inhabitants. Before the dawn of day, a mournful cavalcade moved obscurely out of a postern-gate of the Alhambra, and departed through one of the most retired quarters of the city. It was composed of the family of the unfortunate Boabdil, which he sent off thus privately, that they might not be exposed to the eyes of scoffers, or the exultation of the enemy. The mother of Boabdil, the sultana Ayxa la Horra, rode on in silence, with dejected yet dignified demeanor; but his wife Morayma, and all the females of his household, gave way to loud lamentations, as they looked back upon their favorite abode, now a mass of gloomy towers behind them. They were attended by the ancient domestics of the household, and by a small guard of veteran Moors, loyally attached to the fallen monarch, and who would have sold their lives dearly in defense of his family. The city was yet buried in sleep, as they passed through its silent streets. The guards at the gate shed tears, as they opened it for their departure. They paused not, but proceeded along the banks of the Xenil on the road that leads to the Alpuxarras, until they arrived at a hamlet at some distance from the city, where they halted, and waited until they should be joined by King Boabdil.

The night which had passed so gloomily in the sumptuous halls of the Alhambra, had been one of joyful anticipation in the Christian camp. In the evening proclamation had been made that Granada was to be surrendered on the following day, and the troops were all ordered to assemble at an early hour under their several banners. The cavaliers, pages, and esquires were all charged to array themselves in their richest and most splendid style, for the occasion; and even the royal family determined to lay by the mourning they had recently assumed for the sudden death of the prince of Portugal, the husband of the princess Isabella. In a clause of the capitulation it had been stipulated that the troops destined to take possession, should not traverse the city, but should ascend to the Alhambra by a road opened for the purpose outside of the walls. This was to spare the feelings of the afflicted inhabitants, and to prevent any angry collision between them and their conquerors. So rigorous was Ferdinand in enforcing this precaution, that the soldiers were prohibited under pain of death from leaving the ranks to enter into the city.

The rising sun had scarce shed his rosy beams upon the snowy summits of the Sierra Nevada, when three signal guns boomed heavily from the lofty fortress of the Alhambra. It was the concerted sign that all was ready for the surrender. The Christian army forthwith poured out of the city, or rather camp of Santa Fé, and advanced across the vega. The king and queen, with the prince and princess, the dignitaries and ladies of the court, took the lead, accompanied by the different orders of monks and friars, and surrounded by the royal guards splendidly arrayed. The procession moved slowly forward, and paused at the village of Armilla, at the distance of half a league from the city.

In the mean time, the grand cardinal of Spain, Don Pedro Gonzalez de Mendoza, escorted by three thousand foot and a troop of cavalry, and accompanied by the commander Don Gutierrez de Cardenas, and a number of prelates and hidalgos, crossed the Xenil and proceeded in the advance, to ascend to the Alhambra and take possession of that royal palace and fortress. The road which had been opened for the purpose led by the Puerta de los Molinos, or Gate of Mills, up a defile to the esplanade on the summit of the Hill of Martyrs. At the approach of this detachment, the Moorish king sallied forth from a postern gate of the Alhambra, having left his vizier Yusef Aben Comixa to deliver up the palace. The gate by which he sallied passed through a lofty tower of the outer wall, called the Tower of the Seven Floors (de los siete suelos). He was accompanied by fifty cavaliers, and approached the grand cardinal on foot. The latter immediately alighted, and advanced to meet him with the utmost respect. They stepped aside a few paces, and held a brief conversation in an undertone, when Boabdil, raising his voice, exclaimed, "Go, Señor, and take possession of those fortresses in the name of the powerful sovereigns, to whom God has been pleased to deliver them in reward of their great merits, and in punishment of the sins of the Moors." The grand cardinal sought to console him in his reverses, and offered him the use of his own tent during any time he might sojourn in the camp. Boabdil thanked him for the courteous offer, adding some words of melancholy import, and then taking leave of him gracefully, passed mournfully on to meet the Catholic sovereigns, descending to the vega by the same road by which the cardinal had come. The latter, with the prelates and cavaliers who attended him, entered the Alhambra, the gates of which were thrown wide open by the alcayde Aben Comixa. At the same time the Moorish guards yielded up their arms, and the towers and battlements were taken possession of by the Christian troops.

While these transactions were passing in the Alhambra and its vicinity, the sovereigns remained with their retinue and guards near the village of Armilla, their eyes fixed on the towers of the royal fortress, watching for the appointed signal of possession. The time that had elapsed since the departure of the detachment seemed to them more than necessary for the purpose, and the anxious mind of Ferdinand began to entertain doubts of some commotion in the city. At length they saw the silver cross, the great standard of this crusade, elevated on the Torre de la Vela, or Great Watch-Tower, and sparkling in the sunbeams. This was done by Hernando de Talavera, bishop of Avila. Beside it was planted the pennon of the glorious apostle St. James, and a great shout of "Santiago! Santiago!" rose throughout the army. Lastly was reared the royal standard by the king of arms, with the shout of "Castile! Castile! For King Ferdinand and Queen Isabella!" The words were echoed by the whole army, with acclamations that resounded across the vega. At sight of these signals of possession, the sovereigns sank upon their knees, giving thanks to God for this great triumph; the whole assembled host followed their example, and the choristers of the royal chapel broke forth into the solemn anthem of "*Te Deum laudamus.*"

The king now advanced with a splendid escort of cavalry and the sound of trumpets, until he came to a small mosque near the banks of the Xenil, and not far from the foot of the Hill of Martyrs, which edifice remains to the present day consecrated as the hermitage of St. Sebastian. Here he beheld the unfortunate king of Granada approaching on horseback, at the head of his slender retinue. Boabdil as he drew near made a movement to dismount, but, as had previously been concerted, Ferdinand prevented him. He then offered to kiss the king's hand, which, according to arrangement, was likewise declined, whereupon he leaned forward and kissed the king's right arm; at the same time he delivered the keys of the city with an air of mingled melancholy and resignation: "These keys," said he, "are the last relics of the Arabian empire in Spain: thine, O king, are our trophies, our kingdom, and our person. Such is the will of God! Receive them with the clemency thou hast promised, and which we look for at thy hands." *

King Ferdinand restrained his exultation into an air of serene magnanimity. "Doubt not our promises," replied he, "nor that thou shalt regain from our friendship the prosperity of which the fortune of war has deprived thee."

Being informed that Don Inigo Lopez de Mendoza, the good count of Tendilla, was to be governor of the city, Boabdil drew from his finger a gold ring set with a precious stone, and presented it to the count. "With this ring," said he, "Granada has been governed; take it and govern with it, and God make you more fortunate than I." †

He then proceeded to the village of Armilla, where the queen Isabella remained with her escort and attendants. The queen, like her husband, declined all acts of homage, and received him with her accustomed grace and benignity. She at the same time delivered to him his son, who had been held as a hostage for the fulfillment of the capitulation. Boabdil pressed his child to his bosom with tender emotion, and they seemed mutually endeared to each other by their misfortunes.‡

Having rejoined his family, the unfortunate Boabdil continued

---

* Abarca, *Anales de Aragon*, Reg 30, cap. 3.

† This ring remained in the possession of the descendants of the count until the death of the marques Don Inigo, the last male heir, who died in Malaga without children, in 1656. The ring was then lost through inadvertence and ignorance of its value, Doña Maria, the sister of the marques, being absent in Madrid. Alcantara, lib. 4, cap. 18.

‡ Zurita, *Anales de Aragon*, lib. 20, cap. 92.

on towards the Alpuxarras, that he might not behold the entrance of the Christians into his capital. His devoted band of cavaliers followed him in gloomy silence; but heavy sighs burst from their bosoms, as shouts of joy and strains of triumphant music were borne on the breeze from the victorious army.

Having rejoined his family, Boabdil set forward with a heavy heart for his allotted residence in the Valley of Purchena. At two leagues' distance, the cavalcade, winding into the skirts of the Alpuxarras, ascended an eminence commanding the last view of Granada. As they arrived at this spot, the Moors paused involuntarily, to take a farewell gaze at their beloved city, which a few steps more would shut from their sight forever. Never had it appeared so lovely in their eyes. The sunshine, so bright in that transparent climate, lit up each tower and minaret, and rested gloriously upon the crowning battlements of the Alhambra; while the vega spread its enameled bosom of verdure below, glistening with the silver windings of the Xenil. The Moorish cavaliers gazed with a silent agony of tenderness and grief upon that delicious abode, the scene of their loves and pleasures. While they yet looked, a light cloud of smoke burst forth from the citadel, and presently a peal of artillery, faintly heard, told that the city was taken possession of, and the throne of the Moslem kings was lost forever. The heart of Boabdil, softened by misfortunes and overcharged with grief, could no longer contain itself: "Allah Achbar! God is great!" said he; but the words of resignation died upon his lips, and he burst into tears.

His mother, the intrepid Ayxa, was indignant at his weakness: "You do well," said she, "to weep like a woman for what you failed to defend like a man!"

The vizier Aben Comixa endeavored to console his royal master. "Consider, Señor," said he, "that the most signal misfortunes often render men as renowned as the most prosperous achievements, provided they sustain them with magnanimity."

The unhappy monarch, however, was not to be consoled; his tears continued to flow. "Allah Achbar!" exclaimed he, "when did misfortunes ever equal mine?"

From this circumstance, the hill, which is not far from Padul, took the name of Feg Allah Achbar; but the point of view commanding the last prospect of Granada is known among Spaniards by the name of *El ultimo suspiro del Moro;* or, "The last sigh of the Moor."

CHAPTER C

How the Castilian Sovereigns Took Possession of Granada

QUEEN ISABELLA HAVING joined the king, the royal pair, followed by a triumphant host, passed up the road by the Hill of Martyrs, and thence to the main entrance of the Alhambra. The grand cardinal awaited them under the lofty arch of the great Gate of Justice, accompanied by Don Gutierrez de Cardenas and Aben Comixa. Here King Ferdinand gave the keys which had been delivered up to him into the hands of the queen; they were passed successively into the hands of the prince Juan, the grand cardinal, and finally into those of the count de Tendilla, in whose custody they remained, that brave cavalier having been named alcayde of the Alhambra, and captain-general of Granada.

The sovereigns did not remain long in the Alhambra on this first visit, but leaving a strong garrison there under the count de Tendilla, to maintain tranquillity in the palace and the subjacent city, returned to the camp at Santa Fé.

We must not omit to mention a circumstance attending the surrender of the city, which spoke eloquently to the hearts of the victors. As the royal army had advanced in all the pomp of courtly and chivalrous array, a procession of a different kind came forth to meet it. This was composed of more than five hundred Christian captives, many of whom had languished for years in Moorish dungeons. Pale and emaciated, they came clanking their chains in triumph, and shedding tears of joy. They were received with tenderness by the sovereigns. The king hailed them as good Spaniards, as men loyal and brave, as martyrs to the holy cause; the queen distributed liberal relief among them with her own hands, and they passed on before the squadrons of the army, singing hymns of jubilee.*

The sovereigns forbore to enter the city until it should be fully occupied by their troops, and public tranquillity insured. All this was done under the vigilant superintendence of the count de Tendilla, assisted by the marques of Villena; and the glistening of Christian helms and lances along the walls and bulwarks, and the standards of the faith and of the realm flaunting from the towers, told that the subjugation of the city was complete. The proselyte prince, Cid Hiaya, now known by the Christian appellation of Don Pedrod e Granada Vanegas,† was appointed chief alguazil of the city, and had charge of the Moorish inhabitants; and his son, lately the prince Alnayer, now Alonzo de Granada Vanegas, was appointed admiral of the fleets.

It was on the sixth of January, the day of kings and festival of the Epiphany, that the sovereigns made their triumphal entry with grand military parade. First advanced, we are told, a splendid escort of cavaliers in burnished armor, and superbly mounted. Then followed the prince Juan, glittering with jewels and diamonds; on each side of him, mounted on mules, rode the grand cardinal, clothed in purple, Fray Hernando de Talavera, bishop of Arla, and the archbishop elect of Granada. To these succeeded the queen and her ladies, and the king, managing in galliard style, say the Spanish chronicles, a proud and mettlesome steed (*un caballo arrogante*). Then followed the army in shining columns, with flaunting banners and the inspiring clamor of military music. The king and queen (says the worthy Fray Antonio Agapida) looked, on this occasion, as more than mortal: the venerable ecclesiastics, to whose advice and zeal this glorious

---

* Abarca, lib. sup. Zurita, etc.
† Cid Hiaya was made cavalier of the order of Santiago. He and his son intermarried with the Spanish nobility, and the marqueses of Compotejar are among their descendants. Their portraits, and the portraits of their grandsons, are to be seen in one of the rooms of the Generalife at Granada.

conquest ought in a great measure to be attributed, moved along with hearts swelling with holy exultation, but with chastened and downcast looks of edifying humility; while the hardy warriors, in tossing plumes and shining steel, seemed elevated with a stern joy at finding themselves in possession of this object of so many toils and perils. As the streets resounded with the tramp of steeds and swelling peals of music, the Moors buried themselves in the deepest recesses of their dwellings. There they bewailed in secret the fallen glory of their race, but suppressed their groans, lest they should be heard by their enemies, and increase their triumph.

The royal procession advanced to the principal mosque, which had been consecrated as a cathedral. Here the sovereigns offered up prayers and thanksgivings, and the choir of the royal chapel chanted a triumphant anthem, in which they were joined by all the courtiers and cavaliers. Nothing (says Fray Antonio Agapida) could exceed the thankfulness to God of the pious King Ferdinand, for having enabled him to eradicate from Spain the empire and name of that accursed heathen race, and for the elevation of the cross in that city wherein the impious doctrines of Mahomet had so long been cherished. In the fervor of his spirit, he supplicated from Heaven a continuance of its grace, and that this glorious triumph might be perpetuated.* The prayer of the pious monarch, was responded by the people, and even his enemies were for once convinced of his sincerity.

When the religious ceremonies were concluded, the court ascended to the stately palace of the Alhambra, and entered by the great Gate of Justice. The halls lately occupied by turbaned infidels now rustled with stately dames and Christian courtiers, who wandered with eager curiosity over this far-famed palace, admiring its verdant courts and gushing fountains, its halls decorated with elegant arabesques, and storied with inscriptions, and the splendor of its gilded and brilliantly painted ceilings.

It had been a last request of the unfortunate Boabdil, and one which showed how deeply he felt the transition of his fate, that

* The words of Fray Antonio Agapida are little more than an echo of those of the worthy Jesuit father Mariana (lib. 25, cap. 18).

no person might be permitted to enter or depart by the gate of the Alhambra, through which he had sallied forth to surrender his capital. His request was granted; the portal was closed up, and remains so to the present day—a mute memorial of that event.*

The Spanish sovereigns fixed their throne in the presence-chamber of the palace, so long the seat of Moorish royalty. Hither the principal inhabitants of Granada repaired, to pay them homage and kiss their hands in token of vassalage; and their example was followed by deputies from all the towns and fortresses of the Alpuxarras, which had not hitherto submitted.

Thus terminated the war of Granada, after ten years of incessant fighting; equaling (says Fray Antonio Agapida) the far-famed siege of Troy in duration, and ending, like that, in the capture of the city. Thus ended also the dominion of the Moors in Spain, having endured seven hundred and seventy-eight years, from the memorable defeat of Roderick, the last of the Goths, on the banks of the Guadalete. The authentic Agapida is uncommonly particular in fixing the epoch of this event. This great triumph of our holy Catholic faith, according to his computation, took place in the beginning of January, in the year of our Lord 1492, being 3,655 years from the population of Spain by the patriarch Tubal; 3,797 from the general deluge; 5,453

* Garibay, *Compend. Hist.* lib. 40, cap. 42. The existence of this gateway, and the story connected with it, are perhaps known to few; but were identified, in the researches made to verify this history. The gateway is at the bottom of a tower, at some distance from the main body of the Alhambra. The tower has been rent and ruined by gunpowder, at the time when the fortress was evacuated by the French. Great masses lie around half covered by vines and fig-trees. A poor man, by the name of Matteo Ximenes, who lives in one of the halls among the ruins of the Alhambra, where his family has resided for many generations, pointed out to the author the gateway, still closed up with stones. He remembered to have heard his father and grandfather say, that it had always been stopped up, and that out of it King Boabdil had gone when he surrendered Granada. The route of the unfortunate king may be traced thence across the garden of the convent of Los Martyros, and down a ravine beyond, through a street of Gypsy caves and hovels, by the gate of Los Molinos, and so on to the Hermitage of St. Sebastian. None but an antiquarian, however, will be able to trace it, unless aided by the humble historian of the place, Matteo Ximenes.

from the creation of the world, according to Hebrew calculation; and in the month Rabic, in the eight hundred and ninety-seventh year of the Hegira, or flight of Mahomet; whom may God confound! saith the pious Agapida!

THE ALHAMBRA

·{ ❂❀❂ }·

PALACE OF THE ALHAMBRA

To THE TRAVELLER imbued with a feeling for the historical and poetical, so inseparably intertwined in the annals of *romantic Spain,* the Alhambra is as much an object of devotion as is the Caaba to all true Moslems. How many legends and traditions, true and fabulous,—how many songs and ballads, Arabian and Spanish, of love and war and chivalry, are associated with this Oriental pile! It was the royal abode of the Moorish kings, where, surrounded with the splendors and refinements of Asiatic luxury, they held dominion over what they vaunted as a terrestrial paradise, and made their last stand for empire in Spain. The royal palace forms but a part of a fortress, the walls of which, studded with towers, stretch irregularly round the whole crest of a hill, a spur of the Sierra Nevada or Snowy Mountains, and overlook the city; externally it is a rude congregation of towers and battlements, with no regularity of plan nor grace of architecture, and giving little promise of the grace and beauty which prevail within.

In the time of the Moors the fortress was capable of containing within its outward precincts an army of forty thousand men, and served occasionally as a strong-hold of the sovereigns against their rebellious subjects. After the kingdom had passed into the hands of the Christians, the Alhambra continued to be a royal demesne, and was occasionally inhabited by the Castilian monarchs. The emperor Charles V. commenced a sumptuous palace within its walls, but was deterred from completing it by repeated shocks of earthquakes. The last royal residents were Philip V. and his beautiful queen, Elizabetta of Parma, early in the eighteenth century. Great preparations were made for their reception. The palace and gardens were placed in a state of repair, and

311

a new suite of apartments erected, and decorated by artists brought from Italy. The sojourn of the sovereigns was transient, and after their departure the palace once more became desolate. Still the place was maintained with some military state. The governor held it immediately from the crown, its jurisdiction extended down into the suburbs of the city, and was independent of the captain-general of Granada. A considerable garrison was kept up; the governor had his apartments in the front of the old Moorish palace, and never descended into Granada without some military parade. The fortress, in fact, was a little town of itself, having several streets of houses within its walls, together with a Franciscan convent and a parochial church.

The desertion of the court, however, was a fatal blow to the Alhambra. Its beautiful halls became desolate, and some of them fell to ruin; the gardens were destroyed, and the fountains ceased to play. By degrees the dwellings became filled with a loose and lawless population: contrabandistas, who availed themselves of its independent jurisdiction to carry on a wide and daring course of smuggling, and thieves and rogues of all sorts, who made this their place of refuge whence they might depredate upon Granada and its vicinity. The strong arm of government at length interfered; the whole community was thoroughly sifted; none were suffered to remain but such as were of honest character, and had legitimate right to a residence; the greater part of the houses were demolished and a mere hamlet left, with the parochial church and the Franciscan convent. During the recent troubles in Spain, when Granada was in the hands of the French, the Alhambra was garrisoned by their troops, and the palace was occasionally inhabited by the French commander. With that enlightened taste which has ever distinguished the French nation in their conquests, this monument of Moorish elegance and grandeur was rescued from the absolute ruin and desolation that were overwhelming it. The roofs were repaired, the saloons and galleries protected from the weather, the gardens cultivated, the watercourses restored, the fountains once more made to throw up their sparkling showers; and Spain may thank her invaders for having preserved to her the most beautiful and interesting of her historical monuments.

On the departure of the French they blew up several towers of the outer wall, and left the fortifications scacely tenable. Since that time the military importance of the post is at an end. The garrison is a handful of invalid soldiers, whose principal duty is to guard some of the outer towers, which serve occasionally as a prison of state; and the governor, abandoning the lofty hill of the Alhambra, resides in the centre of Granada, for the more convenient dispatch of his official duties. I cannot conclude this brief notice of the state of the fortress without bearing testimony to the honorable exertions of its present commander, Don Francisco de Serna, who is tasking all the limited resources at his command to put the palace in a state of repair, and by his judicious precautions has for some time arrested its too certain decay. Had his predecessors discharged the duties of their station with equal fidelity, the Alhambra might yet have remained in almost its pristine beauty; were government to second him with means equal to his zeal, this relic of it might still be preserved for many generations to adorn the land, and attract the curious and enlightened of every clime.

Our first object of course, on the morning after our arrival, was a visit to this time-honored edifice; it has been so often, however, and so minutely described by travellers, that I shall not undertake to give a comprehensive and elaborate account of it, but merely occasional sketches of parts, with the incidents and associations connected with them.

Leaving our posada, and traversing the renowned square of the Vivarrambla, once the scene of Moorish jousts and tournaments, now a crowded market-place, we proceeded along the Zacatin, the main street of what, in the time of the Moors, was the Great Bazaar, and where small shops and narrow alleys still retain the Oriental character. Crossing an open place in front of the palace of the captain-general, we ascended a confined and winding street, the name of which reminded us of the chivalric days of Granada. It is called the Calle, or street of the Gomeres, from a Moorish family famous in chronicle and song. This street led up to the Puerta de las Granadas, a massive gateway of Grecian architecture, built by Charles V., forming the entrance to the domains of the Alhambra.

At the gate were two or three ragged superannuated soldiers, dozing on a stone bench, the successors of the Zegris and the Abencerrages; while a tall, meagre varlet, whose rusty-brown cloak was evidently intended to conceal the ragged state of his nether garments, was lounging in the sunshine and gossiping with an ancient sentinel on duty. He joined us as we entered the gate, and offered his services to show us the fortress.

I have a traveller's dislike to officious ciceroni, and did not altogether like the garb of the applicant.

"You are well acquainted with the place, I presume?"

"Ninguno mas; pues señor, soy hijo de la Alhambra."—(Nobody better; in fact, sir, I am a son of the Alhambra!)

The common Spaniards have certainly a most poetical way of expressing themselves. "A son of the Alhambra!" the appellation caught me at once; the very tattered garb of my new acquaintance assumed a dignity in my eyes. It was emblematic of the fortunes of the place, and befitted the progeny of a ruin.

I put some further questions to him, and found that his title was legitimate. His family had lived in the fortress from generation to generation ever since the time of the Conquest. His name was Mateo Ximenes. "Then, perhaps," said I, "you may be a descendant from the great Cardinal Ximenes?"—"Dios Sabe! God knows, Señor! It may be so. We are the oldest family in the Alhambra,—*Christianos Viejos,* old Christians, without any taint of Moor of Jew. I know we belong to some great family or other, but I forget whom. My father knows all about it: he has the coat of arms hanging up in his cottage, up in the fortress." There is not any Spaniard, however poor, but has some claim to high pedigree. The first title of this ragged worthy, however, had completely captivated me; so I gladly accepted the services of the "son of the Alhambra."

We now found ourselves in a deep narrow ravine, filled with beautiful groves, with a steep avenue, and various footpaths winding through it, bordered with stone seats, and ornamented with fountains. To our left we beheld the towers of the Alhambra beetling above us; to our right, on the opposite side of the ravine, we were equally dominated by rival towers on a rocky eminence. These, we were told, were the Torres Vermejos, or vermilion towers, so called from their ruddy hue. No one knows their origin. They are of a date much anterior to the Alhambra: some suppose them to have been built by the Romans; others, by some wandering colony of Phoenicians. Ascending the steep and shady avenue, we arrived at the foot of a huge square Moorish tower, forming a kind of barbican, through which passed the main entrance to the fortress. Within the barbican was another group of veteran invalids, one mounting guard at the portal, while the rest, wrapped in their tattered cloaks, slept on the stone benches. This portal is called the Gate of Justice, from the tribunal held within its porch during the Moslem domination, for the immediate trial of petty causes: a custom common to the Oriental nations, and occasionally alluded to in the Sacred Scriptures. "Judges and officers shalt thou make thee *in all thy gates,* and they shall judge the people with just judgment."

The great vestibule, or porch of the gate, is formed by an immense Arabian arch, of the horseshoe form, which springs to half the height of the tower. On the keystone of this arch is engraven a gigantic hand. Within the vestibule, on the keystone of the portal, is sculptured, in like manner, a gigantic key. Those who pretend to some knowledge of Mohammedan symbols, affirm that the hand is the emblem of doctrine; the five fingers designating the five principal commandments of the creed of Islam, fasting, pilgrimage, alms-giving, ablution, and war against infidels. The key, say they, is the emblem of the faith or of power; the key of Daoud, or David, transmitted to the prophet. "And the key of the house of David will I lay upon his shoulder; so he shall open and none shall shut, and he shall shut and none shall open. (Isaiah xxii:22.) The key we are told was emblazoned on the standard of the Moslems in opposition to the Christian emblem of the cross, when they subdued Spain or Andalusia. It betokened the conquering power invested in the prophet. "He that hath the key of David, he that openeth and no man shutteth; and shutteth and no man openeth." (Rev. iii: 7.)

A different explanation of these emblems, however, was given by the legitimate son of the Alhambra, and one more in unison with the notions of the common people, who attach something of mystery and magic to everything Moorish, and have all kinds of superstitions connected with this old Moslem fortress. According to Mateo, it was a tradition handed down from the oldest inhabitants, and which he had from his father and grandfather, that the hand and key were magical devices on which the fate of the Alhambra depended. The Moorish king who built it was a great magician, or, as some believed, had sold himself to the devil, and had laid the whole fortress under a magic spell. By this means it had remained standing for several years, in defiance of storms and earthquakes, while almost all other buildings of the Moors had fallen to ruin and disappeared. This spell, the tradition went on to say, would last until the hand on the outer arch should reach down and grasp the key, when the whole pile would tumble to pieces, and all the treasures buried beneath it by the Moors would be revealed.

Notwithstanding this ominous prediction, we ventured to pass through the spell-bound gateway, feeling some little assurance against magic art in the protection of the Virgin, a statue of whom we observed above the portal.

After passing through the barbican, we ascended a narrow lane, winding between walls, and came on an open esplanade within the fortress, called the Plaza de los Algibes, or Place of the Cisterns, from great reservoirs which undermine it, cut in the living rock by the Moors to receive the water brought by conduits from the Darro, for the supply of the fortress. Here, also, is a well of immense depth, furnishing the purest and coldest of water,—another monument of the delicate taste of the Moors, who were indefatigable in their exertions to obtain that element in its crystal purity.

In front of this esplanade is the splendid pile commenced by Charles V., and intended, it is said, to eclipse the residence of the Moorish kings. Much of the Oriental edifice intended for the winter season was demolished to make way for this massive pile. The grand entrance was blocked up; so that the present entrance to the Moorish palace is through a simple and almost humble portal in a corner. With all the massive grandeur and architectural merit of the palace of Charles V., we regarded it as an arrogant intruder, and passing by it with a feeling almost of scorn, rang at the Moslem portal.

While waiting for admittance, our self-imposed cicerone, Mateo Ximenes, informed us that the royal palace was intrusted to the care of a worthy old maiden dame called Doña Antonia-Molina, but who, according to Spanish custom, went by the more neighborly appellation of Tia Antonia (Aunt Antonia), who maintained the Moorish halls and gardens in order and showed them to strangers. While we were talking, the door was opened by a plump little black-eyed Andalusian damsel, whom Mateo addressed as Dolores, but who from her bright looks and cheerful disposition evidently merited a merrier name. Mateo informed me in a whisper that she was the niece of Tia Antonia, and I found she was the good fairy who was to conduct us through the enchanted palace. Under her guidance we crossed the threshold, and were at once transported, as if by magic wand, into other times and an oriental realm, and were treading the scenes of Arabian story. Nothing could be in greater contrast than the unpromising exterior of the pile with the scene now before us. We found ourselves in a vast patio or court, one hundred and fifty feet in length, and upwards of eighty feet in breadth, paved with white marble, and decorated at each end with light Moorish peristyles, one of which supported an elegant gallery of fretted architecture. Along the mouldings of the cornices and on various parts of the walls were escutcheons and ciphers, and cufic and Arabic characters in high relief, repeating the pious mottoes of the Moslem monarchs, the builders of the Alhambra, or extolling their grandeur and munificence. Along the centre of the court extended an immense basin or tank (estanque), a hundred and twenty-four feet in length, twenty-seven in breadth, and five in depth, receiving its water from two marble vases. Hence it is called the Court of the Alberca (from al Beerkah, the Arabic for a pond or tank). Great numbers of gold-fish were to be seen gleaming through the waters of the basin, and it was bordered by hedges of roses.

Passing from the court of the Alberca under a Moorish archway, we entered the renowned court of Lions. No part of the edifice gives a more complete idea of its original beauty than this, for none has suffered so little from the ravages of time. In the centre stands the fountain famous in song and story. The alabaster basins still shed their diamond drops; the twelve lions which support them, and give the court its name, still cast forth crystal streams as in the days of Boabdil. The lions, however, are unworthy of their fame, being of miserable sculpture, the work probably of some Christian captive. The court is laid out in flower-beds, instead of its ancient and appropriate pavement of tiles or marble; the alteration, an instance of bad taste, was made by the French when in possession of Granada. Round the four sides of the court are light Arabian arcades of open filigree work, supported by slender pillars of white marble, which it is supposed were originally gilded. The architecture, like that in most parts of the interior of the palace, is characterized by elegance rather than grandeur, bespeaking a delicate and graceful taste, and a disposition to indolent enjoyment. When one looks upon the fairy traces of the peristyles, and the apparently fragile fretwork of the walls, it is difficult to believe that so much has survived the wear and tear of centuries, the shocks of earthquakes, the violence of war, and the quiet, though no less baneful, pilferings of the tasteful traveller: it is almost sufficient to excuse the popular tradition, that the whole is protected by a magic charm.

One one side of the court a rich portal opens into the Hall of the Abencerrages: so called from the gallant cavaliers of that illustrious line who were here perfidiously massacred. There are some who doubt the whole story, but our humble cicerone Mateo pointed out the very wicket of the portal through which they were introduced one by one into the court of Lions, and the white marble fountain in the centre of the hall beside which they were beheaded. He showed us also certain broad ruddy stains on the pavement, traces of their blood, which, according to popular belief, can never be effaced.

Finding we listened to him apparently with easy faith, he added, that there was often heard at night, in the court of Lions, a low confused sound, resembling the murmuring of a multitude; and now and then a faint tinkling, like the distant clank of chains. These sounds were made by the spirits of the murdered Abencerrages; who nightly haunt the scene of their suffering and invoke the vengeance of Heaven on their destroyer.

The sounds in question had no doubt been produced, as I had afterwards an opportunity of ascertaining, by the bubbling currents and tinkling falls of water conducted under the pavement through pipes and channels to supply the fountains; but I was too considerate to intimate such an idea to the humble chronicler of the Alhambra.

Encouraged by my easy credulity, Mateo gave me the following as an undoubted fact, which he had from his grandfather:—

There was once an invalid soldier, who had charge of the Alhambra to show it to strangers; as he was one evening, about twilight, passing through the court of Lions, he heard footsteps on the Hall of the Abencerrages; supposing some strangers to be lingering there, he advanced to attend upon them, when to his astonishment he beheld four Moors richly dressed, with gilded cuirasses and cimeters, and poniards glittering with precious stones. They were walking to and fro, with solemn pace; but paused and beckoned to him. The old soldier, however, took to flight, and could never afterwards be prevailed upon to enter the Alhambra. Thus it is that men sometimes turn their backs upon fortune; for it is the firm opinion of Mateo, that the Moors intended to reveal the place where their treasures lay buried. A successor to the invalid soldier was more knowing; he came to the Alhambra poor; but at the end of a year went off to Malaga, bought houses, set up a carriage, and still lives there, one of the richest as well as oldest men of the place; all which, Mateo sagely surmised, was in consequence of his finding out the golden secret of these phantom Moors.

I now perceived I had made an invaluable acquaintance in this son of the Alhambra, one who knew all the apocryphal history of the place, and firmly believed in it, and whose memory was stuffed with a kind of knowledge for which I have a lurking fancy, but which is too apt to be considered rubbish by less indulgent philosophers. I determined to cultivate the acquaintance of this learned Theban.

Immediately opposite the hall of the Abencerrages, a portal, richly adorned, leads into a hall of less tragical associations. It is light and lofty, exquisitely graceful in its architecture, paved with white marble, and bears the suggestive name of the Hall of the Two Sisters. Some destroy the romance of the name by attributing it to two enormous slabs of alabaster which lie side by side, and form a great part of the pavement: an opinion strongly supported by Mateo Ximenes. Others are disposed to give the name a more poetical significance, as the vague memorial of Moorish beauties who once graced this hall, which was evidently a part of the royal harem. This opinion I was happy to find entertained by our little bright-eyed guide, Dolores, who pointed to a balcony over an inner porch; which gallery, she had been told, belonged to the women's apartment. "You see, señor," said she, "it is all grated and latticed, like the gallery in a convent chapel where the nuns hear mass; for the Moorish kings," added she, indignantly, "shut up their wives just like nuns."

The latticed "jalousies," in fact, still remain, whence the dark-eyed beauties of the harem might gaze unseen upon the zambras and other dances and entertainments of the hall below.

On each side of this hall are recesses or alcoves for ottomans and couches, on which the voluptuous lords of the Alhambra indulged in that dreamy repose so dear to the Orientalists. A cupola or lantern admits a tempered light from above and a free circulation of air; while on one side is heard the refreshing sound of waters from the fountain of the lions, and on the other side the soft plash from the basin in the garden of Lindaraxa.

It is impossible to contemplate this scene, so perfectly Oriental, without feeling the early associations of Arabian romance, and almost expecting to see the white arm of some mysterious princess beckoning from the gallery, or some dark eye sparkling through the lattice. The abode of beauty is here as if it had been inhabited

but yesterday; but where are the two sisters, where the Zoraydas
and Lindaraxas!

An abundant supply of water, brought from the mountains by
old Moorish aqueducts, circulates throughout the palace, supplying its baths and fish pools, sparkling in jets within its halls or
murmuring in channels along the marble pavements. When it has
paid its tribute to the royal pile, and visited its gardens and parterres, it flows down the long avenue leading to the city, tinkling
in rills, gushing in fountains, and maintaining a perpetual verdure
in those groves that embower and beautify the whole hill of the
Alhambra.

Those only who have sojourned in the ardent climates of the
South can appreciate the delights of an abode combining the
breezy coolness of the mountain with the freshness and verdure
of the valley. While the city below pants with the noontide heat,
and the parched Vega trembles to the eye, the delicate airs from
the Sierra Nevada play through these lofty halls, bringing with
them the sweetness of the surrounding gardens. Everything in-
vites to that indolent repose, the bliss of southern climes; and
while the half-shut eye looks out from shaded balconies upon the
glittering landscape, the ear is lulled by the rustling of groves and
the murmur of running streams.

I forbear for the present, however, to describe the other delightful apartments of the palace. My object is merely to give the
reader a general introduction into an abode where, if so disposed,
he may linger and loiter with me day by day until we gradually
become familiar with all its localities.

NOTE ON MORISCO ARCHITECTURE

To an unpractised eye the light relievos and fanciful arabesques which
cover the walls of the Alhambra appear to have been sculptured by hand,
with a minute and patient labor, an inexhaustible variety of detail, yet a
general uniformity and harmony of design truly astonishing; and this may
especially be said of the vaults and cupolas, which are wrought like honey-
combs, or frostwork, with stalactites and pendants which confound the
beholder with the seeming intricacy of their patterns. The astonishment
ceases, however, when it is discovered that this is all stucco-work; plates
of plaster of Paris, cast in moulds and skilfully joined so as to form patterns
of every size and form. This mode of diapering walls with arabesques, and
stuccoing the vaults with grotto-work, was invented in Damascus, but highly

improved by the Moors in Morocco, to whom Saracenic architecture owes its most graceful and fanciful details. The process by which all this tracery was produced was ingeniously simple. The wall in its naked state was divided off by lines crossing at right angles, such as artists use in copying a picture; over these were drawn a succession of interesting segments of circles. By the aid of these the artists could work with celerity and certainty, and from the mere intersection of the plain and curved lines arose the interminable variety of patterns and the general uniformity of their character.*

Much gilding was used in the stucco-work, especially of the cupolas; and the interstices were delicately pencilled with brilliant colors, such as vermilion and lapis lazuli, laid on with the whites of eggs. The primitive colors alone were used, says Ford, by the Egyptians, Greeks, and Arabs, in the early period of art; and they prevail in the Alhambra whenever the artist has been Arabic or Moorish. It is remarkable how much of their original brilliancy remains after the lapse of several centuries.

The lower part of the walls in the saloons, to the height of several feet, is incrusted with glazed tiles, joined like the plates of stucco-work, so as to form various patterns. On some of them are emblazoned the escutcheons of the Moselm kings, traversed with a band and motto. These glazed tiles (azulejos in Spanish, az-zulaj in Arabic) are of Oriental origin; their coolness, cleanliness, and freedom from vermin, render them admirably fitted in sultry climates for paving halls and fountains, incrusting bathing-rooms, and lining the walls of chambers. Ford is inclined to give them great antiquity. From their prevailing colors, sapphire and blue, he deduces that they may have formed the kind of pavements alluded to in the sacred Scriptures:—"There was under his feet as it were a paved work of a sapphire stone" (Exod. xxiv: 10); and again, "Behold I will lay thy stones with fair colors, and lay thy foundations with sapphires" (Isaiah liv: 11).

These glazed or porcelain tiles were introduced into Spain at an early date by the Moslems. Some are to be seen among the Moorish ruins which have been there upwards of eight centuries. Manufactures of them still exist in the Peninsula, and they are much used in the best Spanish houses, especially in the southern provinces, for paving and lining the summer apartments.

The Spaniards introduced them into the Netherlands when they had possession of that country. The people of Holland adopted them with avidity, as wonderfully suited to their passion for household cleanliness; and thus these Oriental inventions, the azulejos of the Spanish, the az-zulaj of the Arabs, have come to be commonly known as Dutch tiles.

* See Urquhart's *Pillars of Hercules,* B. III. C. 8.

LEGEND OF THE ARABIAN ASTROLOGER

IN OLD TIMES, many hundred years ago, there was a Moorish king named Aben Habuz, who reigned over the kingdom of Granada. He was a retired conqueror, that is to say, one who, having in his more youthful days led a life of constant foray and depredation, now that he was grown feeble and superannuated, "languished for repose," and desired nothing more than to live at peace with all the world, to husband his laurels, and to enjoy in quiet the possessions he had wrested from his neighbors.

It so happened, however, that this most reasonable and pacific old monarch had young rivals to deal with; princes full of his early passion for fame and fighting, and who were disposed to call him to account for the scores he had run up with their fathers. Certain distant districts of his own territories, also, which during the days of his vigor he had treated with a high hand, were prone, now that he languished for repose, to rise in rebellion and threaten to invest him in his capital. Thus he had foes on every side; and as Granada is surrounded by wild and craggy mountains, which hide the approach of an enemy, the unfortunate Aben Habuz was kept in a constant state of vigilance and alarm, not knowing in what quarter hostilities might break out.

It was in vain that he built watch-towers on the mountains, and stationed guards at every pass with orders to make fires by night and smoke by day, on the approach of an enemy. His alert foes, baffling every precaution, would break out of some unthought-of defile, ravage his lands beneath his very nose, and then make off with prisoners and booty to the mountains. Was ever peaceable and retried conqueror in a more uncomfortable predicament?

While Aben Habuz was harassed by these perplexities and molestations, an ancient Arabian physician arrived at his court. His gray beard descended to his girdle, and he had every mark of extreme age, yet he had travelled almost the whole way from Egypt on foot, with no other aid than a staff, marked with hieroglyphics.

His fame had preceded him. His name was Ibrahim Ebn Abu Ayub; he was said to have lived ever since the days of Mahomet, and to be son of Abu Ayub; the last of the companions of the Prophet. He had, when a child, followed the conquering army of Amru into Egypt, where he had remained many years studying the dark sciences, and particularly magic, among the Egyptian priests.

It was, moreover, said that he had found out the secret of prolonging life, by means of which he had arrived to the great age of upwards of two centuries, though, as he did not discover the secret until well stricken in years, he could only perpetuate his gray hairs and wrinkles.

This wonderful old man was honorably entertained by the king; who, like most superannuated monarchs, began to take physicians into great favor. He would have assigned him an apartment in his palace, but the astrologer preferred a cave in the side of the hill which rises above the city of Granada, being the same on which the Alhambra has since been built. He caused the cave to be enlarged so as to form a spacious and lofty hall, with a circular hole at the top, through which, as through a well, he could see the heavens and behold the stars even at mid-day. The walls of this hall were covered with Egyptian hieroglyphics with cabalistic symbols, and with the figures of the stars in their signs. This hall he furnished with many implements, fabricated under his directions by cunning artificers of Granada, but the occult properties of which were known only to himself.

In a little while the sage Ibrahim became the bosom counsellor of the king, who applied to him for advice in every emergency. Aben Habuz was once inveighing against the injustice of his neighbors, and bewailing the restless vigilance he had to observe to guard himself against their invasions; when he had finished, the astrologer remained silent for a moment, and then replied, "Know, O king, that when I was in Egypt, I beheld a great marvel devised by a pagan priestess of old. On a mountain, above the city of Borsa, and overlooking the great valley of the Nile, was a figure of a ram, and above it a figure of a cock, both of molten brass, and turning upon a pivot. Whenever the country was threatened with invasion, the ram would turn in the direction of the enemy, and the cock would crow; upon this the inhabitants of the city knew of the danger, and of the quarter from which it was approaching, and could take timely means to guard against it."

"God is great!" exclaimed the pacific Aben Habuz, "what a treasure would be such a ram to keep an eye upon these mountains around me; and then such a cock, to crow in time of danger! Allah Akbar! how securely I might sleep in my palace with such sentinels on the top!"

The astrologer waited until the ecstasies of the king had subsided, and then proceeded.

"After the victorious Amru (may he rest in peace!) had finished his conquest of Egypt, I remained among the priests of the land, studying the rites and ceremonies of their idolatrous faith, and seeking to make myself master of the hidden knowledge for which they are renowned. I was one day seated on the banks of the Nile, conversing with an ancient priest, when he pointed to the mighty pyramids which rose like mountains out of the neighboring desert. 'All that we can teach thee,' said he, 'is nothing to the knowledge locked up in those mighty piles. In the centre of the central pyramid is a sepulchral chamber, in which is enclosed the mummy of the high-priest who aided in rearing that stupendous pile; and with him is buried a wondrous book of knowledge, containing all the secrets of magic and art. This book was given to Adam after his fall, and was handed down from generation to generation to King Solomon the Wise, and by its aid he built the Temple of Jerusalem. How it came into the possession of the builder of the pyramids is known to Him alone who knows all things.'

"When I heard these words of the Egyptian priest, my heart burned to get possession of that book. I could command the services of many of the soldiers of our conquering army, and of a number of the native Egyptians: with these I set to work, and pierced the solid mass of the pyramid, until, after great toil, I came upon one of its interior and hidden passages. Following this up, and threading a fearful labyrinth, I penetrated into the very heart of the pyramids, even to the sepulchral chamber, where the mummy of the high-priest had lain for ages. I broke through the outer cases of the mummy, unfolded its many wrappers and bandages, and at length found the precious volume on its bosom. I seized it with a trembling hand, and groped my way out of the pyramid, leaving the mummy in its dark and silent sepulchre, there to await the final day of resurrection and judgment."

"Son of Abu Ayub" exclaimed Aben Habuz, "thou hast been a great traveller, and seen marvellous things; but of what avail to me is the secret of the pyramid, and the volume of knowledge of the wise Solomon?"

"This it is, O king! By the study of that book I am instructed in all magic arts, and can command the assistance of genii to accomplish my plans. The mystery of the Talisman of Borsa is therefore familiar to me, and such a talisman can I make, nay, one of greater virtues."

"O wise son of Abu Ayub," cried Aben Habuz, "better were such a talisman than all the watch-towers on the hills, and sentinels upon the borders. Give me such a safeguard, and the riches of my treasury are at thy command."

The astrologer immediately set to work to gratify the wishes of the monarch. He caused a great tower to be erected upon the top of the royal palace, which stood on the brow of the hill of the Albaycin. The tower was built of stones brought from Egypt, and taken, it is said, from one of the pyramids. In the upper part of the tower was a circular hall, with windows looking towards every point of the compass, and before each window was a table, on which was arranged, as on a chess-board, a mimic army of horse and foot, with the effigy of the potentate that ruled in that direction, all carved of wood. To each of these tables there was a small lance, no bigger than a bodkin, on which were engraved certain Chaldaic characters. This hall was kept constantly closed, by a gate of brass, with a great lock of steel, the key of which was in possession of the king.

On the top of the tower was a bronze figure of a Moorish horseman, fixed on a pivot, with a shield on one arm, and his lance elevated perpendicularly. The face of this horseman was towards the city, as if keeping guard over it; but if any foe were at hand, the figure would turn in that direction, and would level the lance as if for action.

When this talisman was finished, Aben Habuz was all impatient to try its virtues, and longed as ardently for an invasion as he had ever sighed after repose. His desire was soon gratified. Tidings were brought, early one morning, by the sentinel appointed to watch the tower, that the face of the bronze horseman was turned towards the mountains of Elvira, and that his lance pointed directly against the Pass of Lope.

"Let the drums and trumpets sound to arms, and all Granada be put on the alert," said Aben Habuz.

"O king," said the astrologer, "let not your city be disquieted, nor your warriors called to arms; we need no aid of force to deliver you from your enemies. Dismiss your attendants, and let us proceed alone to the secret hall of the tower."

The ancient Aben Habuz mounted the staircase of the tower, leaning on the arm of the still more ancient Ibrahim Ebn Abu Ayub. They unlocked the brazen door and entered. The window that looked towards the Pass of Lope was open. "In this direction," said the astrologer, "lies the danger; approach, O king, and behold the mystery of the table."

King Aben Habuz approached the seeming chess-board, on which were arranged the small wooden effigies, when, to his surprise, he perceived that they were all in motion. The horses pranced and curveted, the warriors brandished their weapons, and there was a faint sound of drums and trumpets, and the clang of arms, and neighing of steeds; but all no louder, nor more distinct, than the hum of the bee, or the summer-fly, in the drowsy ear of him who lies at noontide in the shade.

"Behold, O king," said the astrologer, "a proof that thy enemies are even now in the field. They must be advancing through yonder mountains, by the Pass of Lope. Would you produce a panic and confusion amongst them, and cause them to retreat without loss of life, strike these effigies with the but-end of this magic lance; would you cause bloody feud and carnage, strike with the point."

A livid streak passed across the countenance of Aben Habuz; he seized the lance with trembling eagerness; his gray beard wagged with exultation as he tottered toward the table: "Son of Abu Ayub," exclaimed he, in chuckling tone, "I think we will have a little blood!"

So saying, he thrust the magic lance into some of the pigmy effigies, and belabored others with the but-end, upon which the former fell as dead upon the board, and the rest turning upon each other, began, pell-mell, a chance-medley fight.

It was with difficulty the astrologer could stay the hand of the most pacific of monarchs, and prevent him from absolutely exterminating his foes; at length he prevailed upon him to leave the tower, and to send out scouts to the mountains by the Pass of Lope.

They returned with the intelligence that a Christian army had advanced through the heart of the Sierra, almost within sight of Granada, where a dissension had broken out among them; they had turned their weapons against each other, and after much slaughter had retreated over the border.

Aben Habuz was transported with joy on thus proving the efficacy of the talisman. "At length," said he, "I shall lead a life of tranquillity, and have all my enemies in my power. O wise son of Abu Ayub, what can I bestow on thee in reward for such a blessing?"

"The wants of an old man and a philosopher, O king, are few and simple; grant me but the means of fitting up my cave as a suitable hermitage, and I am content."

"How noble is the moderation of the truly wise!" exclaimed Aben Habuz, secretly pleased at the cheapness of the recompense. He summoned his treasurer, and bade him dispense whatever sums might be required by Ibrahim to complete and furnish his hermitage.

The astrologer now gave orders to have various chambers hewn out of the solid rock, so as to form ranges of apartments connected with his astrological hall; these he caused to be furnished with luxurious ottomans and divans, and the walls to be hung with the richest silks of Damascus. "I am an old man," said he, "and can no longer rest my bones on stone couches, and these damp walls require covering."

He had baths too constructed, and provided with all kinds of perfumes and aromatic oils. "For a bath," said he, "is necessary to counteract the rigidity of age, and to restore freshness and suppleness to the frame withered by study."

He caused the apartments to be hung with innumerable silver and crystal lamps, which he filled with a fragrant oil prepared according to a receipt discovered by him in the tombs of Egypt. This oil was perpetual in its nature, and diffused a soft radiance like the tempered light of day. "The light of the sun," said he, "is too gairish and violent for the eyes of an old man, and the light of the lamp is more congenial to the studies of a philosopher."

The treasurer of King Aben Habuz groaned at the sums daily demanded to fit up this hermitage, and he carried his complaints to the king. The royal word, however, had been given; Aben Habuz shrugged his shoulders: "We must have patience," said he; "this old man has taken his idea of a philosophic retreat from the interior of the pyramids, and of the vast ruins of Egypt; but all things have an end, and so will the furnishing of his cavern."

The king was in the right; the hermitage was at length complete, and formed a sumptuous subterranean palace. The astrologer expressed himself perfectly content, and, shutting himself up, remained for three whole days buried in study. At the end of that time he appeared again before the treasurer. "One thing more is necessary," said he, "one trifling solace for the intervals of mental labor."

"O wise Ibrahim, I am bound to furnish everything necessary for thy solitude; what more dost thou require?"

"I would fain have a few dancing-women."

"Dancing-women!" echoed the treasurer, with surprise.

"Dancing-women," replied the sage, gravely; "and let them be young and fair to look upon; for the sight of youth and beauty is refreshing. A few will suffice, for I am a philosopher of simple habits and easily satisfied."

While the philosophic Ibrahim Ebn Abu Ayub passed his time thus sagely in his hermitage, the pacific Aben Habuz carried on furious campaigns in effigy in his tower. It was a glorious thing for an old man, like himself, of quiet habits, to have war made easy, and to be enabled to amuse himself in his chamber by brushing away whole armies like so many swarms of flies.

For a time he rioted in the indulgence of his humors, and even taunted and insulted his neighbors, to induce them to make incursions; but by degrees they grew wary from repeated disasters, until no one ventured to invade his territories. For many months the bronze horseman remained on the peace establishment, with his lance elevated in the air; and the worthy old monarch began to repine at the want of his accustomed sport, and to grow peevish at his monotonous tranquillity.

At length, one day, the talismanic horseman veered suddenly round, and lowering his lance, made a dead point towards the mountains of Guadix. Aben Habuz hastened to his tower, but the magic table in that direction remained quiet: not a single warrior was in motion. Perplexed at the circumstance, he sent forth a troop of horse to scour the mountains and reconnoitre. They returned after three days' absence.

"We have searched every mountain pass," said they, "but not a helm nor spear was stirring. All that we have found in the course of our foray, was a Christian damsel of surpassing beauty, sleeping at noontide beside a fountain, whom we have brought away captive."

"A damsel of surpassing beauty!" exclaimed Aben Habuz, his eyes gleaming with animation; "let her be conducted into my presence."

The beautiful damsel was accordingly conducted into his presence. She was arrayed with all the luxury of ornament that had prevailed among the Gothic Spaniards at the time of the Arabian conquest. Pearls of dazzling whiteness were entwined with her raven tresses; and jewels sparkled on her forehead, rivalling the lustre of her eyes. Around her neck was a golden chain, to which was suspended a silver lyre, which hung by her side.

The flashes of her dark refulgent eye were like sparks of fire on the withered yet combustible, heart of Aben Habuz; the swimming voluptuousness of her gait made his senses reel. "Fairest of women," cried he, with rapture, "who and what art thou?"

"The daughter of one of the Gothic princes, who but lately ruled over this land. The armies of my father have been destroyed, as if by magic, among these mountains; he has been driven into exile, and his daughter is a captive."

"Beware, O king!" whispered Ibrahim Ebn Abu Ayub, "this may be one of those northern sorceresses of whom we have heard, who assume the most seductive forms to beguile the unwary. Methinks I read witchcraft in her eye, and sorcery in every movement. Doubtless this is the enemy pointed out by the talisman."

"Son of Abu Ayub," replied the king, "thou art a wise man, I grant, a conjuror for aught I know; but thou art little versed in the ways of woman. In that knowledge will I yield to no man; no, not to the wise Solomon himself, notwithstanding the number of his wives and concubines. As to this damsel, I see no harm in her; she is fair to look upon, and finds favor in my eyes."

"Hearken, O king!" replied the astrologer. "I have given thee many victories by means of my talisman, but have never shared any of the spoil. Give me then this stray captive, to solace me in my solitude with her silver lyre. If she be indeed a sorceress, I have counter spells that set her charms at defiance."

"What! more women!" cried Aben Habuz. "Hast thou not already dancing-women enough to solace thee?"

"Dancing-women have I, it is true, but no singing-women. I would fain have a little minstrelsy to refresh my mind when weary with the toils of study."

"A truce with thy hermit cravings," said the king, impatiently. "This damsel have I marked for my own. I see much comfort in her; even such comfort as David, the father of Solomon the Wise, found in the society of Abishag the Shunamite."

Further solicitations and remonstrances of the astrologer only provoked a more peremptory reply from the monarch, and they parted in high displeasure. The sage shut himself up in his hermitage to brood over his disappointment; ere he departed, however, he gave the king one more warning to beware of his dangerous captive. But where is the old man in love that will listen to counsel? Aben Habuz resigned himself to the full sway of his passion. His only study was how to render himself amiable in the eyes of the Gothic beauty. He had not youth to recommend him, it is true, but then he had riches; and when a lover is old, he is generally generous. The Zacatin of Granada was ransacked for the most precious merchandise of the East; silks, jewels, precious gems, exquisite perfumes, all that Asia and Africa yielded of rich and rare, were lavished upon the princess. All kinds of spectacles and festivities were devised for her entertainment; minstrelsy, dancing, tournaments, bull-fights;—Granada for a time was a scene of perpetual pageant. The Gothic princess regarded all this splendor with the air of one accustomed to magnificence. She received everything as a homage due to her rank, or rather to her beauty; for beauty is more lofty in its exactions even than rank. Nay, she seemed to take a secret pleasure in exciting the monarch to expenses that made his treasury shrink, and then treating his extravagant generosity as a mere matter of course. With all his assiduity and munificence, also, the venerable lover could not flatter himself that he had made any impression on her heart. She never frowned on him, it is true, but then she never smiled. Whenever he began to plead his passion, she struck her silver lyre. There was a mystic charm in the sound. In an instant the monarch began to nod; a drowsiness stole over him, and he gradually sank into a sleep, from which he awoke wonderfully refreshed, but perfectly cooled for the time of his passion. This was very baffling to his suit; but then these slumbers were accompanied by agreeable dreams, which completely inthralled the senses of the drowsy lover; so he continued to dream on, while all Granada scoffed at his infatuation, and groaned at the treasures lavished for a song.

At length a danger burst on the head of Aben Habuz, against which his talisman yielded him no warning. An insurrection broke out in his very capital; his palace was surrounded by an armed rabble, who menaced his life and the life of his Christian paramour. A spark of his ancient warlike spirit was awakened in the breast of the monarch. At the head of a handful of his guards he sallied forth, put the rebels to flight, and crushed the insurrection in the bud.

When quiet was again restored, he sought the astrologer, who still remained shut up in his hermitage, chewing the bitter cud of resentment.

Aben Habuz approached him with a conciliatory tone. "O wise son of Abu Ayub," said he, "well didst thou predict dangers to me from this captive beauty: tell me then, thou who art so quick at foreseeing peril, what I should do to avert it."

"Put from thee the infidel damsel who is the cause."

"Sooner would I part with my kingdom," cried Aben Habuz.

"Thou art in danger of losing both," replied the astrologer.

"Be not harsh and angry, O most profound of philosophers; consider the double distress of a monarch and a lover, and devise some means of protecting me from the evils by which I am menaced. I care not for grandeur, I care not for power, I languish only for repose; would that I had some quiet retreat where I might take refuge from the world, and all its cares, and pomps, and troubles, and devote the remainder of my days to tranquillity and love."

The astrologer regarded him for a moment from under his bushy eyebrows.

"And what wouldst thou give, if I could provide thee such a retreat?"

"Thou shouldst name thy own reward; and whatever it might be, if within the scope of my power, as my soul liveth, it should be thine."

"Thou hast heard, O king, of the garden of Irem, one of the prodigies of Arabia the happy."

"I have heard of that garden; it is recorded in the Koran, even in the chapter entitled 'The Dawn of Day.' I have, moreover, heard marvellous things related of it by pilgrims who had been to Mecca; but I considered them wild fables, such as travellers are wont to tell who have visited remote countries."

"Discredit not, O king, the tales of travellers," rejoined the astrologer, gravely, "for they contain precious rarities of knowledge brought from the ends of the earth. As to the palace and garden of Irem, what is generally told of them is true; I have seen them with mine own eyes;—listen to my adventure, for it has a bearing upon the object of your request.

"In my younger days, when a mere Arab of the desert, I tended my father's camels. In traversing the desert of Aden, one of them strayed from the rest, and was lost. I searched after it for several days, but in vain, until, wearied and faint, I laid myself down at noontide, and slept under a palm-tree by the side of a scanty well. When I awoke I found myself at the gate of a city. I entered, and beheld noble streets, and squares, and market-places; but all were silent and without an inhabitant. I wandered on until I came to a sumptuous palace, with a garden adorned with fountains and fish-ponds, and groves and flowers, and orchards laden with delicious fruit; but still no one was to be seen. Upon which, appalled at this loneliness, I hastened to depart; and, after issuing forth at the gate of the city, I turned to look upon the place, but it was no longer to be seen; nothing but the silent desert extended before my eyes.

"In the neighborhood I met with an aged dervise, learned in the traditions and secrets of the land, and related to him what had befallen me. 'This,' said he, 'is the far-famed garden of Irem, one of the wonders of the desert. It only appears at times to some wanderer like thyself, gladdening him with the sight of towers and palaces and garden-walls overhung with richly-laden fruit-trees, and then vanishes, leaving nothing but a lonely desert. And this is the story of it. In old times, when this country was inhabited by the Addites, King Sheddad, the son of Ad, the great-grandson of Noah, founded here a splendid city. When it was finished, and he saw its grandeur, his heart was puffed up with pride and arrogance, and he determined to build a royal palace, with gardens which should rival all related in the Koran of the celestial paradise. But the curse of heaven fell upon him for his presumption. He and his subjects were swept from the earth, and his splendid city, and palace, and gardens, were laid under a perpetual spell, which hides them from human sight, excepting that they are seen at intervals, by way of keeping his sin in perpetual remembrance.'

"This story, O king, and the wonders I had seen, ever dwelt in my mind; and in after-years, when I had been in Egypt, and was possessed of the book of knowledge of Solomon the Wise, I determined to return and revisit the garden of Irem. I did so, and found it revealed to my instructed sight. I took possession of the palace of Sheddad, and passed several days in his mock paradise. The genii who watch over the place were obedient to my magic power, and revealed to me the spells by which the whole garden had been, as it were, conjured into existence, and by which it was rendered invisible. Such a palace and garden, O king, can I make for thee, even here, on the mountain above thy city. Do I not know all the secret spells? and am I not in possession of the book of knowledge of Solomon the Wise?"

"O wise son of Abu Ayub!" exclaimed Aben Habuz, trembling with eagerness, "thou art a traveller indeed, and hast seen and learned marvellous things! Contrive me such a paradise, and ask any reward, even to the half of my kingdom."

"Alas!" replied the other, "thou knowest I am an old man, and a philosopher, and easily satisfied; all the reward I ask is the first beast of burden, with its load, which shall enter the magic portal of the palace."

The monarch gladly agreed to so moderate a stipulation, and the astrologer began his work. On the summit of the hill, immediately above his subterranean hermitage, he caused a great gateway or barbican to be erected, opening through the centre of a strong tower.

There was an outer vestibule or porch, with a lofty arch, and within it a portal secured by massive gates. On the keystone of the portal the astrologer, with his own hand, wrought the figure of a huge key; and on the keystone of the outer arch of the vestibule, which was loftier than that of the portal, he carved a gigantic hand. These were potent talismans, over which he repeated many sentences in an unknown tongue.

When this gateway was finished, he shut himself up for two days in his astrological hall, engaged in secret incantations; on the third he ascended the hill, and passed the whole day on its summit. At a late hour of the night he came down, and presented himself before Aben Habuz. "At length, O king," said he, "my labor is accomplished. On the summit of the hill stands one of the most delectable palaces that ever the head of man devised, or the heart of man desired. It contains sumptuous halls and galleries, delicious gardens, cool fountains, and fragrant baths; in a word, the whole mountain is converted into a paradise. Like the garden of Irem, it is protected by a mighty charm, which hides it from the view and search of mortals, excepting such as possess the secret of its talismans."

"Enough!" cried Aben Habuz, joyfully, "tomorrow morning with the first light we will ascend and take possession." The happy monarch slept but little that night. Scarcely had the rays of the sun begun to play about the snowy summit of the Sierra Nevada, when he mounted his steed, and, accompanied only by a few chosen attendants, ascended a steep and narrow road leading up the hill. Beside him, on a white palfrey, rode the Gothic princess, her whole dress sparkling with jewels, while round her neck was suspended her silver lyre. The astrologer walked on the other side of the king, assisting his steps with his hieroglyphic staff, for he never mounted steed of any kind.

Aben Habuz looked to see the towers of the palace brightening above him, and the embowered terraces of its gardens stretching along the heights; but as yet nothing of the kind was to be descried. "That is the mystery and safeguard of the place," said the astrologer, "nothing can be discerned until you have passed the spellbound gateway, and been put in possession of the place."

As they approached the gateway, the astrologer paused, and pointed out to the king the mystic hand and key carved upon the portal of the arch. "These," said he, "are the talismans which guard the entrance to this paradise. Until yonder hand shall reach down and seize that key, neither mortal power nor magic artifice can prevail against the lord of this mountain."

While Aben Habuz was gazing, with open mouth and silent wonder, at these mystic talismans, the palfrey of the princess proceeded, and bore her in at the portal, to the very centre of the barbican.

"Behold," cried the astrologer, "my promised reward; the first animal with its burden which should enter the magic gateway."

Aben Habuz smiled at what he considered a pleasantry of the

ancient man; but when he found him to be in earnest, his gray beard trembled with indignation.

"Son of Abu Ayub," said he, sternly, "what equivocation is this? Thou knowest the meaning of my promise: the first beast of burden, with its load, that should enter this portal. Take the strongest mule in my stables, load it with the most precious things of my treasury, and it is thine; but dare not raise thy thoughts to her who is the delight of my heart."

"What need I of wealth?" cried the astrologer, scornfully; "have I not the book of knowledge of Solomon the Wise, and through it the command of the secret treasures of the earth? The princess is mine by right; thy royal word is pledged; I claim her as my own."

The princess looked down haughtily from her palfrey, and a light smile of scorn curled her rosy lip at this dispute between two gray-beards for the possession of youth and beauty. The wrath of the monarch got the better of his discretion. "Base son of the desert," cried he, "thou mayst be master of many arts, but know me for thy master, and presume not to juggle with thy king."

"My master! my king!" echoed the astrologer,—"the monarch of a mole-hill to claim sway over him who possesses the talismans of Solomon! Farewell, Aben Habuz; reign over thy petty kingdom, and revel in thy paradise of fools; for me, I will laugh at thee in my philosophic retirement."

So saying, he seized the bridle of the palfrey, smote the earth with his staff, and sank with the Gothic princess through the centre of the barbican. The earth closed over them, and no trace remained of the opening by which they had descended.

Aben Habuz was struck dumb for a time with astonishment. Recovering himself, he ordered a thousand workmen to dig, with pickaxe and spade, into the ground where the astrologer had disappeared. They digged and digged, but in vain; the flinty bosom of the hill resisted their implements; or if they did penetrate a little way, the earth filled in again as fast as they threw it out. Aben Habuz sought the mouth of the cavern at the foot of the hill, leading to the subterranean palace of the astrologer; but it was nowhere to be found. Where once had been an entrance, was now a solid surface of primeval rock. With the disappearance of

Ibrahim Ebn Abu Ayub ceased the benefit of his talismans. The bronze horseman remained fixed, with his face turned toward the hill, and his spear pointed to the spot where the astrologer had descended, as if there still lurked the deadliest foe of Aben Habuz.

From time to time the sound of music, and the tones of a female voice, could be faintly heard from the bosom of the hill; and a peasant one day brought word to the king, that in the preceding night he had found a fissure in the rock, by which he had crept in, until he looked down into a subterranean hall, in which sat the astrologer, on a magnificent divan, slumbering and nodding to the silver lyre of the princess, which seemed to hold a magic sway over his senses.

Aben Habuz sought the fissure in the rock, but it was again closed. He renewed the attempt to unearth his rival, but all in vain. The spell of the hand and key was too potent to be counteracted by human power. As to the summit of the mountain, the site of the promised palace and garden, it remained a naked waste; either the boasted elysium was hidden from sight by enchantment, or was a mere fable of the astrologer. The world charitably supposed the latter, and some used to call the palace "The King's Folly"; while others named it "The Fool's Paradise."

To add to the chagrin of Aben Habuz, the neighbors whom he had defied and taunted, and cut up at his leisure while master of the talismanic horseman, finding him no longer protected by magic spell, made inroads into his territories from all sides, and the remainder of the life of the most pacific of monarchs was a tissue of turmoils.

At length Aben Habuz died, and was buried. Ages have since rolled away. The Alhambra has been built on the eventful mountain, and in some measure realizes the fabled delights of the garden of Irem. The spell-bound gateway still exists entire, protected no doubt by the mystic hand and key, and now forms the Gate of Justice, the grand entrance to the fortress. Under that gateway, it is said, the old astrologer remains in his subterranean hall, nodding on his divan, lulled by the silver lyre of the princess.

The old invalid sentinels who mount guard at the gate hear the strains occasionally in the summer nights; and, yielding to their soporific power, doze quietly at their posts. Nay, so drowsy an influence pervades the place, that even those who watch by day may generally be seen nodding on the stone benches of the barbican, or sleeping under the neighboring trees; so that in fact it is the drowsiest military post in all Christendom. All this, say the ancient legends, will endure from age to age. The princess will remain captive to the astrologer; and the astrologer, bound up in magic slumber by the princess, until the last day, unless the mystic hand shall grasp the fated key, and dispel the whole charm of this enchanted mountain.

NOTE TO THE ARABIAN ASTROLOGER

Al Makkari, in his history of the Mahommedan Dynasties in Spain, cites from another Arabian writer an account of a talismanic effigy somewhat similar to the one in the foregoing legend.

In Cadiz, says he, there formerly stood a square tower upwards of one hundred cubits high, built of huge blocks of stone, fastened together with clamps of brass. On the top was the figure of a man, holding a staff in his right hand, his face turned to the Atlantic, and pointing with the forefinger of his left hand to the Straits of Gibraltar. It was said to have been set up in ancient times by the Gothic kings of Andalus, as a beacon or guide to navigators. The Moslems of Barbary and Andalus considered it a talisman which exercised a spell over the seas. Under its guidance, swarms of piratical people of a nation called Majus, appeared on the coast in large vessels with a square sail in the bow, and another in the stern. They came every six or seven years: captured everything they met with on the sea;—guided by the statue, they passed through the Straits into the Mediterranean, landed on the coasts of Andalus, laid everything waste with fire and sword; and sometimes carried their depredations on the opposite coasts even as far as Syria.

At length it came to pass in the time of the Civil wars, a Moslem Admiral who had taken possession of Cadiz, hearing that the statue on top of the tower was of pure gold, had it lowered to the ground and broken to pieces: when it proved to be of gilded brass. With the destruction of the idol, the spell over the sea was at an end. From that time forward, nothing more was seen of the piratical people of the ocean, excepting that two of their barks were wrecked on the coast, one at Marsu-l-Majus (the port of the Majus), the other close to the promontory of Al-Aghan.

The maritime invaders above mentioned by Al-Makkari must have been the Northmen.

LEGEND OF THE MOOR'S LEGACY

JUST WITHIN THE FORTRESS of the Alhambra, in front of the royal palace, is a broad open esplanade, called the Place or Square of the Cisterns, (la Plaza de los Algibes,) so called from being undermined by reservoirs of water, hidden from sight, and which have existed from the time of the Moors. At one corner of this esplanade is a Moorish well, cut through the living rock to a great depth, the water of which is cold as ice and clear as crystal. The wells made by the Moors are always in repute, for it is well known what pains they took to penetrate to the purest and sweetest springs and fountains. The one of which we now speak is famous throughout Granada, insomuch that water-carriers, some bearing great water-jars on their shoulders, others driving asses before them laden with earthen vessels, are ascending and descending the steep woody avenues of the Alhambra, from early dawn until a late hour of the night.

Fountains and wells, ever since the scriptural days, have been noted gossiping-places in hot climates; and at the well in question there is a kind of perpetual club kept up during the livelong day, by the invalids, old women, and other curious do-nothing folk of the fortress, who sit here on the stone benches, under an awning spread over the well to shelter the toll-gatherer from the sun, and dawdle over the gossip of the fortress, and question every water-carrier that arrives about the news of the city, and make long comments on everything they hear and see. Not an hour of the day but loitering housewives and idle maid-servants may be seen, lingering, with pitcher on head or in hand, to hear the last of the endless tattle of these worthies.

Among the water-carriers who once resorted to this well, there was a sturdy, strong-backed, bandy-legged little fellow, named Pedro Gil, but called Peregil for shortness. Being a water-carrier, he was a Gallego, or native of Gallicia, of course. Nature seems to have formed races of men, as she has of animals, for different kinds of drudgery. In France the shoeblacks are all Savoyards, the porters of hotels all Swiss, and in the days of hoops and hair-powder in England, no man could give the regular swing to a sedan-chair but a bog-trotting Irishman. So in Spain, the carriers of water and bearers of burdens are all sturdy little natives of Gallicia. No man says, "Get me a porter," but, "Call a Gallego."

To return from this digression, Peregil the Gallego had begun business with merely a great earthen jar which he carried upon his shoulder; by degrees he rose in the world, and was enabled to purchase an assistant of a correspondent class of animals, being a stout shaggy-haired donkey. On each side of this his long-eared aide-de-camp, in a kind of pannier, were slung his water-jars, covered with fig-leaves to protect them from the sun. There was not a more industrious water-carrier in all Granada, nor one more merry withal. The streets rang with his cheerful voice as he trudged after his donkey, singing forth the usual summer note that resounds through the Spanish towns: *"Quien quiere agua— agua mas fria que la nieve?"*—"Who wants water—water colder than snow? Who wants water from the well of the Alhambra, cold as ice and clear as crystal?" When he served a customer with a sparkling glass, it was always with a pleasant word that caused a smile; and if, perchance, it was a comely dame or dimpling damsel, it was always with a sly leer and a compliment to her beauty that was irresistible. Thus Peregil the Gallego was noted through-out all Granada for being one of the civilest, pleasantest, and happiest of mortals. Yet it is not he who sings loudest and jokes most that has the lightest heart. Under all this air of merriment, honest Peregil had his cares and troubles. He had a large family of ragged children to support, who were hungry and clamorous as a nest of young swallows, and beset him with their outcries for food whenever he came home of an evening. He had a helpmate, too, who was anything but a help to him. She had been a village beauty before marriage, noted for her skill at dancing the bolero and rattling the castanets; and she still retained her early propensities, spending the hard earnings of honest Peregil in frippery, and laying the very donkey under requisition for junketing parties into the country on Sundays, and saint's days, and those innumerable holidays which are rather more numerous in Spain than the days of the week. With all this she was a little of a slattern, something more of a lie-abed, and, above all, a gossip of the first water; neglecting house, household, and everything else, to loiter slipshod in the houses of her gossip neighbors.

He, however, who tempers the wind to the shorn lamb, accommodates the yoke of matrimony to the submissive neck. Peregil bore all the heavy dispensations of wife and children with as meek a spirit as his donkey bore the water-jars; and, however he might shake his ears in private, never ventured to question the household virtues of his slattern spouse.

He loved his children, too, even as an owl loves its owlets, seeing in them his own image multiplied and perpetuated; for they were a sturdy, long-backed, bandy-legged little brood. The great pleasure of honest Peregil was, whenever he could afford himself a scanty holiday, and had a handful of maravedis to spare, to take the whole litter forth with him, some in his arms, some tugging at his skirts, and some trudging at his heels, and to treat them to a gambol among the orchards of the Vega, while his wife was dancing with her holiday friends in the Angosturas of the Darro.

It was a late hour one summer night, and most of the water-carriers had desisted from their toils. The day had been uncommonly sultry; the night was one of those delicious moonlights which tempt the inhabitants of southern climes to indemnify themselves for the heat and inaction of the day, by lingering in the open air, and enjoying its tempered sweetness until after midnight. Customers for water were therefore still abroad. Peregil, like a considerate, painstaking father, thought of his hungry children. "One more journey to the well," said he to himself, "to earn a Sunday's puchero for the little ones." So saying, he trudged manfully up the steep avenue of the Alhambra, singing as he went, and now and then bestowing a hearty thwack with a cudgel on the flanks of his donkey, either by way of cadence to the song, or refreshment to the animal; for dry blows serve in lieu of provender in Spain for all beasts of burden.

When arrived at the well, he found it deserted by every one except a solitary stranger in Moorish garb, seated on a stone bench in the moonlight. Peregil paused at first and regarded him with surprise, not unmixed with awe, but the Moor feebly beckoned him to approach. "I am faint and ill," said he; "aid me to return to the city, and I will pay thee double what thou couldst gain by thy jars of water."

The honest heart of the little water-carrier was touched with compassion at the appeal of the stranger. "God forbid," said he, "that I should ask fee or reward for doing a common act of humanity." He accordingly helped the Moor on his donkey, and set off slowly for Granada, the poor Moslem being so weak that it was necessary to hold him on the animal to keep him from falling to the earth.

When they entered the city, the water-carrier demanded whither he should conduct him. "Alas!" said the Moor, faintly, "I have neither home nor habitation; I am a stranger in the land. Suffer me to lay my head this night beneath thy roof, and thou shalt be amply repaid."

Honest Peregil thus saw himself unexpectedly saddled with an infidel guest, but he was too humane to refuse a night's shelter to a fellow-being in so forlorn a plight; so he conducted the Moor to his dwelling. The children, who had sallied forth open-mouthed as usual on hearing the tramp of the donkey, ran back with affright when they beheld the turbaned stranger, and hid themselves behind their mother. The latter stepped forth intrepidly, like a ruffling hen before her brood when a vagrant dog approaches.

"What infidel companion," cried she, "is this you have brought home at this late hour, to draw upon us the eyes of the inquisition?"

"Be quiet, wife," replied the Gallego; "here is a poor sick stranger, without friend or home; wouldst thou turn him forth to perish in the streets?"

The wife would still have remonstrated, for although she lived in a hovel, she was a furious stickler for the credit of her house; the little water-carrier, however, for once was stiffnecked, and refused to bend beneath the yoke. He assisted the poor Moslem to alight, and spread a mat and a sheep-skin for him, on the ground, in the coolest part of the house; being the only kind of bed that his poverty afforded.

In a little while the Moor was seized with violent convulsions, which defied all the ministering skill of the simple water-carrier. The eye of the poor patient acknowledged his kindness. During an interval of his fits he called him to his side, and addressing him in a low voice, "My end," said he, "I fear is at hand. If I die, I bequeath you this box as a reward for your charity:" so saying, he opened his albornoz, or cloak, and showed a small box of sandal-wood, strapped round his body. "God grant, my friend," replied the worthy little Gallego, "that you may live many years to enjoy your treasure, whatever it may be." The Moor shook his head; he laid his hand upon the box, and would have said something more concerning it, but his convulsions returned with increasing violence, and in a little while he expired.

The water-carrier's wife was now as one distracted. "This comes," said she, "of your foolish good-nature, always running into scrapes to oblige others. What will become of us when this corpse is found in our house? We shall be sent to prison as murderers; and if we escape with our lives, shall be ruined by notaries and alguazils."

Poor Peregil was in equal tribulation, and almost repented himself of having done a good deed. At length a thought struck him. "It is not yet day," said he; "I can convey the dead body out of the city, and bury it in the sands on the banks of the Xenil. No one saw the Moor enter our dwelling, and no one will know anything of his death."

So said, so done. The wife aided him; they rolled the body of the unfortunate Moslem in the mat on which he had expired, laid it across the ass, and Peregil set out with it for the banks of the river.

As ill luck would have it, there lived opposite to the water-carrier a barber named Pedrillo Pedrugo, one of the most prying, tattling, and mischief-making of his gossip tribe. He was a weasel-faced, spider-legged varlet, supple and insinuating; the famous barber of Seville could not surpass him for his universal knowledge of the affairs of others, and he had no more power of retention than a sieve. It was said that he slept but with one eye at a time, and kept one ear uncovered, so that even in his sleep he might see and hear all that was going on. Certain it is, he was a sort of scandalous chronicle for the quidnuncs of Granada, and had more customers than all the rest of his fraternity.

This meddlesome barber heard Peregil arrive at an unusual hour at night, and the exclamations of his wife and children. His head was instantly popped out of a little window which served him as a look-out, and he saw his neighbor assist a man in Moorish garb into his dwelling. This was so strange an occurrence, that Pedrillo Pedrugo slept not a wink that night. Every five minutes he was at his loophole, watching the lights that gleamed through the chinks of his neighbor's door, and before daylight he beheld Peregil sally forth with his donkey unusually laden.

The inquisitive barber was in a fidget; he slipped on his clothes, and, stealing forth silently, followed the water-carrier at a distance until he saw him dig a hole in the sandy bank of the Xenil, and bury something that had the appearance of a dead body.

The barber hied him home, and fidgeted about his shop, setting everything upside down, until sunrise. He then took a basin under his arm, and sallied forth to the house of his daily customer the alcalde.

The alcalde was just risen. Pedrillo Pedrugo seated him in a chair, threw a napkin round his neck, put a basin of hot water under his chin, and began to mollify his beard with his fingers.

"Strange doings!" said Pedrugo, who played barber and newsmonger at the same time,—"strange doings! Robbery, and murder, and burial all in one night!"

"Hey!—how!—what is that you say?" cried the alcalde.

"I say," replied the barber, rubbing a piece of soap over the nose and mouth of the dignitary, for a Spanish barber disdains to employ a brush,—"I say that Peregil the Gallego has robbed and murdered a Moorish Mussulman, and buried him, this blessed night. *Maldita sea la noche;*—Accursed be the night for the same!"

"But how do you know all this?" demanded the alcalde.

"Be patient, Señor, and you shall hear all about it," replied Pedrillo, taking him by the nose and sliding a razor over his cheek. He then recounted all that he had seen, going through both operations at that same time, shaving his beard, washing his chin, and wiping him dry with a dirty napkin, while he was robbing, murdering, and burying the Moslem.

Now it so happened that this alcalde was one of the most overbearing, and at the same time most griping and corrupt curmudgeons in all Granada. It could not be denied, however, that he set a high value upon justice, for he sold it at its weight in gold. He presumed the case in point to be one of murder and robbery; doubtless there must be a rich spoil; how was it to be secured into the legitimate hands of the law? for as to merely entrapping the delinquent—that would be feeding the gallows; but entrapping the booty—that would be enriching the judge, and such, according to his creed, was the great end of justice. So thinking, he summoned to his presence his trustiest alguazil—a gaunt, hungry-looking varlet, clad, according to the custom of his order, in the ancient Spanish garb, a broad black beaver turned up at its sides; a quaint ruff; a small black cloak dangling from his shoulders; rusty black under-clothes that set off his spare wiry frame, while in his hand he bore a slender white wand, the dreaded insignia of his office. Such was the legal bloodhound of the ancient Spanish breed, that he put upon the traces of the unlucky water-carrier, and such was his speed and certainty, that he was upon the haunches of poor Peregil before he had returned to his dwelling, and brought both him and his donkey before the dispenser of justice.

The alcalde bent upon him one of the most terrific frowns. "Hark ye, culprit!" roared he, in a voice that made the knees of the little Gallego smite together,—"hark ye, culprit! there is no need of denying thy guilt, everything is known to me. A gallows is the proper reward for the crime thou hast committed, but I am merciful, and readily listen to reason. The man that has been murdered in thy house was a Moor, an infidel, the enemy of our faith. It was doubtless in a fit of religious zeal that thou hast slain him. I will be indulgent, therefore; render up the property of which thou hast robbed him, and we will hush the matter up."

The poor water-carrier called upon all the saints to witness his innocence; alas! not one of them appeared; and if they had, the alcalde would have disbelieved the whole calendar. The water-carrier related the whole story of the dying Moor with the straightforward simplicity of truth, but it was all in vain. "Wilt thou persist in saying," demanded the judge, "that this Moslem had neither gold nor jewels, which were the object of thy cupidity?"

"As I hope to be saved, your worship," replied the water-carrier, "he had nothing but a small box of sandal-wood which he bequeathed to me in reward for my services."

"A box of sandal-wood! a box of sandal-wood!" exclaimed the alcalde, his eyes sparkling at the idea of precious jewels. "And where is this box? were have you concealed it?"

"An' it please your grace," replied the water-carrier, "it is in one of the panniers of my mule, and heartily at the service of your worship."

He had hardly spoken the words, when the keen alguazil darted off, and reappeared in an instant with the mysterious box of sandal-wood. The alcalde opened it with an eager and trembling hand; all pressed forward to gaze upon the treasure it was expected to contain; when, to their disappointment, nothing appeared within, but a parchment scroll, covered with Arabic characters, and an end of a waxen taper.

When there is nothing to be gained by the conviction of a prisoner, justice, even in Spain, is apt to be impartial. The alcalde, having recovered from his disappointment, and found that there was really no booty in the case, now listened dispassionately to the explanation of the water-carrier, which was corroborated by the testimony of his wife. Being convinced, therefore, of his innocence, he discharged him from arrest; nay more, he permitted him to carry off the Moor's legacy, the box of sandal-wood and its contents, as the well-merited reward of his humanity; but he retained his donkey in payment of costs and charges.

Behold the unfortunate little Gallego reduced once more to the necessity of being his own water-carrier, and trudging up to the well of the Alhambra with a great earthen jar upon his shoulder.

As he toiled up the hill in the heat of a summer noon, his usual good-humor forsook him. "Dog of an alcalde!" would he cry, "to rob a poor man of the means of his subsistence, of the best friend he had in the world!" And then at the remembrance of the beloved companion of his labors, all the kindness of his nature would break forth. "Ah, donkey of my heart!" would he exclaim, resting his burden on a stone, and wiping the sweat from his brow, —"ah, donkey of my heart! I warrant me thou thinkest of thy old master! I warrant me thou missest the water-jars—poor beast."

To add to his afflictions, his wife received him, on his return home, with whimperings and repinings; she had clearly the vantage-ground of him, having warned him not to commit the egregious act of hospitality which had brought on him all these misfortunes; and, like a knowing woman, she took every occasion to throw her superior sagacity in his teeth. If her children lacked food, or needed a new garment, she could answer with a sneer, "Go to your father—he is heir to king Chico of the Alhambra: ask him to help you out of the Moor's strong box."

Was ever poor mortal so soundly punished for having done a good action? The unlucky Peregil was grieved in flesh and spirit, but still he bore meekly with the railings of his spouse. At length, one evening, when, after a hot day's toil, she taunted him in the usual manner, he lost all patience. He did not venture to retort upon her, but his eye rested upon the box of sandal-wood, which lay on a shelf with lid half open, as if laughing in mockery at his vexation. Seizing it up, he dashed it with indignation to the floor. "Unlucky was the day that I ever set eyes on thee," he cried, "or sheltered thy master beneath my roof!"

As the box struck the floor, the lid flew wide open, and the parchment scroll rolled forth.

Peregil sat regarding the scroll for some time in moody silence. At length rallying his ideas, "Who knows," thought he, "but this writing may be of some importance, as the Moor seems to have guarded it with such care?" Picking it up therefore, he put it in his bosom, and the next morning, as he was crying water through the streets, he stopped at the shop of a Moor, a native of Tangiers, who sold trinkets and perfumery in the Zacatin, and asked him to explain the contents.

The Moor read the scroll attentively, then stroked his beard and smiled. "This manuscript," said he, "is a form of incantation for the recovery of hidden treasure that is under the power of enchantment. It is said to have such virtue that the strongest bolts and bars, nay the adamantine rock itself, will yield before it!"

"Bah!" cried the little Gallego, "what is all that to me? I am no enchanter, and know nothing of buried treasure." So saying, he shouldered his water-jar, left the scroll in the hands of the Moor, and trudged forward on his daily rounds.

That evening, however, as he rested himself about twilight at the well of the Alhambra, he found a number of gossips assembled at the place, and their conversation, as is not unusual at that shadowy hour, turned upon old tales and traditions of a supernatural nature. Being all poor as rats, they dwelt with peculiar fondness upon the popular theme of enchanted riches left by the Moors in various parts of the Alhambra. Above all, they concurred in the belief that there were great treasures buried deep in the earth under the tower of the seven floors.

These stories made an unusual impression on the mind of the honest Peregil, and they sank deeper and deeper into his thoughts as he returned alone down the darkling avenues. "If, after all, there should be treasure hid beneath that tower; and if the scroll I left with the Moor should enable me to get at it!" In the sudden ecstasy of the thought he had wellnigh let fall his water-jar.

That night he tumbled and tossed, and could scarcely get a wink of sleep for the thoughts that were bewildering his brain. Bright and early he repaired to the shop of the Moor, and told him all that was passing in his mind. "You can read Arabic," said he; "suppose we go together to the tower, and try the effect of the charm; if it fails, we are no worse off than before; but if it succeeds we will share equally all the treasure we may discover."

"Hold," replied the Moslem; "this writing is not sufficient of itself; it must be read at midnight, by the light of a taper singularly compounded and prepared, the ingredients of which are not within my reach. Without such a taper the scroll is of no avail."

"Say no more!" cried the little Gallego; "I have such a taper at hand, and will bring it here in a moment." So saying, he hastened home, and soon returned with the end of yellow wax taper that he had found in the box of sandal-wood.

The Moor felt it and smelt to it. "Here are rare and costly perfumes," said he, "combined with this yellow wax. This is the kind of taper specified in the scroll. While this burns, the strongest walls and most secret caverns will remain open. Woe to him, however, who lingers within until it be extinguished. He will remain enchanted with the treasure."

It was now agreed between them to try the charm that very night. At a late hour, therefore, when nothing was stirring but bats and owls, they ascended the woody hill of the Alhambra, and approached that awful tower, shrouded by trees and rendered formidable by so many traditionary tales. By the light of a lantern they groped their way through bushes, and over fallen stones, to the door of a vault beneath the tower. With fear and trembling they descended a flight of steps cut into the rock. It led to an empty chamber, damp and drear, from which another flight of steps led to a deeper vault. In this way they descended for several flights, leading into as many vaults, one below the other, but the floor of the fourth was solid; and though, according to tradition, there remained three vaults still below, it was said to be impossible to penetrate further, the residue being shut up by strong enchantment. The air of this vault was damp and chilly, and had an earthy smell, and the light scarce cast forth any rays. They paused here for a time, in breathless suspense, until they faintly heard the clock of the watch-tower strike midnight; upon this they lit the waxen taper, which diffused an odor of myrrh and frankincense and storax.

The Moor began to read in a hurried voice. He had scarce finished when there was a noise as of subterraneous thunder. The earth shook, and the floor, yawning open, disclosed a flight of steps. Trembling with awe, they descended, and by the light of the lantern found themselves in another vault covered with Arabic inscriptions. In the centre stood a great chest, secured with seven bands of steel, at each end of which sat an enchanted Moor in armor, but motionless as a statue, being controlled by the power of the incantation. Before the chest were several jars filled with gold and silver and precious stones. In the largest of these they thrust their arms up to the elbow, and at every dip hauled forth handfuls of broad yellow pieces of Moorish gold, or bracelets and ornaments of the same precious metal, while occasionally a necklace of Oriental pearl would stick to their fingers. Still they trembled and breathed short while cramming their pockets with the spoils; and cast many a fearful glance at the two enchanted Moors, who sat grim and motionless, glaring upon them with unwinking eyes. At length, struck with a sudden panic at some fancied noise, they both rushed up the staircase, tumbled over one another into the upper apartment, overturned and extinguished the waxen taper, and the pavement again closed with a thundering sound.

Filled with dismay, they did not pause until they had groped their way out of the tower, and beheld the stars shining through the trees. Then seating themselves upon the grass, they divided the spoil, determining to content themselves for the present with this mere skimming of the jars, but to return on some future night and drain them to the bottom. To make sure of each other's good faith, also, they divided the talismans between them, one retaining the scroll and the other the taper; this done, they set off with light hearts and well-lined pockets for Granada.

As they wended their way down the hill, the shrewd Moor whispered a word of counsel in the ear of the simple little water-carrier.

"Friend Peregil," said he, "all this affair must be kept a profound secret until we have secured the treasure, and conveyed it out of harm's way. If a whisper of it gets to the ear of the alcalde, we are undone!"

"Certainly," replied the Gallego, "nothing can be more true."

"Friend Peregil," said the Moor, "you are a discreet man, and I make no doubt can keep a secret; but you have a wife."

"She shall not know a word of it," replied the little water-carrier, sturdily.

"Enough," said the Moor, "I depend upon thy discretion and thy promise."

Never was promise more positive and sincere; but, alas! what

man can keep a secret from his wife? Certainly not such a one as
Peregil the water-carrier, who was one of the most loving and
tractable of husbands. On his return home, he found his wife
moping in a corner. "Mighty well," cried she as he entered, "you've
come at last, after rambling about until this hour of the night. I
wonder you have not brought home another Moor as a house-
mate." Then bursting into tears, she began to wring her hands and
smite her breast. "Unhappy woman that I am!" exclaimed she,
"what will become of me? My house stripped and plundered by
lawyers and alguazils; my husband a do-no-good, that no longer
brings home bread to his family, but goes rambling about day
and night, with infidel Moors! O my children! my children! what
will become of us? We shall all have to beg in the streets!"

Honest Peregil was so moved by the distress of his spouse, that
he could not help whimpering also. His heart was as full as his
pocket, and not to be restrained. Thrusting his hand into the latter
he hauled forth three or four broad gold pieces, and slipped them
into her bosom. The poor woman stared with astonishment, and
could not understand the meaning of this golden shower. Before
she could recover her surprise, the little Gallego drew forth a
chain of gold and dangled it before her, capering with exultation,
his mouth distended from ear to ear.

"Holy Virgin protect us!" exclaimed the wife. "What hast thou
been doing, Peregil? surely thou hast not been committing murder
and robbery!"

The idea scarce entered the brain of the poor woman, than it
became a certainty with her. She saw a prison and a gallows
in the distance, and a little bandy-legged Gallego hanging pendent
from it; and, overcome by the horrors conjured up by her imagination, fell into violent hysterics.

What could the poor man do? He had no other means of pacifying his wife, and dispelling the phantoms of her fancy, than by
relating the whole story of his good fortune. This, however, he
did not do until he had exacted from her the most solemn promise
to keep it a profound secret from every living being.

To describe her joy would be impossible. She flung her arms
round the neck of her husband, and almost strangled him with

her caresses. "Now, wife," exclaimed the little man with honest exultation, "what say you now to the Moor's legacy? Henceforth never abuse me for helping a fellow-creature in distress."

The honest Gallego retired to his sheep-skin mat, and slept as soundly as if on a bed of down. Not so his wife; she emptied the whole contents of his pockets upon the mat, and sat counting gold pieces of Arabic coin, trying on necklaces and earrings, and fancying the figure she should one day make when permitted to enjoy her riches.

On the following morning the honest Gallego took a broad golden coin, and repaired with it to a jeweller's shop in the Zacatin to offer it for sale, pretending to have found it among the ruins of the Alhambra. The jeweller saw that it had an Arabic inscription, and was of the purest gold; he offered, however, but a third of its value, with which the water-carrier was perfectly content. Peregil now bought new clothes for his little flock, and all kinds of toys, together with ample provisions for a hearty meal, and returning to his dwelling, set all his children dancing around him, while he capered in the midst, the happiest of fathers.

The wife of the water-carrier kept her promise of secrecy with surprising strictness. For a whole day and a half she went about with a look of mystery and a heart swelling almost to bursting, yet she held her peace, though surrounded by her gossips. It is true, she could not help giving herself a few airs, apologized for her ragged dress, and talked of ordering a new basquina all trimmed with gold lace and bugles, and a new lace mantilla. She threw out hints of her husband's intention of leaving off his trade of water-carrying, as it did not altogether agree with his health. In fact she thought they should all retire to the country for the summer, that the children might have the benefit of the mountain air, for there was no living in the city in this sultry season.

The neighbors stared at each other, and thought the poor woman had lost her wits; and her airs and graces and elegant pretensions were the theme of universal scoffing and merriment among her friends, the moment her back was turned.

If she restrained herself abroad, however, she indemnified herself at home, and putting a string of rich Oriental pearls round her neck, Moorish bracelets on her arms, and an aigrette of diamonds on her head, sailed backwards and forwards in her slattern rags about the room, now and then stopping to admire herself in a broken mirror. Nay, in the impulse of her simple vanity, she could not resist, on one occasion, showing herself at the window to enjoy the effect of her finery on the passers-by.

As the fates would have it, Pedrillo Pedrugo, the meddlesome barber, was at this moment sitting idly in his shop on the opposite side of the street, when his ever-watchful eye caught the sparkle of a diamond. In an instant he was at his loophole reconnoitring the slattern spouse of the water-carrier, decorated with the splendor of an eastern bride. No sooner had he taken an accurate inventory of her ornaments, than he posted off with all speed to the alcalde. In a little while the hungry alguazil was again on the scent, and before the day was over the unfortunate Peregil was once more dragged into the presence of the judge.

"How is this, villain!" cried the alcalde, in a furious voice. "You told me that the infidel who died in your house left nothing behind but an ampty coffer, and now I hear of your wife flaunting in her rags decked out with pearls and diamonds. Wretch that thou art! prepare to render up the spoils of thy miserable victim, and to swing on the gallows that is already tired of waiting for thee."

The terrified water-carrier fell on his knees, and made a full relation of the marvellous manner in which he had gained his wealth. The alcalde, the alguazil, and the inquisitive barber listened with greedy ears to this Arabian tale of enchanted treasure. The alguazil was dispatched to bring the Moor who had assisted in the incantation. The Moslem entered half frightened out of his wits at finding himself in the hands of the harpies of the law. When he beheld the water-carrier standing with sheepish looks and downcast countenance, he comprehended the whole matter. "Miserable animal," said he, as he passed near him, "did I not warn thee against babbling to thy wife?"

The story of the Moor coincided exactly with that of his colleague; but the alcalde affected to be slow of belief, and threw out menaces of imprisonment and rigorous investigation.

"Softly, good Señor Alcalde," said the Mussulman, who by this time had recovered his usual shrewdness and self-possession. "Let us not mar fortune's favors in the scramble for them. Nobody knows anything of this matter but ourselves; let us keep the secret. There is wealth enough in the cave to enrich us all. Promise a fair division, and all shall be produced; refuse, and the cave shall remain forever closed."

The alcalde consulted apart with the alguazil. The latter was an old fox in his profession. "Promise anything," said he, "until you get possession of the treasure. You may then seize upon the whole, and if he and his accomplice dare to murmur, threaten them with the fagot and the stake as infidels and sorcerers."

The alcalde relished the advice. Smoothing his brow and turning to the Moor, "This is a strange story," said he, "and may be true, but I must have ocular proof of it. This very night you must repeat the incantation in my presence. If there be really such treasure, we will share it amicably between us, and say nothing further of the matter; if ye have deceived me, expect no mercy at my hands. In the mean time you must remain in custody."

The Moor and the water-carrier cheerfully agreed to these conditions, satisfied that the event would prove the truth of their words.

Towards midnight the alcalde sallied forth secretly, attended by the alguazil and the meddlesome barber, all strongly armed. They conducted the Moor and the water-carrier as prisoners, and were provided with the stout donkey of the latter to bear off the expected treasure. They arrived at the tower without being observed, and tying the donkey to a fig-tree, descended into the fourth vault of the tower.

The scroll was produced, the yellow waxen taper lighted, and the Moor read the form of incantation. The earth trembled as before, and the pavement opened with a thundering sound, disclosing the narrow flight of steps. The alcalde, the alguazil, and the barber were struck aghast, and could not summon courage to descend. The Moor and the water-carrier entered the lower vault, and found the two Moors seated as before, silent and motionless. They removed two of the great jars, filled with golden coin and precious stones. The water-carrier bore them up one by one upon his shoulders, but though a strong-backed little man, and accustomed to carry burdens, he staggered beneath their weight, and found, when slung on each side of his donkey, they were as much as the animal could bear.

"Let us be content for the present," said the Moor, "here is as much treasure as we can carry off without being perceived, and enough to make us all wealthy to our heart's desire."

"Is there more treasure remaining behind?" demanded the alcalde.

"The greatest prize of all," said the Moor, "a huge coffer bound with bands of steel, and filled with pearls and precious stones."

"Let us have up the coffer by all means," cried the grasping alcalde.

"I will descend for no more," said the Moor, doggedly; "enough is enough for a reasonable man—more is superfluous."

"And I," said the water-carrier, "will bring up no further burden to break the back of my poor donkey."

Finding commands, threats, and entreaties equally vain, the alcalde turned to his two adherents. "Aid me," said he, "to bring up the coffer, and its contents shall be divided between us." So saying, he descended the steps, followed with trembling reluctance by the alguazil and the barber.

No sooner did the Moor behold them fairly earthed than he extinguished the yellow taper; the pavement closed with its usual crash, and the three worthies remained buried in its womb.

He then hastened up the different flight of steps, nor stopped until in the open air. The little water-carrier followed him as fast as his short legs would permit.

"What hast thou done?" cried Peregil, as soon as he could recover breath. "The alcalde and the other two are shut up in the vault."

"It is the will of Allah!" said the Moor, devoutly.

"And will you not release them?" demanded the Gallego.

"Allah forbid!" replied the Moor, smoothing his beard. "It is written in the book of fate that they shall remain enchanted until some future adventurer arrive to break the charm. The will of God be done!" so saying, he hurled the end of the waxen taper far among the gloomy thickets of the glen.

There was now no remedy; so the Moor and the water-carrier proceeded with the richly laden donkey toward the city, nor could honest Peregil refrain from hugging and kissing his long-eared fellow-laborer, thus restored to him from the clutches of the law; and, in fact, it is doubtful which gave the simple-hearted little man most joy at the moment, the gaining of the treasure, or the recovery of the donkey.

The two partners in good luck divided their spoil amicably and fairly, except that the Moor, who had a little taste for trinketry, made out to get into his heap the most of the pearls and precious stones and other baubles, but then he always gave the water-carrier in lieu magnificent jewels of massy gold, of five times the size, with which the latter was heartily content. They took care not to linger within reach of accidents, but made off to enjoy their wealth undisturbed in other countries. The Moor returned to Africa, to his native city of Tangiers, and the Gallego, with his wife, his children, and his donkey, made the best of his way to Portugal. Here, under the admonition and tuition of his wife, he became a personage of some consequence, for she made the worthy little man array his long body and short legs in doublet and hose, with a feather in his hat and a sword by his side, and laying aside his familiar appellation of Peregil, assume the more sonorous title of Don Pedro Gil: his progeny grew up a thriving and merry-hearted, though short and bandy-legged generation, while Señora Gil, befringed, belaced, and betasselled from her head to her heels, with glittering rings on every finger, became a model of slattern fashion and finery. As to the alcalde and his adjuncts, they remained shut up under the great tower of the seven floors, and there they remain spellbound at the present day. Whenever there shall be a lack in Spain of pimping barbers, sharking alguazils, and corrupt alcaldes, they may be sought after; but if they have to wait until such time for their deliverance, there is danger of their enchantment enduring until doomsday.

LEGEND OF THE ROSE
OF THE ALHAMBRA

FOR SOME TIME after the surrender of Granada by the Moors, that delightful city was a frequent and favorite residence of the Spanish sovereigns, until they were frightened away by successive shocks of earthquakes, which toppled down various houses, and made the old Moslem towers rock to their foundation.

Many, many years then rolled away, during which Granada was rarely honored by a royal guest. The palaces of the nobility remained silent and shut up; and the Alhambra, like a slighted beauty, sat in mournful desolation among her neglected gardens. The tower of the Infantas, once the residence of the three beautiful Moorish princesses, partook of the general desolation; the spider spun her web athwart the gilded vault, and bats and owls nestled in those chambers that had been graced by the presence of Zayda, Zorayda, and Zorahayda. The neglect of this tower may have been partly owing to some superstitious notions of the neighbors. It was rumored that the spirit of the youthful Zorahayda, who had perished in that tower, was often seen by moonlight seated beside the fountain in the hall, or moaning about the battlements, and that the notes of her silver lute would be heard at midnight by wayfarers passing along the glen.

At length the city of Granada was once more welcomed by the royal presence. All the world knows that Philip V. was the first Bourbon that swayed the Spanish sceptre. All the world knows that he married, in second nuptials, Elizabetta or Isabella (for they are the same), the beautiful princess of Parma; and all the world knows that by this chain of contingencies a French prince and an Italian princess were seated together on the Spanish throne. For a visit of this illustrious pair, the Alhambra was repaired and fitted up with all possible expedition. The arrival of the court changed the whole aspect of the lately deserted palace. The clangor of drum and trumpet, the tramp of steed about the avenues and outer court, the glitter of arms and display of banners about barbican and battlement, recalled the ancient and warlike glories of the fortress. A softer spirit, however, reigned within the royal palace. There was the rustling of robes and the cautious tread and murmuring voice of reverential courtiers about the antechambers; a loitering of pages and maids of honor about the gardens, and the sound of music stealing from open casements.

Among those who attended in the train of the monarchs was a favorite page of the queen, named Ruyz de Alarcon. To say that he was a favorite page of the queen was at once to speak his eulogium, for every one in the suite of the stately Elizabetta was chosen for grace, and beauty, and accomplishments. He was just turned of eighteen, light and lithe of form, and graceful as a young Antinous. To the queen he was all deference and respect, yet he was at heart a roguish stripling, petted and spoiled by the ladies about the court, and experienced in the ways of women far beyond his years.

This loitering page was one morning rambling about the groves of the Generalife, which overlook the grounds of the Alhambra. He had taken with him for his amusement a favorite gerfalcon of the queen. In the course of his rambles, seeing a bird rising from a thicket, he unhooded the hawk and let him fly. The falcon towered high in the air, made a swoop at his quarry, but missing it, soared away, regardless of the calls of the page. The latter followed the truant bird with his eye, in its capricious flight, until he saw it alight upon the battlements of a remote and lonely tower, in the outer wall of the Alhambra, built on the edge of a ravine that separated the royal fortress from the grounds of the Generalife. It was in fact the "Tower of the Princesses."

The page descended into the ravine and approached the tower, but it had no entrance from the glen, and its lofty height rendered any attempt to scale it fruitless. Seeking one of the gates of the fortress, therefore, he made a wide circuit to that side of the tower facing within the walls.

A small garden, enclosed by a trellis-work of reeds overhung with myrtle, lay before the tower. Opening a wicket, the page passed between beds of flowers and thickets of roses to the door.

It was closed and bolted. A crevice in the door gave him a peep into the interior. There was a small Moorish hall with fretted walls, light marble columns, and an alabaster fountain surrounded with flowers. In the centre hung a gilt cage containing a singing-bird; beneath it, on a chair, lay a tortoise-shell cat among reels of silk and other articles of female labor, and a guitar decorated with ribbons leaned against the fountain.

Ruyz de Alarcon was struck with these traces of female taste and elegance in a lonely, and, as he had supposed, deserted tower. They reminded him of the tales of enchanted halls current in the Alhambra; and the tortoise-shell cat might be some spell-bound princess.

He knocked gently at the door. A beautiful face peeped out from a little window above, but was instantly withdrawn. He waited, expecting that the door would be opened, but he waited in vain; no footstep was to be heard within—all was silent. Had his senses deceived him, or was this beautiful apparition the fairy of the tower? He knocked again, and more loudly. After a little while the beaming face once more peeped forth; it was that of a blooming damsel of fifteen.

The page immediately doffed his plumed bonnet, and entreated in the most courteous accents to be permitted to ascend the tower in pursuit of his falcon.

"I dare not open the door, Señor," replied the little damsel, blushing, "my aunt has forbidden it."

"I do beseech you, fair maid—it is the favorite falcon of the queen: I dare not return to the palace without it."

"Are you then one of the cavaliers of the court?"

"I am, fair maid; but I shall lose the queen's favor and my place, if I lose this hawk."

"Santa Maria! It is against you cavaliers of the court my aunt has charged me especially to bar the door."

"Against wicked cavaliers doubtless, but I am none of these, but a simple, harmless page, who will be ruined and undone if you deny me this small request."

The heart of the little damsel was touched by the distress of the page. It was a thousand pities he sound be ruined for the want of so trifling a boon. Surely too he could not be one of those dangerous beings whom her aunt had described as a species of cannibal, ever on the prowl to make prey of thoughtless damsels; he was gentle and modest, and stood so entreatingly with cap in hand, and looked so charming.

The sly page saw that the garrison began to waver, and redoubled his entreaties in such moving terms that it was not in the nature of mortal maiden to deny him; so the blushing little warden of the tower descended, and opened the door with a trembling hand, and if the page had been charmed by a mere glimpse of her countenance from the window, he was ravished by the full-length portrait now revealed to him.

Her Andalusian bodice and trim basquiña set off the round but delicate symmetry of her form, which was as yet scarce verging into womanhood. Her glossy hair was parted on her forehead with scrupulous exactness, and decorated with a fresh plucked rose, according to the universal custom of the country. It is true her complexion was tinged by the ardor of a southern sun, but it served to give richness to the mantling bloom of her cheek, and to heighten the lustre of her melting eyes.

Ruyz de Alarcon beheld all this with a single glance, for it became him not to tarry; he merely murmured his acknowledgments, and then bounded lightly up the spiral staircase in quest of his falcon.

He soon returned with the truant bird upon his fist. The damsel, in the mean time, had seated herself by the fountain in the hall, and was winding silk; but in her agitation she let fall the reel upon the pavement. The page sprang and picked it up, then dropping gracefully on one knee, presented it to her; but seizing the hand extended to receive it, imprinted on it a kiss more fervent and devout than he had ever imprinted on the fair hand of his sovereign.

"Ave Maria, Señor!" exclaimed the damsel, blushing still deeper with confusion and surprise, for never before had she received such a salutation.

The modest page made a thousand apologies, assuring her it

was the way at court of expressing the most profound homage and respect.

Her anger, if anger she felt, was easily pacified, but her agitation and embarrassment continued, and she sat blushing deeper and deeper, with her eyes cast down upon her work, entangling the silk which she attempted to wind.

The cunning page saw the confusion in the opposite camp, and would fain have profited by it, but the fine speeches he would have uttered died upon his lips; his attempts at gallantry were awkward and ineffectual; and to his surprise, the adroit page, who had figured with such grace and effrontery among the most knowing and experienced ladies of the court, found himself awed and abashed in the presence of a simple damsel of fifteen.

In fact, the artless maiden, in her own modesty and innocence, had guardians more effectual than the bolts and bars prescribed by her vigilant aunt. Still, where is the female bosom proof against the first whisperings of love? The little damsel, with all her artlessness, instinctively comprehended all that the faltering tongue of the page failed to express, and her heart was fluttered at beholding, for the first time, a lover at her feet—and such a lover!

The diffidence of the page, though genuine, was short-lived, and he was recovering his usual ease and confidence, when a shrill voice was heard at a distance.

"My aunt is returning from mass!" cried the damsel in affright: "I pray you, Señor, depart."

"Not until you grant me that rose from your hair as a remembrance."

She hastily untwisted the rose from her raven locks. "Take it," cried she, agitated and blushing, "but pray begone."

The page took the rose, and at the same time covered with kisses the fair hand that gave it. Then, placing the flower in his bonnet, and taking the falcon upon his fist, he bounded off through the garden, bearing away with him the heart of the gentle Jacinta.

When the vigilant aunt arrived at the tower, she remarked the agitation of her niece, and an air of confusion in the hall; but a word of explanation sufficed. "A ger-falcon had pursued his prey into the hall."

"Mercy on us! to think of a falcon flying into the tower. Did ever one hear of so saucy a hawk? Why, the very bird in the cage is not safe!"

The vigilant Fredegonda was one of the most wary of ancient spinsters. She had a becoming terror and distrust of what she denominated "the opposite sex," which had gradually increased through a long life of celibacy. Not that the good lady had ever suffered from their wiles, nature having set up a safeguard in her face that forbade all trespass upon her premises; but ladies who have least cause to fear for themselves are most ready to keep a watch over their more tempting neighbors.

The niece was the orphan of an officer who had fallen in the wars. She had been educated in a convent, and had recently been transferred from her sacred asylum to the immediate guardianship of her aunt, under whose overshadowing care she vegetated in obscurity, like an opening rose blooming beneath a brier. Nor indeed is this comparison entirely accidental; for, to tell the truth, her fresh and dawning beauty had caught the public eye, even in her seclusion, and, with that poetical turn common to the people of Andalusia, the peasantry of the neighborhood had given her the appellation of "the Rose of the Alhambra."

The wary aunt continued to keep a faithful watch over her tempting little niece as long as the court continued at Granada, and flattered herself that her vigilance had been successful. It is true the good lady was now and then discomposed by the tinkling of guitars and chanting of love-ditties from the moonlit groves beneath the tower; but she would exhort her niece to shut her ears against such idle minstrelsy, assuring her that it was one of the arts of the opposite sex, by which simple maids were often lured to their undoing. Alas! what chance with a simple maid has a dry lecture against a moonlight serenade?

At length king Philip cut short his sojourn at Granada, and suddenly departed with all his train. The vigilant Fredegonda watched the royal pageant as it issued forth from the Gate of Justice, and descended the great avenue leading to the city. When the last banner disappeared from her sight, she returned exulting to her tower, for all her cares were over. To her surprise, a light

Arabian steed pawed the ground at the wicket-gate of the garden;
—to her horror she saw through the thickets of roses a youth in
gaily embroidered dress, at the feet of her niece. At the sound of
her footsteps he gave a tender adieu, bounded lightly over the
barrier of reeds and myrtles, sprang upon his horse, and was out
of sight in an instant.

The tender Jacinta, in the agony of her grief, lost all thought
of her aunt's displeasure. Throwing herself into her arms, she
broke forth into sobs and tears.

"Ay de mi!" cried she; "he's gone!—he's gone!—he's gone!
and I shall never see him more!"

"Gone!—who is gone?—what youth is that I saw at your feet?"

"A queen's page, aunt, who came to bid me farewell."

"A queen's page, child!" echoed the vigilant Fredegonda,
faintly, "and when did you become acquainted with the queen's
page?"

"The morning that the ger-falcon came into the tower. It was
the queen's ger-falcon, and he came in pursuit of it."

"Ah silly, silly girl! know that there are no ger-falcons half
so dangerous as these young prankling pages, and it is precisely
such simple birds as thee that they pounce upon."

The aunt was at first indignant at learning that in despite of her
boasted vigilance, a tender intercourse had been carried on by
the youthful lovers, almost beneath her eye; but when she found
that her simple-hearted niece, though thus exposed, without the
protection of bolt or bar, to all the machinations of the opposite
sex, had come forth unsinged from the fiery ordeal, she consoled
herself with the persuasion that it was owing to the chaste and
cautious maxims in which she had, as it were, steeped her to the
very lips.

While the aunt laid this soothing unction to her pride, the niece
treasured up the oft-repeated vows of fidelity of the page. But
what is the love of restless, roving man? A vagrant stream that
dallies for a time with each flower upon its bank, then passes on,
and leaves them all in tears.

Days, weeks, months elapsed, and nothing more was heard
of the page. The pomegranate ripened, the vine yielded up its

fruit, the autumnal rains descended in torrents from the mountains; the Sierra Nevada became covered with a snowy mantle, and wintry blasts howled through the halls of the Alhambra—still he came not. The winter passed away. Again the genial spring burst forth with song and blossom and balmy zephyr; the snows melted from the mountains, until none remained but on the lofty summit of Nevada, glistening through the sultry summer air. Still nothing was heard of the forgetful page.

In the mean time the poor little Jacinta grew pale and thoughtful. Her former occupations and amusements were abandoned, her silk lay entangled, her guitar unstrung, her flowers were neglected, the notes of her bird unheeded, and her eyes, once so bright, were dimmed with secret weeping. If any solitude could be devised to foster the passion of a love-lorn damsel, it would be such a place as the Alhambra, where everything seems disposed to produce tender and romantic reveries. It is a very paradise for lovers: how hard then to be alone in such a paradise—and not merely alone, but forsaken!

"Alas, silly child!" would the staid and immaculate Fredegonda say, when she found her niece in one of her desponding moods— "did I not warn thee against the wiles and deceptions of these men? What couldst thou expect, too, from one of a haughty and aspiring family—thou an orphan, the descendant of a fallen and impoverished line? Be assured, if the youth were true, his father, who is one of the proudest nobles about the court, would prohibit his union with one so humble and portionless as thou. Pluck up thy resolution, therefore, and drive these idle notions from thy mind."

The words of the immaculate Fredegonda only served to increase the melancholy of her niece, but she sought to indulge it in private. At a late hour one midsummer night, after her aunt had retired to rest, she remained alone in the hall of the tower, seated beside the alabaster fountain. It was here that the faithless page had first knelt and kissed her hand; it was here that he had often vowed eternal fidelity. The poor little damsel's heart was overladen with sad and tender recollections, her tears began to flow, and slowly fell drop by drop into the fountain. By degrees the crystal water became agitated, and—bubble—bubble—bubble—boiled up and was tossed about, until a female figure, richly clad in Moorish robes, slowly rose to view.

Jacinta was so frightened that she fled from the hall, and did not venture to return. The next morning she related what she had seen to her aunt, but the good lady treated it as a fantasy of her troubled mind, or supposed she had fallen asleep and dreamt beside the fountain. "Thou hast been thinking of the story of the three Moorish princesses that once inhabited this tower," continued she, "and it has entered into thy dreams."

"What story, aunt? I know nothing of it."

"Thou hast certainly heard of the three princesses, Zayda, Zorayda, and Zorahayda, who were confined in this tower by the king their father, and agreed to fly with three Christian cavaliers. The two first accomplished their escape, but the third failed in her resolution, and, it is said, died in this tower."

"I now recollect to have heard of it," said Jacinta, "and to have wept over the fate of the gentle Zorahayda."

"Thou mayest well weep over her fate," continued the aunt, "for the lover of Zorahayda was thy ancestor. He long bemoaned his Moorish love; but time cured him of his grief, and he married a Spanish lady, from whom thou art descended."

Jacinta ruminated upon these words. "That what I have seen is no fantasy of the brain," said she to herself, "I am confident. If indeed it be the spirit of the gentle Zorahayda, which I have heard lingers about this tower, of what should I be afraid? I'll watch by the fountain to-night—perhaps the visit will be repeated."

Towards midnight, when everything was quiet, she again took her seat in the hall. As the bell in the distant watch-tower of the Alhambra struck the midnight hour, the fountain was again agitated; and bubble—bubble—bubble—it tossed about the waters until the Moorish female again rose to view. She was young and beautiful; her dress was rich with jewels, and in her hand she held a silver lute. Jacinta trembled and was faint, but was reassured by the soft and plaintive voice of the apparition, and the sweet expression of her pale, melancholy countenance.

"Daughter of mortality," said she, "what aileth thee? Why do thy tears trouble my fountain, and thy sighs and plaints disturb the quiet watches of the night?"

"I weep because of the faithlessness of man, and I bemoan my solitary and forsaken state."

"Take comfort; thy sorrows may yet have an end. Thou beholdest a Moorish princess, who, like thee, was unhappy in her love. A Christian knight, thy ancestor, won my heart, and would have borne me to his native land and to the bosom of his church. I was a convert in my heart, but I lacked courage equal to my faith, and lingered till too late. For this the evil genii are permitted to have power over me, and I remain enchanted in this tower until some pure Christian will deign to break the magic spell. Wilt thou undertake the task?"

"I will," replied the damsel, trembling.

"Come hither then, and fear not; dip thy hand in the fountain, sprinkle the water over me, and baptize me after the manner of thy faith; so shall the enchantment be dispelled, and my troubled spirit have repose."

The damsel advanced with faltering steps, dipped her hand in the fountain, collected water in the palm, and sprinkled it over the pale face of the phantom.

The latter smiled with ineffable benignity. She dropped her silver lute at the feet of Jacinta, crossed her white arms upon her bosom, and melted from sight, so that it seemed merely as if a shower of dew-drops had fallen into the fountain.

Jacinta retired from the hall filled with awe and wonder. She scarcely closed her eyes that night; but when she awoke at daybreak out of a troubled slumber, the whole appeared to her like a distempered dream. On descending into the hall, however, the truth of the vision was established, for beside the fountain she beheld the silver lute glittering in the morning sunshine.

She hastened to her aunt, to relate all that had befallen her, and called her to behold the lute as a testimonial of the reality of her story. If the good lady had any lingering doubts, they were removed when Jacinta touched the instrument, for she drew forth such ravishing tones as to thaw even the frigid bosom of the immaculate Fredegonda, that region of eternal winter, into a genial flow. Nothing but supernatural melody could have produced such an effect.

The extraordinary power of the lute became every day more and more apparent. The wayfarer passing by the tower was detained, and, as it were, spell-bound, in breathless ecstasy. The very birds gathered in the neighboring trees, and hushing their own strains, listened in charmed silence.

Rumor soon spread the news abroad. The inhabitants of Granada thronged to the Alhambra to catch a few notes of the transcendent music that floated about the tower of Las Infantas.

The lovely little minstrel was at length drawn forth from her retreat. The rich and powerful of the land contended who should entertain and do honor to her; or rather, who should secure the charms of her lute to draw fashionable throngs to their saloons. Wherever she went her vigilant aunt kept a dragon watch at her elbow, awing the throngs of impassioned admirers who hung in raptures on her strains. The report of her wonderful powers spread from city to city. Malaga, Seville, Cordova, all became successively mad on the theme; nothing was talked of throughout Andalusia but the beautiful minstrel of the Alhambra. How could it be otherwise among a people so musical and gallant as the Andalusians, when the lute was magical in its powers, and the minstrel inspired by love!

While all Andalusia was thus music mad, a different mood prevailed at the court of Spain. Philip V., as is well known, was a miserable hypochondriac, and subject to all kinds of fancies. Sometimes he would keep to his bed for weeks together, groaning under imaginary complaints. At other times he would insist upon abdicating his throne, to the great annoyance of his royal spouse, who had a strong relish for the splendors of a court and the glories of a crown, and guided the sceptre of her imbecile lord with an expert and steady hand.

Nothing was found to be so efficacious in dispelling the royal megrims as the power of music; the queen took care, therefore, to have the best performers, both vocal and instrumental, at hand,

and retained the famous Italian singer Farinelli about the court as a kind of royal physician.

At the moment we treat of, however, a freak had come over the mind of this sapient and illustrious Bourbon that surpassed all former vagaries. After a long spell of imaginary illness, which set all the strains of Farinelli and the consultations of a whole orchestra of court-fiddlers at defiance, the monarch fairly, in idea, gave up the ghost, and considered himself absolutely dead.

This would have been harmless enough, and even convenient both to his queen and courtiers, had he been content to remain in the quietude befitting a dead man; but to their annoyance he insisted upon having the funeral ceremonies performed over him, and, to their inexpressible perplexity, began to grow impatient, and to revile bitterly at them for negligence and disrespect, in leaving him unburied. What was to be done? To disobey the king's positive commands was monstrous in the eyes of the obsequious courtiers of a punctilious court—but to obey him, and bury him alive would be downright regicide!

In the midst of this fearful dilemma a rumor reached the court of the female minstrel who was turning the brains of all Andalusia. The queen dispatched missions in all haste to summon her to St. Ildefonso, where the court at that time resided.

Within a few days, as the queen with her maids of honor was walking in those stately gardens, intended, with their avenues and terraces and fountains, to eclipse the glories of Versailles, the far-famed minstrel was conducted into her presence. The imperial Elizabetta gazed with surprise at the youthful and unpretending appearance of the little being that had set the world madding. She was in her picturesque Andalusian dress, her silver lute in hand, and stood with modest and downcast eyes, but with a simplicity and freshness of beauty that still bespoke her "the Rose of the Alhambra."

As usual she was accompanied by the evervigilant Fredegonda, who gave the whole history of her parentage and descent to the inquiring queen. If the stately Elizabetta had been interested by the appearance of Jacinta, she was still more pleased when she learnt that she was of a meritorious though impoverished line, and that her father had bravely fallen in the service of the crown. "If thy powers equal their renown," said she, "and thou canst cast forth this evil spirit that possesses thy sovereign, thy fortunes shall henceforth be my care, and honors and wealth attend thee."

Impatient to make trial of her skill, she led the way at once to the apartment of the moody monarch.

Jacinta followed with downcast eyes through files of guards and crowds of courtiers. They arrived at length at a great chamber hung with black. The windows were closed to exclude the light of day: a number of yellow wax tapers in silver sconces diffused a lugubrious light, and dimly revealed the figures of mutes in mourning dresses, and courtiers who glided about with noiseless step and woe-begone visage. In the midst of a funeral bed or bier, his hands folded on his breast, and the tip of his nose just visible, lay extended this would-be-buried monarch.

The queen entered the chamber in silence, and pointing to a footstool in an obscure corner, beckoned to Jacinta to sit down and commence.

At first she touched her lute with a faltering hand, but gathering confidence and animation as she proceeded, drew forth such soft aërial harmony, that all present could scarce believe it mortal. As to the monarch, who had already considered himself in the world of spirits, he set it down for some angelic melody or the music of the spheres. By degrees the theme was varied, and the voice of the minstrel accompanied the instrument. She poured forth one of the legendary ballads treating of the ancient glories of the Alhambra and the achievements of the Moors. Her whole soul entered into the theme, for with the recollections of the Alhambra was associated the story of her love. The funeral-chamber resounded with the animating strain. It entered into the gloomy heart of the monarch. He raised his head and gazed around: he sat up on his couch, his eye began to kindle—at length, leaping upon the floor, he called for sword and buckler.

The triumph of music, or rather of the enchanted lute, was complete; the demon of melancholy was cast forth; and, as it were, a dead man brought to life. The windows of the apartment were thrown open; the glorious effulgence of Spanish sunshine burst into the late lugubrious chamber; all eyes sought the lovely enchantress, but the lute had fallen from her hand, she had sunk upon the earth, and the next moment was clasped to the bosom of Ruyz de Alarcon.

The nuptials of the happy couple were celebrated soon afterwards with great splendor, and the Rose of the Alhambra became the ornament and delight of the court. "But hold—not so fast"— I hear the reader exclaim; "this is jumping to the end of a story at a furious rate! First let us know how Ruyz de Alarcon managed to account to Jacinta for his long neglect?" Nothing more easy; the venerable, time-honored excuse, the opposition to his wishes by a proud, pragmatical old father: besides, young people who really like one another soon come to an amicable understanding, and bury all past grievances when once they meet.

But how was the proud, pragmatical old father reconciled to the match?

Oh! as to that, his scruples were easily overcome by a word or two from the queen; especially as dignities and rewards were showered upon the blooming favorite of royalty. Besides, the lute of Jacinta, you know, possessed a magic power, and could control the most stubborn head and hardest breast.

And what came of the enchanted lute?

Oh, that is the most curious matter of all, and plainly proves the truth of the whole story. That lute remained for some time in the family, but was purloined and carried off, as was supposed, by the great singer Farinelli, in pure jealousy. At his death it passed into other hands in Italy, who were ignorant of its mystic powers, and melting down the silver, transferred the strings to an old Cremona fiddle. The strings still retain something of their magic virtues. A word in the reader's ear, but let it go no further: that fiddle is now bewitching the whole world,—it is the fiddle of Paganini!

A TOUR ON THE PRAIRIES

CHAPTER VII

News of the Rangers—The Count and His Indian Squire—Halt in the Woods—Woodland Scene—Osage Village—Osage Visitors at Our Evening Camp

IN THE MORNING EARLY, (Oct. 12,) the two Creeks who had been sent express by the commander of Fort Gibson, to stop the company of rangers, arrived at our encampment on their return. They had left the company encamped about fifty miles distant, in a fine place on the Arkansas, abounding in game, where they intended to await out arrival. This news spread animation throughout our party, and we set out on our march, at sunrise, with renewed spirit.

In mounting our steeds, the young Osage attempted to throw a blanket upon his wild horse. The fine, sensitive animal took fright, reared and recoiled. The attitudes of the wild horse and the almost naked savage would have formed studies for a painter or a statuary.

I often pleased myself, in the course of our march, with noticing the appearance of the young Count and his newly enlisted follower, as they rode before me. Never was preux chavalier better suited with an esquire. The Count was well mounted, and, as I have before observed, was a bold and graceful rider. He was fond, too, of caracoling his horse, and dashing about in the buoyancy of youthful spirits. His dress was a gay Indian hunting-frock, of dressed deer-skin, setting well to the shape, dyed of a beautiful purple, and fancifully embroidered with silks of various colors; as if it had been the work of some Indian beauty, to decorate a favorite chief. With this he wore leathern pantaloons and moccasons, a foraging-cap, and a double-barrelled gun slung by a bandoleer athwart his back: so that he was quite a picturesque figure as he managed gracefully his spirited steed.

The young Osage would ride close behind him on his wild and beautifully mottled horse, which was decorated with crimson tufts of hair. He rode, with his finely shaped head and bust naked; his blanket being girt round his waist. He carried his rifle in one hand, and managed his horse with the other, and seemed ready to dash off at a moment's warning, with his youthful leader, on any madcap foray or scamper. The Count, with the sanguine anticipations of youth, promised himself many hardy adventures and exploits in company with his youthful "brave," when we should get among the buffaloes, in the Pawnee hunting-grounds.

After riding some distance, we crossed a narrow, deep stream, upon a solid bridge, the remains of an old beaver dam; the industrious community which had constructed it had all been destroyed. Above us, a streaming flight of wild geese, high in air, and making a vociferous noise, gave note of the waning year.

About half-past ten o'clock we made a halt in a forest, where there was abundance of the pea-vine. Here we turned the horses loose to graze. A fire was made, water procured from an adjacent spring, and in a short time our little Frenchman, Tonish, had a pot of coffee prepared for our refreshment. While partaking of it, we were joined by an old Osage, one of a small hunting party who had recently passed this way. He was in search of his horse, which had wandered away, or been stolen. Our half-breed, Beatte, made a wry face on hearing of Osage hunters in this direction. "Until we pass those hunters," said he, "we shall see no buffaloes. They frighten away everything like a prairie on fire."

The morning repast being over, the party amused themselves in various ways. Some shot with their rifles at a mark, others lay asleep half buried in the deep bed of foliage, with their heads resting on their saddles; others gossiped round the fire at the foot of a tree, which sent up wreaths of blue smoke among the branches. The horses banqueted luxuriously on the pea-vines, and some lay down and rolled amongst them.

We were overshadowed by lofty trees, with straight, smooth trunks, like stately columns; and as the glancing rays of the sun shone through the transparent leaves, tinted with the many-colored hues of autumn, I was reminded of the effect of sunshine among the stained windows and clustering columns of a Gothic cathedral. Indeed there is a grandeur and solemnity in our spacious forests of the West, that awaken in me the same feeling I have experienced in those vast and venerable piles, and the sound of the wind sweeping through them supplies occasionally the deep breathings of the organ.

About noon the bugle sounded to horse, and we were again on the march, hoping to arrive at the encampment of the rangers before night; as the old Osage had assured us it was not above ten or twelve miles distant. In our course through a forest, we passed by a lonely pool, covered with the most magnificent water-lilies I had ever beheld; among which swam several wood-ducks, one of the most beautiful of water-fowl, remarkable for the gracefulness and brilliancy of its plumage.

After proceeding some distance farther, we came down upon the banks of the Arkansas, at a place where tracks of numerous horses, all entering the water, showed where a party of Osage hunters had recently crossed the river on their way to the buffalo range. After letting our horses drink in the river, we continued along its bank for a space, and then across prairies, where we saw a distant smoke, which we hoped might proceed from the encampment of the rangers. Following what we supposed to be their trail, we came to a meadow in which were a number of horses grazing: they were not, however, the horses of the troop. A little farther on, we reached a straggling Osage village, on the banks of the Arkansas. Our arrival created quite a sensation. A number of old men came forward and shook hands with us all severally; while the women and children huddled together in groups, staring at us wildly, chattering and laughing among themselves. We found that all the young men of the village had departed on a hunting expedition, leaving the women and children and old men behind.

Here the Commissioner made a speech from on Horseback; informing his hearers of the purport of his mission, to promote a general peace among the tribes of the West, and urging them to lay aside all warlike and bloodthirsty notions, and not to make any wanton attacks upon the Pawnees. This speech being interpreted by Beatte, seemed to have a most pacifying effect upon the multitude, who promised faithfully that, as far as in them lay, the peace should not be disturbed; and indeed their age and sex gave some reason to trust that they would keep their word.

Still hoping to reach the camp of the rangers before nightfall, we pushed on until twilight, when we were obliged to halt on the borders of a ravine. The rangers bivouacked under trees, at the bottom of the dell, while we pitched our tent on a rocky knoll near a running stream. The night came on dark and overcast, with flying clouds, and much appearance of rain. The fires of the rangers burnt brightly in the dell, and threw strong masses of light upon the robber-looking groups that were cooking, eating, and drinking around them. To add to the wildness of the scene, several Osage Indians, visitors from the village we had passed, were mingled among the men. Three of them came and seated themselves by our fire. They watched everything that was going on round them in silence, and looked like figures of monumental bronze. We gave them food, and, what they most relished, coffee; for the Indians partake in the universal fondness for this beverage, which pervades the West. When they had made their supper, they stretched themselves side by side before the fire, and began a low nasal chant, drumming with their hands upon their breasts by way of accompaniment. Their chant seemed to consist of regular staves, every one terminating, not in a melodious cadence, but in the abrupt interjection huh! uttered almost like a hiccup. This chant, we were told by our interpreter, Beatte, related to ourselves, our appearance, our treatment of them, and all that they knew of our plans. In one part they spoke of the young Count, whose animated character and eagerness for Indian enterprise had struck their fancy, and they indulged in some waggery about him and the young Indian beauties, that produced great merriment among our half-breeds.

This mode of improvising is common throughout the savage tribes; and in this way, with a few simple inflections of the voice, they chant all their exploits in war and hunting, and occasionally indulge in a vein of comic humor and dry satire, to which the Indians appear to me much more prone than is generally imagined.

In fact, the Indians that I have had an opportunity of seeing in real life are quite different from those described in poetry. They are by no means the stoics that they are represented; taciturn, unbending, without a tear or a smile. Taciturn they are, it is true, when in company with white men, whose good-will they distrust, and whose language they do not understand; but the white man is equally taciturn under like circumstances. When the Indians are among themselves, however, there cannot be greater gossips. Half their time is taken up in talking over their adventures in war and hunting, and in telling whimsical stories. They are great mimics and buffoons, also, and entertain themselves excessively at the expense of the whites with whom they have associated, and who have supposed them impressed with profound respect for their grandeur and dignity. They are curious observers, noting everything in silence, but with a keen and watchful eye; occasionally exchanging a glance or a grunt with each other, when anything particularly strikes them; but reserving all comments until they are alone. Then it is that they give full scope to criticism, satire, mimicry, and mirth.

In the course of my journey along the frontier I have had repeated opportunities of noticing their excitability and boisterous merriment at their games; and have occasionally noticed a group of Osages sitting round a fire until a late hour of the night, engaged in the most animated and lively conversation; and at times making the woods resound with peals of laughter. As to tears, they have them in abundance, both real and affected; at times they make a merit of them. No one weeps more bitterly or profusely at the death of a relative or friend; and they have stated times when they repair to howl and lament at their graves. I have heard doleful wailings at daybreak, in the neighboring Indian villages, made by some of the inhabitants, who go out at that hour into the fields to mourn and weep for the dead: at such times, I am told, the tears will stream down their cheeks in torrents.

As far as I can judge, the Indian of poetical fiction is, like the shepherd of pastoral romance, a mere personification of imaginary attributes.

The nasal chant of our Osage guests gradually died away; they covered their heads with their blankets and fell fast asleep, and in a little while all was silent, excepting the pattering of scattered rain-drops upon our tent.

In the morning our Indian visitors breakfasted with us, but the young Osage who was to act as esquire to the Count in his knight-errantry on the prairies, was nowhere to be found. His wild horse, too, was missing, and, after many conjectures, we came to the conclusion that he had taken "Indian leave" of us in the night. We afterwards ascertained that he had been persuaded so to do by the Osages we had recently met with; who had represented to him the perils that would attend him in an expedition to the Pawnee hunting-grounds, where he might fall into the hands of the implacable enemies of his tribe; and, what was scarcely less to be apprehended, the annoyances to which he would be subjected from the capricious and overbearing conduct of the white men; who, as I have witnessed in my own short experience, are prone to treat the poor Indians as little better than brute animals. Indeed, he had had a specimen of it himself in the narrow escape he made from the infliction of "Lynch's law," by the hard-winking worthy of the frontier, for the flagitious crime of finding a stray horse.

The disappearance of the youth was generally regretted by our party, for we had all taken a great fancy to him from his handsome, frank, and manly appearance, and the easy grace of his deportment. He was indeed a native-born gentleman. By none, however, was he so much lamented as by the young Count, who thus suddenly found himself deprived of his esquire. I regretted the departure of the Osage for his own sake, for we should have cherished him throughout the expedition, and I am convinced,

from the munificent spirit of his patron, he would have returned
to his tribe laden with wealth of beads and trinkets and Indian
blankets.

CHAPTER VIII

The Honey Camp

THE WEATHER, WHICH HAD been rainy in the night, having
held up, we resumed our march at seven o'clock in the morning,
in confident hope of soon arriving at the encampment of the
rangers. We had not ridden above three or four miles when we
came to a large tree which had recently been felled by an axe,
for the wild honey contained in the hollow of its trunk, several
broken flakes of which still remained. We now felt sure that the
camp could not be far distant. About a couple of miles farther
some of the rangers set up a shout, and pointed to a number of
horses grazing in a woody bottom. A few paces brought us to the
brow of an elevated ridge, whence we looked down upon the encampment. It was a wild bandit, or Robin Hood, scene. In a beautiful open forest, traversed by a running stream, were booths of
bark and branches, and tents of blankets,—temporary shelters
from the recent rain, for the rangers commonly bivouac in the
open air. There were groups of rangers in every kind of uncouth
garb. Some were cooking at large fires made at the feet of trees;
some were stretching and dressing deer-skins; some were shooting
at a mark, and some lying about on the grass. Venison jerked, and
hung on frames, was drying over the embers in one place; in another lay carcasses recently brought in by the hunters. Stacks of
rifles were leaning against the trunks of the trees, and saddles,
bridles, and powder-horns hanging above them, while the horses
were grazing here and there among the thickets.

Our arrival was greeted with acclamation. The rangers crowded about their comrades to inquire the news from the fort. For our own part, we were received in frank simple hunter's style by Captain Bean, the commander of the company; a man about forty years of age, vigorous and active. His life had been chiefly passed on the frontier, occasionally in Indian warfare so that he was a thorough woodsman, and a first-rate hunter. He was equipped in character; in leathern hunting-shirt and leggins, and a leathern foraging-cap.

While we were conversing with the Captain, a veteran huntsman approached, whose whole appearance struck me. He was of the middle size, but tough and weather-proved; a head partly bald and garnished with loose iron-gray locks, and a fine black eye, beaming with youthful spirit. His dress was similar to that of the Captain; a rifle-shirt and leggins of dressed deer-skin, that had evidently seen service; a powder-horn was slung by his side, a hunting-knife stuck in his belt, and in his hand was an ancient and trusty rifle, doubtless as dear to him as a bosom-friend. He asked permission to go hunting, which was readily granted. "That's old Ryan," said the Captain, when he had gone; "there's not a better hunter in the camp; he's sure to bring in game."

In a little while our pack-horses were unloaded and turned loose to revel among the pea-vines. Our tent was pitched; our fire made; the half of a deer had been sent to us from the Captain's lodge; Beatte brought in a couple of wild turkeys; the spits were laden, and the camp-kettle crammed with meat; and, to crown our luxuries, a basin filled with great flakes of delicious honey, the spoils of a plundered bee-tree, was given us by one of the rangers.

Our little Frenchman, Tonish, was in an ecstasy, and tucking up his sleeves to the elbows, set to work to make a display of his culinary skill, on which he prided himself almost as much as upon his hunting, his riding, and his warlike prowess.

CHAPTER IX

A Bee-Hunt

THE BEAUTIFUL FOREST in which we were encamped abounded
in bee-trees; that is to say, trees in the decayed trunks of which
wild bees had established their hives. It is surprising in what
countless swarms the bees have overspread the Far West within
but a moderate number of years. The Indians consider them the
harbinger of the white man, as the buffalo is of the red man; and
say that, in proportion as the bee advances, the Indian and buffalo retire. We are always accustomed to associate the hum of the
bee-hive with the farm-house and flower-garden, and to consider
those industrious little animals as connected with the busy haunts
of man; and I am told that the wild bee is seldom to be met with
at any great distance from the frontier. They have been the her-
alds of civilization, steadfastly preceding it as it advanced from
the Atlantic borders, and some of the ancient settlers of the West
pretend to give the very year when the honey-bee first crossed
the Mississippi. The Indians with surprise found the mouldering
trees of their forests suddenly teeming with ambrosial sweets, and
nothing, I am told, can exceed the greedy relish with which they
banquet for the first time upon this unbought luxury of the wilderness.

At present the honey-bee swarms in myriads, in the noble
groves and forests which skirt and intersect the prairies, and extend along the alluvial bottoms of the rivers. It seems to me as
if these beautiful regions answer literally to the description of
the land of promise, "a land flowing with milk and honey"; for
the rich pasturage of the prairies is calculated to sustain herds of
cattle as countless as the sands upon the sea-shore, while the flowers with which they are enamelled render them a very paradise
for the nectar-seeking bee.

We had not been long in the camp when a party set out in
quest of a bee-tree; and, being curious to witness the sport, I

gladly accepted an invitation to accompany them. The party was headed by a veteran bee-hunter, a tall, lank fellow in homespun garb that hung loosely about his limbs, and a straw hat shaped not unlike a bee-hive; a comrade, equally uncouth in garb, and without a hat, straddled along at his heels, with a long rifle on his shoulder. To these succeeded half a dozen others, some with axes and some with rifles, for no one stirs far from the camp without his firearms, so as to be ready either for wild deer or wild Indian.

After proceeding some distance, we came to an open glade on the skirts of the forest. Here our leader halted, and then advanced quietly to a low bush, on the top of which I perceived a piece of honey-comb. This I found was the bait or lure for the wild bees. Several were humming about it, and diving into its cells. When they had laden themselves with honey, they would rise into the air, and dart off in a straight line, almost with the velocity of a bullet. The hunters watched attentively the course they took, and then set off in the same direction, stumbling along over twisted roots and fallen trees, with their eyes turned up to the sky. In this way they traced the honey-laden bees to their hive, in the hollow trunk of a blasted oak, where, after buzzing about for a moment, they entered a hole about sixty feet from the ground.

Two of the bee-hunters now plied their axes vigorously at the foot of the tree, to level it with the ground. The mere spectators and amateurs, in the meantime, drew off to a cautious distance, to be out of the way of the falling of the tree and the vengeance of its inmates. The jarring blows of the axe, seemed to have no effect in alarming or disturbing this most industrious community. They continued to ply at their usual occupations, some arriving full freighted into port, others sallying forth on new expeditions, like so many merchantmen in a money-making metropolis, little suspicious of impending bankruptcy and downfall. Even a loud crack which announced the disrupture of the trunk, failed to divert their attention from the intense pursuit of gain; at length down came the tree with a tremendous crash, bursting open from end to end, and displaying all the horded treasures of the commonwealth.

One of the hunters immediately ran up with a wisp of lighted hay as a defense against the bees. The latter, however, made no attack and sought no revenge; they seemed stupefied by the catastrophe and unsuspicious of its cause, and remained crawling and buzzing about the ruins without offering us any molestation. Every one of the party now fell to, with spoon and hunting-knife, to scoop out the flakes of honey-comb with which the hollow trunk was stored. Some of them were of old date and a deep brown color, others were beautifully white, and the honey in their cells was almost limpid. Such of the combs as were entire were placed in camp-kettles to be conveyed to the encampment; those which had been shivered in the fall were devoured upon the spot. Every stark bee-hunter was to be seen with a rich morsel in his hand, dripping about his fingers, and disappearing as rapidly as a cream tart before the holiday appetite of a schoolboy.

Nor was it the bee-hunters alone that profited by the downfall of this industrious community: as if the bees would carry through the similitude of their habits with those of laborious and gainful man, I beheld numbers from rival hives, arriving on eager wing, to enrich themselves with the ruins of their neighbors. These busied themselves as eagerly and cheerfully as so many wreckers on an Indiaman that has been driven on shore; plunging into the cells of the broken honey-combs, banqueting greedily on the spoil, and then winging their way full freighted to their homes. As to the poor proprietors of the ruin, they seemed to have no heart to do anything, not even to taste the nectar that flowed around them; but crawled backwards and forwards, in vacant desolation, as I have seen a poor fellow with his hands in his pockets, whistling vacantly and despondingly about the ruins of his house that had been burnt.

It is difficult to describe the bewilderment and confusion of the bees of the bankrupt hive who had been absent at the time of the catastrophe, and who arrived from time to time, with full cargoes from abroad. At first they wheeled about in the air, in the place where the fallen tree had once reared its head, astonished at finding it all a vacuum. At length, as if comprehending their disaster, they settled down in clusters on a dry branch of a neighboring tree, whence they seemed to contemplate the pros-

trate ruin, and to buzz forth doleful lamentations over the downfall of their republic. It was a scene on which the "melancholy
Jacques" might have moralized by the hour.

We now abandoned the place, leaving much honey in the hollow of the tree. "It will all be cleared off by varmint," said one of
the rangers. "What vermin?" asked I. "Oh, bears, and skunks,
and raccoons, and 'possums. The bears is the knowingest varmint
for finding out a bee-tree in the world. They'll gnaw for days together at the trunk till they make a hole big enough to get in
their paws, and then they'll haul out honey, bees, and all."

CHAPTER X

Amusements in the Camp—Consultations—Hunters' Fare and Feasting—
Evening Scenes—Camp Melody—The Fate of an Amateur Owl

ON RETURNING TO THE CAMP, we found it a scene of the greatest
hilarity. Some of the rangers were shooting at a mark, others were
leaping, wrestling, and playing at prison-bars. They were mostly
young men, on their first expedition, in high health and vigor,
and buoyant with anticipations; and I can conceive nothing more
likely to set the youthful blood into a flow than a wild wood-life
of the kind, and the range of a magnificent wilderness, abounding
with game, and fruitful of adventure. We send our youth abroad
to grow luxurious and effeminate in Europe; it appears to me that
a previous tour on the prairies would be more likely to produce
that manliness, simplicity, and self-dependence most in unison
with our political institutions.

While the young men were engaged in these boisterous amusements, a graver set, composed of the Captain, the Doctor, and
other sages and leaders of the camp, were seated or stretched out
on the grass, round a frontier map, holding a consultation about
our position, and the course we were to pursue.

Our plan was to cross the Arkansas just above where the Red Fork falls into it, then to keep westerly, until we should pass through a grand belt of open forest, called the Cross Timber, which ranges nearly north and south from the Arkansas to Red River; after which we were to keep a southerly course towards the latter river.

Our half-breed, Beatte, being an experienced Osage hunter, was called into the consultation. "Have you ever hunted in this direction?" said the Captain. "Yes," was the laconic reply.

"Perhaps, then, you can tell us in which direction lies the Red Fork?"

"If you keep along yonder, by the edge of the prairie, you will come to a bald hill, with a pile of stones upon it."

"I have noticed that hill as I was hunting," said the Captain.

"Well! those stones were set up by the Osages as a landmark: from that spot you may have a sight of the Red Fork."

"In that case," cried the Captain, "we shall reach the Red Fork to-morrow; then cross the Arkansas above it, into the Pawnee country, and then in two days we shall crack buffalo bones!"

The idea of arriving at the adventurous hunting-grounds of the Pawnees, and of coming upon the traces of the buffaloes, made every eye sparkle with animation. Our further conversation was interrupted by the sharp report of a rifle at no great distance from the camp.

"That's old Ryan's rifle," exclaimed the Captain; "there's a buck down, I'll warrant!" nor was he mistaken; for, before long, the veteran made his appearance, calling upon one of the younger rangers to return with him, and aid in bringing home the carcass.

The surrounding country, in fact, abounded with game, so that the camp was overstocked with provisions, and, as no less than twenty bee-trees had been cut down in the vicinity, every one revelled in luxury. With the wasteful prodigality of hunters, there was a continual feasting, and scarce any one put by provision for the morrow. The cooking was conducted in hunters' style: the meat was stuck upon tapering spits of dogwood, which were thrust perpendicularly into the ground, so as to sustain the joint before the fire, where it was roasted or broiled with all its juices retained in it in a manner that would have tickled the palate of the most experienced gourmand. As much could not be said in favor of the bread. It was little more than a paste made of flour and water, and fried like fritters, in lard: though some adopted a ruder style, twisting it round the ends of sticks, and thus roasting it before the fire. In either way, I have found it extremely palatable on the prairies. No one knows the true relish of food until he has a hunter's appetite.

Before sunset, we were summoned by little Tonish to a sumptuous repast. Blankets had been spread on the ground near to the fire, upon which we took our seats. A large dish, or bowl, made from the root of a maple-tree, and which we had purchased at the Indian village, was placed on the ground before us, and into it were emptied the contents of one of the camp-kettles, consisting of a wild turkey hashed, together with slices of bacon and lumps of dough. Beside it was placed another bowl of similar ware, containing an ample supply of fritters. After we had discussed the hash, two wooden spits, on which the ribs of a fat buck were broiling before the fire, were removed and planted in the ground before us, with a triumphant air, by little Tonish. Having no dishes, we had to proceed in hunters' style, cutting off strips and slices with our hunting knives, and dipping them in salt and pepper. To do justice to Tonish's cookery, however, and to the keen sauce of the prairies, never have I tasted venison so delicious. With all this, our beverage was coffee, boiled in a camp-kettle, sweetened with brown sugar, and drunk out of tin cups: and such was the style of our banqueting throughout this expedition, whenever provisions were plenty, and as long as flour and coffee and sugar held out.

As the twilight thickened into night, the sentinels were marched forth to their stations around the camp: an indispensable precaution in a country infested by Indians. The encampment now presented a picturesque appearance. Camp-fires were blazing and smouldering here and there among the trees, with groups of rangers round them; some seated or lying on the ground, others standing in the ruddy glare of the flames, or in shadowy relief. At some of the fires there was much boisterous mirth, where peals of laughter were mingled with loud ribald jokes and uncouth exclamations; for the troop was evidently a raw, undisciplined band, levied among the wild youngsters of the frontier, who had enlisted, some for the sake of roving adventure, and some for the purpose of getting a knowledge of the country. Many of them were the neighbors of their officers, and accustomed to regard them with the familiarity of equals and companions. None of them had any idea of the restraint and decorum of a camp, or ambition to acquire a name for exactness in a profession in which they had no intention of continuing.

While this boisterous merriment prevailed at some of the fires, there suddenly rose a strain of nasal melody from another, at which a choir of "vocalists" were uniting their voices in a most lugubrious psalm-tune. This was led by one of the lieutenants; a tall, spare man, who we were informed had officiated as school-master, singing-master, and occasionally as Methodist preacher, in one of the villages of the frontier. The chant rose solemnly and sadly in the night air, and reminded me of the description of similar canticles in the camps of the Covenanters; and, indeed, the strange medley of figures and faces and uncouth garbs congregated together in our troop would not have disgraced the banners of Praise-God Barebone.

In one of the intervals of this nasal psalmody an amateur owl, as if in competition, began his dreary hooting. Immediately there was a cry throughout the camp of "Charley's owl! Charley's owl!" It seems this "obscure bird" had visited the camp every night, and had been fired at by one of the sentinels, a half-witted lad named Charley; who, on being called up for firing when on duty, excused himself by saying, that he understood that owls made uncommonly good soup.

One of the young rangers mimicked the cry of this bird of wisdom, who, with a simplicity little consonant with his character, came hovering within sight, and alighted on the naked branch of a tree lit up by the blaze of our fire. The young Count immediately seized his fowling-piece, took fatal aim, and in a twinkling the poor bird of ill omen came fluttering to the ground. Charley was now called upon to make and eat his dish of owl-soup, but declined, as he had not shot the bird.

In the course of the evening I paid a visit to the Captain's fire. It was composed of huge trunks of trees, and of sufficient magnitude to roast a buffalo whole. Here were a number of the prime hunters and leaders of the camp, some sitting, some standing, and others lying on skins or blankets before the fire, telling old frontier stories about hunting and Indian warfare.

As the night advanced, we perceived above the trees, to the west, a ruddy glow flushing up the sky.

"That must be a prairie set on fire by the Osage hunters," said the Captain.

"It is at the Red Fork," said Beatte, regarding the sky. "It seems but three miles distant, yet it perhaps is twenty."

About half-past eight o'clock, a beautiful pale light gradually sprang up in the east, a precursor of the rising moon. Drawing off from the Captain's lodge, I now prepared for the night's repose. I had determined to abandon the shelter of the tent, and henceforth to bivouac like the rangers. A bear-skin spread at the foot of a tree was my bed, with a pair of saddle-bags for a pillow. Wrapping myself in blankets, I stretched myself on this hunter's couch, and soon fell into a sound and sweet sleep, from which I did not awake until the bugle sounded at daybreak.

CHAPTER XXIX

The Grand Prairie—A Buffalo Hunt

AFTER PROCEEDING about two hours in a southerly direction, we emerged towards mid-day from the dreary belt of the Cross Timber, and to our infinite delight beheld "the Great Prairie," stretching to the right and left before us. We could distinctly trace the meandering course of the Main Canadian, and various smaller streams, by the strips of green forests that bordered them.

The landscape was vast and beautiful. There is always an expansion of feeling in looking upon these boundless and fertile wastes; but I was doubly conscious of it after emerging from our "close dungeon of innumerous boughs."

From a rising ground Beatte pointed out the place where he and his comrades had killed the buffaloes; and we beheld several black objects moving in the distance, which he said were part of the herd. The Captain determined to shape his course to a woody bottom about a mile distant, and to encamp there for a day or two, by way of having a regular buffalo-hunt, and getting a supply of provisions. As the troop defiled along the slope of the hill towards the camping-ground, Beatte proposed to my messmates and myself, that we should put ourselves under his guidance, promising to take us where we should have plenty of sport. Leaving the line of march, therefore, we diverged towards the prairie; traversing a small valley, and ascending a gentle swell of land. As we reached the summit, we beheld a gang of wild horses about a mile off. Beatte was immediately on the alert, and no longer thought of buffalo-hunting. He was mounted on his powerful half-wild horse, with a lariat coiled at the saddle-bow, and set off in pursuit; while we remained on a rising ground watching his manœuvres with great solicitude. Taking advantage of a strip of woodland, he stole quietly along, so as to get close to them before he was perceived. The moment they caught sight of him a grand scamper took place. We watched him skirting along the horizon like a privateer in full chase of a merchantman; at length he passed over the brow of a ridge, and down into a shallow valley; in a few moments he was on the opposite hill, and close upon one of the horses. He was soon head and head, and appeared to be trying to noose his prey; but they both disappeared again below the hill, and we saw no more of them. It turned out afterwards that he had noosed a powerful horse, but could not hold him, and had lost his lariat in the attempt.

While we were waiting for his return, we perceived two buffalo bulls descending a slope, towards a stream, which wound through a ravine fringed with trees. The young Count and myself endeavored to get near them under covert of the trees. They discovered us while we were yet three or four hundred yards off, and turning about, retreated up the rising ground. We urged our horses across the ravine, and gave chase. The immense weight of head and shoulders causes the buffalo to labor heavily up-hill; but it accelerates his descent. We had the advantage, therefore, and gained rapidly upon the fugitives, though it was difficult to get our horses to approach them, their very scent inspiring them with terror. The Count, who had a double-barrelled gun loaded with ball, fired, but it missed. The bulls now altered their course, and galloped down-hill with headlong rapidity. As they ran in different directions, we each singled one and separated. I was provided with a brace of veteran brass-barrelled pistols, which I had borrowed at Fort Gibson, and which had evidently seen some service. Pistols are very effective in buffalo hunting, as the hunter can ride up close to the animal, and fire it while at full speed; whereas the long heavy rifles used on the frontier, cannot be easily managed, nor discharged with accurate aim from horseback. My object, therefore, was to get within pistol-shot of the buffalo. This was no very easy matter. I was well mounted on a horse of excellent speed and bottom, that seemed eager for the chase, and soon overtook the game; but the moment he came nearly parallel, he would keep sheering off, with ears forked and pricked forward, and every symptom of aversion and alarm. It was no wonder. Of all animals, a buffalo, when close pressed by the hunter, has an aspect the most diabolical. His two short black horns curve out of a huge frontlet of shaggy hair; his eyes glow like coals; his mouth is open; his tongue parched and drawn up into a half crescent; his tail is erect, and tufted and whisking about in the air: he is a perfect picture of mingled rage and terror.

It was with difficulty I urged my horse sufficiently near, when, taking aim, to my chagrin both pistols missed fire. Unfortunately the locks of these veteran weapons were so much worn, that in the gallop the priming had been shaken out of the pans. At the snapping of the last pistol I was close upon the buffalo, when, in his despair, he turned round with a sudden snort, and rushed upon me. My horse wheeled about as if on a pivot, made a convulsive spring, and, as I had been leaning on one side with pistol extended, I came near being thrown at the feet of the buffalo.

Three or four bounds of the horse carried us out of the reach of the enemy, who, having merely turned in desperate self-defence, quickly resumed his flight. As soon as I could gather in my panic-stricken horse, and prime the pistols afresh, I again spurred in pursuit of the buffalo, who had slackened his speed to take breath. On my approach he again set off full tilt, heaving himself forward with a heavy rolling gallop, dashing with headlong precipitation through brakes and ravines, while several deer and wolves, startled from their coverts by his thundering career, ran helter-skelter to right and left across the waste.

A gallop across the prairies in pursuit of game is by no means so smooth a career as those may imagine who have only the idea of an open level plain. It is true, the prairies of the hunting-ground are not so much entangled with flowering plants and long herbage as the lower prairies, and are principally covered with short buffalo-grass; but they are diversified by hill and dale, and where most level, are apt to be cut up by deep rifts and ravines, made by torrents after rains; and which, yawning from an even surface, are almost like pitfalls in the way of the hunter, checking him suddenly when in full career, or subjecting him to the risk of limb and life. The plains, too, are beset by burrowing-holes of small animals, in which the horse is apt to sink to the fetlock, and throw both himself and his rider. The late rain had covered some parts of the prairie, where the ground was hard, with a thin sheet of water, through which the horse had to splash his way. In other parts there were innumerable shallow hollows, eight or ten feet in diameter, made by the buffaloes, who wallow in sand and mud like swine. These being filled with water, shone like mirrors, so that the horse was continually leaping over them or springing on one side. We had reached, too, a rough part of the prairie, very much broken and cut up; the buffalo, who was running for life, took no heed to his course, plunging down break-neck ravines, where it was necessary to skirt the borders in search of a safer descent. At length we came to where a winter stream had torn a deep chasm across the whole prairie, leaving open jagged rocks, and forming a long glen bordered by steep crumbling cliffs of mingled stone and clay. Down one of these the buffalo flung himself, half tumbling, half leaping, and then scuttled along the bottom; while I, seeing all further pursuit useless, pulled up, and gazed quietly after him from the border of the cliff, until he disappeared amidst the windings of the ravine.

Nothing now remained but to turn my steed and rejoin my companions. Here at first was some little difficulty. The ardor of the chase had betrayed me into a long, heedless gallop. I now found myself in the midst of a lonely waste, in which the prospect was bounded by undulating swells of land, naked and uniform where, from the deficiency of landmarks and distinct features, an inexperienced man may become bewildered, and lose his way as readily as in the wastes of the ocean. The day, too, was overcast, so that I could not guide myself by the sun; my only mode was to retrace the track my horse had made in coming, though this I would often lose sight of, where the ground was covered with parched herbage.

To one unaccustomed to it, there is something inexpressibly lonely in the solitude of a prairie. The loneliness of a forest seems nothing to it. There the view is shut in by trees, and the imagination is left free to picture some livelier scene beyond. But here we have an immense extent of landscape without a sign of human existence. We have the consciousness of being far, far beyond the bounds of human habitation; we feel as if moving in the midst of a desert world. As my horse lagged slowly back over the scenes of our late scamper, and the delirium of the chase had passed away, I was peculiarly sensible to these circumstances. The silence of the waste was now and then broken by the cry of a distant flock of pelicans, stalking like spectres about a shallow pool; sometimes by the sinister croaking of a raven in the air, while occasionally a scoundrel wolf would scour off from before me, and, having attained a safe distance, would sit down and howl and whine with tones that gave a dreariness to the surrounding solitude.

After pursuing my way for some time, I descried a horseman on the edge of a distant hill, and soon recognized him to be the

Count. He had been equally unsuccessful with myself; we were shortly after rejoined by our worthy comrade, the Virtuoso, who, with spectacles on nose, had made two or three ineffectual shots from horseback.

We determined not to seek the camp until we had made one more effort. Casting our eyes about the surrounding waste, we descried a herd of buffalo about two miles distant, scattered apart, and quietly grazing near a small strip of trees and bushes. It required but little stretch of fancy to picture them so many cattle grazing on the edge of a common, and that the grove might shelter some lonely farm-house.

We now formed our plan to circumvent the herd, and by getting on the other side of them, to hunt them in the direction where we knew our camp to be situated: otherwise, the pursuit might take us to such a distance as to render it impossible to find our way back before nightfall. Taking a wide circuit, therefore, we moved slowly and cautiously, pausing occasionally when we saw any of the herd desist from grazing. The wind fortunately set from them, otherwise they might have scented us and have taken the alarm. In this way we succeeded in getting round the herd without disturbing it. It consisted of about forty head; bulls, cows, and calves. Separating to some distance from each other, we now approached slowly in a parallel line, hoping by degrees to steal near without exciting attention. They began, however, to move off quietly, stopping at every step or two to graze, when suddenly a bull, that, unobserved by us, had been taking his siesta under a clump of trees to our left, roused himself from his lair, and hastened to join his companions. We were still at a considerable distance, but the game had taken the alarm. We quickened our pace; they broke into a gallop, and now commenced a full chase.

As the ground was level, they shouldered along with great speed, following each other in a line; two or three bulls bringing up the rear, the last of whom, from his enormous size and venerable frontlet, and beard of sunburnt hair, looked like the patriarch of the herd, and as if he might long have reigned the monarch of the prairie.

There is a mixture of the awful and the comic in the look of these huge animals, as they bear their great bulk forwards, with an up and down motion of the unwieldy head and shoulders, their tail cocked up like the cue of Pantaloon in a pantomime, the end whisking about in a fierce yet whimsical style, and their eyes glaring venomously with an expression of fright and fury.

For some time I kept parallel with the line, without being able to force my horse within pistol-shot, so much had he been alarmed by the assault of the buffalo in the preceding chase. At length I succeeded, but was again balked by my pistols missing fire. My companions, whose horses were less fleet and more wayworn, could not overtake the herd; at length Mr. L., who was in the rear of the line, and losing ground, levelled his double-barrelled gun, and fired a long raking shot. It struck a buffalo just above the loins, broke its backbone, and brought it to the ground. He stopped and alighted to dispatch his prey, when, borrowing his gun, which had yet a charge remaining in it, I put my horse to his speed, again overtook the herd which was thundering along, pursued by the Count. With my present weapon there was no need of urging my horse to such close quarters; galloping along parallel, therefore, I singled out a buffalo, and by a fortunate shot brought it down on the spot. The ball had struck a vital part; it could not move from the place where it fell, but lay there struggling in mortal agony, while the rest of the herd kept on their headlong career across the prairie.

Dismounting, I now fettered my horse to prevent his straying, and advanced to contemplate my victim. I am nothing of a sportsman; I had been prompted to this unwonted exploit by the magnitude of the game and the excitement of an adventurous chase. Now that the excitement was over, I could not but look with commiseration upon the poor animal that lay struggling and bleeding at my feet. His very size and importance, which had before inspired me with eagerness, now increased my compunction. It seemed as if I had inflicted pain in proportion to the bulk of my victim, and as if there were a hundred-fold greater waste of life than there would have been in the destruction of an animal of inferior size.

To add to these after-qualms of conscience, the poor animal

lingered in his agony. He had evidently received a mortal wound, but death might be long in coming. It would not do to leave him here to be torn piecemeal, while yet alive, by the wolves that had already snuffed his blood, and were skulking and howling at a distance, and waiting for my departure; and by the ravens that were flapping about, croaking dismally in the air. It became now an act of mercy to give him his quietus, and put him out of his misery. I primed one of the pistols, therefore, and advanced close up to the buffalo. To inflict a wound thus in cold blood, I found a totally different thing from firing in the heat of the chase. Taking aim, however, just behind the fore-shoulder, my pistol for once proved true; the ball must have passed through the heart, for the animal gave one convulsive throe and expired.

While I stood meditating and moralizing over the wreck I had so wantonly produced, with my horse grazing near me, I was rejoined by my fellow-sportsman the Virtuoso, who, being a man of universal adroitness, and withal more experienced and hardened in the gentle art of "venerie," soon managed to carve out the tongue of the buffalo, and delivered it to me to bear back to the camp as a trophy.

ASTORIA

·{❧❀❧}·

CHAPTER XXII

WHILE MR. HUNT was diligently preparing for his arduous journey, some of his men began to lose heart at the perilous prospect before them; but before we accuse them of want of spirit, it is proper to consider the nature of the wilderness into which they were about to adventure. It was a region almost as vast and trackless as the ocean, and, at the time of which we treat, but little known, excepting through the vague accounts of Indian hunters. A part of their route would lay across an immense tract, stretching north and south for hundreds of miles along the foot of the Rocky Mountains, and drained by the tributary streams of the Missouri and the Mississippi. This region, which resembles one of the immeasurable steppes of Asia, has not inaptly been termed "the great American desert." It spreads forth into undulating and treeless plains, and desolate sandy wastes wearisome to the eye from their extent and monotony, and which are supposed by geologists to have formed the ancient floor of the ocean, countless ages since, when its primeval waves beat against the granite bases of the Rocky Mountains.

It is a land where no man permanently abides; for, in certain seasons of the year there is no food either for the hunter or his steed. The herbage is parched and withered; the brooks and streams are dried up; the buffalo, the elk and the deer have wandered to distant parts, keeping within the verge of expiring verdure, and leaving behind them a vast uninhabited solitude, seamed by ravines, the beds of former torrents, but now serving only to tantalize and increase the thirst of the traveller.

Occasionally the monotony of this vast wilderness is interrupted by mountainous belts of sand and limestone, broken into confused masses; with precipitous cliffs and yawning ravines, looking like the ruins of a world; or is traversed by lofty and barren ridges of rock, almost impassable, like those denominated the Black Hills. Beyond these rise the stern barriers of the Rocky Mountains, the limits, as it were, of the Atlantic world. The rugged defiles and deep valleys of this vast chain form sheltering places for restless and ferocious bands of savages, many of them the remnants of tribes, once inhabitants of the prairies, but broken up by war and violence, and who carry into their mountain haunts the fierce passions and reckless habits of desperadoes.

Such is the nature of this immense wilderness of the far West; which apparently defies cultivation, and the habitation of civilized life. Some portions of it along the rivers may partially be subdued by agriculture, others may form vast pastoral tracts, like those of the East; but it is to be feared that a great part of it will form a lawless interval between the abodes of civilized man, like the wastes of the ocean or the deserts of Arabia; and, like them, be subject to the depredations of the marauder. Here may spring up new and mongrel races, like new formations in geology, the amalgamation of the "debris" and "abrasions" of former races, civilized and savage; the remains of broken and almost extinguished tribes; the descendants of wandering hunters and trappers; of fugitives from the Spanish and American frontiers; of adventurers and desperadoes of every class and country, yearly ejected from the bosom of society into the wilderness. We are contributing incessantly to swell this singular and heterogeneous cloud of wild population that is to hang about our frontier, by the transfer of whole tribes from the east of the Mississippi to the great wastes of the far West. Many of these bear with them the smart of real or fancied injuries; many consider themselves expatriated beings, wrongfully exiled from their hereditary homes, and the sepulchres of their fathers, and cherish a deep and abiding animosity against the race that has dispossessed them. Some may gradually become pastoral hordes, like those rude and migratory people, half shepherd, half warrior, who, with their flocks and herds, roam the plains of upper Asia; but others, it is to be apprehended, will become predatory bands, mounted on the fleet steeds of the prairies, with the open plains for their marauding grounds, and the mountains for their retreats and lurking-places. Here they may resemble those great hordes of the North, "Gog and Magog with their bands," that haunted the gloomy imaginations of the prophets. "A great company and a mighty host, all riding upon horses, and warring upon those nations which were at rest, and dwelt peaceably, and had gotten cattle and goods."

The Spaniards changed the whole character and habits of the Indians when they brought the horse among them. In Chili, Tucuman, and other parts, it has converted them, we are told, into Tartar-like tribes, and enabled them to keep the Spaniards out of their country, and even to make it dangerous for them to venture far from their towns and settlements. Are we not in danger of producing some such state of things in the boundless regions of the far West. That these are not mere fanciful and extravagant suggestions we have sufficient proofs in the dangers already experienced by the traders to the Spanish mart of Santa Fé, and to the distant posts of the fur companies. These are obliged to proceed in armed caravans, and are subject to murderous attacks from bands of Pawnees, Comanches, and Blackfeet, that come scouring upon them in their weary march across the plains, or lie in wait for them among the passes of the mountains.

We are wandering, however, into excursive speculations, when our intention was merely to give an idea of the nature of the wilderness which Mr. Hunt was about to traverse; and which at that time was far less known than at present; though it still remains in a great measure an unknown land. We cannot be surprised, therefore, that some of the least resolute of his party should feel dismay at the thoughts of adventuring into this perilous wilderness under the uncertain guidance of three hunters, who had merely passed once through the country and might have forgotten the landmarks. Their apprehensions were aggravated by some of Lisa's followers, who, not being engaged in the expedition, took a mischievous pleasure in exaggerating its dangers. They painted in strong colors, to the poor Canadian voyageurs, the risk they would run of perishing with hunger and thirst; of being cut off by war-parties of the Sioux who scoured the plains; of having their horses stolen by the Upsarokas or Crows, who infested the skirts of the

Rocky Mountains; or of being butchered by the Blackfeet, who lurked among the defiles. In a word, there was little chance of their getting alive across the mountains; and even if they did, those three guides knew nothing of the howling wilderness that lay beyond.

The apprehensions thus awakened in the minds of some of the men came well nigh proving detrimental to the expedition. Some of them determined to desert, and to make their way back to St. Louis. They accordingly purloined several weapons and a barrel of gunpowder, as ammunition for their enterprise, and buried them in the river bank, intending to seize one of the boats, and make off in the night. Fortunately their plot was overheard by John Day, the Kentuckian, and communicated to the partners, who took quiet and effectual means to frustrate it.

The dangers to be apprehended from the Crow Indians had not been overrated by the camp gossips. These savages, through whose mountain haunts the party would have to pass, were noted for daring and excursive habits, and great dexterity in horse stealing. Mr. Hunt, therefore, considered himself fortunate in having met with a man who might be of great use to him in any intercourse he might have with the tribe. This was a wandering individual named Edward Rose, whom he had picked up somewhere on the Missouri—one of those anomalous beings found on the frontier, who seem to have neither kin nor country. He had lived some time among the Crows, so as to become acquainted with their language and customs; and was, withal, a dogged, sullen, silent fellow, with a sinister aspect, and more of the savage than the civilized man in his appearance. He was engaged to serve in general as a hunter, but as guide and interpreter when they should reach the country of the Crows.

On the 18th of July, Mr. Hunt took up his line of march by land from the Arickara village, leaving Mr. Lisa and Mr. Nuttall there, where they intended to await the expected arrival of Mr. Henry from the Rocky Mountains. As to Messrs. Bradbury and Breckenridge they had departed some days previously, on a voyage down the river to St. Louis, with a detachment from Mr. Lisa's party. With all his exertions, Mr. Hunt had been unable to obtain

a sufficient number of horses for the accommodation of all his people. His cavalcade consisted of eighty-two horses, most of them
heavily laden with Indian goods, beaver traps, ammunition,
Indian corn, corn meal and other necessaries. Each of the partners was mounted, and a horse was allotted to the interpreter,
Pierre Dorion, for the transportation of his luggage and his two
children. His squaw, for the most part of the time, trudged on
foot, like the residue of the party; nor did any of the men show
more patience and fortitude than this resolute woman in enduring
fatigue and hardship.

The veteran trappers and voyageurs of Lisa's party shook their
heads as their comrades set out, and took leave of them as of
doomed men; and even Lisa himself gave it as his opinion, after
the travellers had departed, they would never reach the shores of
the Pacific, but would either perish with hunger in the wilderness,
or be cut off by the savages.

CHAPTER XXIII

THE COURSE TAKEN by Mr. Hunt was at first to the northwest,
but soon turned and kept generally to the southwest, to avoid the
country infested by the Blackfeet. His route took him across some
of the tributary streams of the Missouri, and over immense prairies, bounded only by the horizon, and destitute of trees. It was
now the height of summer, and these naked plains would be in-
tolerable to the traveller were it not for the breezes which sweep
over them during the fervor of the day, bringing with them tem-
pering airs from the distant mountains. To the prevalence of these
breezes, and to the want of all leafy covert, may we also attribute
the freedom from those flies and other insects so tormenting to
man and beast during the summer months, in the lower plains,
which are bordered and interspersed with woodland.

The monotony of these immense landscapes, also, would be as

wearisome as that of the ocean, were it not relieved in some degree by the purity and elasticity of the atmosphere, and the
beauty of the heavens. The sky has that delicious blue for which
the sky of Italy is renowned; the sun shines with a splendor un-
obscured by any cloud or vapor, and a starlight night on the prairies is glorious. This purity and elasticity of atmosphere increases
as the traveller approaches the mountains and gradually rises into
more elevated prairies.

On the second day of the journey, Mr. Hunt arranged the party
into small and convenient messes, distributing among them the
camp kettles. The encampments at night were as before; some
sleeping under tents, and others bivouacking in the open air. The
Canadians proved as patient of toil and hardship on the land
as on the water; indeed, nothing could surpass the patience and
good-humor of these men upon the march. They were the cheerful
drudges of the party, loading and unloading the horses, pitching
the tents, making the fires, cooking; in short, performing all those
household and menial offices which the Indians usually assign to
the squaws; and, like the squaws, they left all the hunting and
fighting to others. A Canadian has but little affection for the ex
ercise of the rifle.

The progress of the party was but slow for the first few days.
Some of the men were indisposed; Mr. Crooks, especially, was so
unwell that he could not keep on his horse. A rude kind of litter
was, therefore, prepared for him, consisting of two long poles,
fixed, one on each side of two horses, with a matting between
them, on which he reclined at full length, and was protected from
the sun by a canopy of boughs.

On the evening of the 23d (July) they encamped on the banks
of what they term Big River; and here we cannot but pause to
lament the stupid, commonplace, and often ribald names entailed
upon the rivers and other features of the great West, by traders
and settlers. As the aboriginal tribes of these magnificent regions
are yet in existence, the Indian names might easily be recovered;
which, beside being in general more sonorous and musical, would
remain mementoes of the primitive lords of the soil, of whom in a
little while scarce any traces will be left. Indeed, it is to be wished

that the whole of our country could be rescued, as much as possible, from the wretched nomenclature inflicted upon it, by ignorant and vulgar minds; and this might be done, in a great degree, by restoring the Indian names, wherever significant and euphonious. As there appears to be a spirit of research abroad in respect to our aboriginal antiquities, we would suggest, as a worthy object of enterprise, a map, or maps, of every part of our country, giving the Indian names wherever they could be ascertained. Whoever achieves such an object worthily, will leave a monument to his own reputation.

To return from this digression. As the travellers were now in a country abounding with buffalo, they remained for several days encamped upon the banks of Big River, to obtain a supply of provisions, and to give the invalids time to recruit.

On the second day of their sojourn, as Ben Jones, John Day, and others of the hunters were in pursuit of game, they came upon an Indian camp on the open prairie, near to a small stream which ran through a ravine. The tents or lodges were of dressed buffalo skins, sewn together and stretched on tapering pine poles, joined at top, but radiating at bottom, so as to form a circle capable of admitting fifty persons. Numbers of horses were grazing in the neighborhood of the camp, or straying at large in the prairie; a sight most acceptable to the hunters. After reconnoitring the camp for some time, they ascertained it to belong to a band of Cheyenne Indians, the same that had sent a deputation to the Arickaras. They received the hunters in the most friendly manner; invited them to their lodges, which were more cleanly than Indian lodges are prone to be, and set food before them with true uncivilized hospitality. Several of them accompanied the hunters back to the camp, when a trade was immediately opened. The Cheyennes were astonished and delighted to find a convoy of goods and trinkets thus brought into the very heart of the prairie; while Mr. Hunt and his companions were overjoyed to have an opportunity of obtaining a further supply of horses from these equestrian savages.

During a fortnight that the travellers lingered at this place, their encampment was continually thronged by the Cheyennes.

They were a civil, well-behaved people, cleanly in their persons and decorous in their habits. The men were tall, straight and vigorous, with aquiline noses, and high cheek bones. Some were almost as naked as ancient statues, and might have stood as models for a statuary; others had leggins and moccasins of deer skin, and buffalo robes, which they threw gracefully over their shoulders. In a little while, however, they began to appear in more gorgeous array, tricked out in the finery obtained from the white men; bright cloths, brass rings, beads of various colors; and happy was he who could render himself hideous with vermilion.

The travellers had frequent occasion to admire the skill and grace with which these Indians managed their horses. Some of them made a striking display when mounted; themselves and their steeds decorated in gala style; for the Indians often bestow more finery upon their horses than upon themselves. Some would hang around the necks, or rather on the breasts of their horses, the most precious ornaments they had obtained from the white men; others interwove feathers in their manes and tails. The Indian horses, too, appear to have an attachment to their wild riders, and indeed it is said that the horses of the prairies readily distinguish an Indian from a white man by the smell, and give a preference to the former. Yet the Indians, in general, are hard riders, and, however they may value their horses, treat them with great roughness and neglect. Occasionally the Cheyennes joined the white hunters in pursuit of the elk and buffalo; and when in the ardor of the chase, spared neither themselves nor their steeds, scouring the prairies at full speed, and plunging down precipices and frightful ravines that threatened the necks of both horse and horseman. The Indian steed, well trained to the chase, seems as mad as his rider, and pursues the game as eagerly as if it were his natural prey, on the flesh of which he was to banquet.

The history of the Cheyennes is that of many of those wandering tribes of the prairies. They were the remnant of a once powerful people called the Shaways, inhabiting a branch of the Red River which flows into Lake Winnipeg. Every Indian tribe has some rival tribe with which it wages implacable hostility. The deadly enemies of the Shaways were the Sioux, who, after a long course of warfare, proved too powerful for them, and drove them across the Missouri. They again took root near the Warricanne Creek, and established themselves there in a fortified village.

The Sioux still followed them with deadly animosity; dislodged them from their village, and compelled them to take refuge in the Black Hills, near the upper waters of the Sheyenne or Cheyenne River. Here they lost even their name, and became known among the French colonists by that of the river they frequented.

The heart of the tribe was now broken; its numbers were greatly thinned by their harassing wars. They no longer attempted to establish themselves in any permanent abode that might be an object of attack to their cruel foes. They gave up the cultivation of the fruits of the earth, and became a wandering tribe, subsisting by the chase, and following the buffalo in its migrations.

Their only possessions were horses, which they caught on the prairies, or reared, or captured on predatory incursions into the Mexican territories, as has already been mentioned. With some of these they repaired once a year to the Arickara villages, exchanged them for corn, beans, pumpkins, and articles of European merchandise, and then returned into the heart of the prairies.

Such are the fluctuating fortunes of these savage nations. War, famine, pestilence, together or singly, bring down their strength and thin their numbers. Whole tribes are rooted up from their native places, wander for a time about these immense regions, become amalgamated with other tribes, or disappear from the face of the earth. There appears to be a tendency to extinction among all the savage nations; and this tendency would seem to have been in operation among the aboriginals of this country long before the advent of the white men, if we nay judge from the traces and traditions of ancient populousness in regions which were silent and deserted at the time of the discovery; and from the mysterious and perplexing vestiges of unknown races, predecessors of those found in actual possession, and who must long since have become gradually extinguished or been destroyed. The whole history of the aboriginal population of this country, however, is an enigma, and a grand one—will it ever be solved?

CHAPTER XXIV

ON THE SIXTH OF AUGUST the travellers bade farewell to the friendly band of Cheyennes, and resumed their journey. As they had obtained thirty-six additional horses by their recent traffic, Mr. Hunt made a new arrangement. The baggage was made up in smaller loads. A horse was allotted to each of the six prime hunters, and others were distributed among the voyageurs, a horse for every two, so that they could ride and walk alternately. Mr. Crooks being still too feeble to mount the saddle, was carried on a litter.

Their march this day lay among singular hills and knolls of an indurated red earth, resembling brick, about the bases of which were scattered pumice stones and cinders, the whole bearing traces of the action of fire. In the evening they encamped on a branch of Big River.

They were now out of the tract of country infested by the Sioux, and had advanced such a distance into the interior that Mr. Hunt no longer felt apprehensive of the desertion of any of his men. He was doomed, however, to experience new cause of anxiety. As he was seated in his tent after nightfall, one of the men came to him privately, and informed him that there was mischief brewing in the camp. Edward Rose, the interpreter, whose sinister looks we have already mentioned, was denounced by this secret informer as a designing, treacherous scoundrel, who was tampering with the fidelity of certain of the men, and instigating them to a flagrant piece of treason. In the course of a few days they would arrive at the mountainous district infested by the Upsarokas or Crows, the tribe among which Rose was to officiate as interpreter. His plan was that several of the men should join with him, when in that neighborhood, in carrying off a number of the horses with their packages of goods, and deserting to those savages. He assured them of good treatment among the Crows, the principal chiefs and warriors of whom he knew; they would soon become great men among them, and have the finest women, and the daughters of the chiefs for wives; and the horses and goods they carried off would make them rich for life.

The intelligence of this treachery on the part of Rose gave much disquiet to Mr. Hunt, for he knew not how far it might be effective among his men. He had already had proofs that several of them were disaffected to the enterprise, and loath to cross the mountains. He knew also that savage life had charms for many of them, especially the Canadians, who were prone to intermarry and domesticate themselves among the Indians.

And here a word or two concerning the Crows may be of service to the reader, as they will figure occasionally in the succeeding narration.

The tribe consists of four bands, which have their nestling-places in fertile, well-wooded valleys, lying among the Rocky Mountains, and watered by the Big Horse River and its tributary streams; but, though these are properly their homes, where they shelter their old people, their wives, and their children, the men of the tribe are almost continually on the foray and the scamper. They are, in fact, notorious marauders and horse-stealers; crossing and recrossing the mountains, robbing on the one side, and conveying their spoils to the other. Hence, we are told, is derived their name, given to them on account of their unsettled and predatory habits; winging their flight, like the crows, from one side of the mountains to the other, and making free booty of every thing that lies in their way. Horses, however, are the especial objects of their depredations, and their skill and audacity in stealing them are said to be astonishing. This is their glory and delight; an accomplished horse-stealer fills up their idea of a hero. Many horses are obtained by them, also, in barter from tribes in and beyond the mountains. They have an absolute passion for this noble animal; beside which he is with them an important object of traffic. Once a year they make a visit to the Mandans, Minatrees, and other tribes of the Missouri, taking with them droves of horses which they exchange for guns, ammunition, trinkets, vermilion, cloths of bright colors, and various other articles of European

manufacture. With these they supply their own wants and caprices, and carry on the internal trade for horses already mentioned.

The plot of Rose to rob and abandon his countrymen when in
the heart of the wilderness, and to throw himself into the hands
of a horde of savages, may appear strange and improbable to those
unacquainted with the singular and anomalous characters that are
to be found about the borders. This fellow, it appears, was one of
those desperadoes of the frontiers, outlawed by their crimes, who
combine the vices of civilized and savage life, and are ten times
more barbarous than the Indians with whom they consort. Rose
had formerly belonged to one of the gangs of pirates who infested
the islands of the Mississippi, plundering boats as they went up
and down the river, and who sometimes shifted the scene of their
robberies to the shore, waylaying travellers as they returned by
land from New Orleans with the proceeds of their downward
voyage, plundering them of their money and effects, and often
perpetrating the most atrocious murders.

These hordes of villains being broken up and dispersed, Rose
had betaken himself to the wilderness, and associated himself with
the Crows, whose predatory habits were congenial with his own,
had married a woman of the tribe, and, in short, had identified
himself with those vagrant savages.

Such was the worthy guide and interpreter, Edward Rose. We
give his story, however, not as it was known to Mr. Hunt and his
companions at the time, but as it has been subsequently ascertained. Enough was known of the fellow and his dark and per-
fidious character to put Mr. Hunt upon his guard: still, as there
was no knowing how far his plans might have succeeded, and as
any rash act might blow the mere smouldering sparks of treason
into a sudden blaze, it was thought advisable by those with whom
Mr. Hunt consulted, to conceal all knowledge or suspicion of the
meditated treachery, but to keep up a vigilant watch upon the
movements of Rose, and a strict guard upon the horses at night.

CHAPTER XXV

THE PLAINS OVER WHICH the travellers were journeying continued to be destitute of trees or even shrubs; insomuch that they had to use the dung of the buffalo for fuel, as the Arabs of the desert use that of the camel. This substitute for fuel is universal among the Indians of these upper prairies, and is said to make a fire equal to that of turf. If a few chips are added, it throws out a cheerful and kindly blaze.

These plains, however, had not always been equally destitute of wood, as was evident from the trunks of the trees which the travellers repeatedly met with, some still standing, others lying about in broken fragments, but all in a fossil state, having flourished in times long past. In these singular remains, the original grain of the wood was still so distinct that they could be ascertained to be the ruins of oak trees. Several pieces of the fossil wood were selected by the men to serve as whetstones.

In this part of the journey there was no lack of provisions, for the prairies were covered with immense herds of buffalo. These, in general, are animals of peaceful demeanor, grazing quietly like domestic cattle; but this was the season when they are in heat, and when the bulls are usually fierce and pugnacious. There was accordingly a universal restlessness and commotion throughout the plain; and the amorous herds gave utterance to their feelings in low bellowings that resounded like distant thunder. Here and there fierce duellos took place between rival enamorados; butting their huge shagged fronts together, goring each other with their short black horns, and tearing up the earth with their feet in perfect fury.

In one of the evening halts, Pierre Dorion, the interpreter, together with Carson and Gardpie, two of the hunters, were missing, nor had they returned by morning. As it was supposed they had wandered away in pursuit of buffalo, and would readily find the track of the party, no solicitude was felt on their account. A fire was left burning, to guide them by its column of smoke, and the travellers proceeded on their march. In the evening a signal fire was made on a hill adjacent to the camp, and in the morning it was replenished with fuel so as to last throughout the day. These signals are usual among the Indians, to give warnings to each other, or to call home straggling hunters; and such is the transparency of the atmosphere in those elevated plains, that a slight column of smoke can be discerned from a great distance, particularly in the evenings. Two or three days elapsed, however, without the reappearance of the three hunters; and Mr. Hunt slackened his march to give them time to overtake him.

A vigilant watch continued to be kept upon the movements of Rose, and of such of the men as were considered doubtful in their loyalty; but nothing occurred to excite immediate apprehensions. Rose evidently was not a favorite among his comrades, and it was hoped that he had not been able to make any real partisans.

On the 10th of August they encamped among hills, on the highest peak of which Mr. Hunt caused a huge pyre of pine wood to be made, which soon sent up a great column of flame that might be seen far and wide over the prairies. This fire blazed all night, and was amply replenished at daybreak; so that the towering pillar of smoke could not but be descried by the wanderers if within the distance of a day's journey.

It is a common occurrence in these regions, where the features of the country so much resemble each other, for hunters to lose themselves and wander for many days, before they can find their way back to the main body of their party. In the present instance, however, a more than common solicitude was felt, in consequence of the distrust awakened by the sinister designs of Rose.

The route now became excessively toilsome, over a ridge of steep rocky hills, covered with loose stones. These were intersected by deep valleys, formed by two branches of Big River, coming from the south of west, both of which they crossed. These streams were bordered by meadows, well stocked with buffaloes. Loads of meat were brought in by the hunters; but the travellers were rendered dainty by profusion, and would cook only the choice pieces.

They had now travelled for several days at a very slow rate, and had made signal-fires and left traces of their route at every stage, yet nothing was heard or seen of the lost men. It began to be feared that they might have fallen into the hands of some lurking band of savages. A party numerous as that of Mr. Hunt, with a long train of pack-horses, moving across open plains or naked hills, is discoverable at a great distance by Indian scouts, who spread the intelligence rapidly to various points, and assemble their friends to hang about the skirts of the travellers, steal their horses, or cut off any stragglers from the main body.

Mr. Hunt and his companions were more and more sensible how much it would be in the power of this sullen and daring vagabond Rose, to do them mischief, when they should become entangled in the defiles of the mountains, with the passes of which they were wholly unacquainted, and which were infested by his freebooting friends, the Crows. There, should he succeed in seducing some of the party into his plans, he might carry off the best horses and effects, throw himself among his savage allies, and set all pursuit at defiance. Mr. Hunt resolved, therefore, to frustrate the knave, divert him, by management, from his plans, and make it sufficiently advantageous for him to remain honest. He took occasion, accordingly, in the course of conversation, to inform Rose that, having engaged him chiefly as a guide and interpreter through the country of the Crows, they would not stand in need of his services beyond. Knowing, therefore, his connection by marriage with that tribe, and his predilection for a residence among them, they would put no restraint upon his will, but, whenever they met with a party of that people, would leave him at liberty to remain among his adopted brethren. Furthermore, that, in thus parting with him, they would pay him half a year's wages in consideration of his past services, and would give him a horse, three beaver traps, and sundry other articles calculated to set him up in the world.

This unexpected liberality, which made it nearly as profitable and infinitely less hazardous for Rose to remain honest than to play the rogue, completely disarmed him. From that time his whole deportment underwent a change. His brow cleared up and appeared more cheerful; he left off his sullen, skulking habits, and made no further attempts to tamper with the faith of his comrades.

On the 13th of August Mr. Hunt varied his course, and inclined westward, in hopes of falling in with the three lost hunters; who, it was now thought, might have kept to the right hand of Big River. This course soon brought him to a fork of the Little Missouri, about a hundred yards wide, and resembling the great river of the same name in the strength of its current, its turbid water, and the frequency of drift-wood and sunken trees.

Rugged mountains appeared ahead, crowding down to the water edge, and offering a barrier to further progress on the side they were ascending. Crossing the river, therefore, they encamped on its northwest bank, where they found good pasturage and buffalo in abundance. The weather was overcast and rainy, and a general gloom pervaded the camp; the voyageurs sat smoking in groups, with their shoulders as high as their heads, croaking their foreboding, when suddenly towards evening a shout of joy gave notice that the lost men were found. They came slowly lagging into the camp, with weary looks, and horses jaded and wayworn. They had, in fact, been for several days incessantly on the move. In their hunting excursion on the prairies they had pushed so far in pursuit of buffalo, as to find it impossible to retrace their steps over plains trampled by innumerable herds; and were baffled by the monotony of the landscape in their attempts to recall landmarks. They had ridden to and fro until they had almost lost the points of the compass, and become totally bewildered; nor did they ever perceive any of the signal fires and columns of smoke made by their comrades. At length, about two days previously, when almost spent by anxiety and hard riding, they came, to their great joy, upon the "trail" of the party, which they had since followed up steadily.

Those only, who have experienced the warm cordiality that grows up between comrades in wild and adventurous expeditions of the kind, can picture to themselves the hearty cheering with which the stragglers were welcomed to the camp. Every one crowded round them to ask questions, and to hear the story of their mishaps; and even the squaw of the moody half-breed,

Pierre Dorion, forgot the sternness of his domestic rule, and the
conjugal discipline of the cudgel, in her joy at his safe return.

CHAPTER XXVI

MR. HUNT AND HIS PARTY were now on the skirts of the Black
Hills, or Black Mountains, as they are sometimes called; an
extensive chain, lying about a hundred miles east of the Rocky
Mountains, and stretching in a northeast direction from the south
fork of the Nebraska, or Platte River, to the great north bend of
the Missouri. The Sierra or ridge of the Black Hills, in fact, forms
the dividing line between the waters of the Missouri and those
of the Arkansas and the Mississippi, and gives rise to the Cheyenne,
the Little Missouri, and several tributary streams of the Yellowstone.

The wild recesses of these hills, like those of the Rocky Mountains, are retreats and lurking-places for broken and predatory
tribes, and it was among them that the remnant of the Cheyenne
tribe took refuge, as has been stated, from their conquering enemies, the Sioux.

The Black Hills are chiefly composed of sandstone, and in many
places are broken into savage cliffs and precipices, and present
the most singular and fantastic forms; sometimes resembling
towns and castellated fortresses. The ignorant inhabitants of
plains are prone to clothe the mountains that bound their horizon
with fanciful and superstitious attributes. Thus the wandering
tribes of the prairies, who often behold clouds gathering round
the summits of these hills, and lightning flashing, and thunder
pealing from them, when all the neighboring plains are serene and
sunny, consider them the abode of the genii or thunder-spirits who
fabricate storms and tempests. On entering their defiles, therefore,
they often hang offerings on the trees, or place them on the rocks,
to propitiate the invisible "lords of the mountains," and procure

good weather and successful hunting; and they attach unusual significance to the echoes which haunt the precipices. This superstition may also have arisen, in part, from a natural phenomenon of a singular nature. In the most calm and serene weather, and at all times of the day or night, successive reports are now and then heard among these mountains, resembling the discharge of several pieces of artillery. Similar reports were heard by Messrs. Lewis and Clarke in the Rocky Mountains, which they say were attributed by the Indians to the bursting of the rich mines of silver contained in the bosom of the mountains.

In fact, these singular explosions have received fanciful explanations from learned men, and have not been satisfactorily accounted for even by philosophers. They are said to occur frequently in Brazil. Vasconcelles, a Jesuit father, describes one which he heard in the Sierra, or mountain region of Piratininga, and which he compares to the discharges of a park of artillery. The Indians told him that it was an explosion of stones. The worthy father had soon a satisfactory proof of the truth of their information, for the very place was found where a rock had burst and exploded from its entrails a stony mass, like a bomb-shell, and of the size of a bull's heart. This mass was broken either in its ejection or its fall, and wonderful was the internal organization revealed. It had a shell harder even than iron; within which were arranged, like the seeds of a pomegranate, jewels of various colors; some transparent as crystal; others of a fine red, and others of mixed hues. The same phenomenon is said to occur occasionally in the adjacent province of Guayra, where stones of the bigness of a man's hand are exploded, with a loud noise, from the bosom of the earth, and scatter about glittering and beautiful fragments that look like precious gems, but are of no value.

The Indians of the Orellanna, also, tell of horrible noises heard occasionally in the Paraguaxo, which they consider the throes and groans of the mountain, endeavoring to cast forth the precious stones hidden within its entrails. Others have endeavored to account for these discharges of "mountain artillery" on humbler principles; attributing them to the loud reports made by the disruption and fall of great masses of rock, reverberated and prolonged by the echoes; others, to the disengagement of hydrogen, produced by subterraneous beds of coal in a state of ignition. In whatever way this singular phenomenon may be accounted for, the existence of it appears to be well established. It remains one of the lingering mysteries of nature which throw something of a supernatural charm over her wild mountain solitudes; and we doubt whether the imaginative reader will not rather join with the poor Indian in attributing it to the thunder-spirits, or the guardian genii of unseen treasures, than to any commonplace physical cause.

Whatever might be the supernatural influences among these mountains, the travellers found their physical difficulties hard to cope with. They made repeated attempts to find a passage through or over the chain, but were as often turned back by impassable barriers. Sometimes a defile seemed to open a practicable path, but it would terminate in some wild chaos of rocks and cliffs, which it was impossible to climb. The animals of these solitary regions were different from those they had been accustomed to. The blacktailed deer would bound up the ravines on their approach, and the bighorn would gaze fearlessly down upon them from some impending precipice, or skip playfully from rock to rock. These animals are only to be met with in mountainous regions. The former is larger than the common deer, but its flesh is not equally esteemed by hunters. It has very large ears, and the tip of the tail is black, from which it derives its name.

The bighorn is so named from its horns; which are of a great size, and twisted like those of a ram. It is called by some the argali, by others the ibex, though differing from both of these animals. The Mandans call it the ahsahta, a name much better than the clumsy appellation which it generally bears. It is of the size of a small elk, or large deer, and of a dun color, excepting the belly and round the tail, where it is white. In its habits it resembles the goat, frequenting the rudest precipices; cropping the herbage from their edges; and like the chamois, bounding lightly and securely among dizzy heights, where the hunter dares not venture. It is difficult therefore, to get within shot of it. Ben Jones the hunter, however, in one of the passes of the Black Hills, succeeded in bringing down a bighorn from the verge of a precipice, the flesh of which was pronounced by the gormands of the camp to have the flavor of excellent mutton.

Baffled in his attempts to traverse this mountain chain, Mr. Hunt skirted along it to the southwest, keeping it on the right; and still in hopes of finding an opening. At an early hour one day, he encamped in a narrow valley on the banks of a beautifully clear but rushy pool; surrounded by thickets bearing abundance of wild cherries, currants, and yellow and purple gooseberries.

While the afternoon's meal was in preparation, Mr. Hunt and Mr. M'Kenzie ascended to the summit of the nearest hill, from whence, aided by the purity and transparency of the evening atmosphere, they commanded a vast prospect on all sides. Below them extended a plain, dotted with innumerable herds of buffalo. Some were lying down among the herbage, others roaming in their unbounded pastures, while many were engaged in fierce contests like those already described, their low bellowings reaching the ear like the hoarse murmurs of the surf on a distant shore.

Far off in the west they descried a range of lofty mountains printing the clear horizon, some of them evidently capped with snow. These they supposed to be the Big horn Mountains, so called from the animal of that name, with which they abound. They are a spur of the great Rocky chain. The hill from whence Mr. Hunt had this prospect was, according to his computation, about two hundred and fifty miles from the Arickara village.

On returning to the camp, Mr. Hunt found some uneasiness prevailing among the Canadian voyageurs. In straying among the thickets they had beheld tracks of grizzly bears in every direction, doubtless attracted thither by the fruit. To their dismay, they now found that they had encamped in one of the favorite resorts of this dreaded animal. The idea marred all the comfort of the encampment. As night closed, the surrounding thickets were peopled with terrors; insomuch that, according to Mr. Hunt, they could not help starting at every little breeze that stirred the bushes.

The grizzly bear is the only really formidable quadruped of our continent. He is the favorite theme of the hunters of the far

West, who describe him as equal in size to a common cow and of prodigious strength. He makes battle if assailed, and often, if pressed by hunger, is the assailant. If wounded, he becomes furious and will pursue the hunter. His speed exceeds that of a man but is inferior to that of a horse. In attacking he rears himself on his hind legs, and springs the length of his body. Woe to horse or rider that comes within the sweep of his terrific claws, which are sometimes nine inches in length, and tear everything before them.

At the time we are treating of, the grizzly bear was still frequent on the Missouri and in the lower country, but, like some of the broken tribes of the prairie, he has gradually fallen back before his enemies, and is now chiefly to be found in the upland regions, in rugged fastnesses like those of the Black Hills and the Rocky Mountains. Here he lurks in caverns, or holes which he had digged in the sides of hills, or under the roots and trunks of fallen trees. Like the common bear, he is fond of fruits, and mast, and roots, the latter of which he will dig up with his fore claws. He is carnivorous also, and will even attack and conquer the lordly buffalo, dragging his huge carcass to the neighborhood of his den, that he may prey upon it at his leisure.

The hunters, both white and red men, consider this the most heroic game. They prefer to hunt him on horseback, and will venture so near as sometimes to singe his hair with the flash of the rifle. The hunter of the grizzly bear, however, must be an experienced hand, and know where to aim at a vital part; for of all quadrupeds, he is the most difficult to be killed. He will receive repeated wounds without flinching, and rarely is a shot mortal unless through the head or heart.

That the dangers apprehended from the grizzly bear, at this night encampment, were not imaginary, was proved on the following morning. Among the hired men of the party was one William Cannon, who had been a soldier at one of the frontier posts, and entered into the employ of Mr. Hunt at Mackinaw. He was an inexperienced hunter and a poor shot, for which he was much bantered by his more adroit comrades. Piqued at their raillery, he had been practicing ever since he had joined the ex-

pedition, but without success. In the course of the present afternoon, he went forth by himself to take a lesson in venerie, and,
to his great delight, had the good fortune to kill a buffalo. As he
was a considerable distance from the camp, he cut out the tongue
and some of the choice bits, made them into a parcel, and slinging
them on his shoulders by a strap passed round his forehead, as
the voyageurs carry packages of goods, set out all glorious for the
camp, anticipating a triumph over his brother hunters. In passing
through a narrow ravine, he heard a noise behind him, and looking
round beheld, to his dismay, a grizzly bear in full pursuit, apparently attracted by the scent of the meat. Cannon had heard so
much of the invulnerability of this tremendous animal, that he
never attempted to fire, but, slipping the strap from his forehead,
let go the buffalo meat and ran for his life. The bear did not stop
to regale himself with the game, but kept on after the hunter. He
had nearly overtaken him when Cannon reached a tree, and,
throwing down his rifle, scrambled up it. The next instant Bruin
was at the foot of the tree; but, as this species of bear does not
climb, he contented himself with turning the chase into a blockade.
Night came on. In the darkness Cannon could not perceive whether
or not the enemy maintained his station; but his fears pictured
him rigorously mounting guard. He passed the night, therefore,
in the tree, a prey to dismal fancies. In the morning the bear was
gone. Cannon warily descended the tree, gathered up his gun, and
made the best of his way back to the camp, without venturing to
look after his buffalo meat.

While on this theme we will add another anecdote of an adventure with a grizzly bear, told of John Day, the Kentucky
hunter, but which happened at a different period of the expedition.
Day was hunting in company with one of the clerks of the company,
a lively youngster, who was a great favorite with the veteran, but
whose vivacity he had continually to keep in check. They were
in search of deer, when suddenly a huge grizzly bear emerged from
a thicket about thirty yards distant, rearing himself upon his
hind legs with a terrific growl, and displaying a hideous array of
teeth and claws. The rifle of the young man was leveled in an
instant, but John Day's iron hand was as quickly upon his arm.

"Be quiet, boy! be quiet!" exclaimed the hunter between his clenched teeth, and without turning his eyes from the bear. They remained motionless. The monster regarded them for a time, then, lowering himself on his fore paws, slowly withdrew. He had not gone many paces before he again returned, reared himself on his hind legs, and repeated his menace. Day's hand was still on the arm of his young companion; he again pressed it hard, and kept repeating between his teeth, "Quiet, boy!—keep quiet!—keep quiet!"—though the latter had not made a move since his first prohibition. The bear again lowered himself on all fours, retreated some twenty yards further, and again turned, reared, showed his teeth, and growled. This third menace was too much for the game spirit of John Day. "By Jove!" exclaimed he, "I can stand this no longer," and in an instant a ball from his rifle whizzed into the foe. The wound was not mortal; but, luckily, it dismayed instead of enraging the animal, and he retreated into the thicket.

Day's young companion reproached him for not practicing the caution which he enjoined upon others. "Why, boy," replied the veteran, "caution is caution, but one must not put up with too much, even from a bear. Would you have me suffer myself to be bullied all day by a varmint?"

CHAPTER XXVII

FOR THE TWO FOLLOWING DAYS, the travellers pursued a westerly course for thirty-four miles along a ridge of country dividing the tributary waters of the Missouri and the Yellowstone. As landmarks they guided themselves by the summits of the far distant mountains, which they supposed to belong to the Bighorn chain. They were gradually rising into a higher temperature, for the weather was cold for the season, with a sharp frost in the night, and ice of an eighth of an inch in thickness.

On the twenty-second of August, early in the day, they came

upon the trail of a numerous band. Rose and the other hunters examined the foot-prints with great attention, and determined it to be the trail of a party of Crows, returning from an annual trading visit to the Mandans. As this trail afforded more commodious travelling, they immediately struck into it, and followed it for two days. It led them over rough hills, and through broken gullies, during which time they suffered great fatigue from the ruggedness of the country. The weather, too, which had recently been frosty, was now oppressively warm, and there was a great scarcity of water, insomuch that a valuable dog belonging to Mr. M'Kenzie died of thirst.

At one time they had twenty-five miles of painful travel, without a drop of water, until they arrived at a small running stream. Here they eagerly slaked their thirst; but, this being allayed, the calls of hunger became equally importunate. Ever since they had got among these barren and arid hills, where there was a deficiency of grass, they had met with no buffaloes; those animals keeping in the grassy meadows near the streams. They were obliged, therefore, to have recourse to their corn meal, which they reserved for such emergencies. Some, however, were lucky enough to kill a wolf, which they cooked for supper, and pronounced excellent food.

The next morning they resumed their wayfaring, hungry and jaded, and had a dogged march of eighteen miles among the same kind of hills. At length they emerged upon a stream of clear water, one of the forks of Power River, and to their great joy beheld once more wide grassy meadows, stocked with herds of buffalo. For several days they kept along the banks of the river, ascending it about eighteen miles. It was a hunter's paradise; the buffaloes were in such abundance that they were enabled to kill as many as they pleased, and to jerk a sufficient supply of meat for several day's journeying. Here, then, they reveled and reposed after their hungry and weary travel, hunting and feasting, and reclining upon the grass. Their quiet, however, was a little marred by coming upon traces of Indians, who, they concluded, must be Crow; they were therefore obliged to keep a more vigilant watch than ever upon their horses. For several days they had been directing their march towards the lofty mountain descried by Mr. Hunt and Mr. M'Kenzie on the 17th of August, the height of which rendered it a landmark over a vast extent of country. At first it had appeared to them solitary and detached; but as they advanced towards it, it proved to be the principal summit of a chain of mountains. Day by day it varied in form, or rather its lower peaks, and the summits of others of the chain emerged above the clear horizon, and finally the inferior line of hills which connected most of them rose to view. So far, however, are objects discernible in the pure atmosphere of these elevated plains, that, from the place where they first descried the main mountain, they had to travel a hundred and fifty miles before they reached its base. Here they encamped on the 30th of August, having come nearly four hundred miles since leaving the Arickara village.

The mountain which now towered above them was one of the Bighorn chain, bordered by a river, of the same name, and extending for a long distance rather east of north and west of south. It was a part of the great system of granite mountains which forms one of the most important and striking features of North America, stretching parallel to the coast of the Pacific from the Isthmus of Panama almost to the Arctic Ocean; and presenting a corresponding chain to that of the Andes in the southern hemisphere. This vast range has acquired, from its rugged and broken character and its summits of naked granite, the appellation of the Rocky Mountains, a name by no means distinctive, as all elevated ranges are rocky. Among the early explorers it was known as the range of Chippewyan Mountains, and this Indian name is the one it is likely to retain in poetic usage. Rising from the midst of vast plains and prairies, traversing several degrees of latitude, dividing the waters of the Atlantic and the Pacific, and seeming to bind with diverging ridges the level regions on its flanks, it has been figuratively termed the backbone of the northern continent.

The Rocky Mountains do not present a range of uniform elevation, but rather groups and occasionally detached peaks. Though some of these rise to the region of perpetual snows, and are upwards of eleven thousand feet in real altitude, yet their height from their immediate basis is not so great as might be imagined, as they swell up from elevated plains, several thousand feet above the level of the ocean. These plains are often of a desolate sterility; mere sandy wastes, formed of the detritus of the granite heights, destitute of trees and herbage, scorched by the ardent and reflected rays of the summer's sun, and in winter swept by chilling blasts from the snow-clad mountains. Such is a great part of that vast region extending north and south along the mountains, several hundred miles in width, which has not improperly been termed the Great American Desert. It is a region that almost discourages all hope of cultivation, and can only be traversed with safety by keeping near the streams which intersect it. Extensive plains likewise occur among the higher regions of the mountains, of considerable fertility. Indeed, these lofty plats of table-land seem to form a peculiar feature in the American continents. Some occur among the Cordilleras of the Andes, where cities and towns, and cultivated farms are to be seen eight thousand feet above the level of the sea.

The Rocky Mountains, as we have already observed, occur sometimes singly or in groups, and occasionally in collateral ridges. Between these are deep valleys, with small streams winding through them, which find their way into the lower plains, augmenting as they proceed, and ultimately discharging themselves into those vast rivers, which traverse the prairies like great arteries and drain the continent.

While the granitic summits of the Rocky Mountains are bleak and bare, many of the inferior ridges are scantily clothed with scrubbed pines, oaks, cedar, and furze. Various parts of the mountains also bear traces of volcanic action. Some of the interior valleys are strewed with scoria and broken stones, evidently of volcanic origin; the surrounding rocks bear the like character, and vestiges of extinguished craters are to be seen on the elevated heights.

We have already noticed the superstitious feelings with which the Indians regard the Black Hills; but this immense range of mountains, which divides all that they know of the world, and gives birth to such mighty rivers, is still more an object of awe and veneration. They call it "the crest of the world," and think that Wacondah, or the master of life, as they designate the Supreme Being, has his residence among these aerial heights. The tribes on the eastern prairies call them the mountains of the setting sun. Some of them place the "happy hunting-grounds," their ideal paradise, among the recesses of these mountains; but say that they are invisible to living men. Here also is the "Land of Souls," in which are the "towns of the free and generous spirits," where those who have pleased the master of life while living, enjoy after death all manner of delights.

Wonders are told of these mountains by the distant tribes, whose warriors or hunters have ever wandered in their neighborhood. It is thought by some that, after death, they will have to travel to these mountains and ascend one of their highest and most rugged peaks, among rocks and snows and tumbling torrents. After many moons of painful toil they will reach the summit, from whence they will have a view over the land of souls. There they will see the happy hunting-grounds, with the souls of the brave and good living in tents in green meadows, by bright running streams, or hunting the herds of buffalo, and elk, and deer, which have been slain on earth. There, too, they will see the villages or towns of the free and generous spirits brightening in the midst of delicious prairies. If they have acquitted themselves well while living, they will be permitted to descend and enjoy this happy country; if otherwise they will but be tantalized with this prospect of it, and then hurled back from the mountain to wander about the sandy plains, and endure the eternal pangs of unsatisfied thirst and hunger.